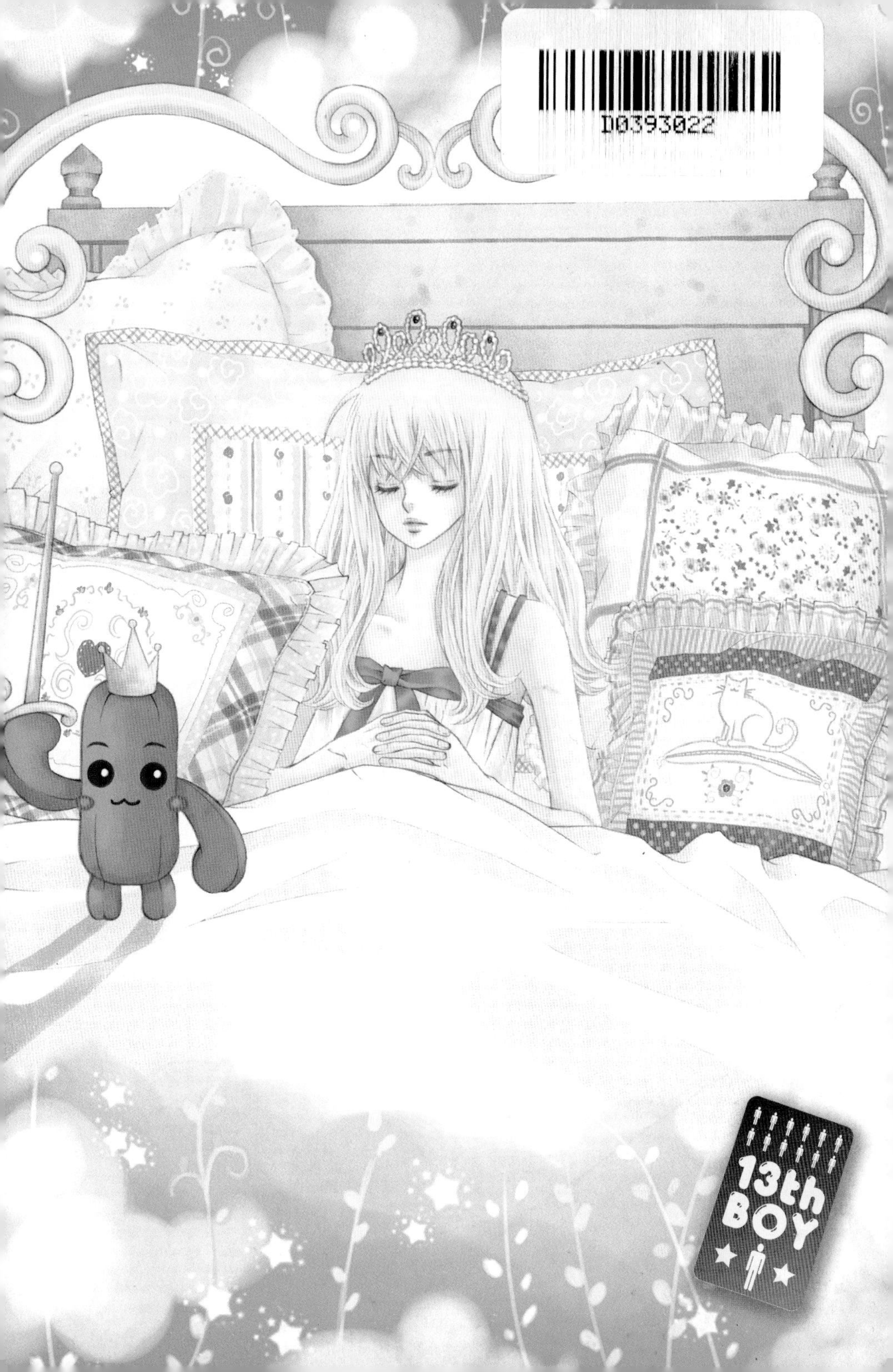
13th
BOY

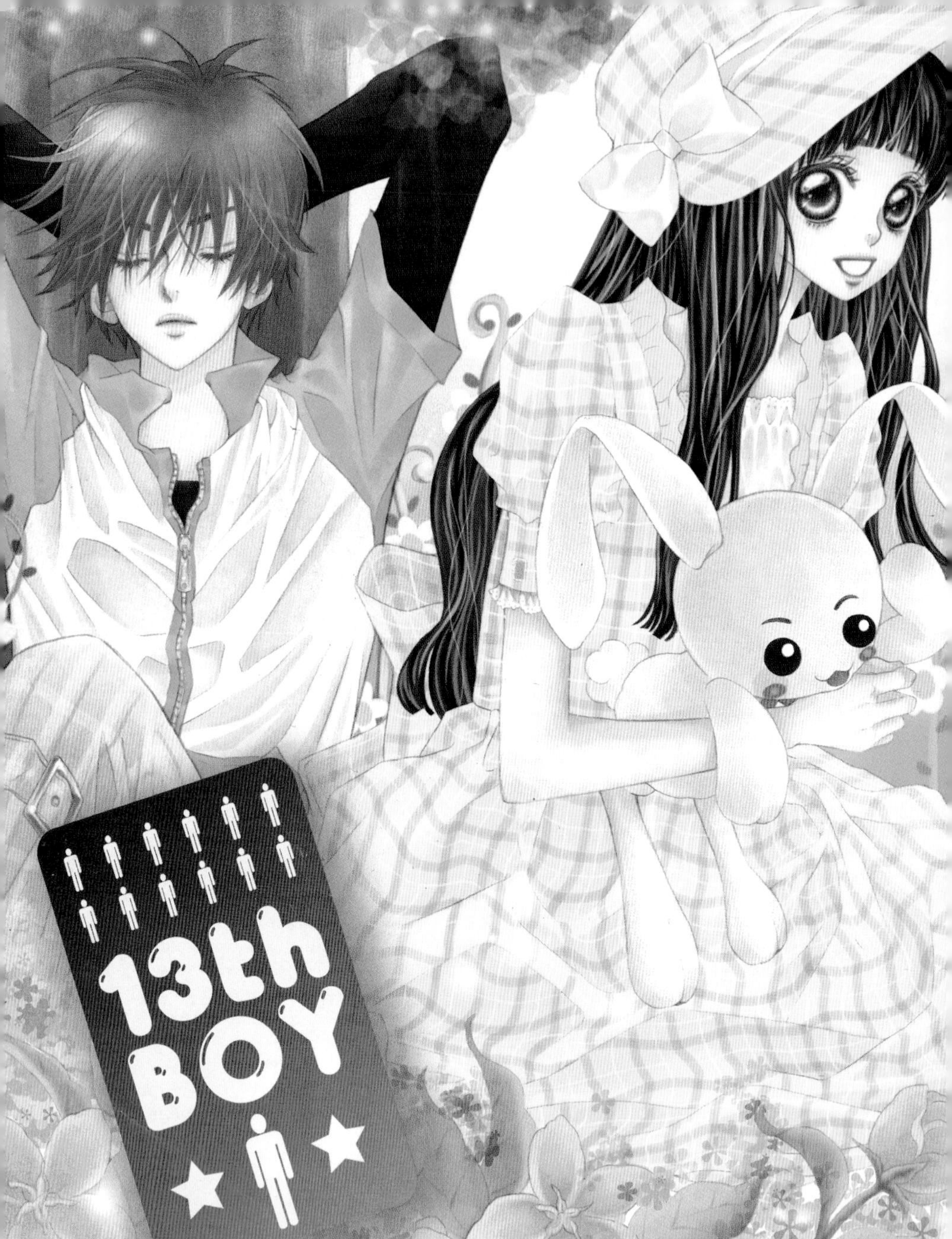
13th
BOY

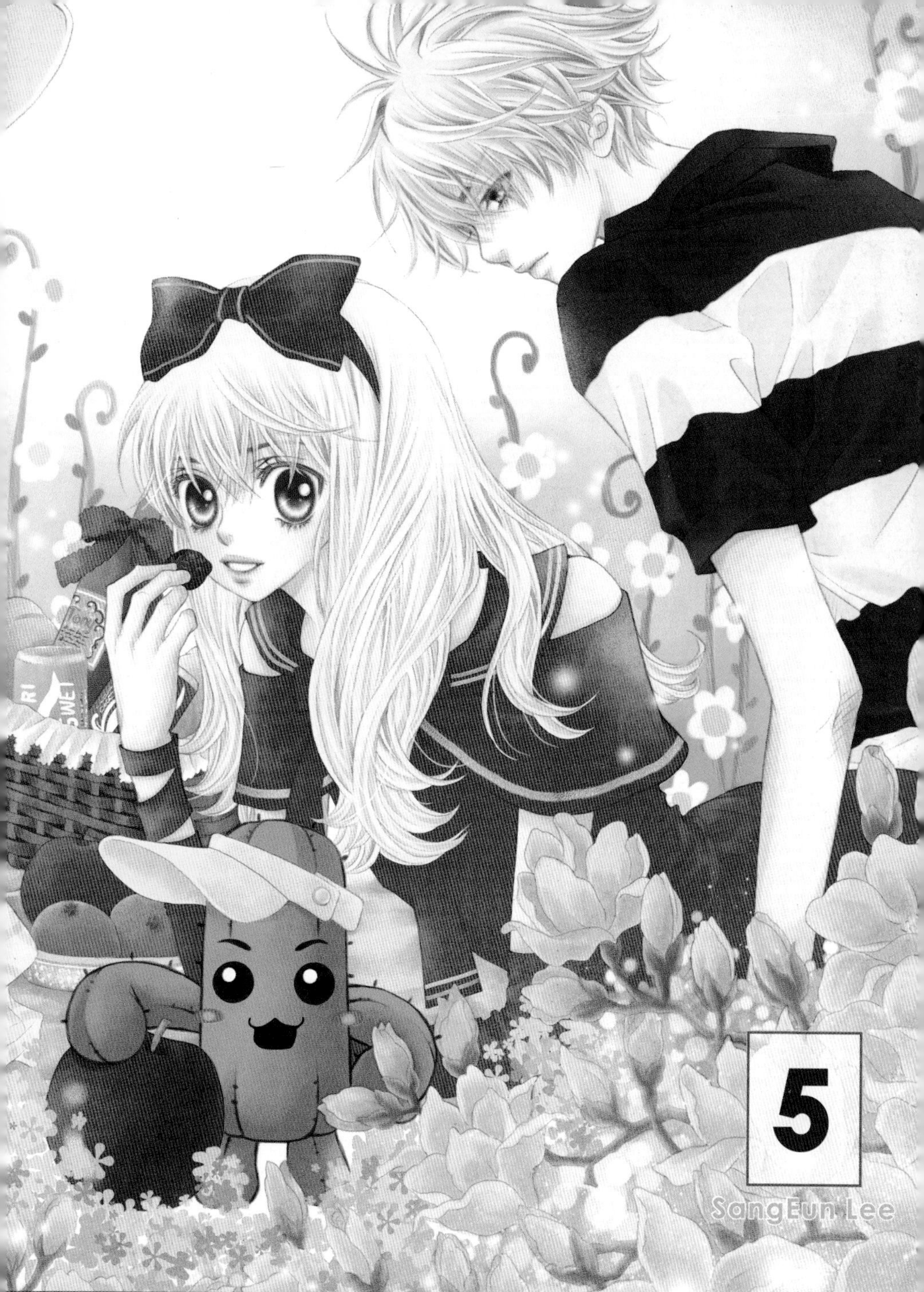
5
SangEun Lee

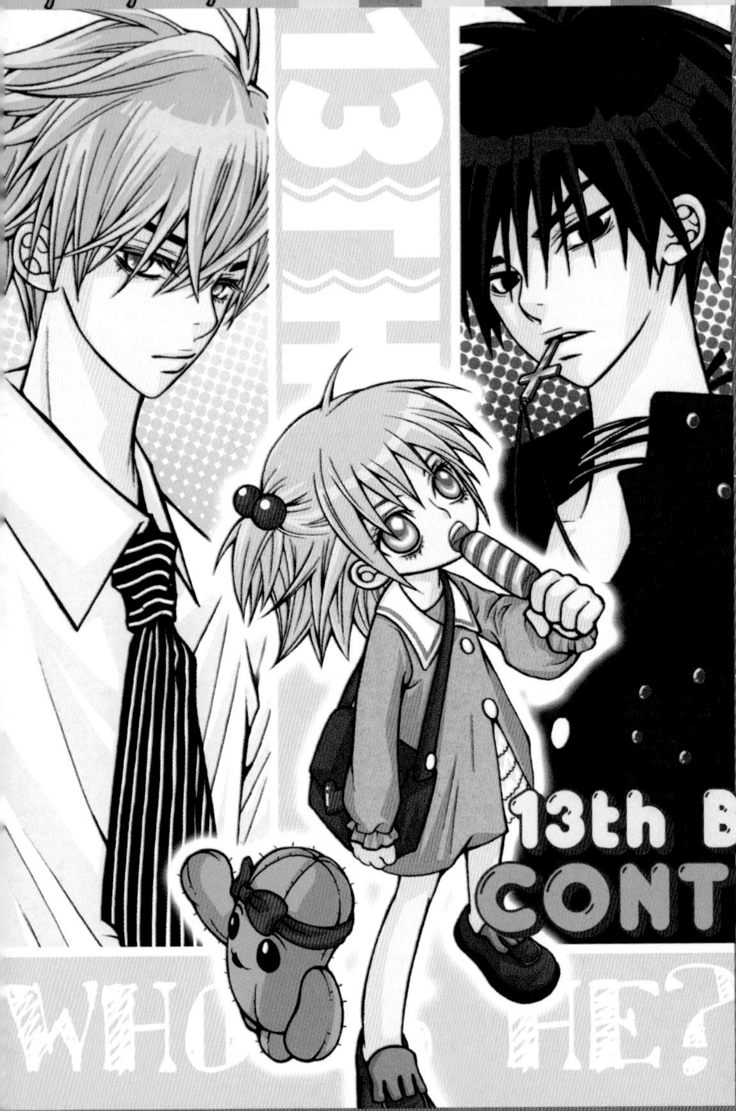
13TH
WHO
HE?

13th BOY♥ CONTENTS

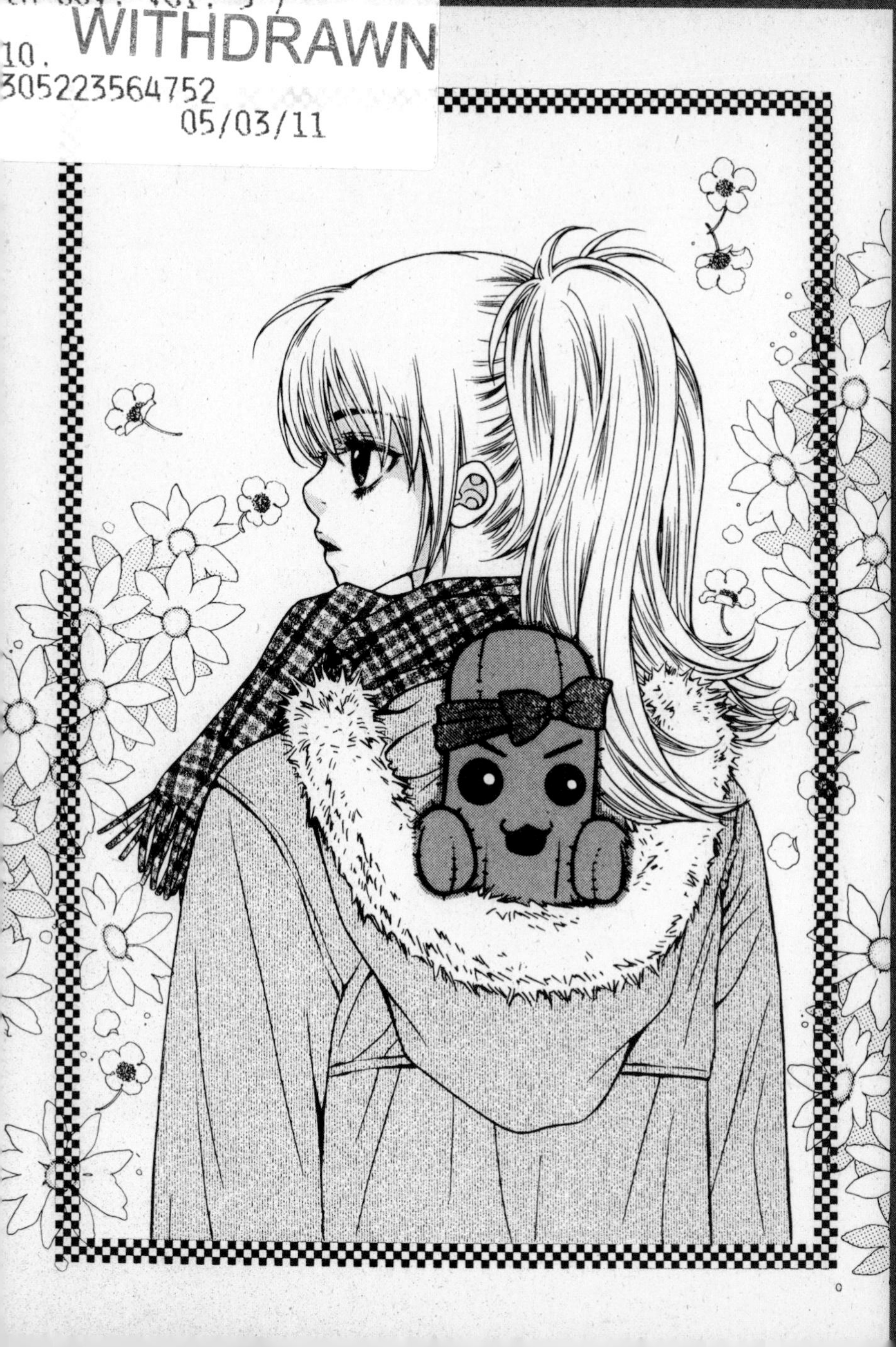

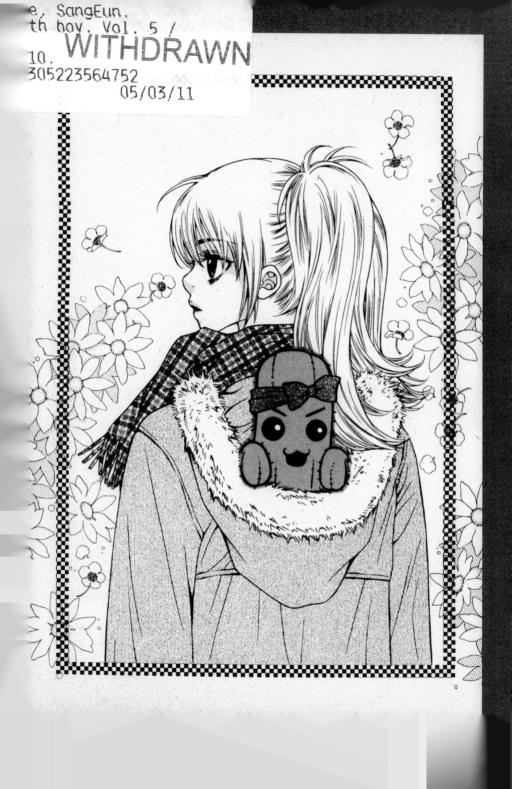

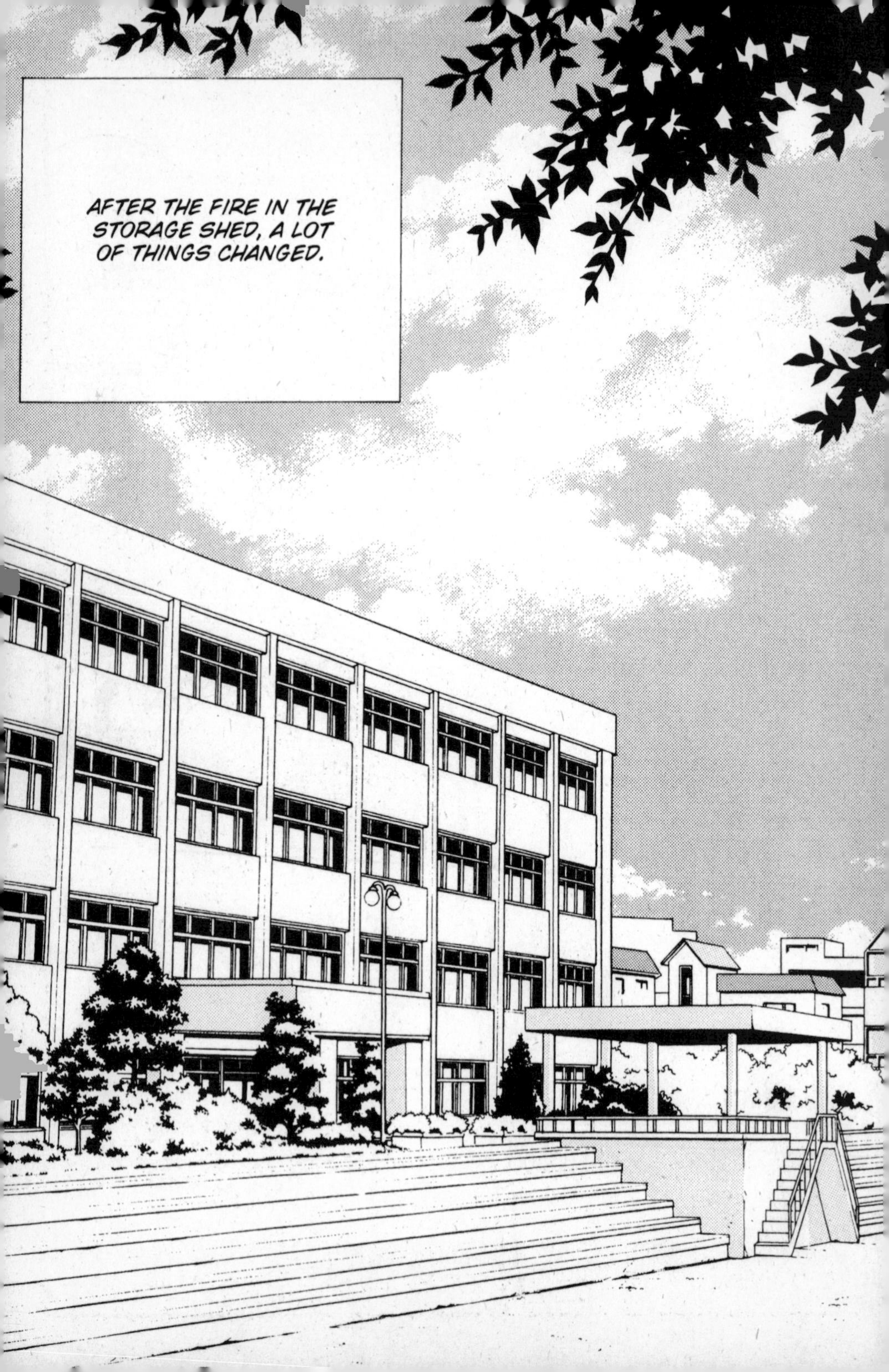
AFTER THE FIRE IN THE STORAGE SHED, A LOT OF THINGS CHANGED.

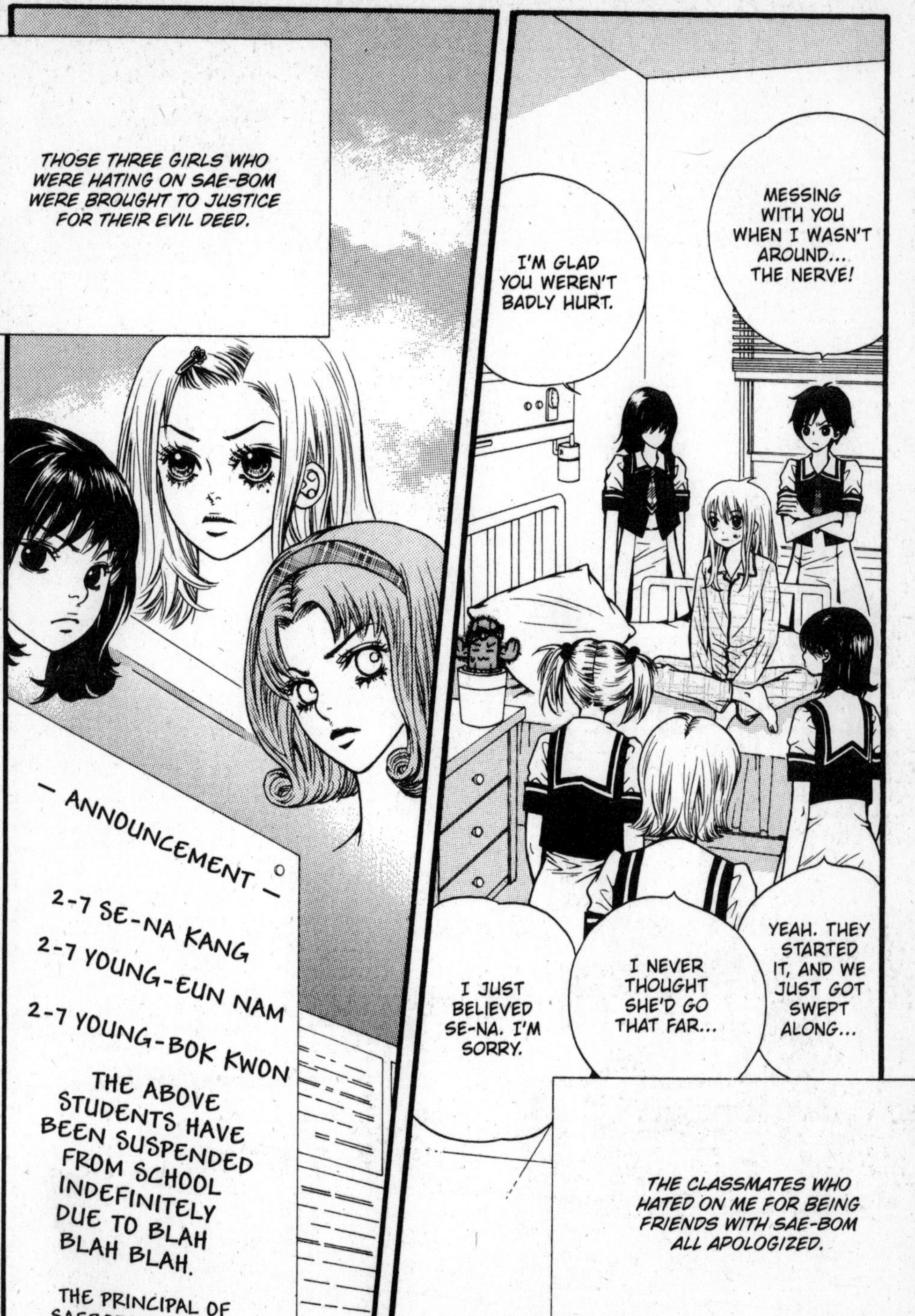
THOSE THREE GIRLS WHO WERE HATING ON SAE-BOM WERE BROUGHT TO JUSTICE FOR THEIR EVIL DEED.
— ANNOUNCEMENT —
2-7 SE-NA KANG
2-7 YOUNG-EUN NAM
2-7 YOUNG-BOK KWON
THE ABOVE STUDENTS HAVE BEEN SUSPENDED FROM SCHOOL INDEFINITELY DUE TO BLAH BLAH BLAH.
THE PRINCIPAL OF SAEBORAM JUNIOR HIGH SCHOOL
I'M GLAD YOU WEREN'T BADLY HURT.
MESSING WITH YOU WHEN I WASN'T AROUND... THE NERVE!
I JUST BELIEVED SE-NA. I'M SORRY.
I NEVER THOUGHT SHE'D GO THAT FAR...
YEAH. THEY STARTED IT, AND WE JUST GOT SWEPT ALONG...
THE CLASSMATES WHO HATED ON ME FOR BEING FRIENDS WITH SAE-BOM ALL APOLOGIZED.

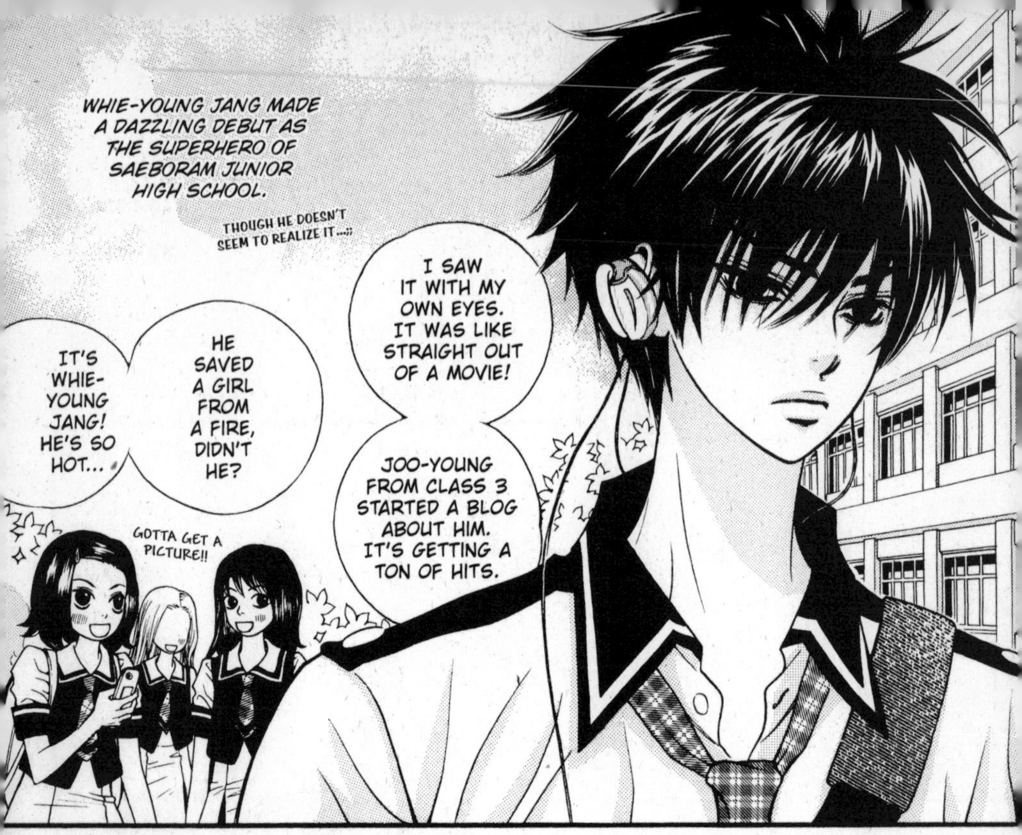
WHIE-YOUNG JANG MADE A DAZZLING DEBUT AS THE SUPERHERO OF SAEBORAM JUNIOR HIGH SCHOOL.
THOUGH HE DOESN'T SEEM TO REALIZE IT...;;
IT'S WHIE-YOUNG JANG! HE'S SO HOT...
HE SAVED A GIRL FROM A FIRE, DIDN'T HE?
I SAW IT WITH MY OWN EYES. IT WAS LIKE STRAIGHT OUT OF A MOVIE!
JOO-YOUNG FROM CLASS 3 STARTED A BLOG ABOUT HIM. IT'S GETTING A TON OF HITS.
GOTTA GET A PICTURE!!
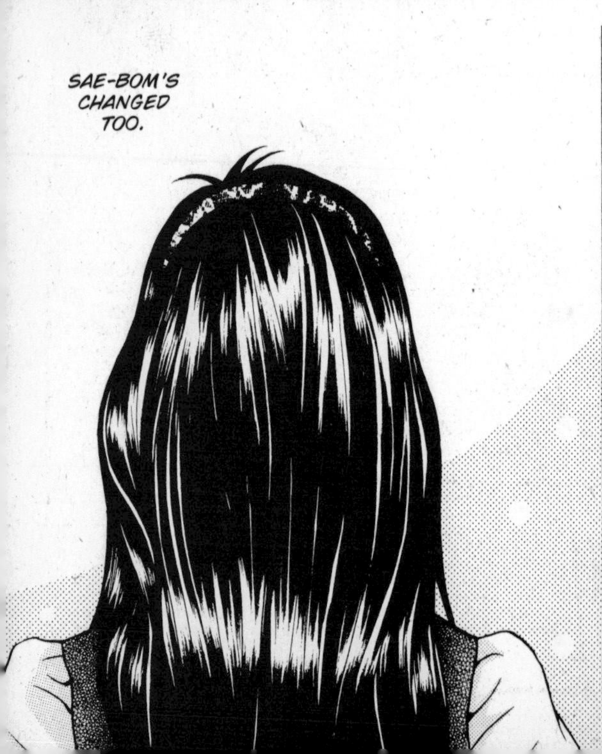
SAE-BOM'S CHANGED TOO.
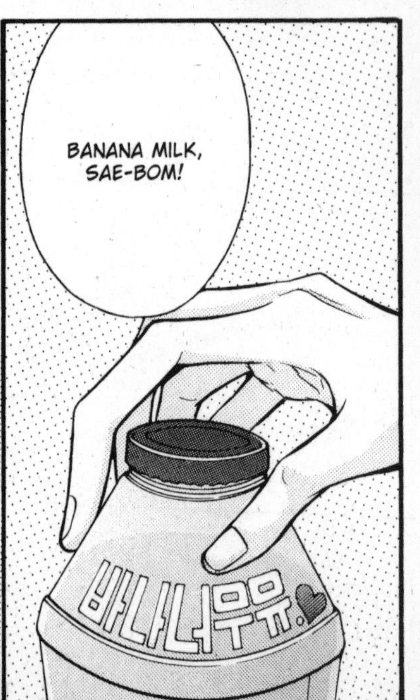
BANANA MILK, SAE-BOM!
BOTTLE: BANANOMILK.♥

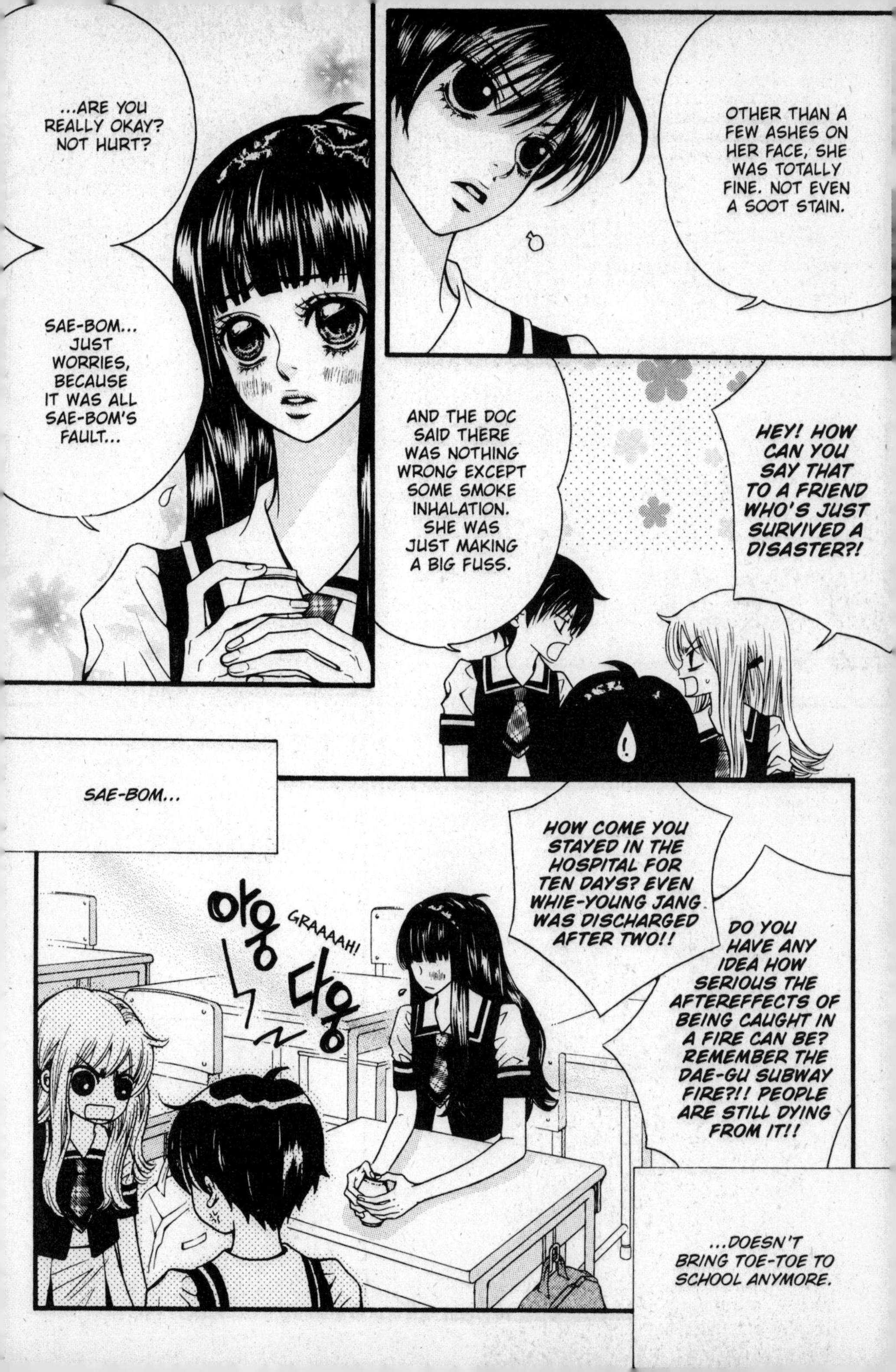
...ARE YOU REALLY OKAY? NOT HURT?
SAE-BOM... JUST WORRIES, BECAUSE IT WAS ALL SAE-BOM'S FAULT...
OTHER THAN A FEW ASHES ON HER FACE, SHE WAS TOTALLY FINE. NOT EVEN A SOOT STAIN.
AND THE DOC SAID THERE WAS NOTHING WRONG EXCEPT SOME SMOKE INHALATION. SHE WAS JUST MAKING A BIG FUSS.
HEY! HOW CAN YOU SAY THAT TO A FRIEND WHO'S JUST SURVIVED A DISASTER?!
SAE-BOM...
HOW COME YOU STAYED IN THE HOSPITAL FOR TEN DAYS? EVEN WHIE-YOUNG JANG WAS DISCHARGED AFTER TWO!!
야옹
GRAAAAH!
다옹
DO YOU HAVE ANY IDEA HOW SERIOUS THE AFTEREFFECTS OF BEING CAUGHT IN A FIRE CAN BE? REMEMBER THE DAE-GU SUBWAY FIRE?!! PEOPLE ARE STILL DYING FROM IT!!
...DOESN'T BRING TOE-TOE TO SCHOOL ANYMORE.

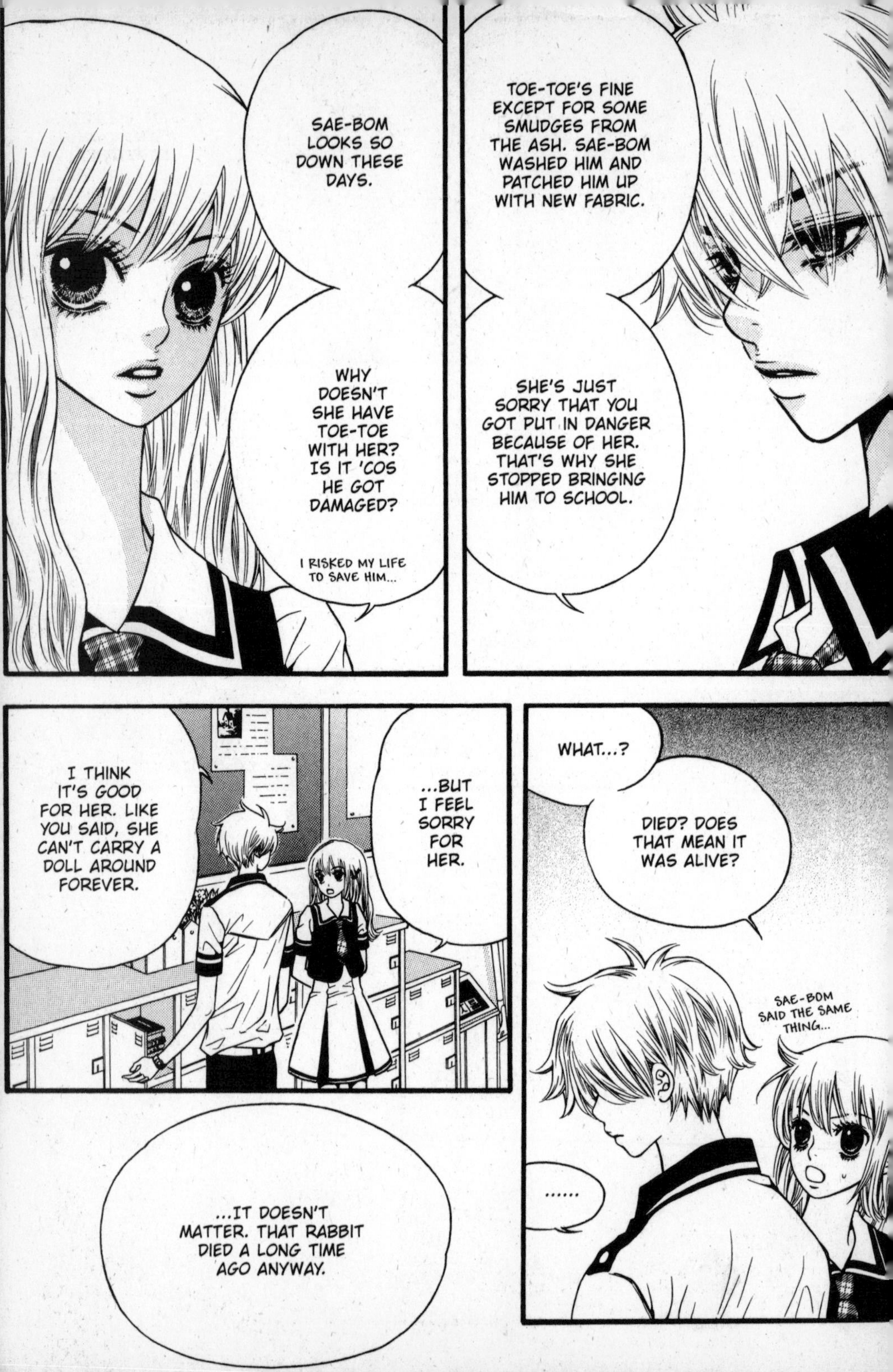
SAE-BOM LOOKS SO DOWN THESE DAYS.
WHY DOESN'T SHE HAVE TOE-TOE WITH HER? IS IT 'COS HE GOT DAMAGED?
I RISKED MY LIFE TO SAVE HIM...
TOE-TOE'S FINE EXCEPT FOR SOME SMUDGES FROM THE ASH. SAE-BOM WASHED HIM AND PATCHED HIM UP WITH NEW FABRIC.
SHE'S JUST SORRY THAT YOU GOT PUT IN DANGER BECAUSE OF HER. THAT'S WHY SHE STOPPED BRINGING HIM TO SCHOOL.
I THINK IT'S GOOD FOR HER. LIKE YOU SAID, SHE CAN'T CARRY A DOLL AROUND FOREVER.
...BUT I FEEL SORRY FOR HER.
...IT DOESN'T MATTER. THAT RABBIT DIED A LONG TIME AGO ANYWAY.
WHAT...?
DIED? DOES THAT MEAN IT WAS ALIVE?
SAE-BOM SAID THE SAME THING...
......

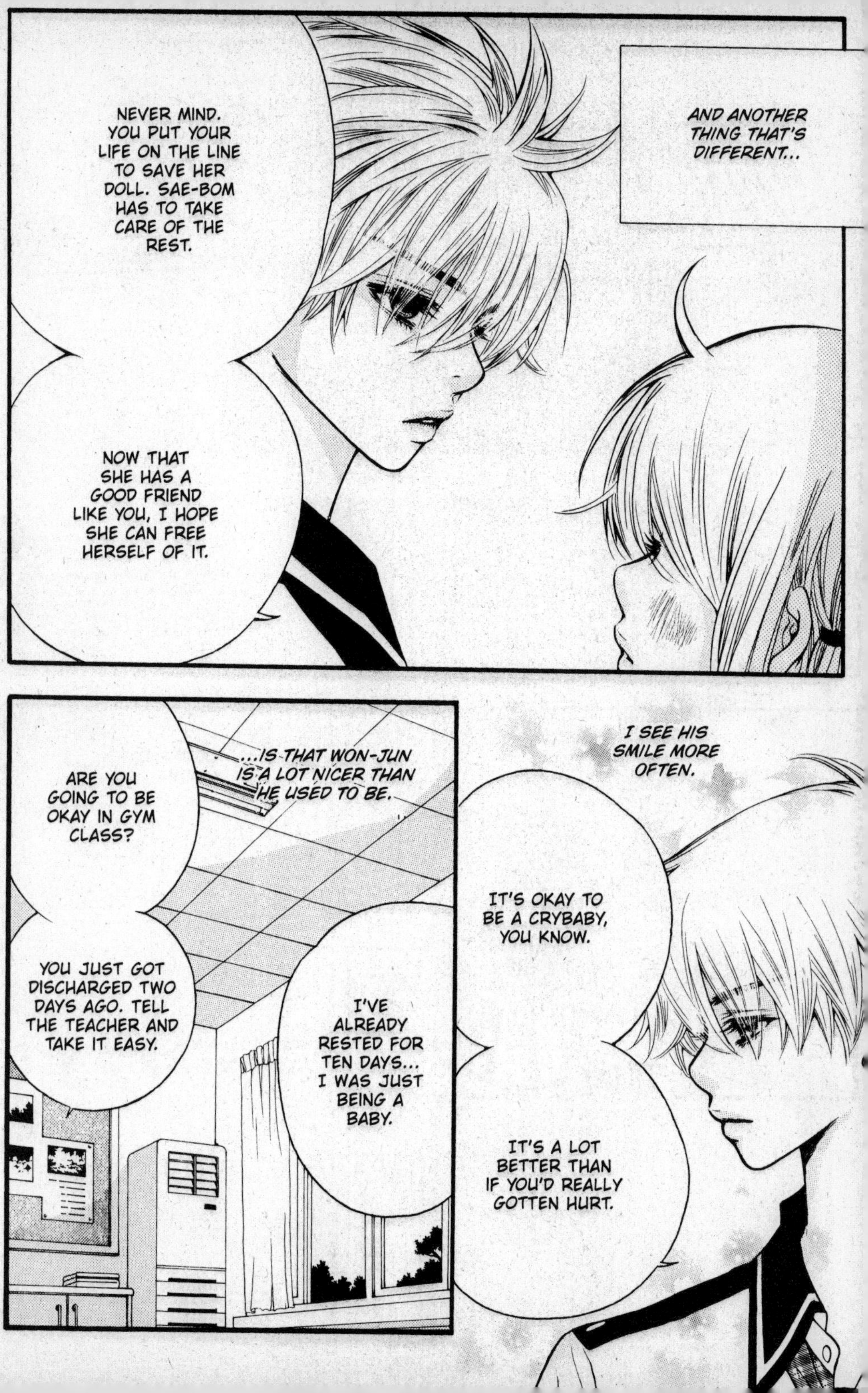
NEVER MIND. YOU PUT YOUR LIFE ON THE LINE TO SAVE HER DOLL. SAE-BOM HAS TO TAKE CARE OF THE REST.
AND ANOTHER THING THAT'S DIFFERENT...
NOW THAT SHE HAS A GOOD FRIEND LIKE YOU, I HOPE SHE CAN FREE HERSELF OF IT.
...IS THAT WON-JUN IS A LOT NICER THAN HE USED TO BE.
ARE YOU GOING TO BE OKAY IN GYM CLASS?
YOU JUST GOT DISCHARGED TWO DAYS AGO. TELL THE TEACHER AND TAKE IT EASY.
I'VE ALREADY RESTED FOR TEN DAYS... I WAS JUST BEING A BABY.
I SEE HIS SMILE MORE OFTEN.
IT'S OKAY TO BE A CRYBABY, YOU KNOW.
IT'S A LOT BETTER THAN IF YOU'D REALLY GOTTEN HURT.

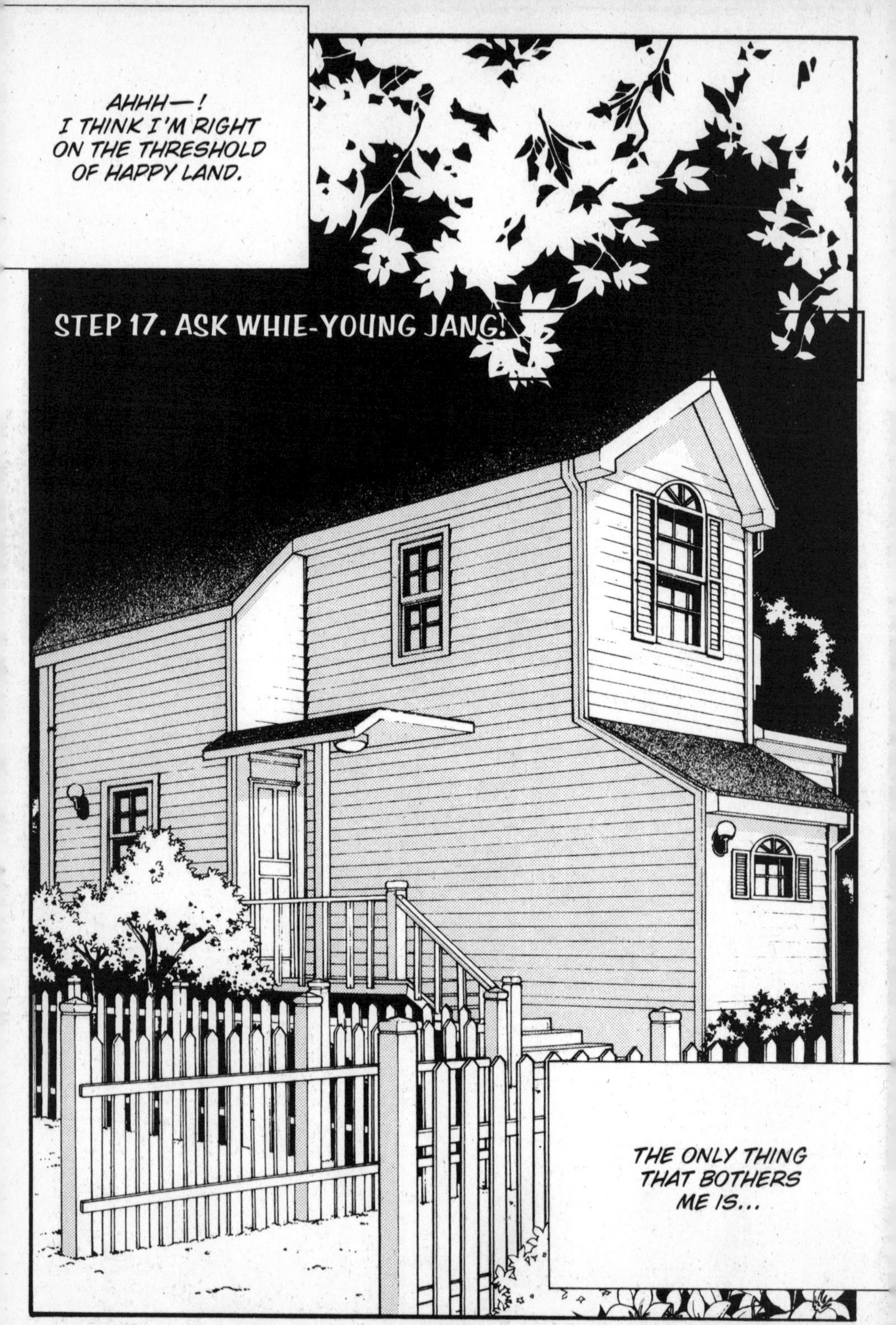
AHHH—!
I THINK I'M RIGHT
ON THE THRESHOLD
OF HAPPY LAND.
STEP 17. ASK WHIE-YOUNG JANG!
THE ONLY THING
THAT BOTHERS
ME IS...

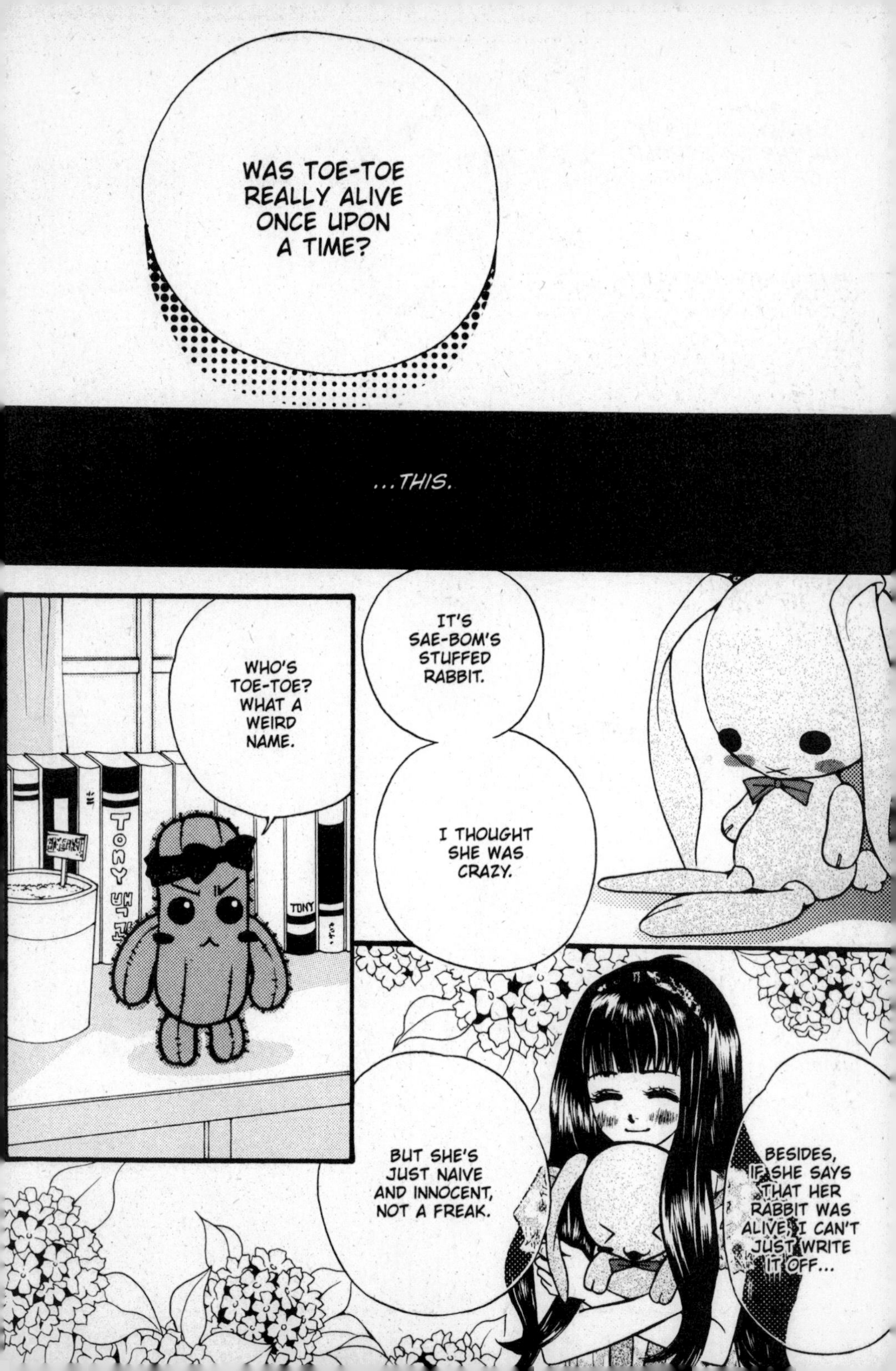
WAS TOE-TOE REALLY ALIVE ONCE UPON A TIME?
...THIS.
WHO'S TOE-TOE? WHAT A WEIRD NAME.
IT'S SAE-BOM'S STUFFED RABBIT.
I THOUGHT SHE WAS CRAZY.
TONY
TONY
BUT SHE'S JUST NAIVE AND INNOCENT, NOT A FREAK.
BESIDES, IF SHE SAYS THAT HER RABBIT WAS ALIVE, I CAN'T JUST WRITE IT OFF...

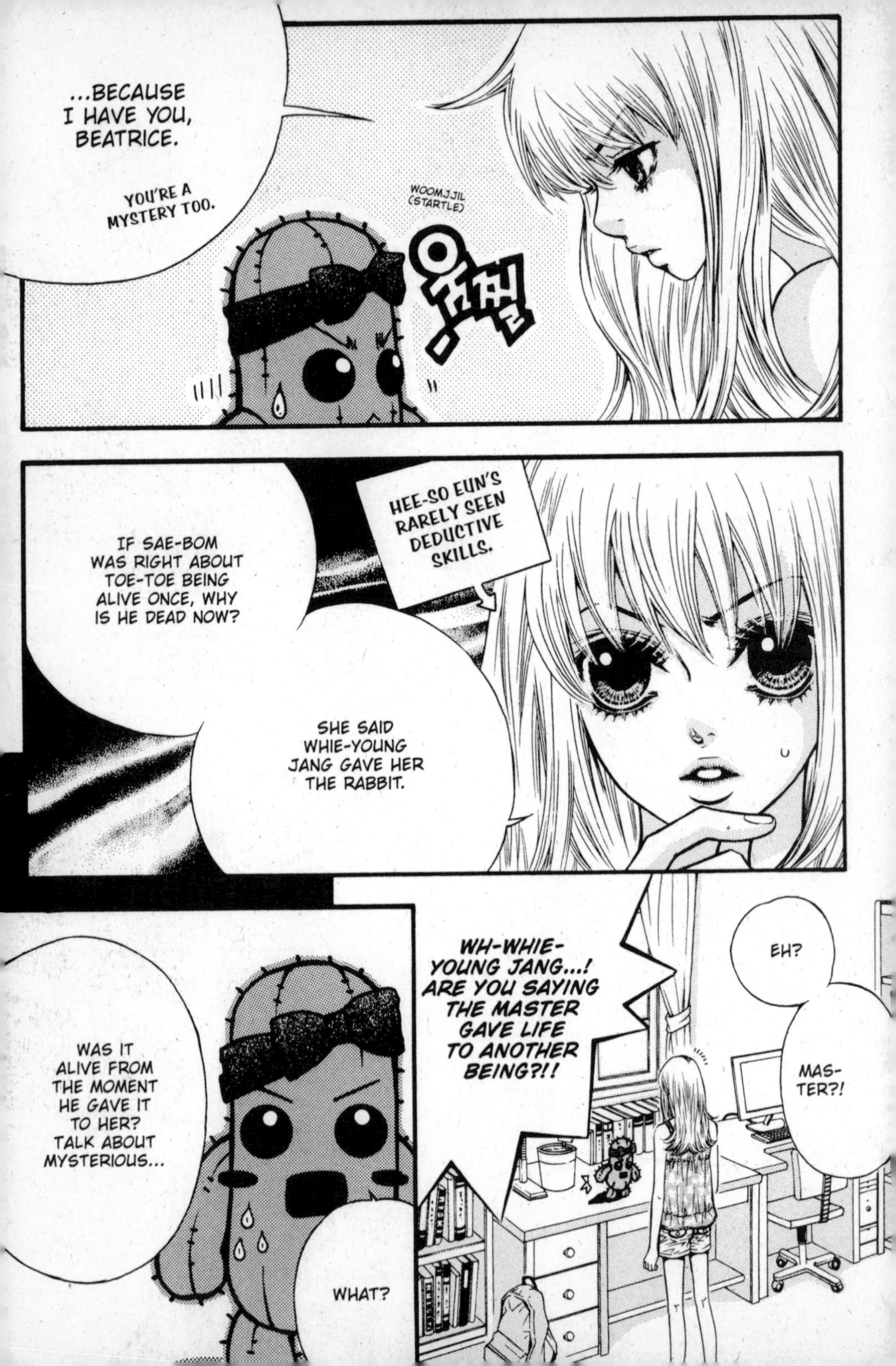
...BECAUSE I HAVE YOU, BEATRICE.
YOU'RE A MYSTERY TOO.
WOOMJJIL (STARTLE)
IF SAE-BOM WAS RIGHT ABOUT TOE-TOE BEING ALIVE ONCE, WHY IS HE DEAD NOW?
HEE-SO EUN'S RARELY SEEN DEDUCTIVE SKILLS.
SHE SAID WHIE-YOUNG JANG GAVE HER THE RABBIT.
WAS IT ALIVE FROM THE MOMENT HE GAVE IT TO HER? TALK ABOUT MYSTERIOUS...
WHAT?
WH-WHIE-YOUNG JANG...! ARE YOU SAYING THE MASTER GAVE LIFE TO ANOTHER BEING?!!
EH?
MAS-TER?!

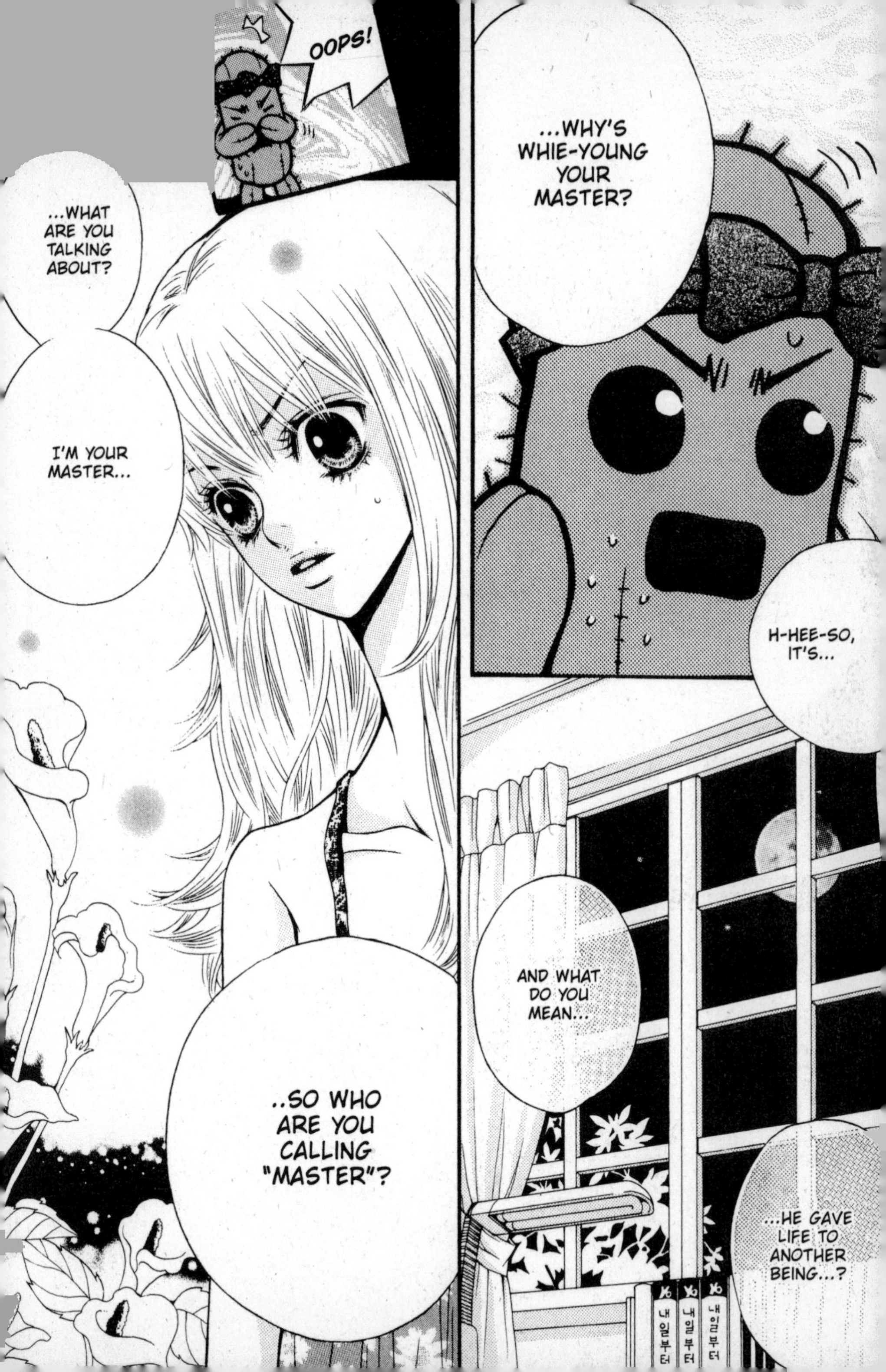
OOPS!
...WHAT ARE YOU TALKING ABOUT?
I'M YOUR MASTER...
..SO WHO ARE YOU CALLING "MASTER"?
...WHY'S WHIE-YOUNG YOUR MASTER?
H-HEE-SO, IT'S...
AND WHAT DO YOU MEAN...
...HE GAVE LIFE TO ANOTHER BEING...?
내일부터
내일부터
내일부터

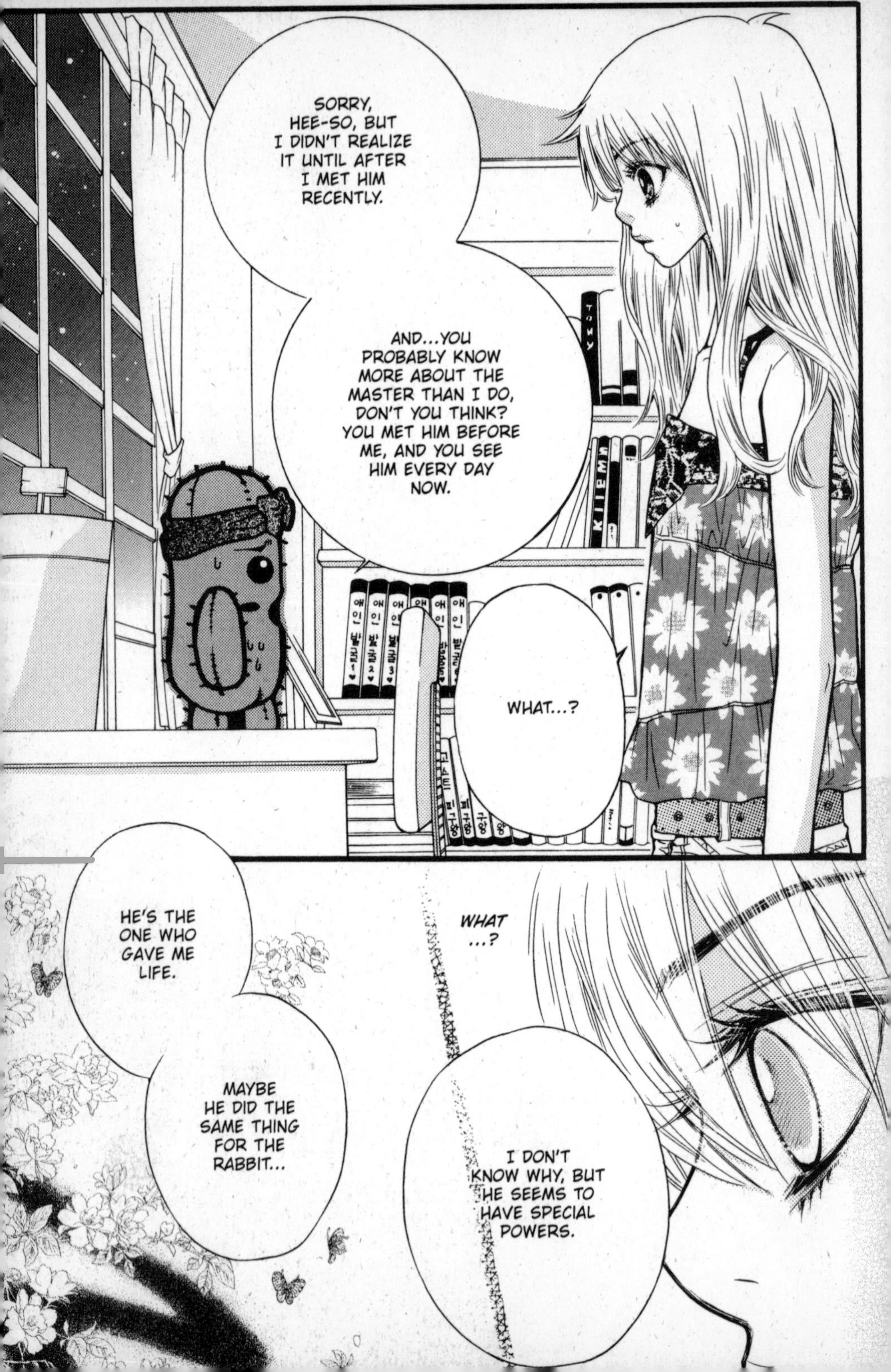
SORRY, HEE-SO, BUT I DIDN'T REALIZE IT UNTIL AFTER I MET HIM RECENTLY.
AND...YOU PROBABLY KNOW MORE ABOUT THE MASTER THAN I DO, DON'T YOU THINK? YOU MET HIM BEFORE ME, AND YOU SEE HIM EVERY DAY NOW.
WHAT...?
HE'S THE ONE WHO GAVE ME LIFE.
MAYBE HE DID THE SAME THING FOR THE RABBIT...
WHAT ...?
I DON'T KNOW WHY, BUT HE SEEMS TO HAVE SPECIAL POWERS.

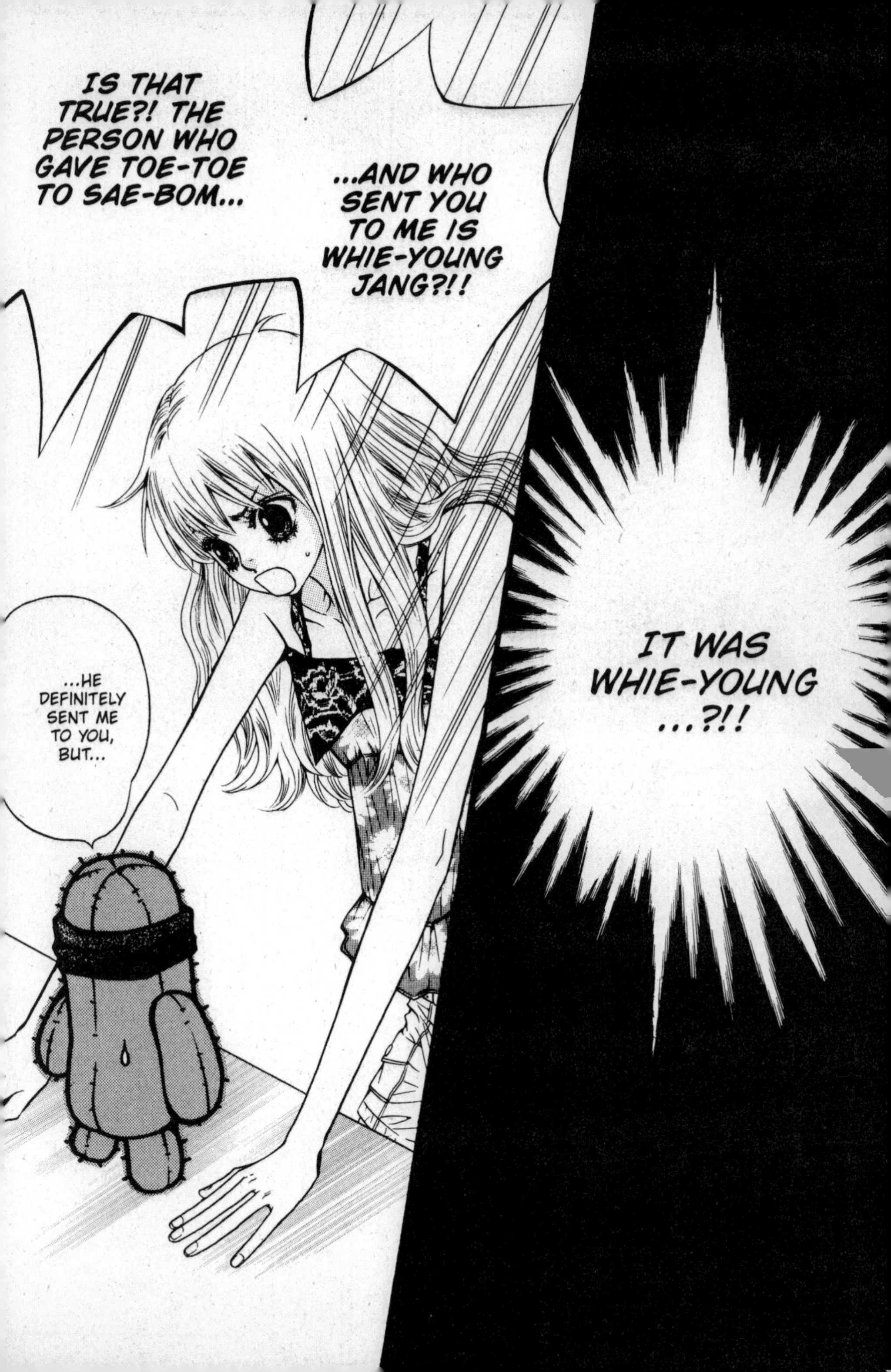
IS THAT TRUE?! THE PERSON WHO GAVE TOE-TOE TO SAE-BOM...
...AND WHO SENT YOU TO ME IS WHIE-YOUNG JANG?!!
...HE DEFINITELY SENT ME TO YOU, BUT...
IT WAS WHIE-YOUNG ...?!!

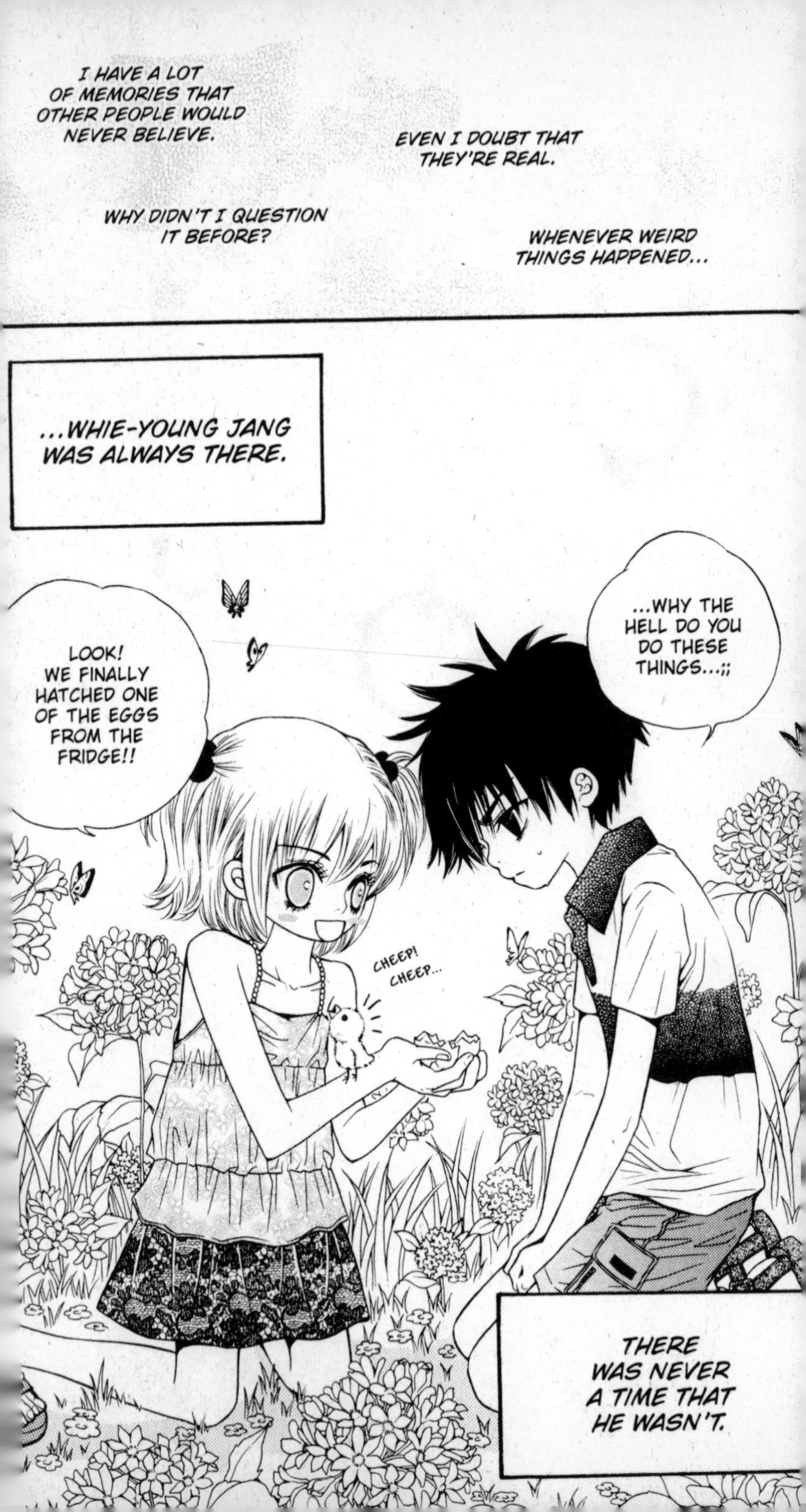
I HAVE A LOT OF MEMORIES THAT OTHER PEOPLE WOULD NEVER BELIEVE.
EVEN I DOUBT THAT THEY'RE REAL.
WHY DIDN'T I QUESTION IT BEFORE?
WHENEVER WEIRD THINGS HAPPENED...
...WHIE-YOUNG JANG WAS ALWAYS THERE.
LOOK! WE FINALLY HATCHED ONE OF THE EGGS FROM THE FRIDGE!!
...WHY THE HELL DO YOU DO THESE THINGS...;;
CHEEP! CHEEP...
THERE WAS NEVER A TIME THAT HE WASN'T.

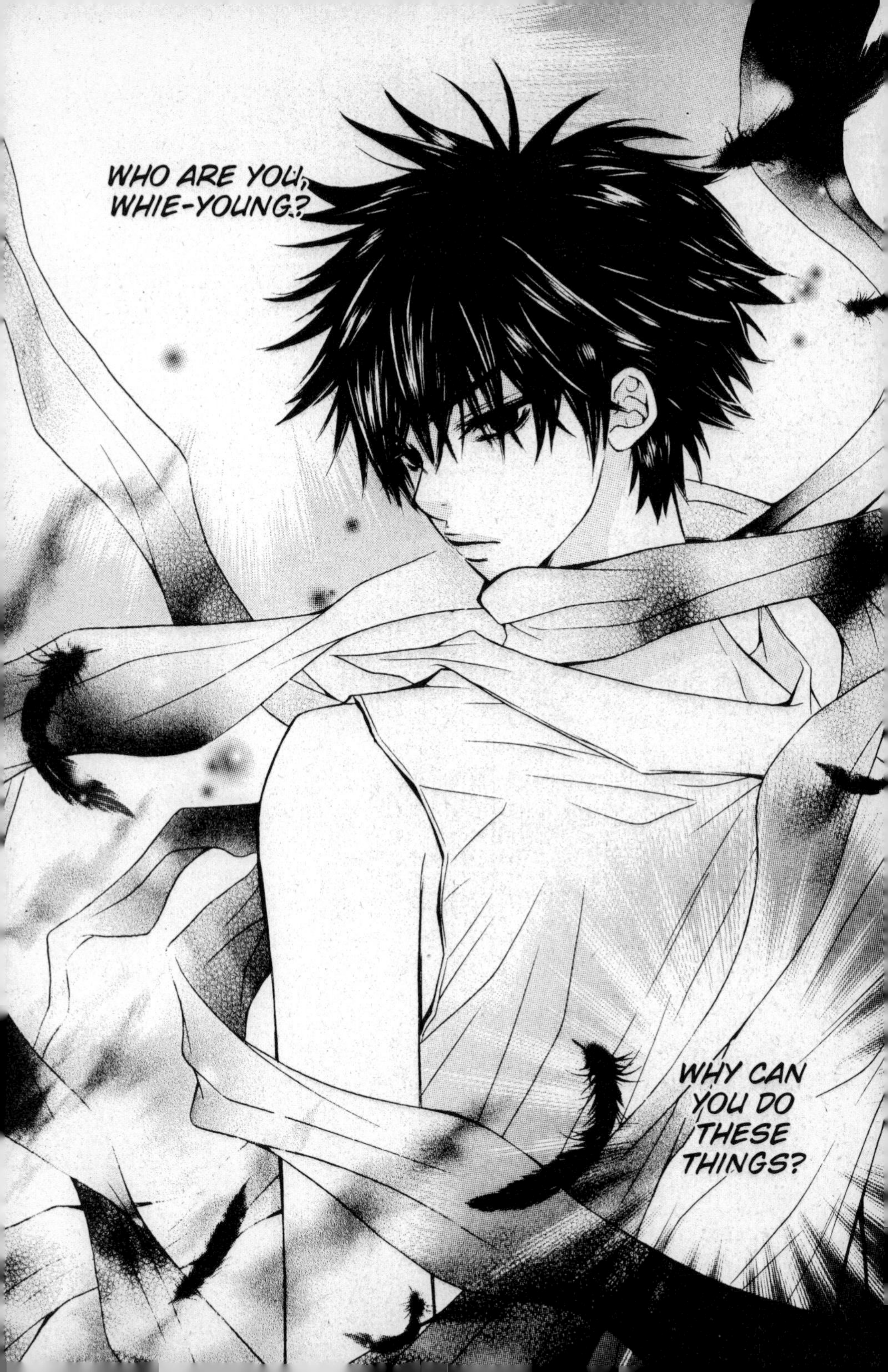
WHO ARE YOU, WHIE-YOUNG?
WHY CAN YOU DO THESE THINGS?

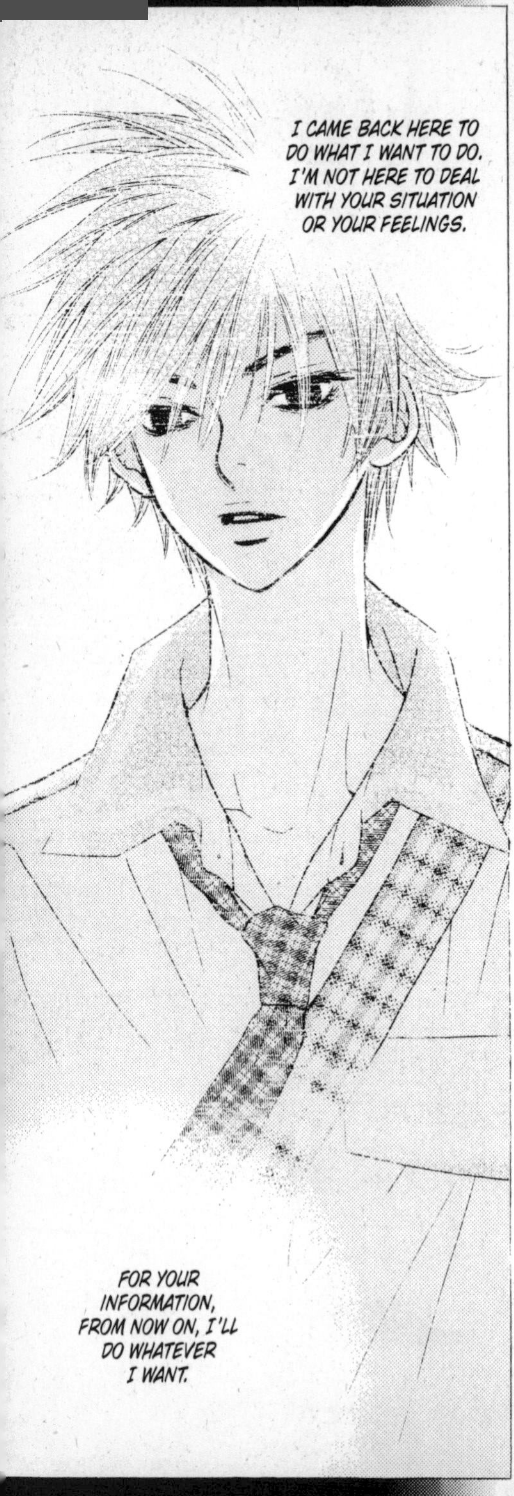
I CAME BACK HERE TO DO WHAT I WANT TO DO. I'M NOT HERE TO DEAL WITH YOUR SITUATION OR YOUR FEELINGS.
FOR YOUR INFORMATION, FROM NOW ON, I'LL DO WHATEVER I WANT.
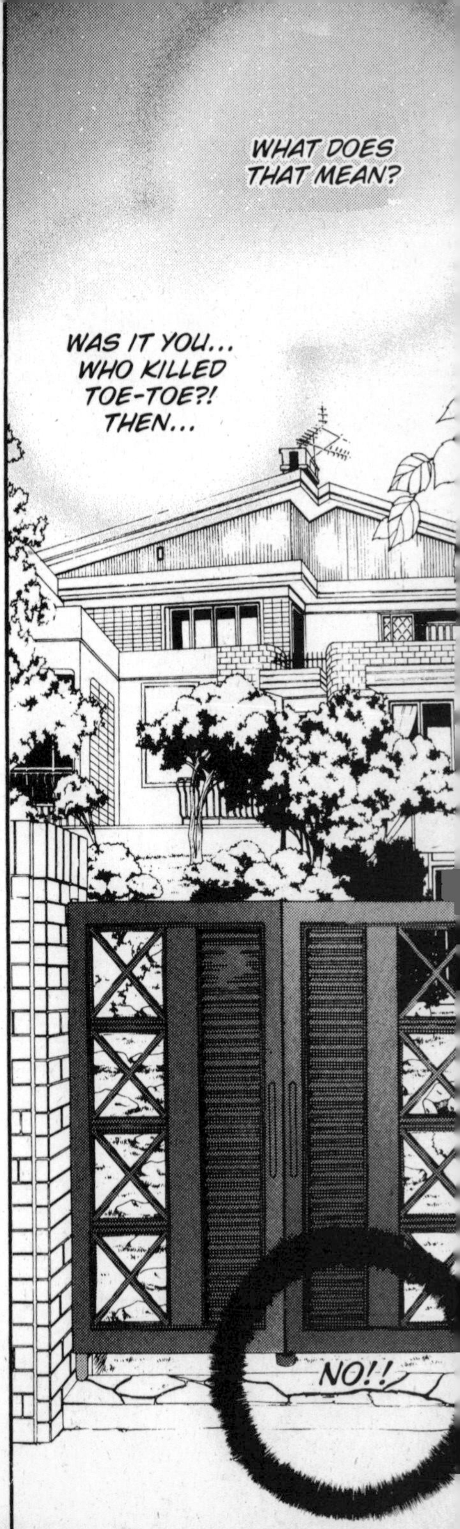
WHAT DOES THAT MEAN?
WAS IT YOU... WHO KILLED TOE-TOE?! THEN...
NO!!

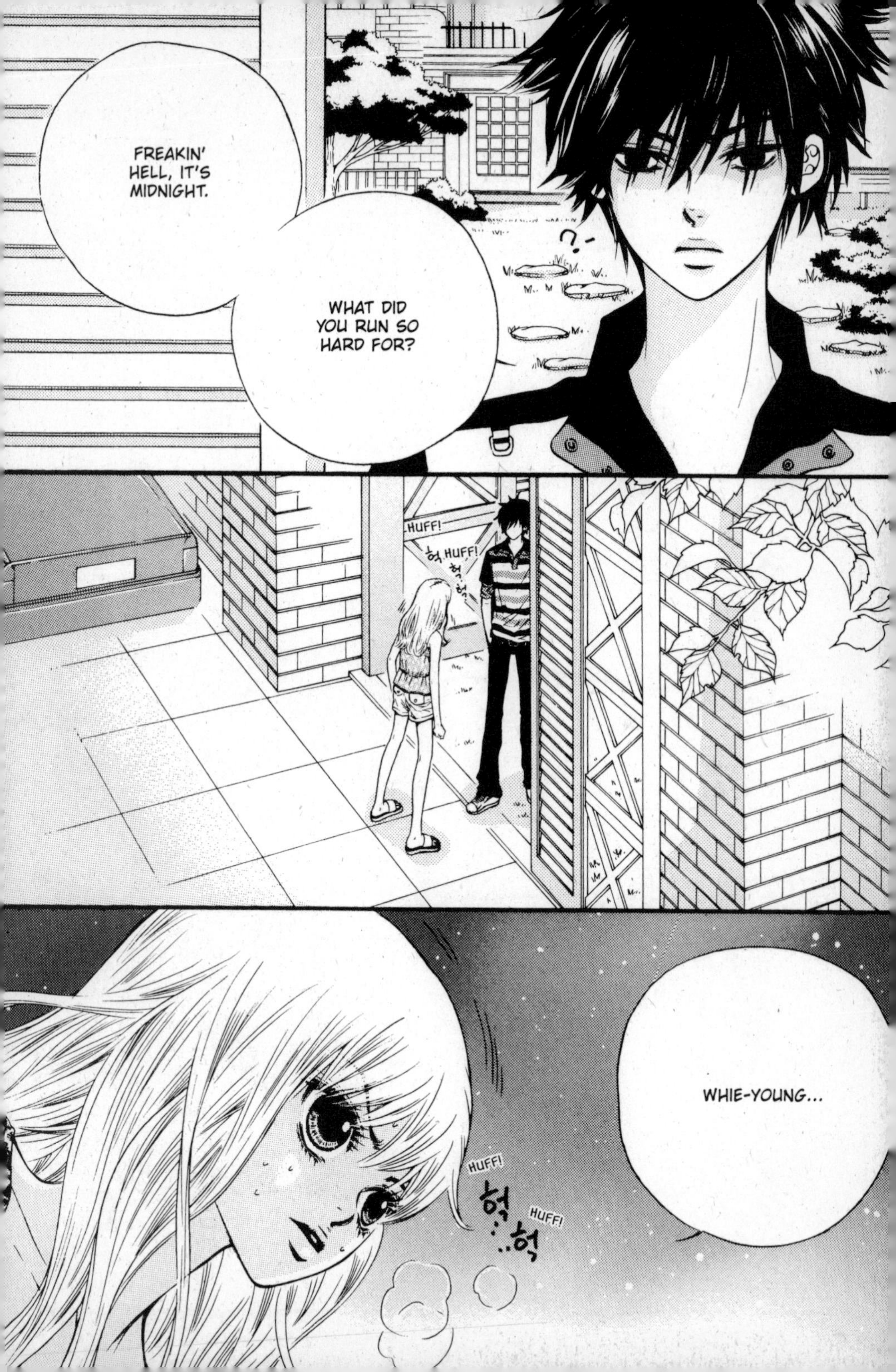
FREAKIN' HELL, IT'S MIDNIGHT.
WHAT DID YOU RUN SO HARD FOR?
HUFF!
헉 HUFF!
헉 헉
HUFF!
헉
HUFF!
..헉
WHIE-YOUNG...

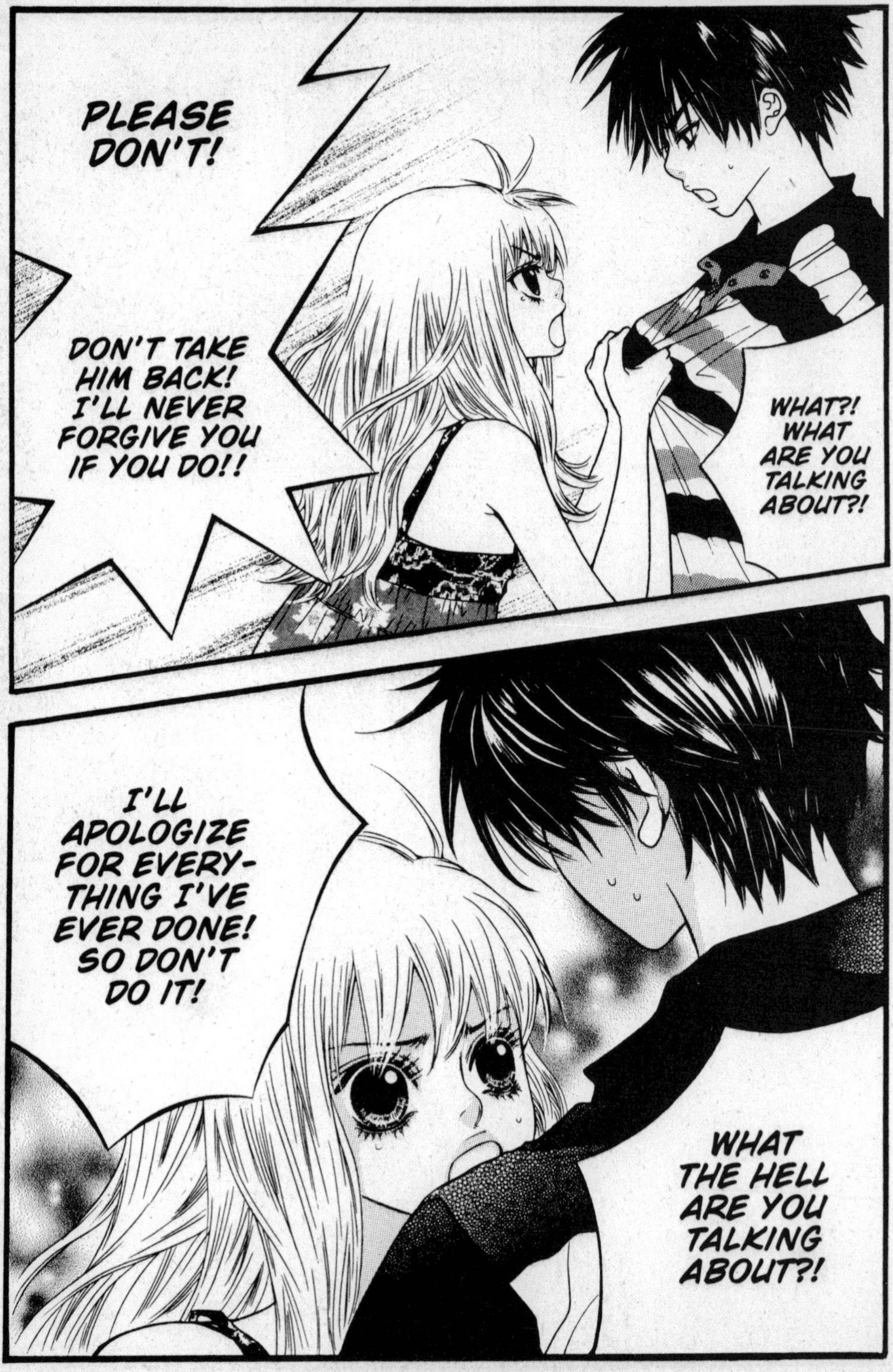
PLEASE DON'T!
DON'T TAKE HIM BACK! I'LL NEVER FORGIVE YOU IF YOU DO!!
WHAT?! WHAT ARE YOU TALKING ABOUT?!
I'LL APOLOGIZE FOR EVERY-THING I'VE EVER DONE! SO DON'T DO IT!
WHAT THE HELL ARE YOU TALKING ABOUT?!

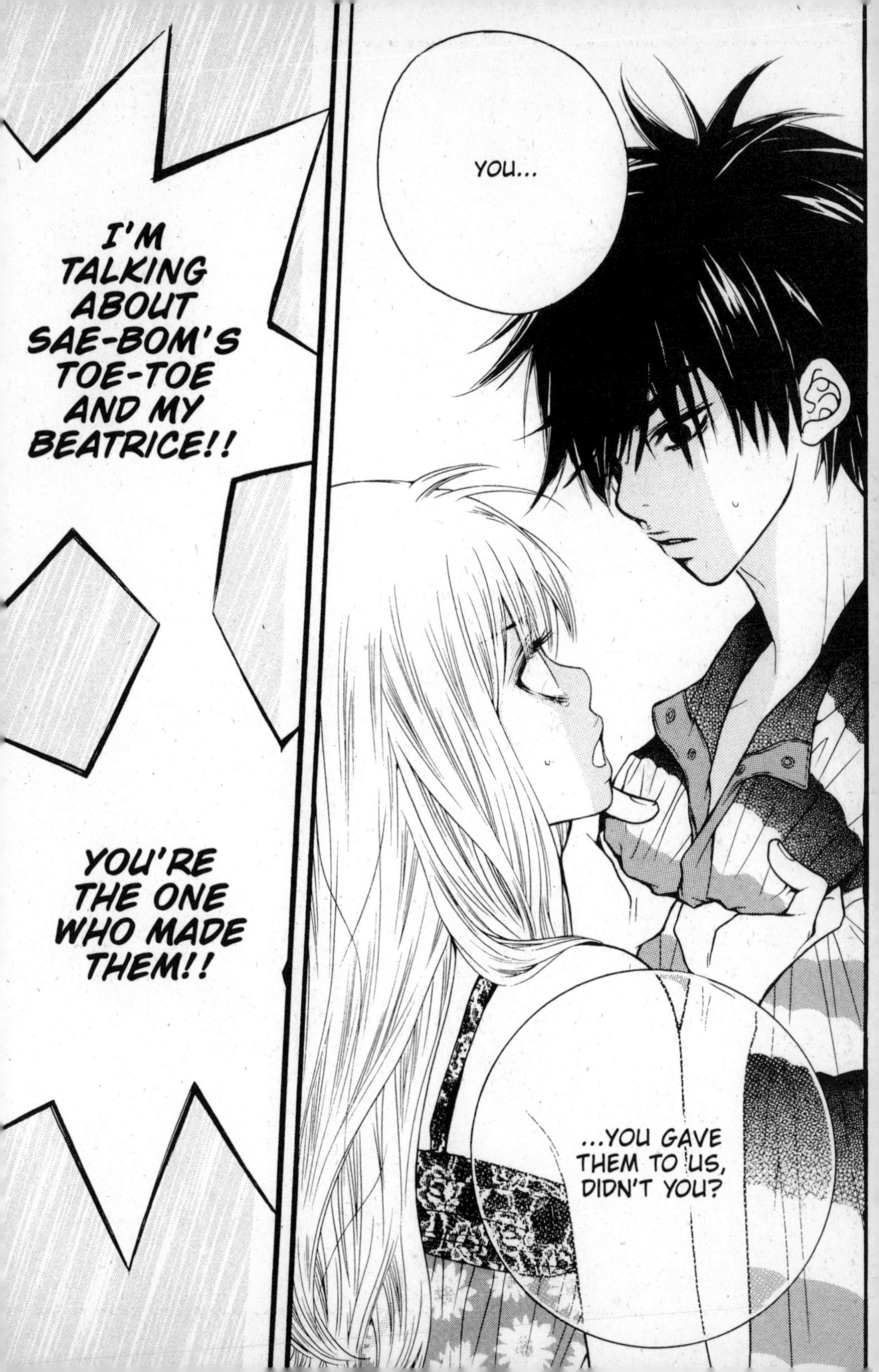
I'M TALKING ABOUT SAE-BOM'S TOE-TOE AND MY BEATRICE!!
YOU'RE THE ONE WHO MADE THEM!!
YOU...
...YOU GAVE THEM TO US, DIDN'T YOU?

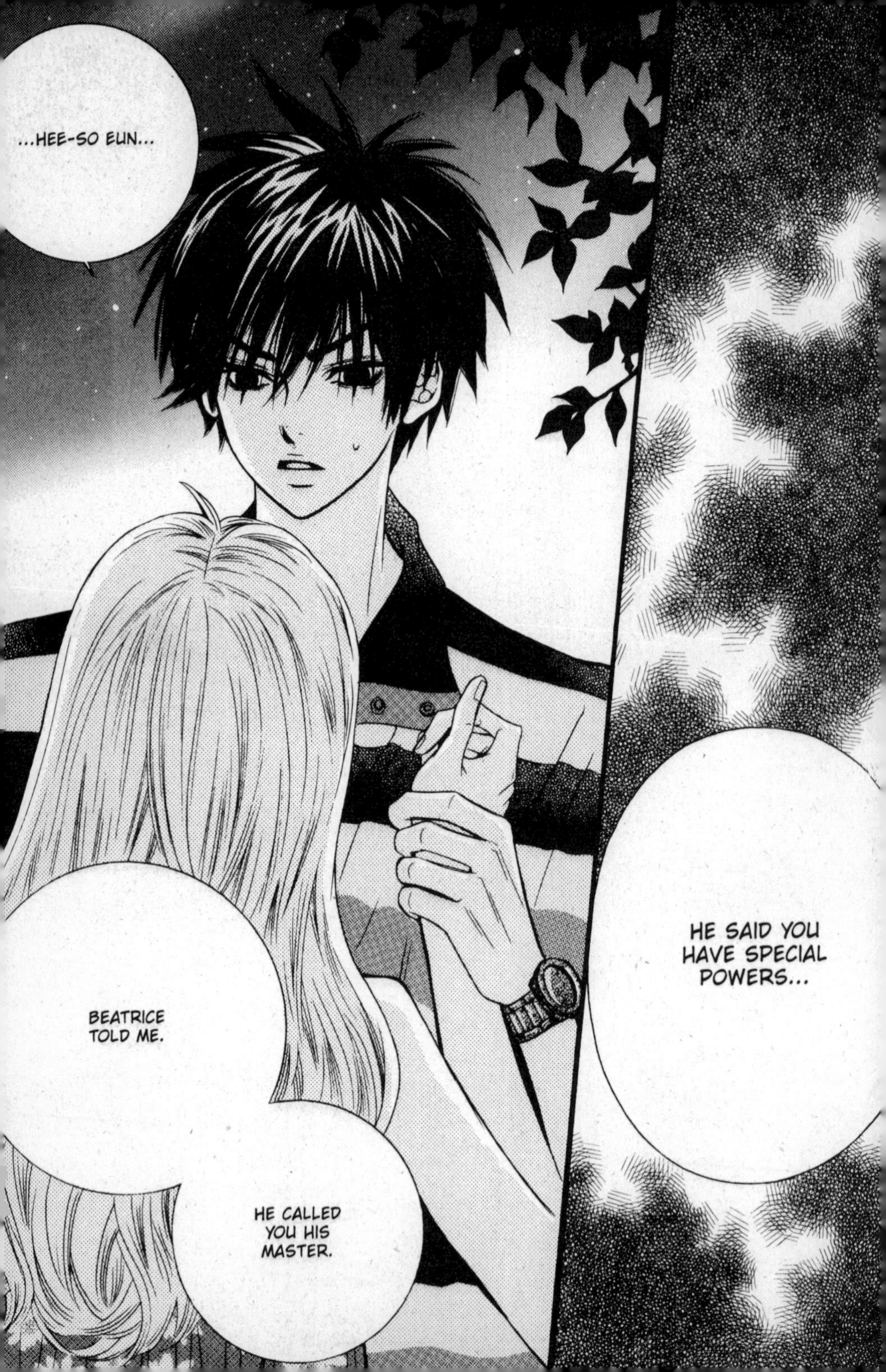
...HEE-SO EUN...
BEATRICE TOLD ME.
HE CALLED YOU HIS MASTER.
HE SAID YOU HAVE SPECIAL POWERS...

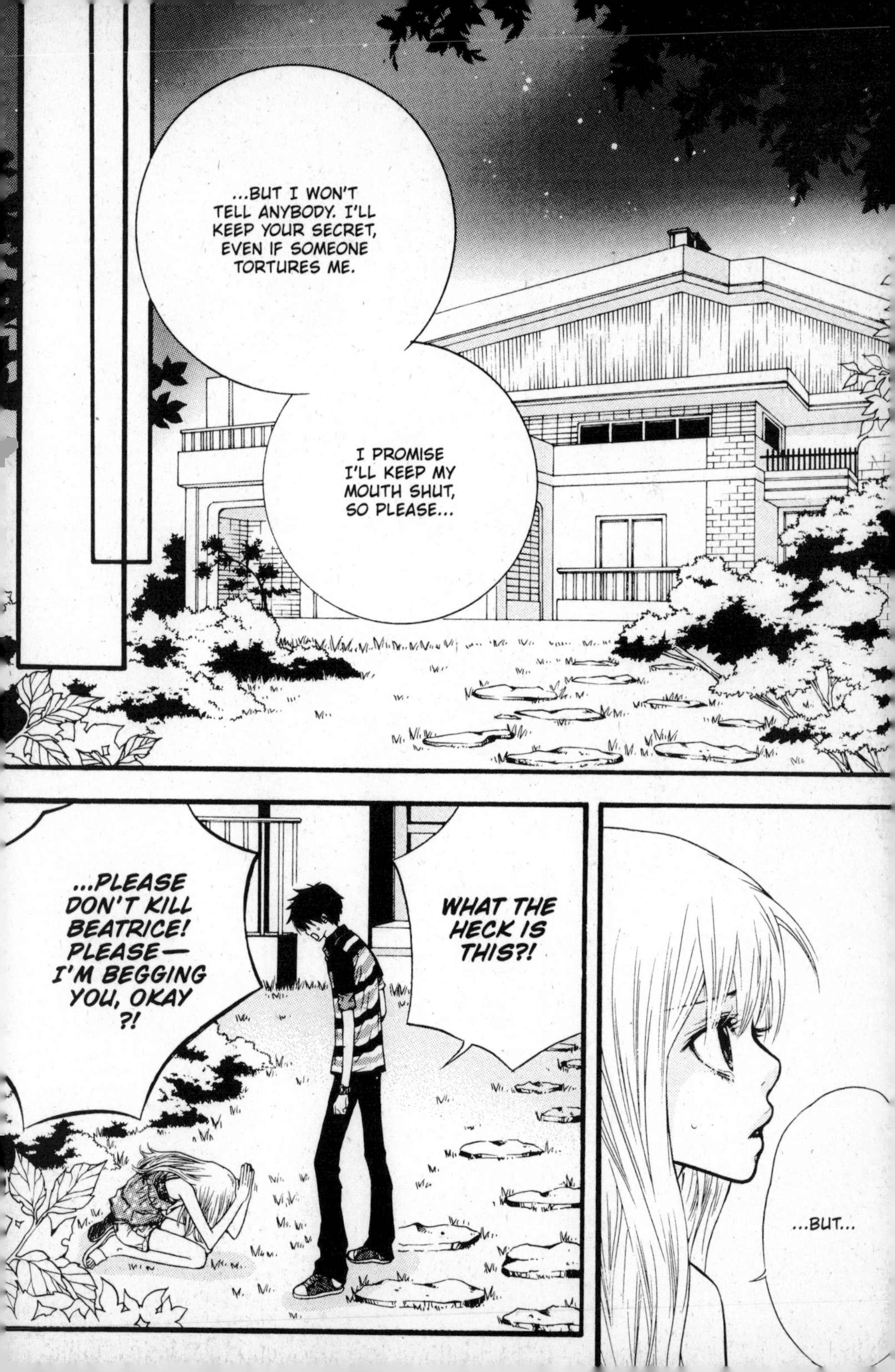
...BUT I WON'T TELL ANYBODY. I'LL KEEP YOUR SECRET, EVEN IF SOMEONE TORTURES ME.
I PROMISE I'LL KEEP MY MOUTH SHUT, SO PLEASE...
...PLEASE DON'T KILL BEATRICE! PLEASE—I'M BEGGING YOU, OKAY?!
WHAT THE HECK IS THIS?!
...BUT...

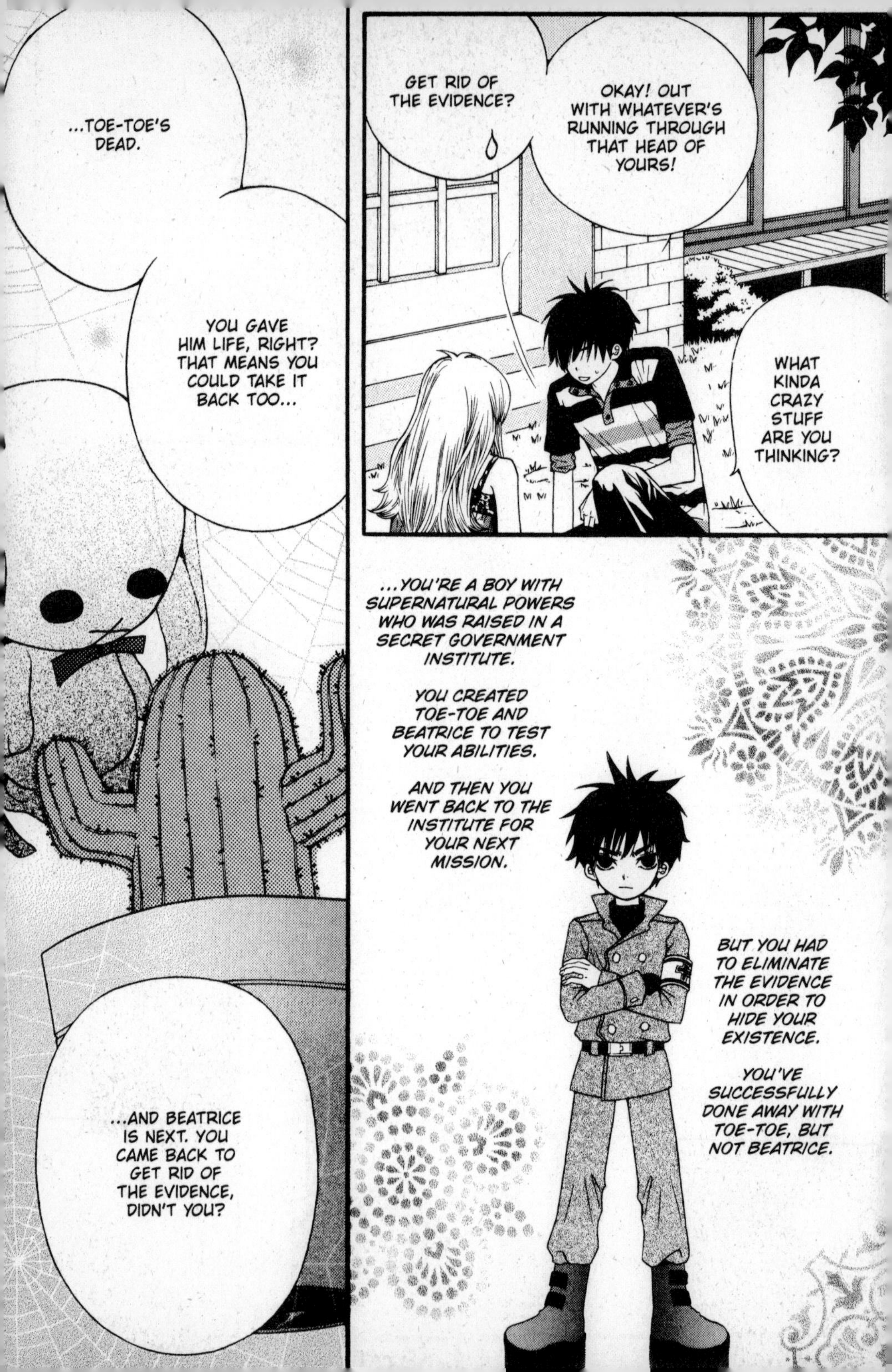
...TOE-TOE'S DEAD.
YOU GAVE HIM LIFE, RIGHT? THAT MEANS YOU COULD TAKE IT BACK TOO...
...AND BEATRICE IS NEXT. YOU CAME BACK TO GET RID OF THE EVIDENCE, DIDN'T YOU?
GET RID OF THE EVIDENCE?
OKAY! OUT WITH WHATEVER'S RUNNING THROUGH THAT HEAD OF YOURS!
WHAT KINDA CRAZY STUFF ARE YOU THINKING?
...YOU'RE A BOY WITH SUPERNATURAL POWERS WHO WAS RAISED IN A SECRET GOVERNMENT INSTITUTE.
YOU CREATED TOE-TOE AND BEATRICE TO TEST YOUR ABILITIES.
AND THEN YOU WENT BACK TO THE INSTITUTE FOR YOUR NEXT MISSION.
BUT YOU HAD TO ELIMINATE THE EVIDENCE IN ORDER TO HIDE YOUR EXISTENCE.
YOU'VE SUCCESSFULLY DONE AWAY WITH TOE-TOE, BUT NOT BEATRICE.

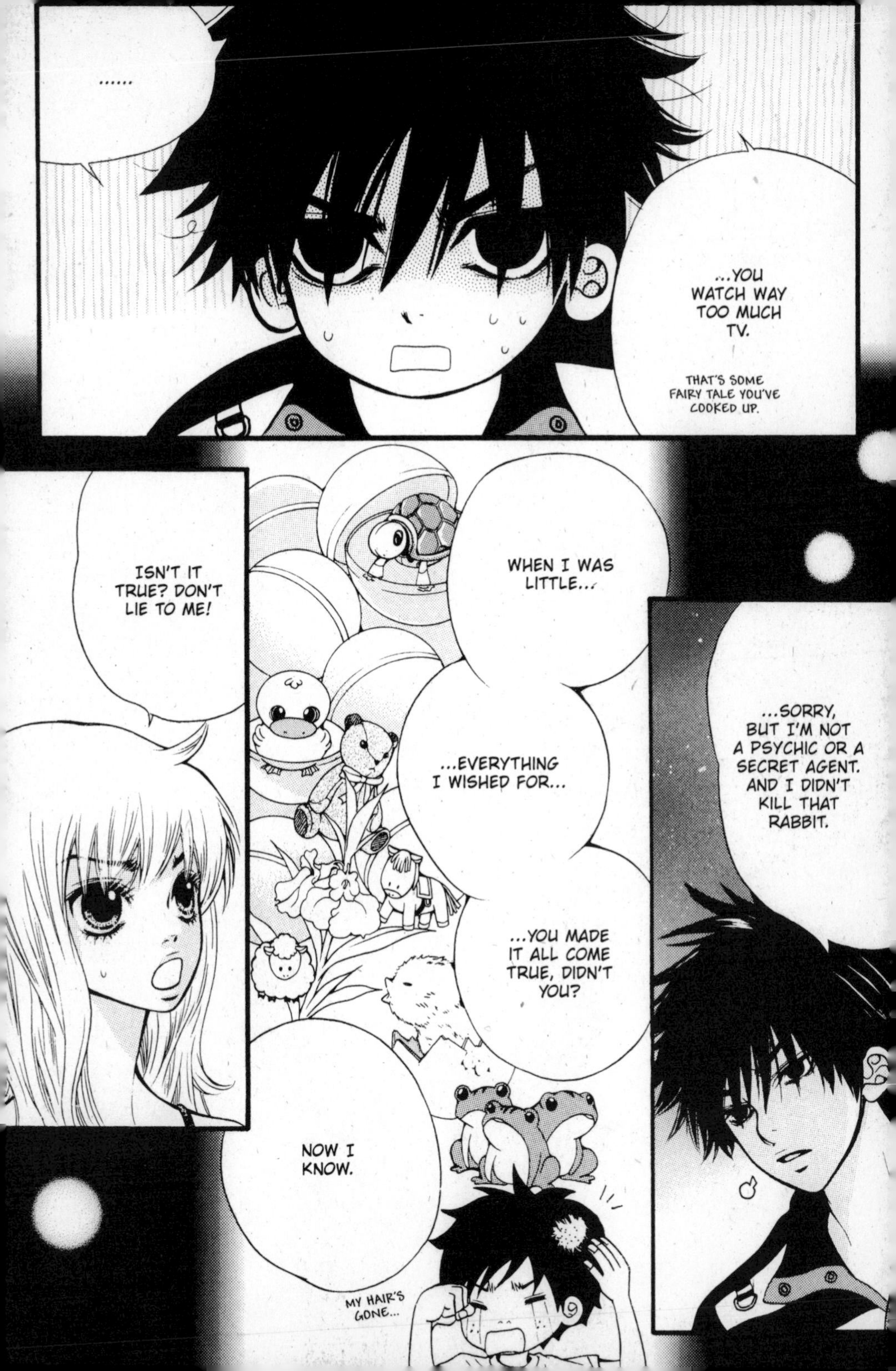
......
...YOU WATCH WAY TOO MUCH TV.
THAT'S SOME FAIRY TALE YOU'VE COOKED UP.
ISN'T IT TRUE? DON'T LIE TO ME!
WHEN I WAS LITTLE...
...EVERYTHING I WISHED FOR...
...YOU MADE IT ALL COME TRUE, DIDN'T YOU?
NOW I KNOW.
MY HAIR'S GONE...
...SORRY, BUT I'M NOT A PSYCHIC OR A SECRET AGENT. AND I DIDN'T KILL THAT RABBIT.

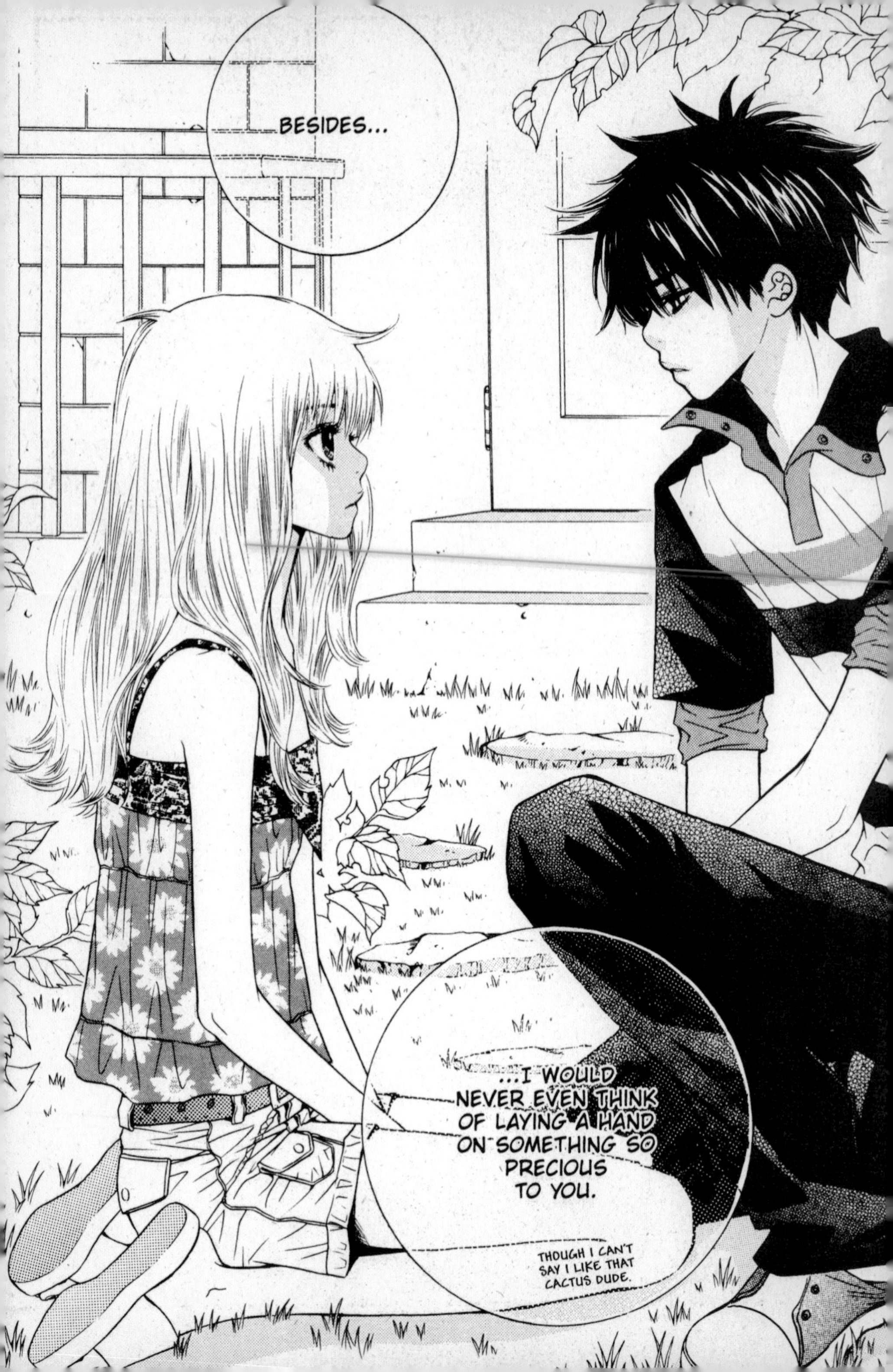
BESIDES...
...I WOULD NEVER EVEN THINK OF LAYING A HAND ON SOMETHING SO PRECIOUS TO YOU.
THOUGH I CAN'T SAY I LIKE THAT CACTUS DUDE.

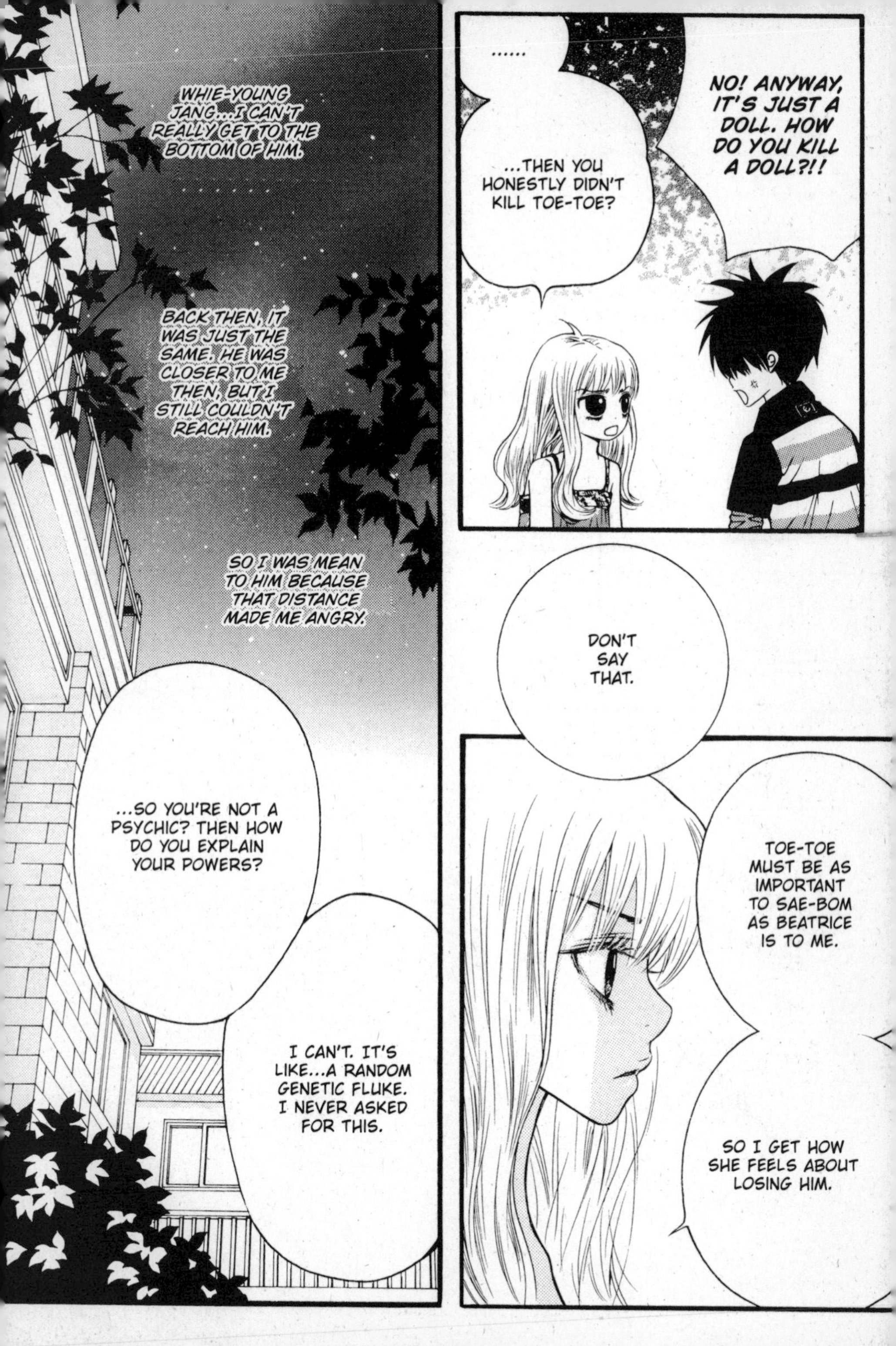
WHIE-YOUNG JANG...I CAN'T REALLY GET TO THE BOTTOM OF HIM.
BACK THEN, IT WAS JUST THE SAME. HE WAS CLOSER TO ME THEN, BUT I STILL COULDN'T REACH HIM.
SO I WAS MEAN TO HIM BECAUSE THAT DISTANCE MADE ME ANGRY.
...SO YOU'RE NOT A PSYCHIC? THEN HOW DO YOU EXPLAIN YOUR POWERS?
I CAN'T. IT'S LIKE...A RANDOM GENETIC FLUKE. I NEVER ASKED FOR THIS.
......
...THEN YOU HONESTLY DIDN'T KILL TOE-TOE?
NO! ANYWAY, IT'S JUST A DOLL. HOW DO YOU KILL A DOLL?!!
DON'T SAY THAT.
TOE-TOE MUST BE AS IMPORTANT TO SAE-BOM AS BEATRICE IS TO ME.
SO I GET HOW SHE FEELS ABOUT LOSING HIM.

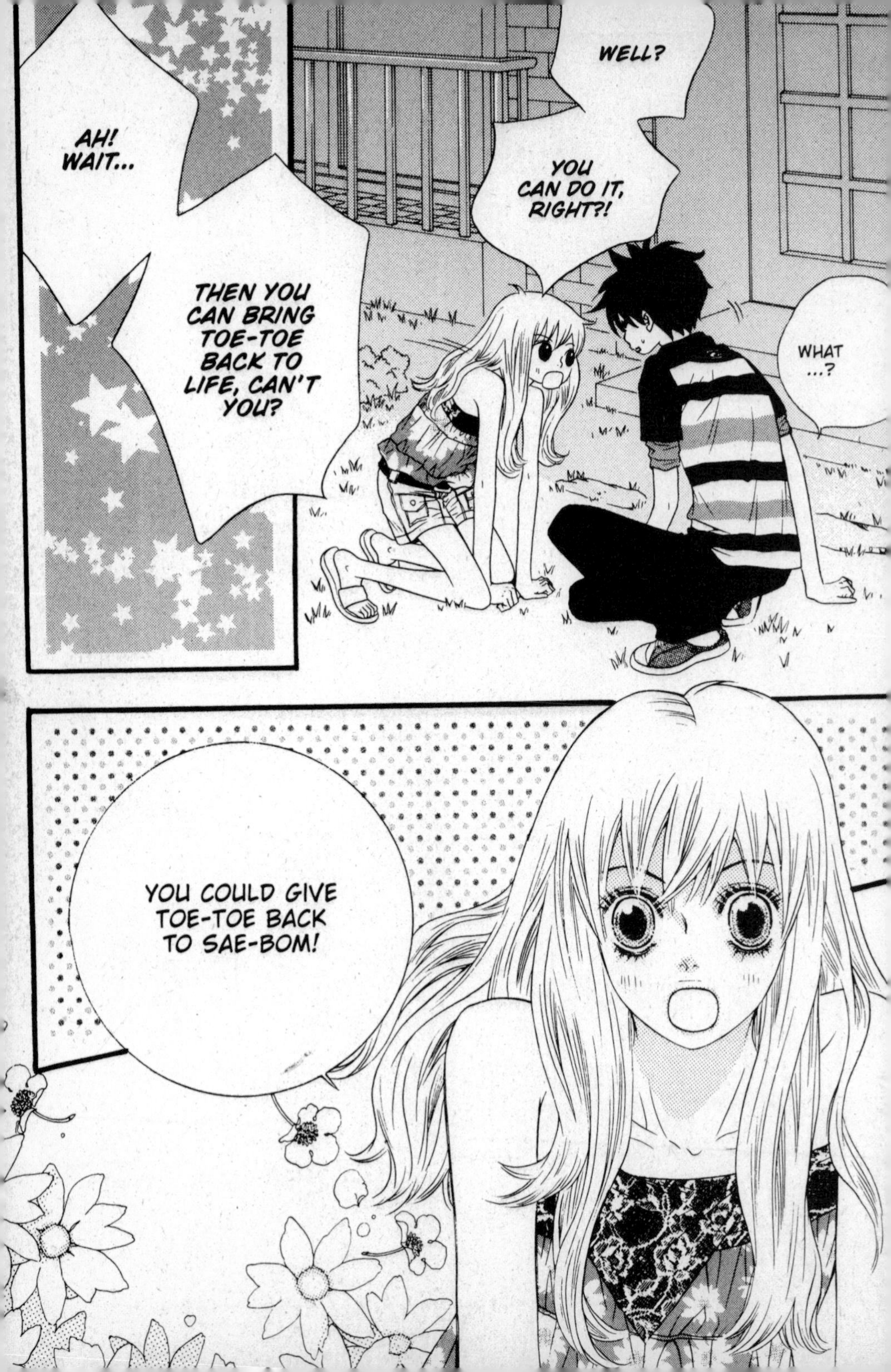
AH! WAIT...
THEN YOU CAN BRING TOE-TOE BACK TO LIFE, CAN'T YOU?
WELL?
YOU CAN DO IT, RIGHT?!
WHAT ...?
YOU COULD GIVE TOE-TOE BACK TO SAE-BOM!

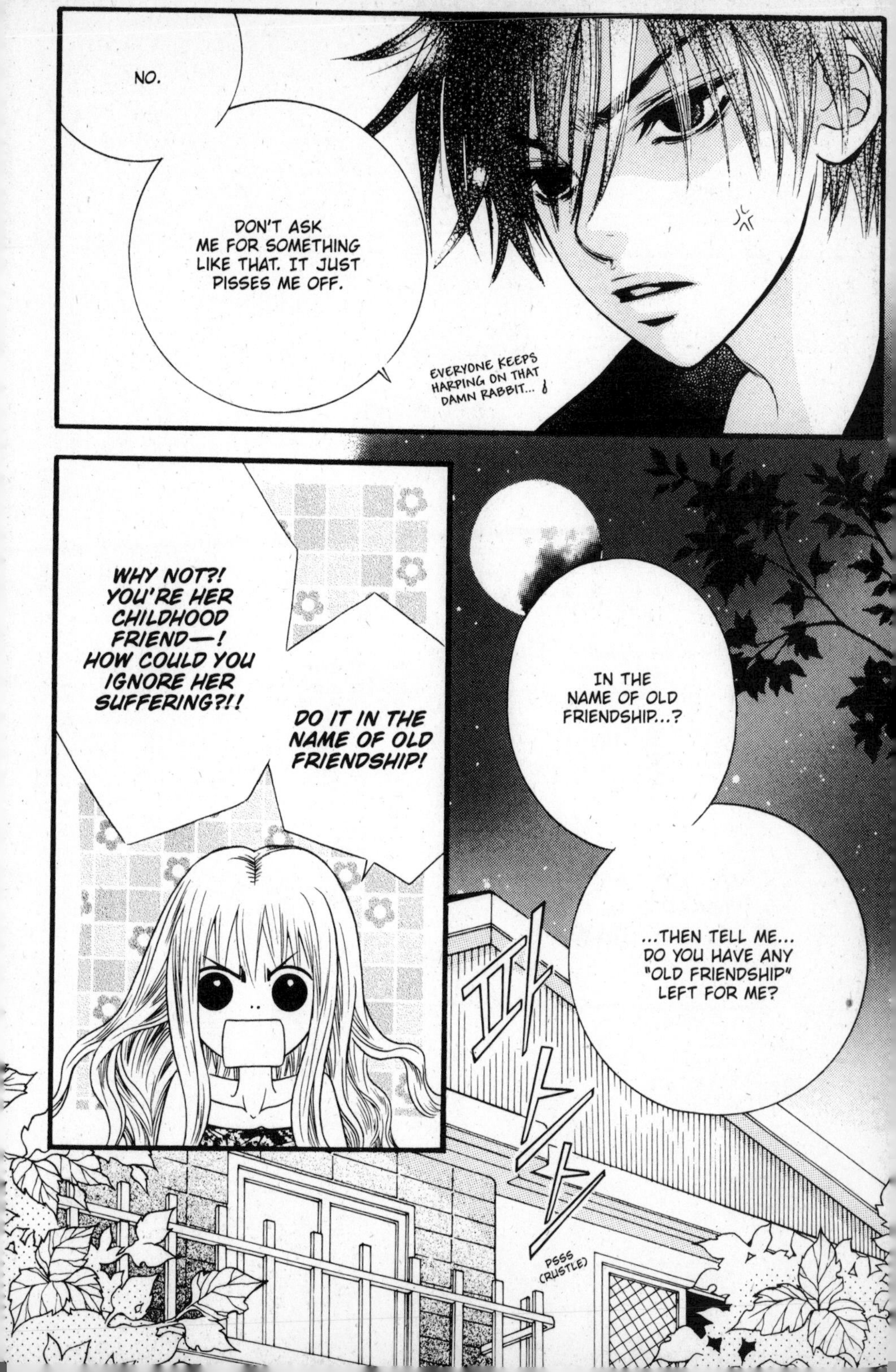
NO.
DON'T ASK ME FOR SOMETHING LIKE THAT. IT JUST PISSES ME OFF.
EVERYONE KEEPS HARPING ON THAT DAMN RABBIT...
WHY NOT?! YOU'RE HER CHILDHOOD FRIEND—! HOW COULD YOU IGNORE HER SUFFERING?!!
DO IT IN THE NAME OF OLD FRIENDSHIP!
IN THE NAME OF OLD FRIENDSHIP...?
...THEN TELL ME... DO YOU HAVE ANY "OLD FRIENDSHIP" LEFT FOR ME?
PSSS (RUSTLE)

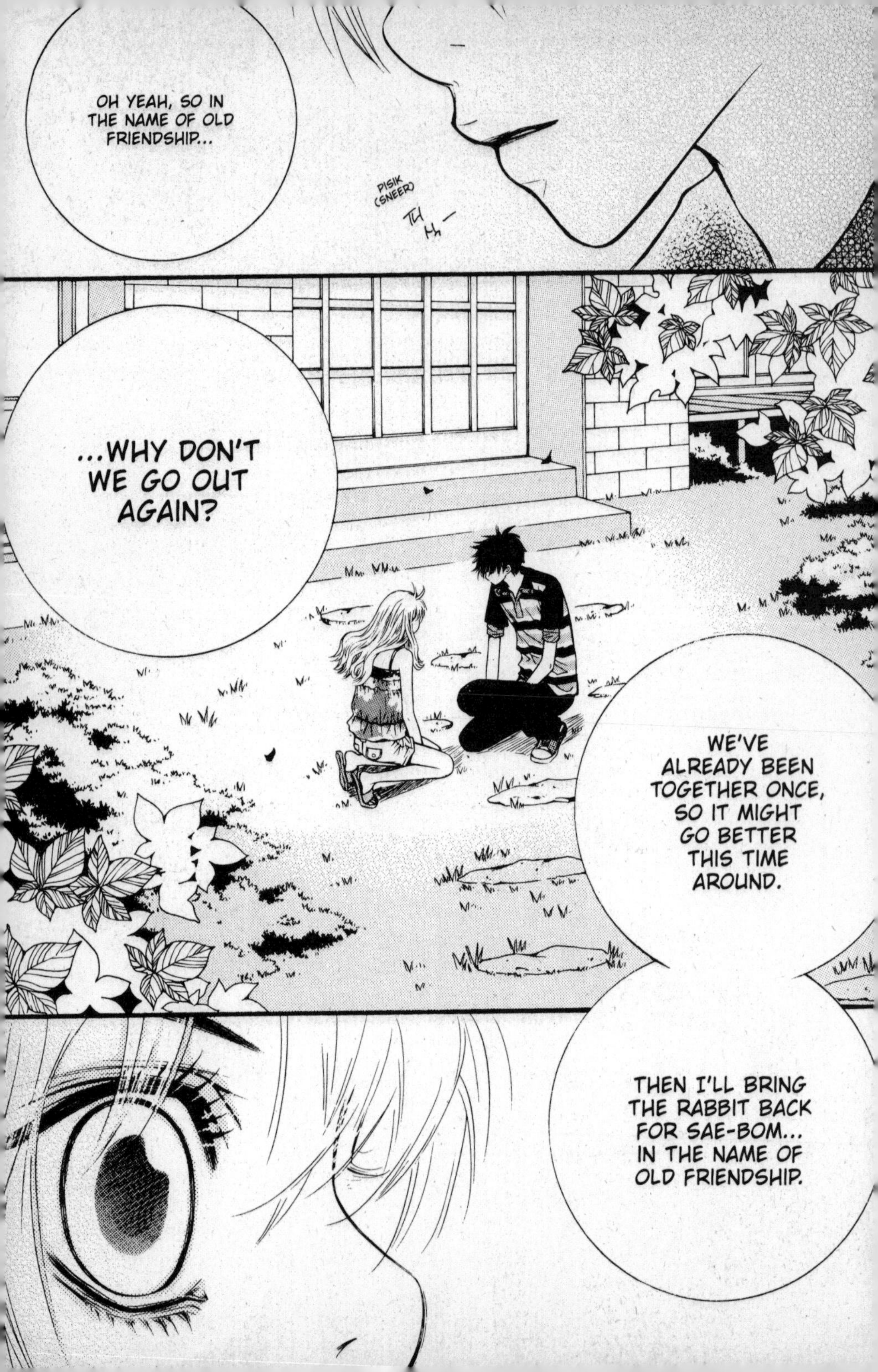
OH YEAH, SO IN THE NAME OF OLD FRIENDSHIP...
PISIK (SNEER)
...WHY DON'T WE GO OUT AGAIN?
WE'VE ALREADY BEEN TOGETHER ONCE, SO IT MIGHT GO BETTER THIS TIME AROUND.
THEN I'LL BRING THE RABBIT BACK FOR SAE-BOM... IN THE NAME OF OLD FRIENDSHIP.

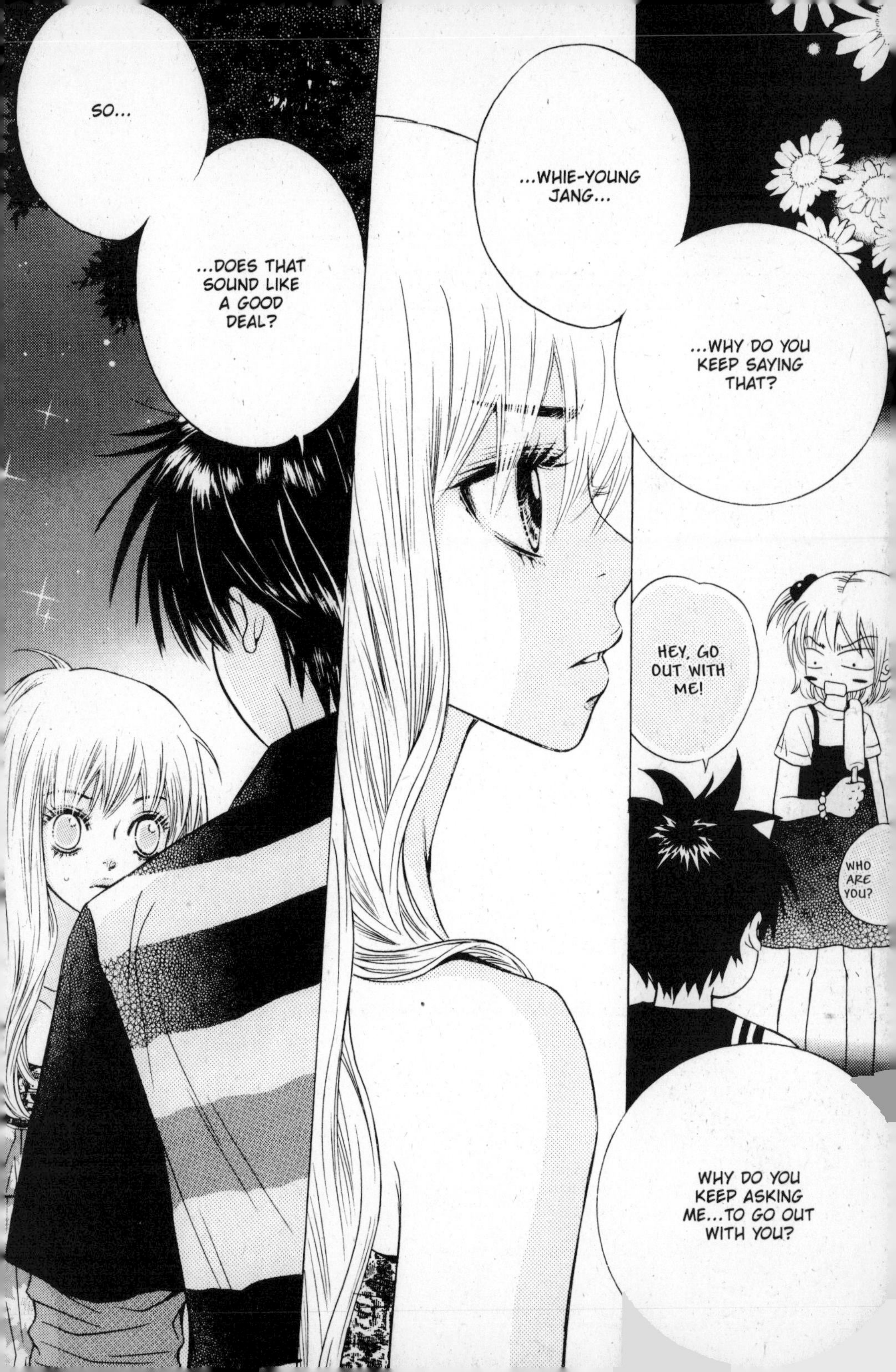
SO...
...DOES THAT SOUND LIKE A GOOD DEAL?
...WHIE-YOUNG JANG...
...WHY DO YOU KEEP SAYING THAT?
HEY, GO OUT WITH ME!
WHO ARE YOU?
WHY DO YOU KEEP ASKING ME...TO GO OUT WITH YOU?

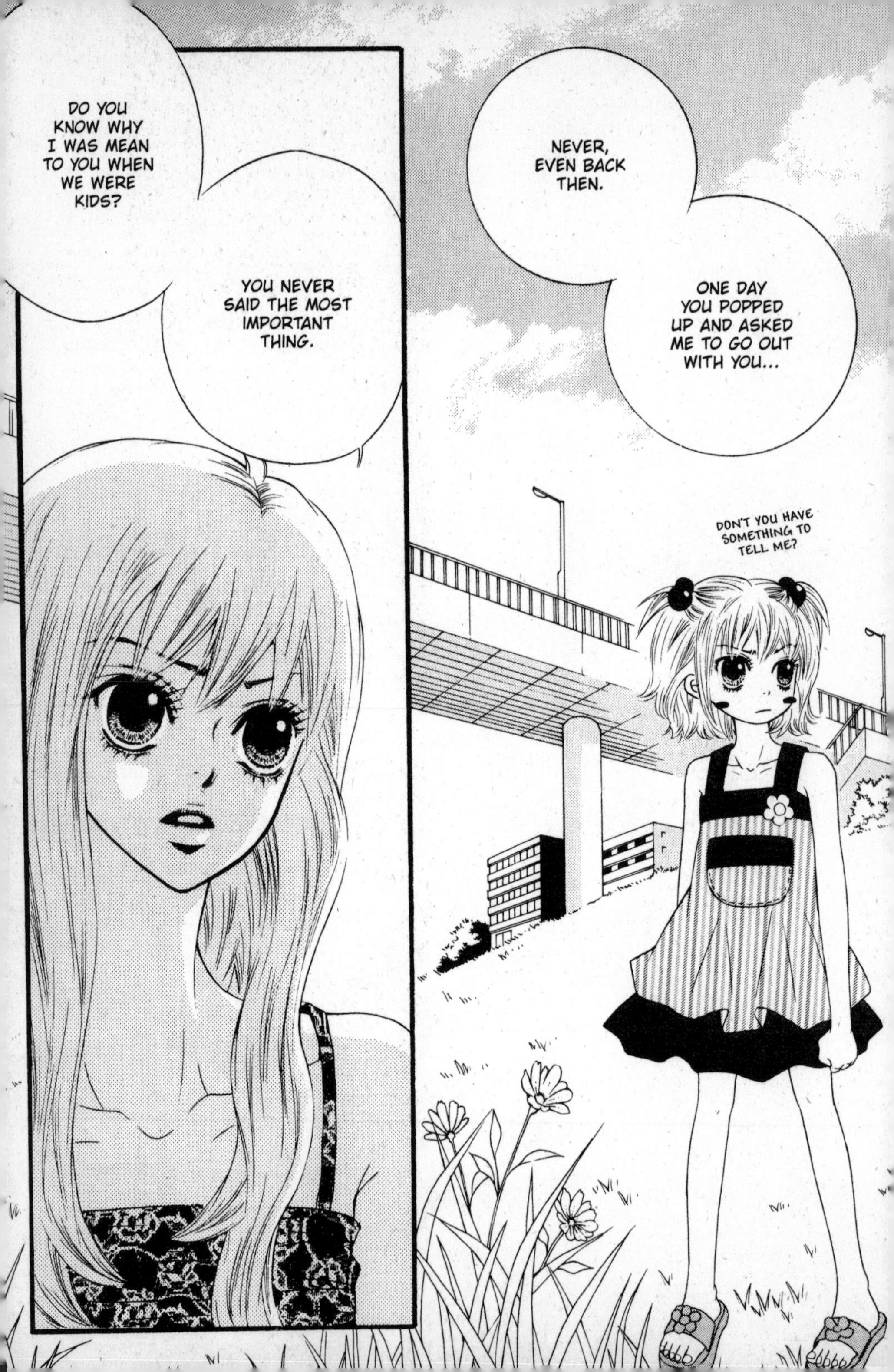
DO YOU KNOW WHY I WAS MEAN TO YOU WHEN WE WERE KIDS?
YOU NEVER SAID THE MOST IMPORTANT THING.
NEVER, EVEN BACK THEN.
ONE DAY YOU POPPED UP AND ASKED ME TO GO OUT WITH YOU...
DON'T YOU HAVE SOMETHING TO TELL ME?

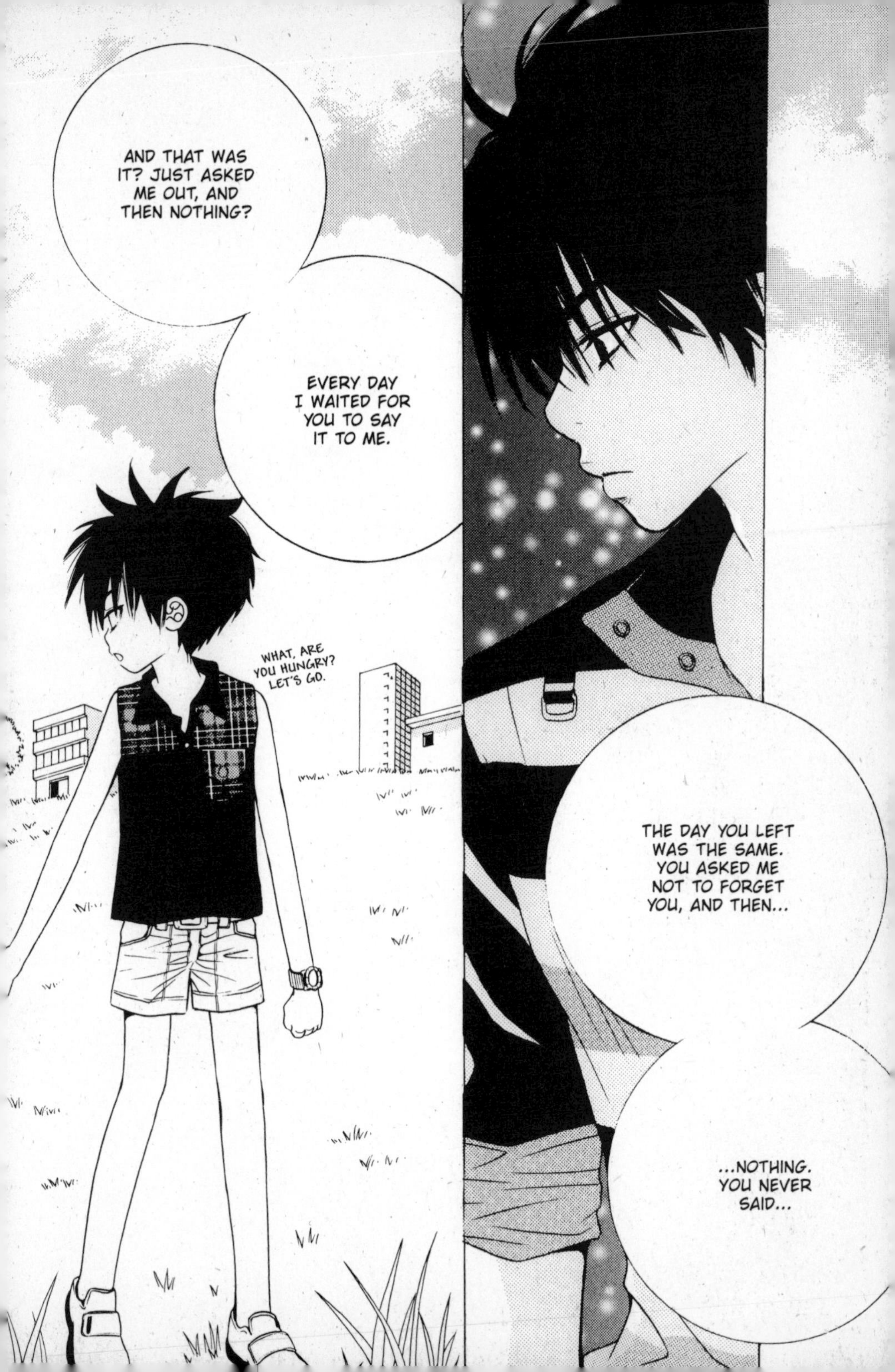
AND THAT WAS IT? JUST ASKED ME OUT, AND THEN NOTHING?
EVERY DAY I WAITED FOR YOU TO SAY IT TO ME.
WHAT, ARE YOU HUNGRY? LET'S GO.
THE DAY YOU LEFT WAS THE SAME. YOU ASKED ME NOT TO FORGET YOU, AND THEN...
...NOTHING. YOU NEVER SAID...

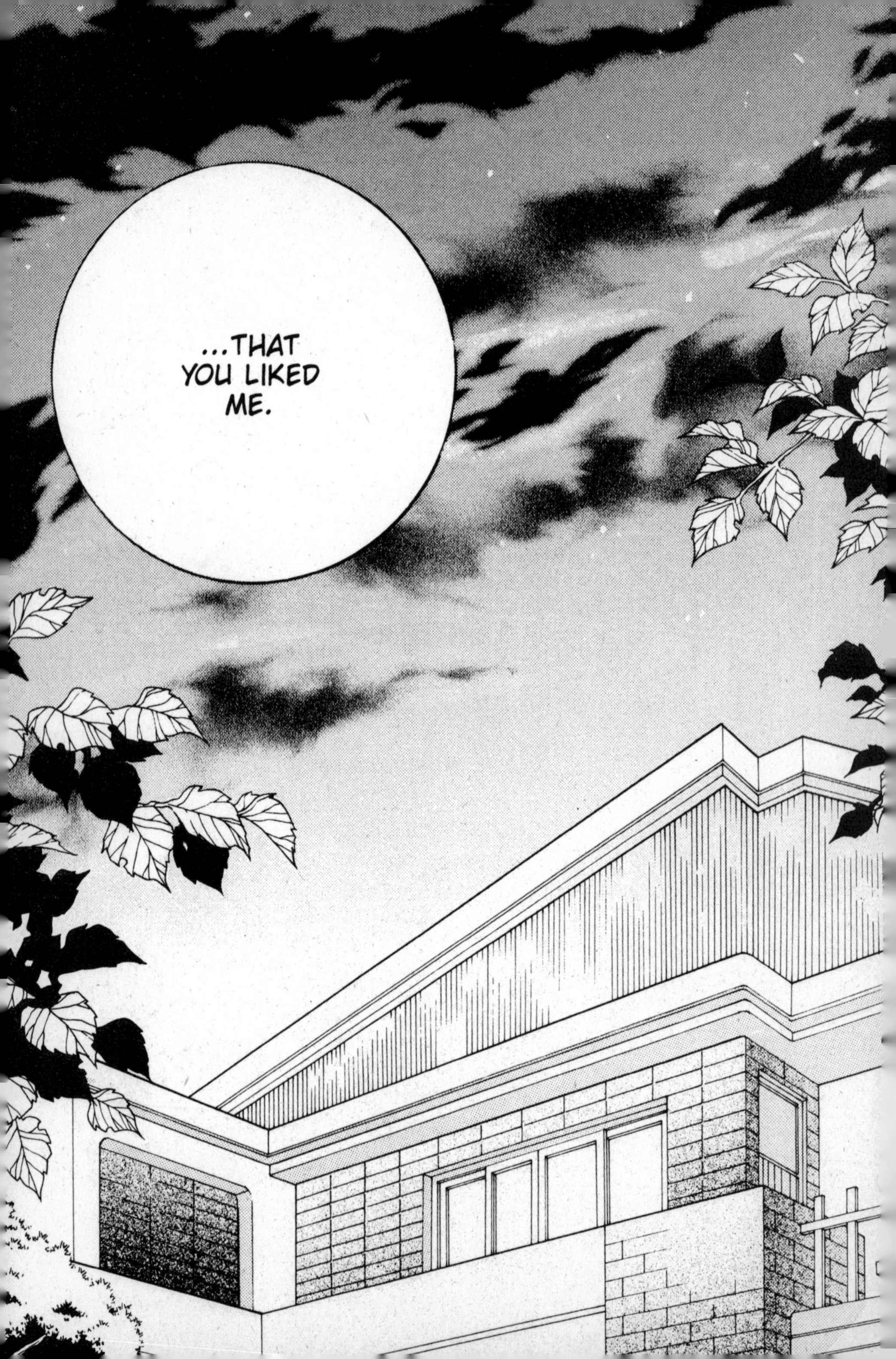
...THAT YOU LIKED ME.

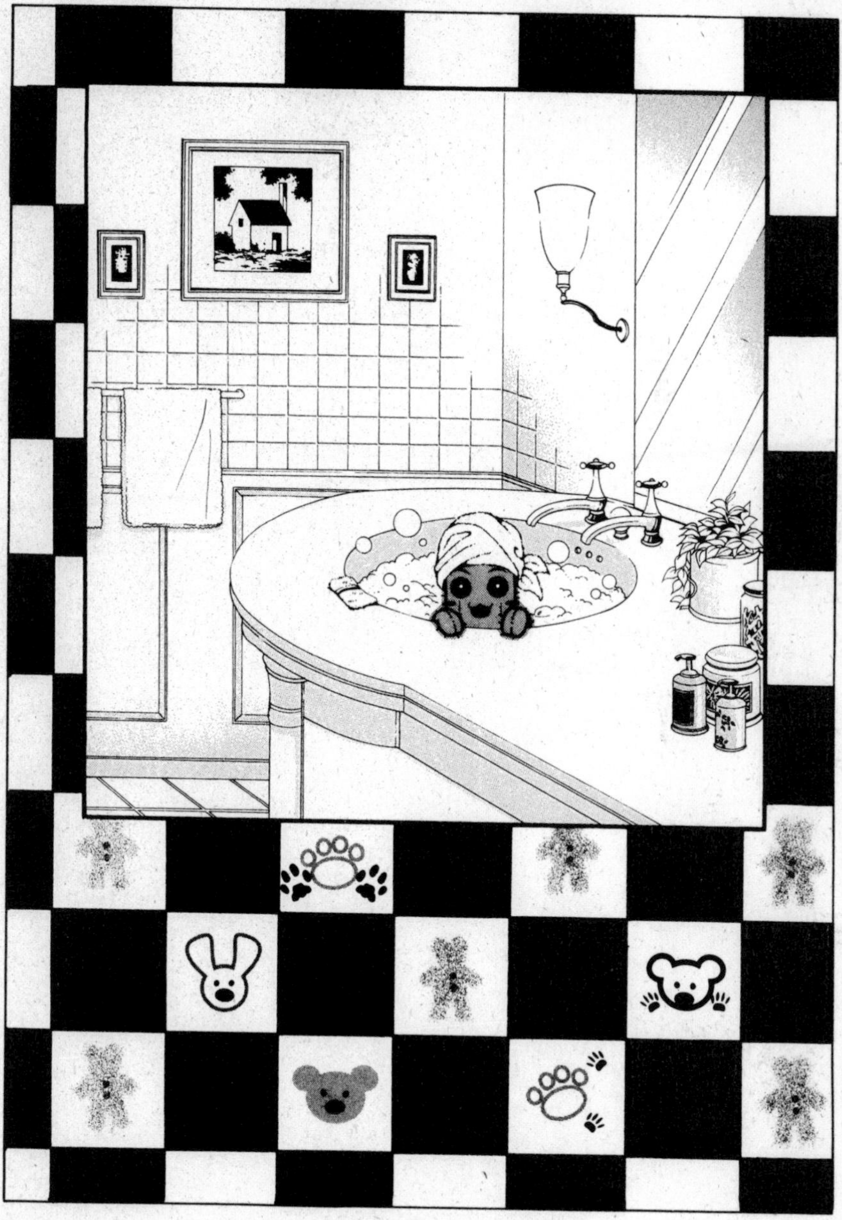

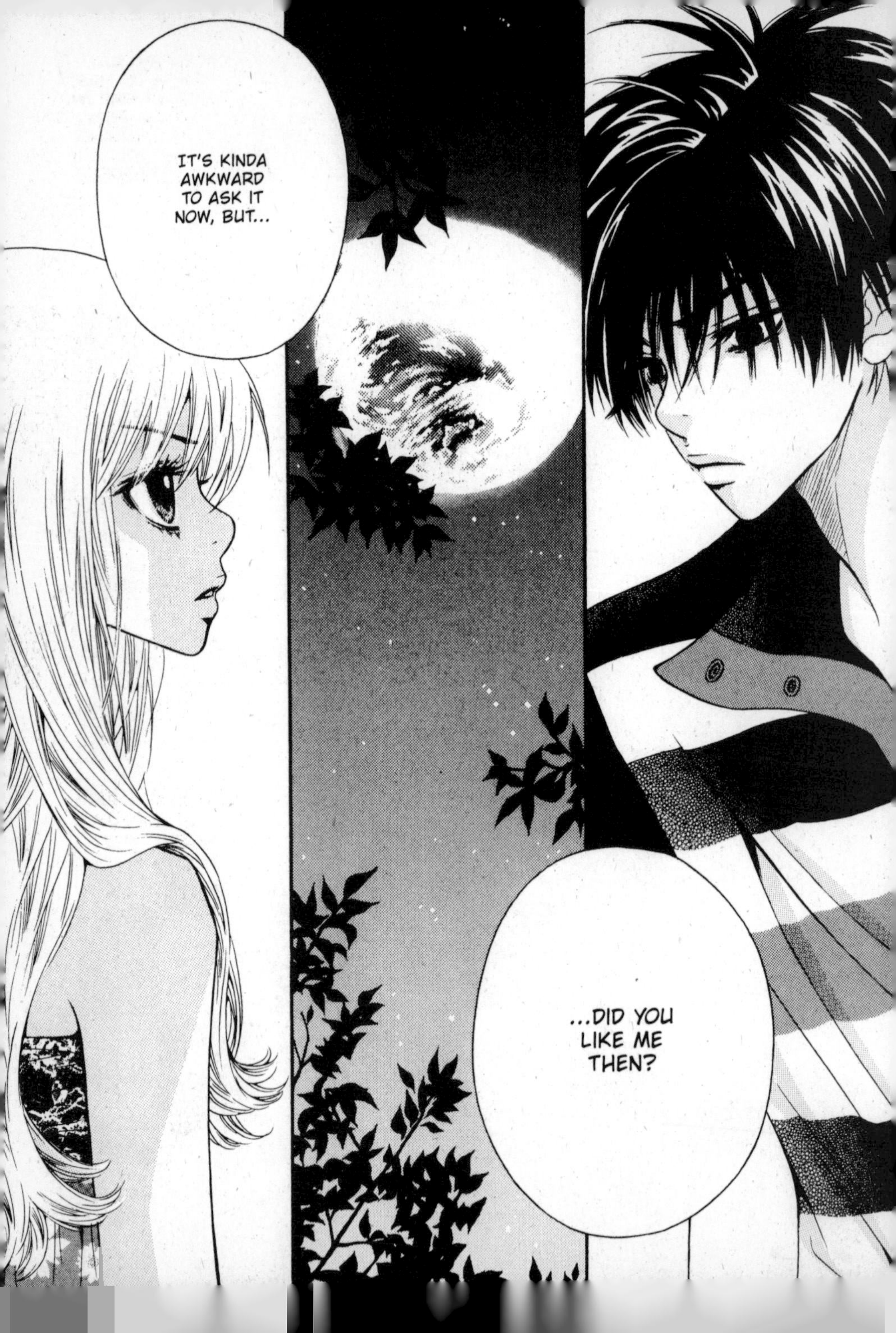
IT'S KINDA AWKWARD TO ASK IT NOW, BUT...
...DID YOU LIKE ME THEN?

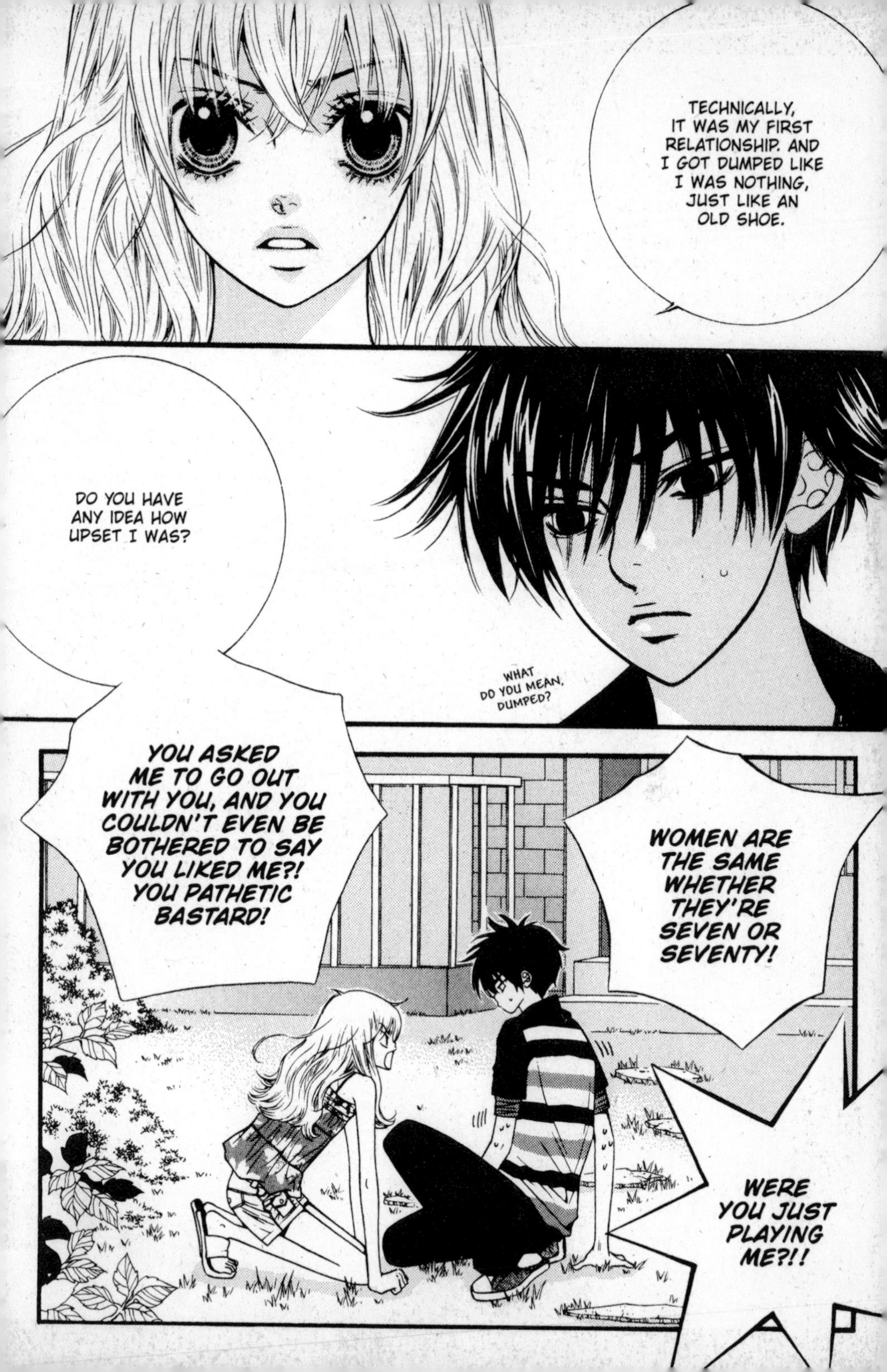
TECHNICALLY, IT WAS MY FIRST RELATIONSHIP. AND I GOT DUMPED LIKE I WAS NOTHING, JUST LIKE AN OLD SHOE.
DO YOU HAVE ANY IDEA HOW UPSET I WAS?
WHAT DO YOU MEAN, DUMPED?
YOU ASKED ME TO GO OUT WITH YOU, AND YOU COULDN'T EVEN BE BOTHERED TO SAY YOU LIKED ME?! YOU PATHETIC BASTARD!
WOMEN ARE THE SAME WHETHER THEY'RE SEVEN OR SEVENTY!
WERE YOU JUST PLAYING ME?!!

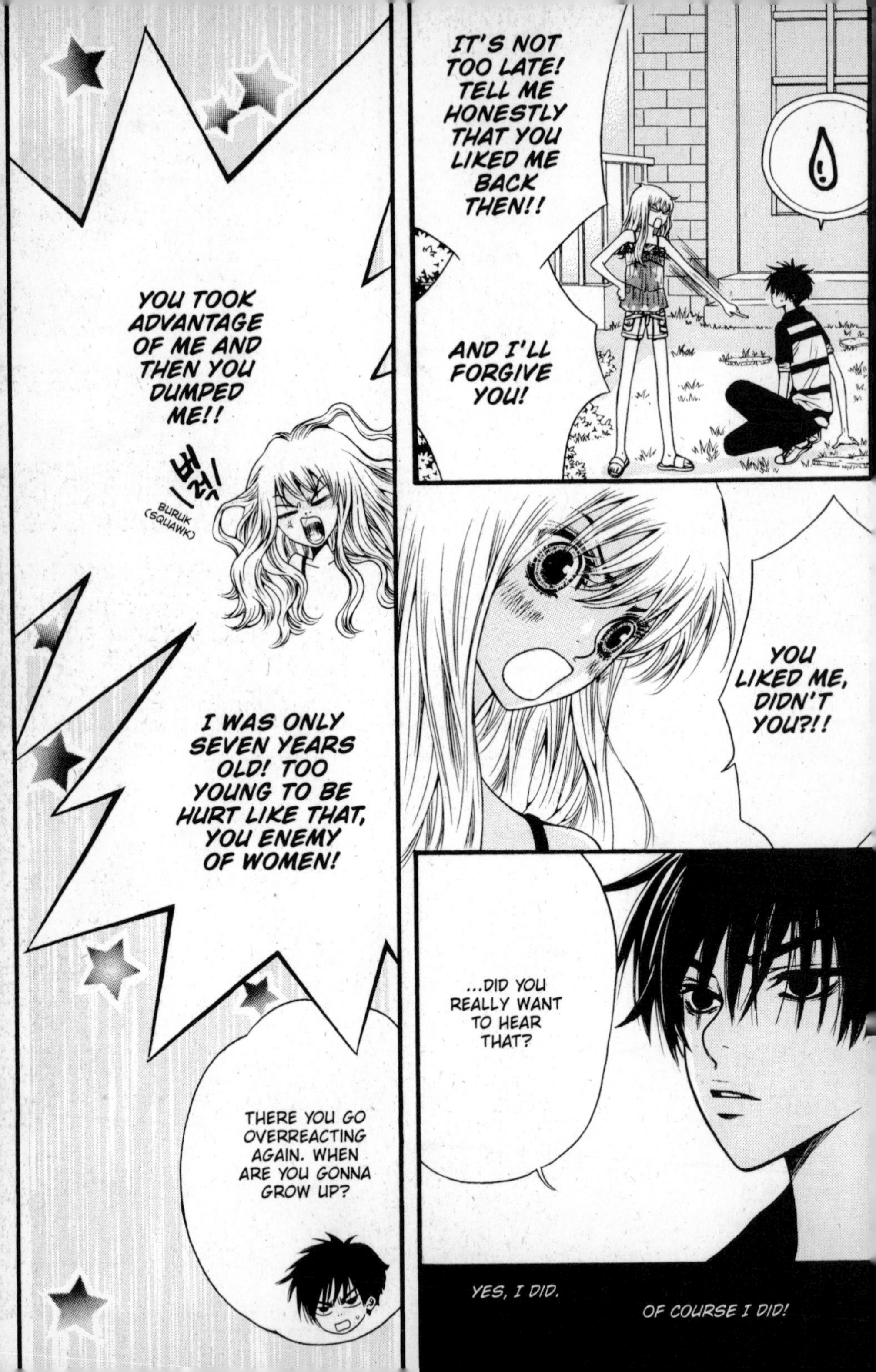
YOU TOOK ADVANTAGE OF ME AND THEN YOU DUMPED ME!!
BURUK (SQUAWK)
I WAS ONLY SEVEN YEARS OLD! TOO YOUNG TO BE HURT LIKE THAT, YOU ENEMY OF WOMEN!
THERE YOU GO OVERREACTING AGAIN. WHEN ARE YOU GONNA GROW UP?
IT'S NOT TOO LATE! TELL ME HONESTLY THAT YOU LIKED ME BACK THEN!!
AND I'LL FORGIVE YOU!
YOU LIKED ME, DIDN'T YOU?!!
...DID YOU REALLY WANT TO HEAR THAT?
YES, I DID.
OF COURSE I DID!

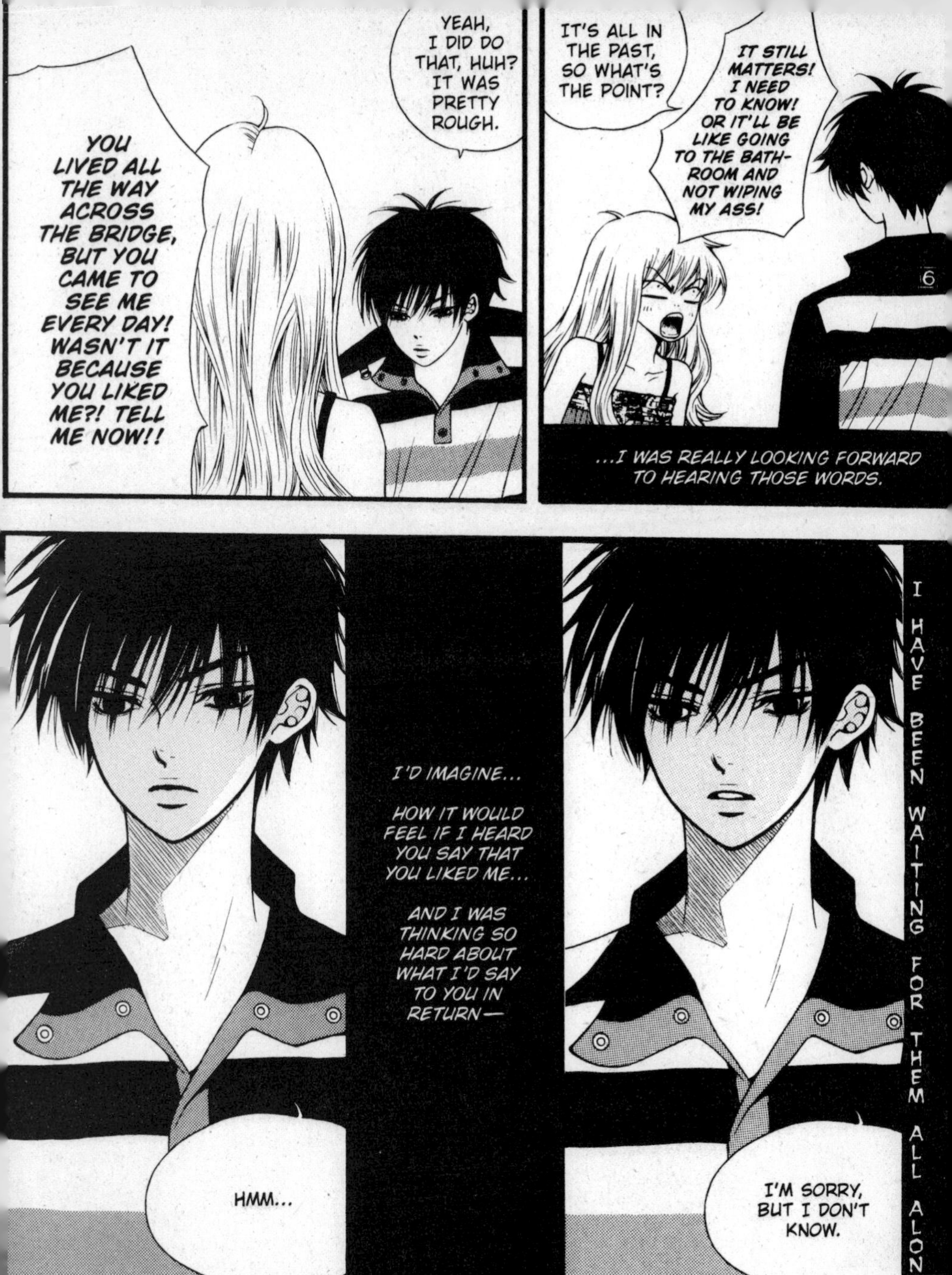
YOU LIVED ALL THE WAY ACROSS THE BRIDGE, BUT YOU CAME TO SEE ME EVERY DAY! WASN'T IT BECAUSE YOU LIKED ME?! TELL ME NOW!!
YEAH, I DID DO THAT, HUH? IT WAS PRETTY ROUGH.
IT'S ALL IN THE PAST, SO WHAT'S THE POINT?
IT STILL MATTERS! I NEED TO KNOW! OR IT'LL BE LIKE GOING TO THE BATH-ROOM AND NOT WIPING MY ASS!
...I WAS REALLY LOOKING FORWARD TO HEARING THOSE WORDS.
HMM...
I'D IMAGINE...
HOW IT WOULD FEEL IF I HEARD YOU SAY THAT YOU LIKED ME...
AND I WAS THINKING SO HARD ABOUT WHAT I'D SAY TO YOU IN RETURN—
I'M SORRY, BUT I DON'T KNOW.
I HAVE BEEN WAITING FOR THEM ALL ALONG!

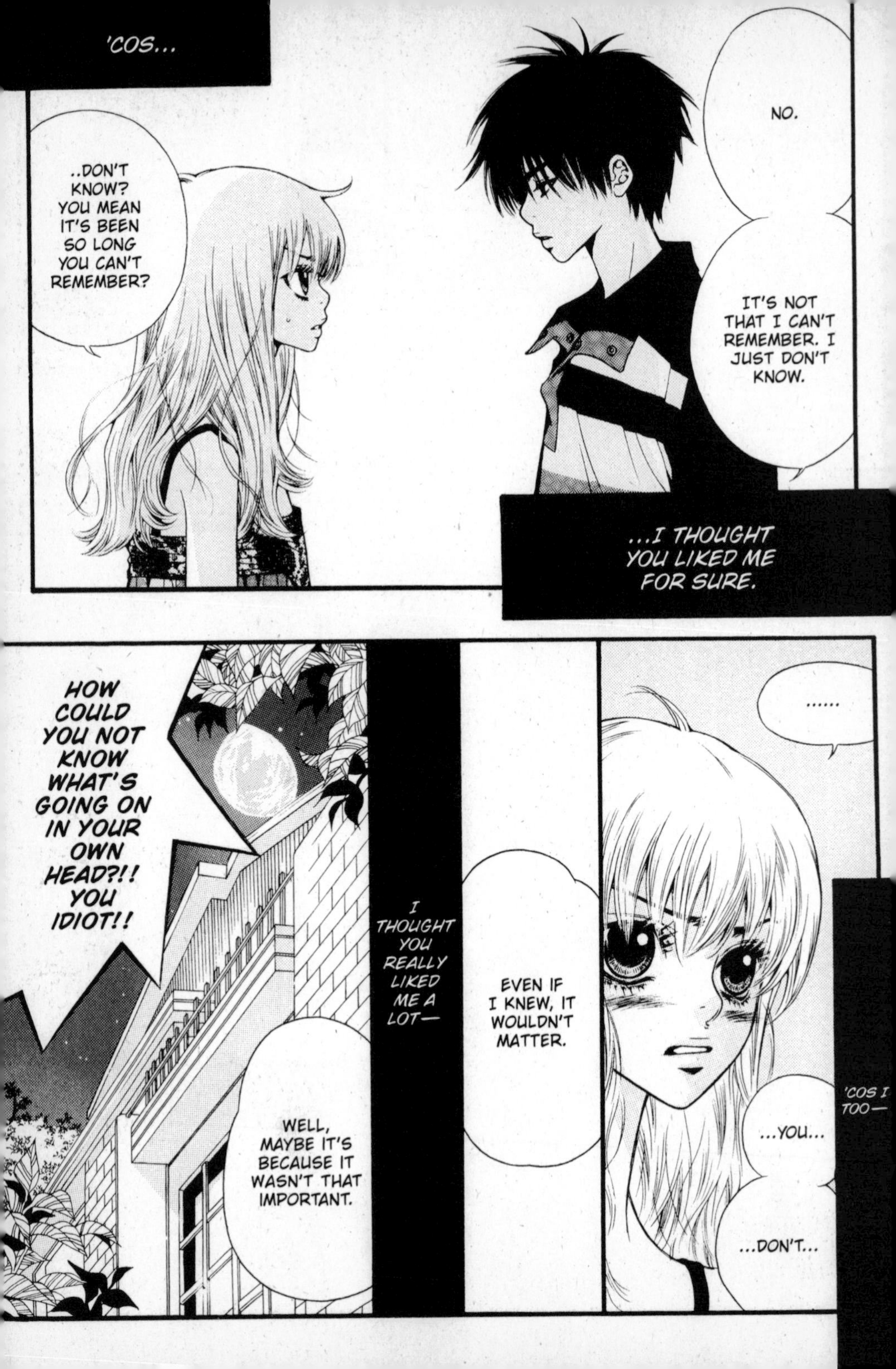
'COS...
..DON'T KNOW? YOU MEAN IT'S BEEN SO LONG YOU CAN'T REMEMBER?
NO.
IT'S NOT THAT I CAN'T REMEMBER. I JUST DON'T KNOW.
...I THOUGHT YOU LIKED ME FOR SURE.
HOW COULD YOU NOT KNOW WHAT'S GOING ON IN YOUR OWN HEAD?!! YOU IDIOT!!
WELL, MAYBE IT'S BECAUSE IT WASN'T THAT IMPORTANT.
I THOUGHT YOU REALLY LIKED ME A LOT—
EVEN IF I KNEW, IT WOULDN'T MATTER.
......
...YOU...
...DON'T...
'COS I TOO—

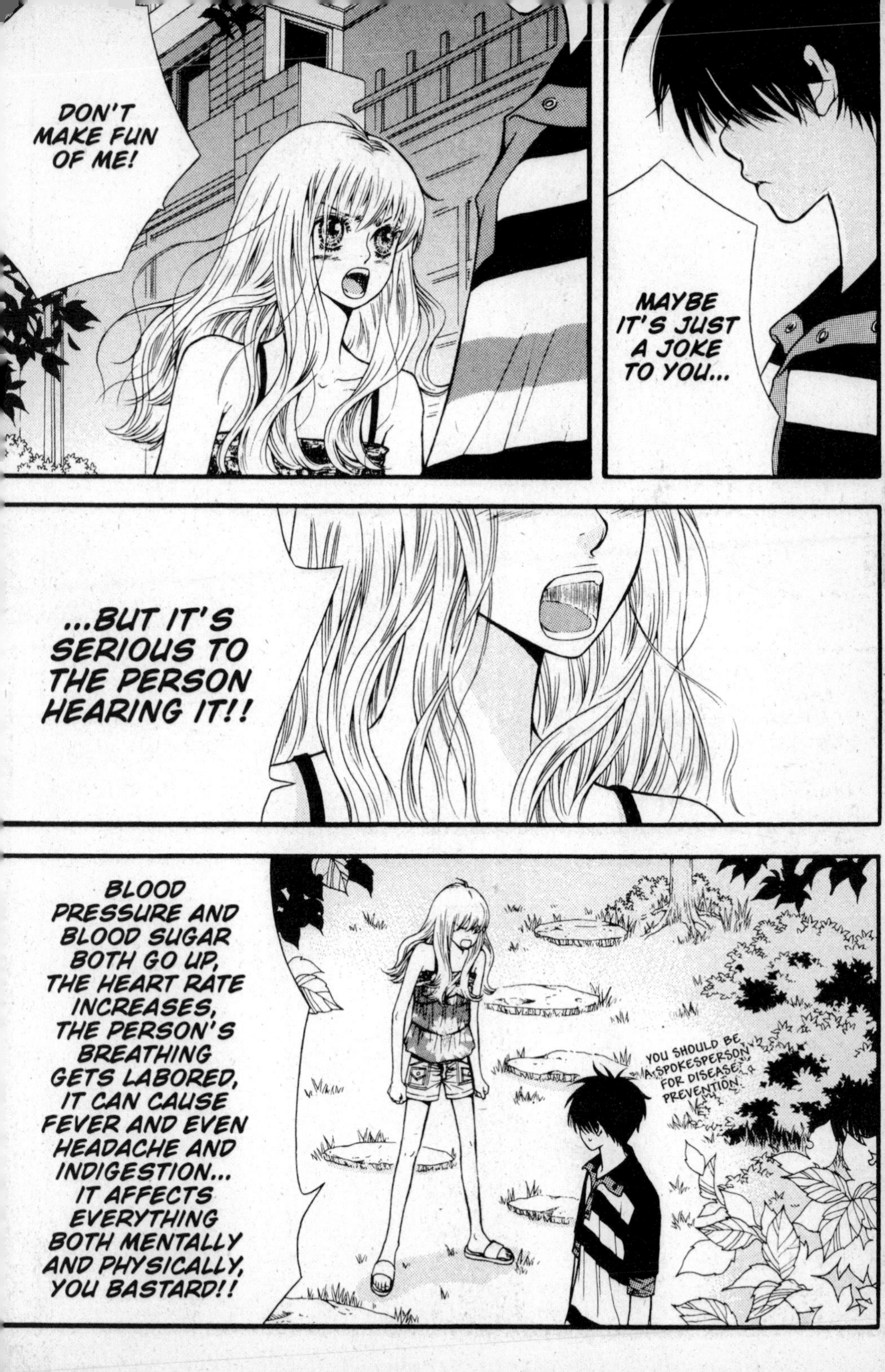
DON'T MAKE FUN OF ME!
MAYBE IT'S JUST A JOKE TO YOU...
...BUT IT'S SERIOUS TO THE PERSON HEARING IT!!
BLOOD PRESSURE AND BLOOD SUGAR BOTH GO UP, THE HEART RATE INCREASES, THE PERSON'S BREATHING GETS LABORED, IT CAN CAUSE FEVER AND EVEN HEADACHE AND INDIGESTION... IT AFFECTS EVERYTHING BOTH MENTALLY AND PHYSICALLY, YOU BASTARD!!
YOU SHOULD BE A SPOKESPERSON FOR DISEASE PREVENTION.

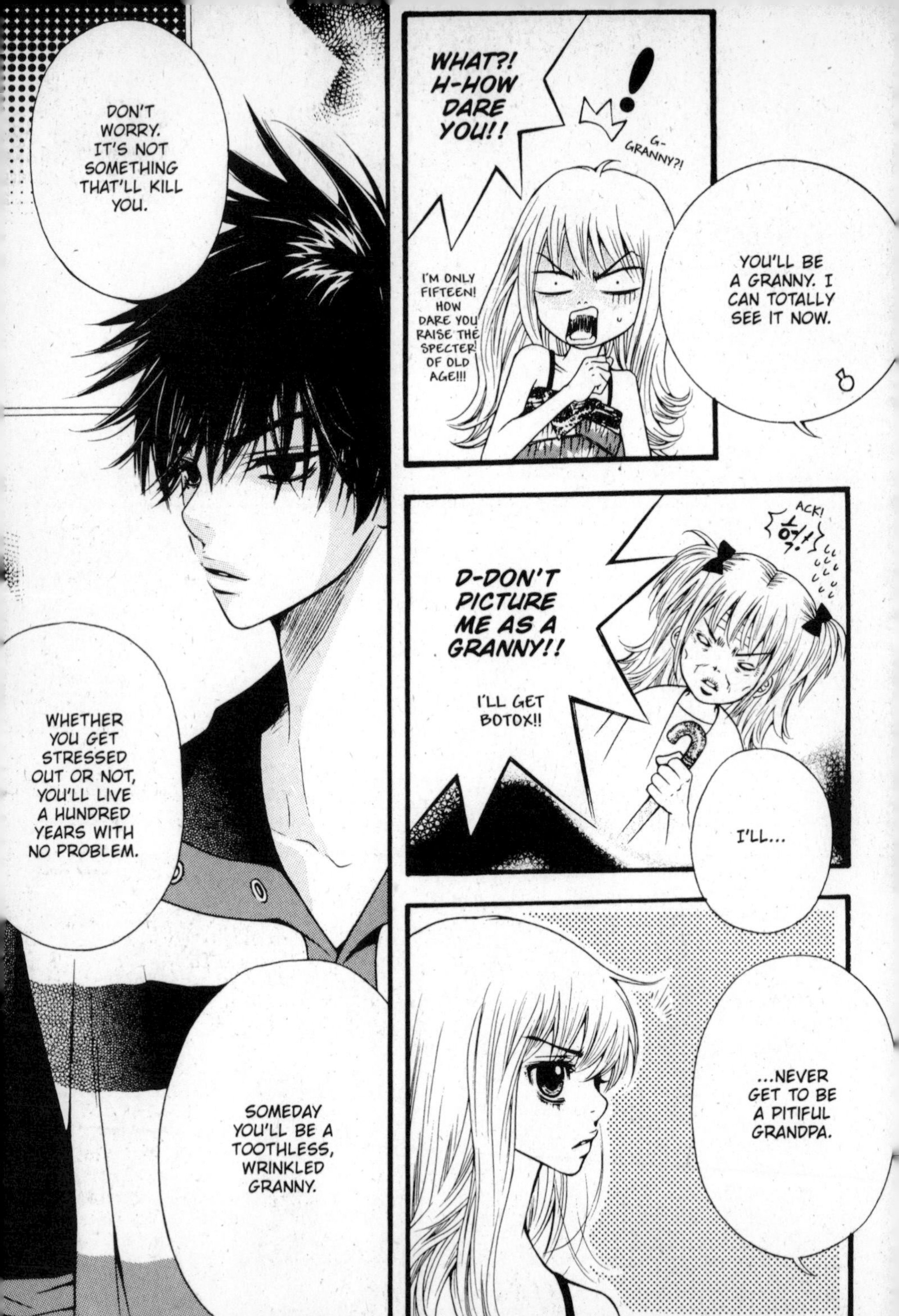
DON'T WORRY. IT'S NOT SOMETHING THAT'LL KILL YOU.
WHETHER YOU GET STRESSED OUT OR NOT, YOU'LL LIVE A HUNDRED YEARS WITH NO PROBLEM.
SOMEDAY YOU'LL BE A TOOTHLESS, WRINKLED GRANNY.
WHAT?! H-HOW DARE YOU!!
G-GRANNY?!
I'M ONLY FIFTEEN! HOW DARE YOU RAISE THE SPECTER OF OLD AGE!!!
YOU'LL BE A GRANNY. I CAN TOTALLY SEE IT NOW.
ACK!
D-DON'T PICTURE ME AS A GRANNY!!
I'LL GET BOTOX!!
I'LL...
...NEVER GET TO BE A PITIFUL GRANDPA.

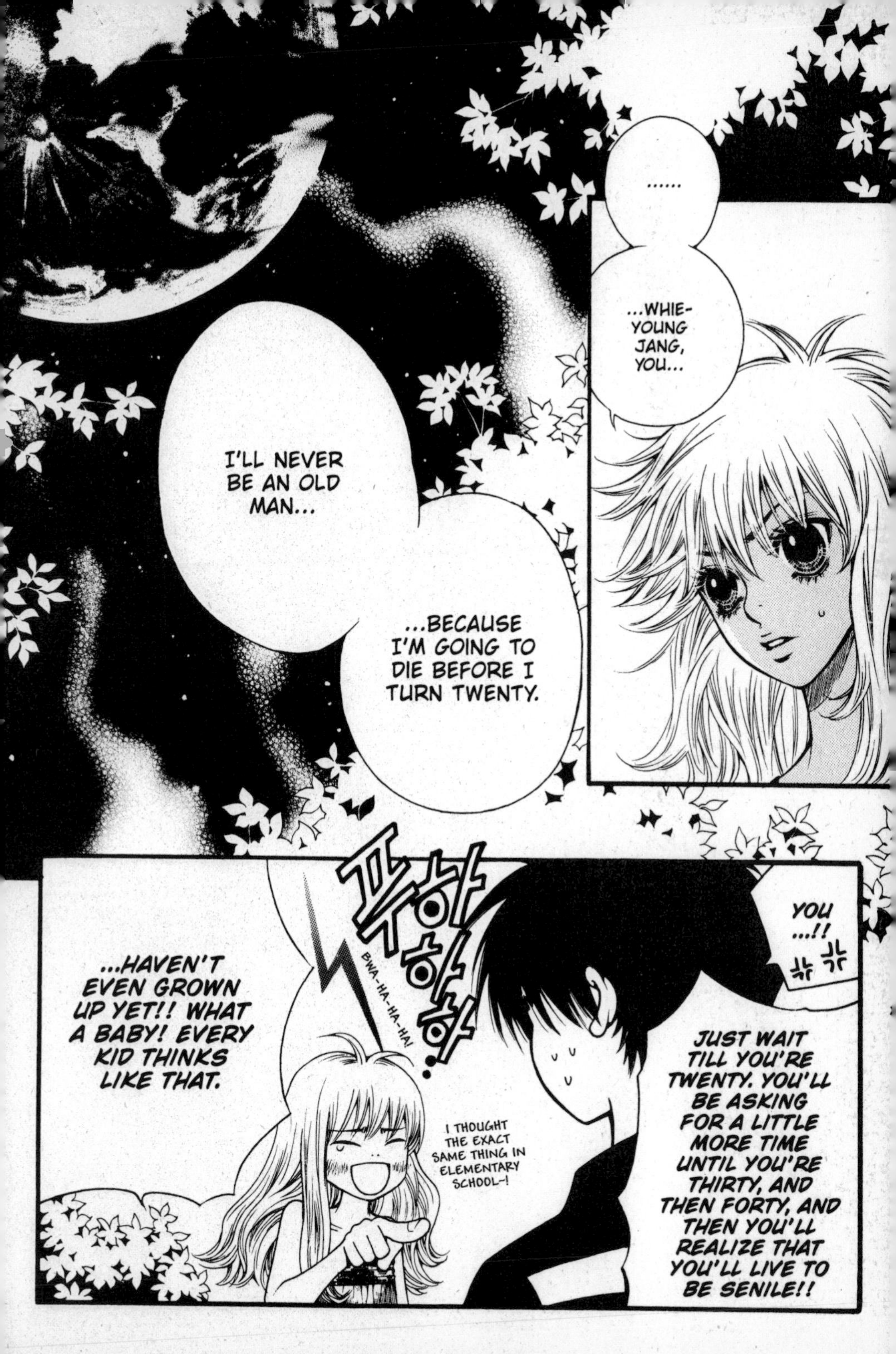
I'LL NEVER BE AN OLD MAN...
...BECAUSE I'M GOING TO DIE BEFORE I TURN TWENTY.
......
...WHIE-YOUNG JANG, YOU...
...HAVEN'T EVEN GROWN UP YET!! WHAT A BABY! EVERY KID THINKS LIKE THAT.
푸하하하!
BWA-HA-HA-HA!
YOU ...!!
I THOUGHT THE EXACT SAME THING IN ELEMENTARY SCHOOL-!
JUST WAIT TILL YOU'RE TWENTY. YOU'LL BE ASKING FOR A LITTLE MORE TIME UNTIL YOU'RE THIRTY, AND THEN FORTY, AND THEN YOU'LL REALIZE THAT YOU'LL LIVE TO BE SENILE!!

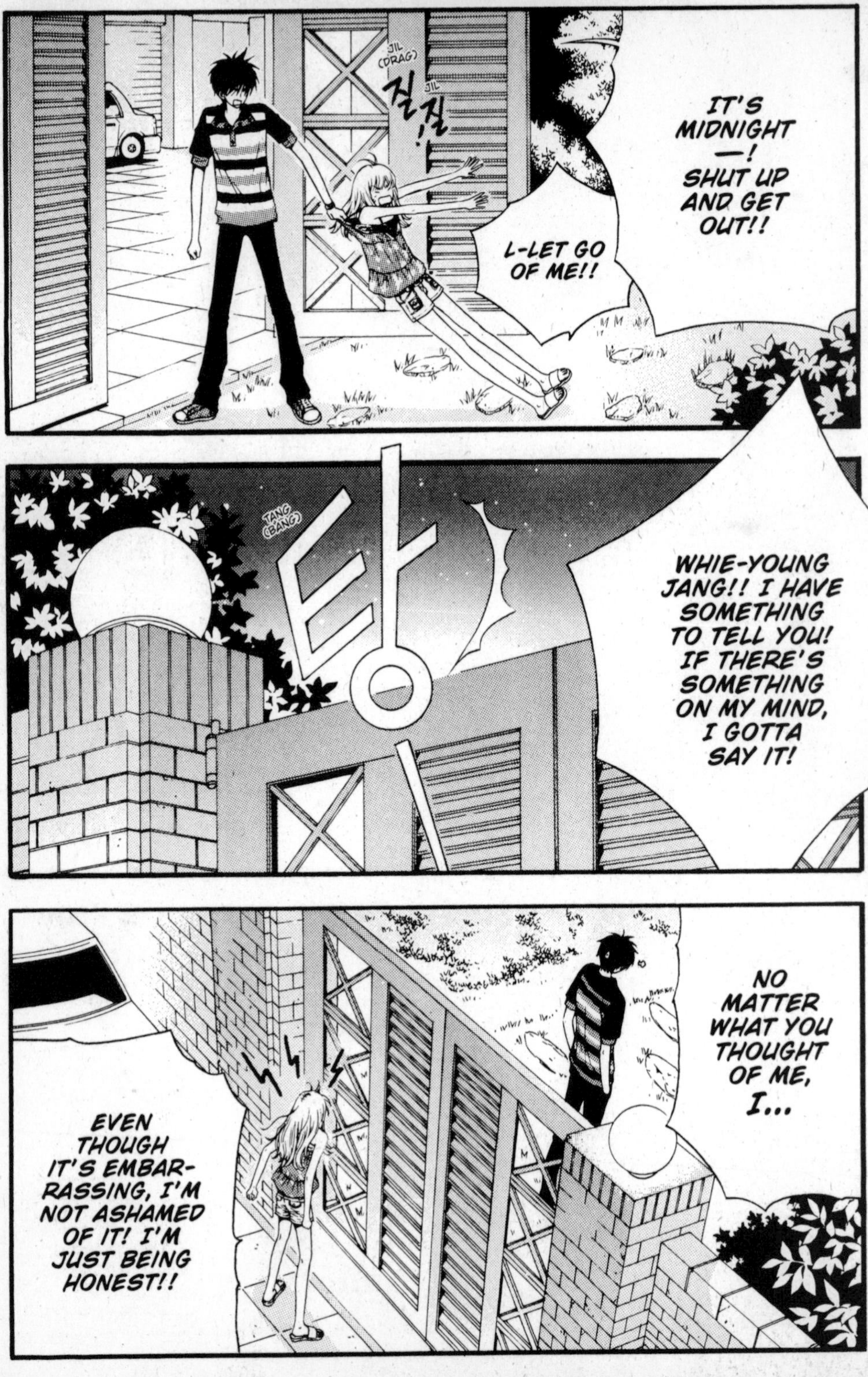
JIL (DRAG)
질 JIL 질!
L-LET GO OF ME!!
IT'S MIDNIGHT—! SHUT UP AND GET OUT!!
TANG (BANG)
탕
WHIE-YOUNG JANG!! I HAVE SOMETHING TO TELL YOU! IF THERE'S SOMETHING ON MY MIND, I GOTTA SAY IT!
EVEN THOUGH IT'S EMBAR-RASSING, I'M NOT ASHAMED OF IT! I'M JUST BEING HONEST!!
NO MATTER WHAT YOU THOUGHT OF ME, I...

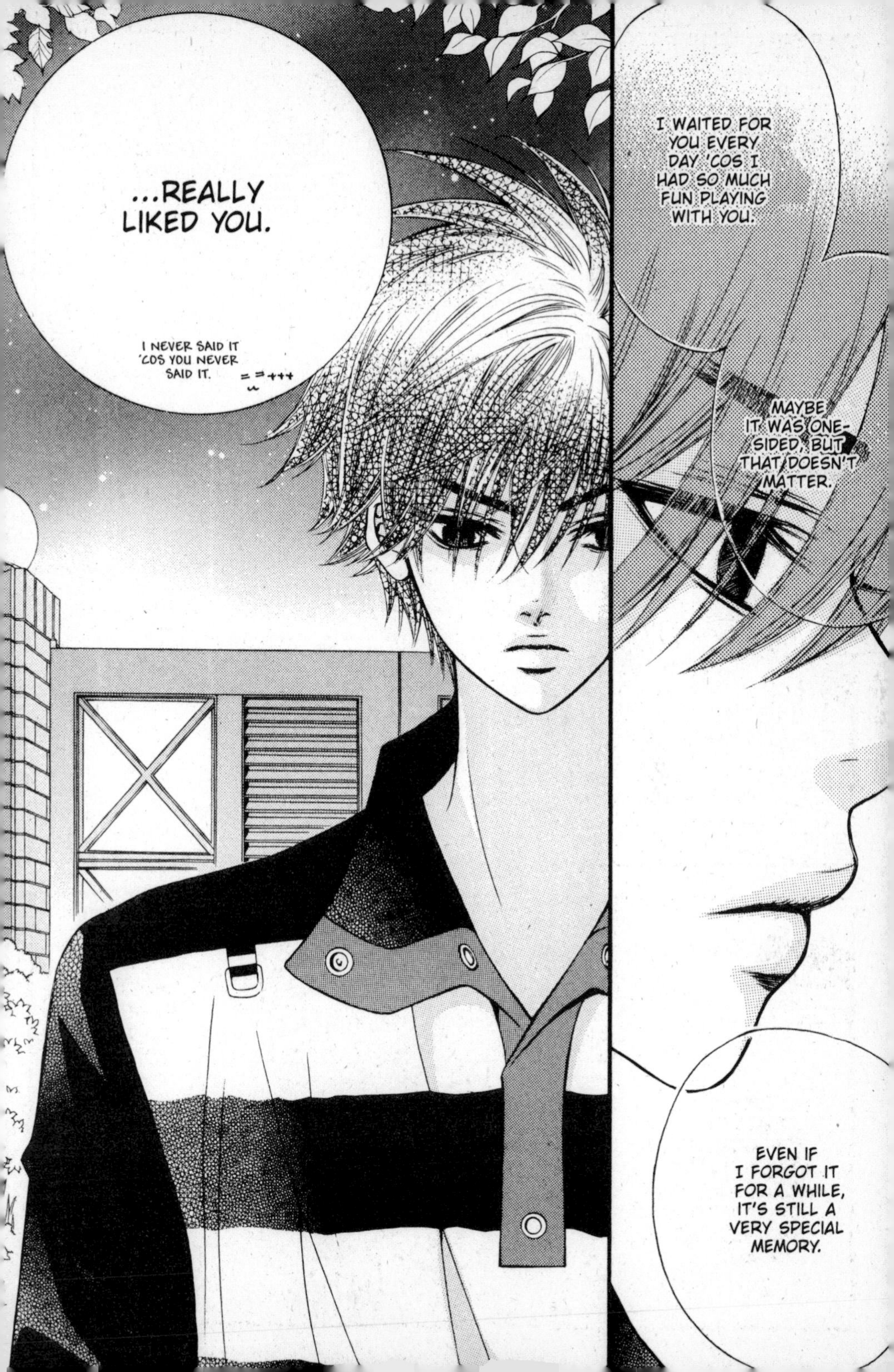
...REALLY LIKED YOU.
I NEVER SAID IT 'COS YOU NEVER SAID IT.
I WAITED FOR YOU EVERY DAY 'COS I HAD SO MUCH FUN PLAYING WITH YOU.
MAYBE IT WAS ONE-SIDED, BUT THAT DOESN'T MATTER.
EVEN IF I FORGOT IT FOR A WHILE, IT'S STILL A VERY SPECIAL MEMORY.

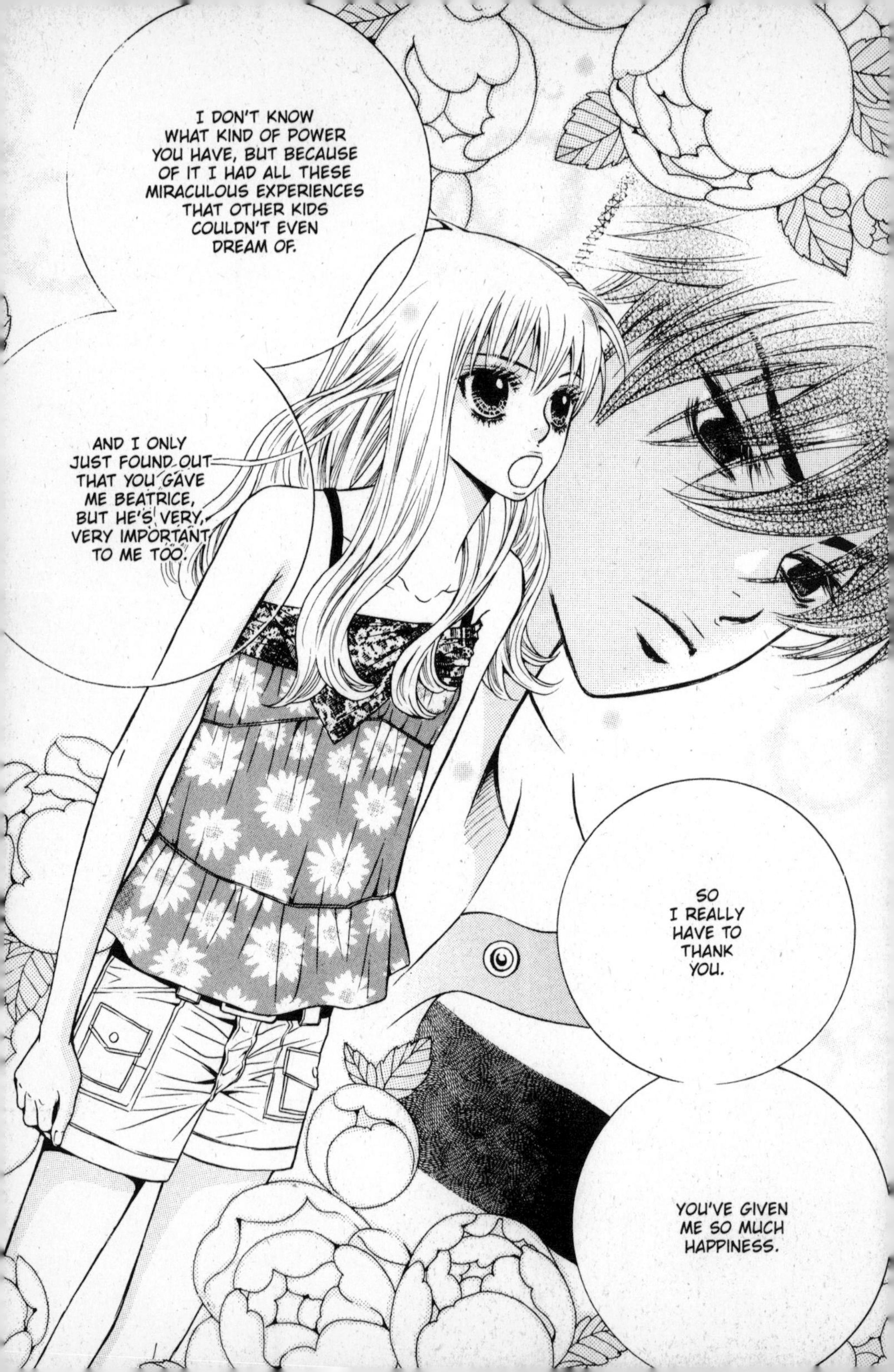
I DON'T KNOW WHAT KIND OF POWER YOU HAVE, BUT BECAUSE OF IT I HAD ALL THESE MIRACULOUS EXPERIENCES THAT OTHER KIDS COULDN'T EVEN DREAM OF.
AND I ONLY JUST FOUND OUT THAT YOU GAVE ME BEATRICE, BUT HE'S VERY, VERY IMPORTANT TO ME TOO.
SO I REALLY HAVE TO THANK YOU.
YOU'VE GIVEN ME SO MUCH HAPPINESS.

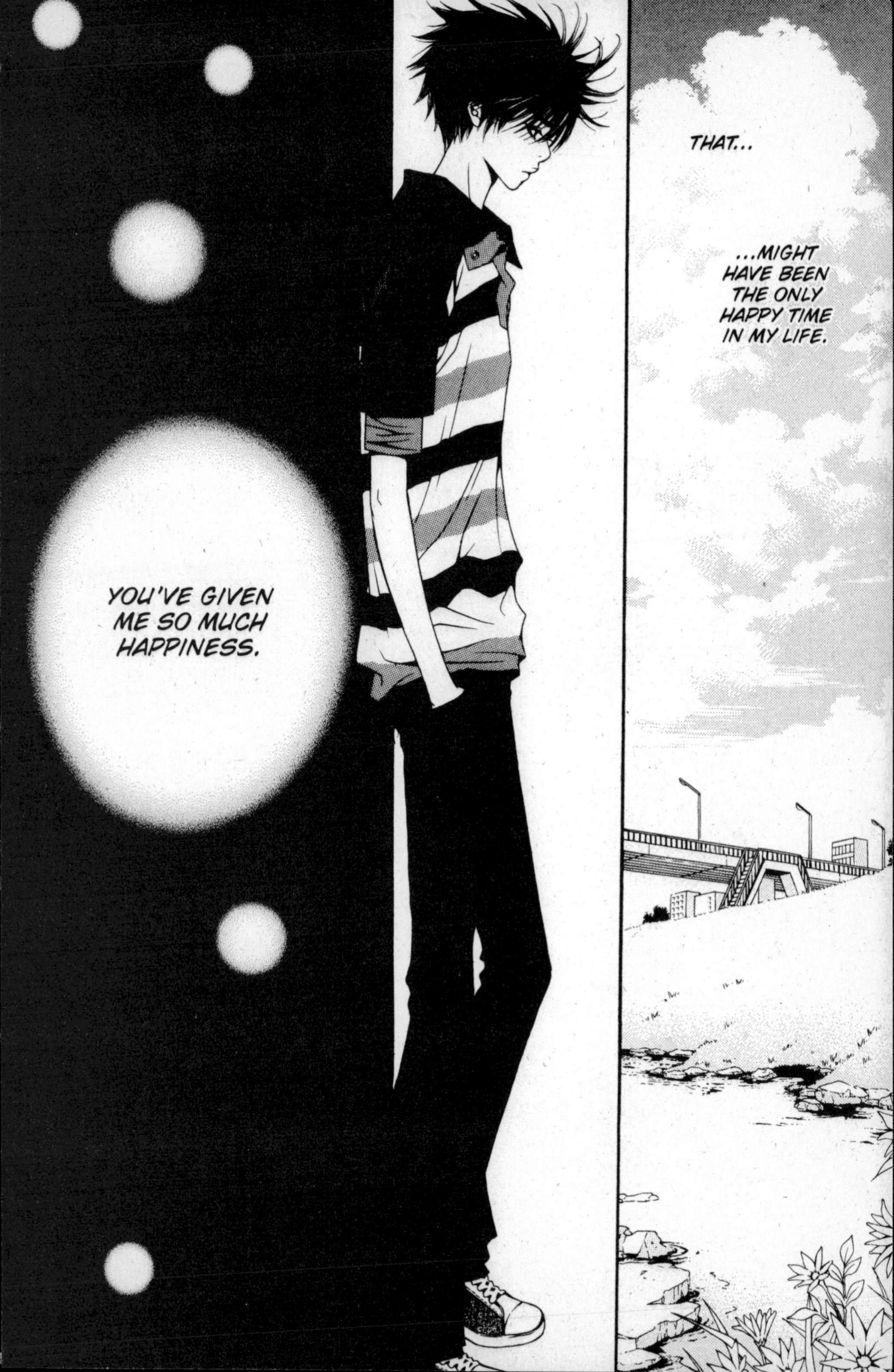
YOU'VE GIVEN ME SO MUCH HAPPINESS.
THAT...
...MIGHT HAVE BEEN THE ONLY HAPPY TIME IN MY LIFE.

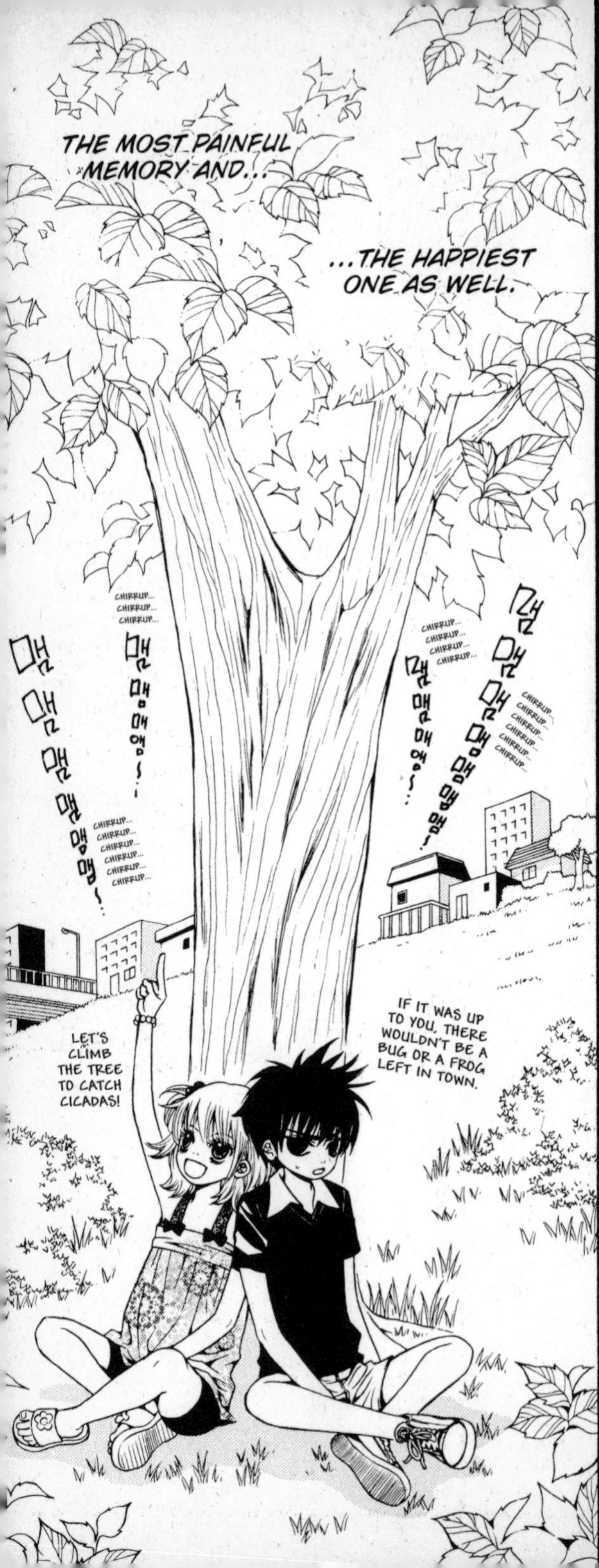
THE MOST PAINFUL MEMORY AND...
...THE HAPPIEST ONE AS WELL.
CHIRRUP... CHIRRUP... CHIRRUP...
CHIRRUP... CHIRRUP... CHIRRUP... CHIRRUP... CHIRRUP...
CHIRRUP... CHIRRUP... CHIRRUP... CHIRRUP...
CHIRRUP... CHIRRUP... CHIRRUP... CHIRRUP... CHIRRUP... CHIRRUP...
LET'S CLIMB THE TREE TO CATCH CICADAS!
IF IT WAS UP TO YOU, THERE WOULDN'T BE A BUG OR A FROG LEFT IN TOWN.
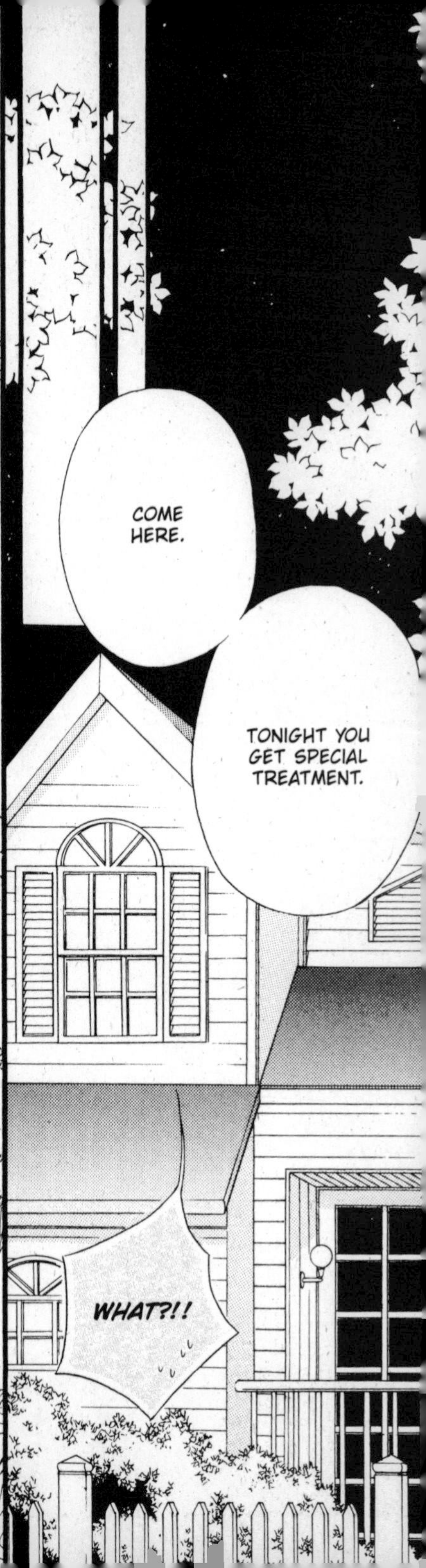
COME HERE.
TONIGHT YOU GET SPECIAL TREATMENT.
WHAT?!!

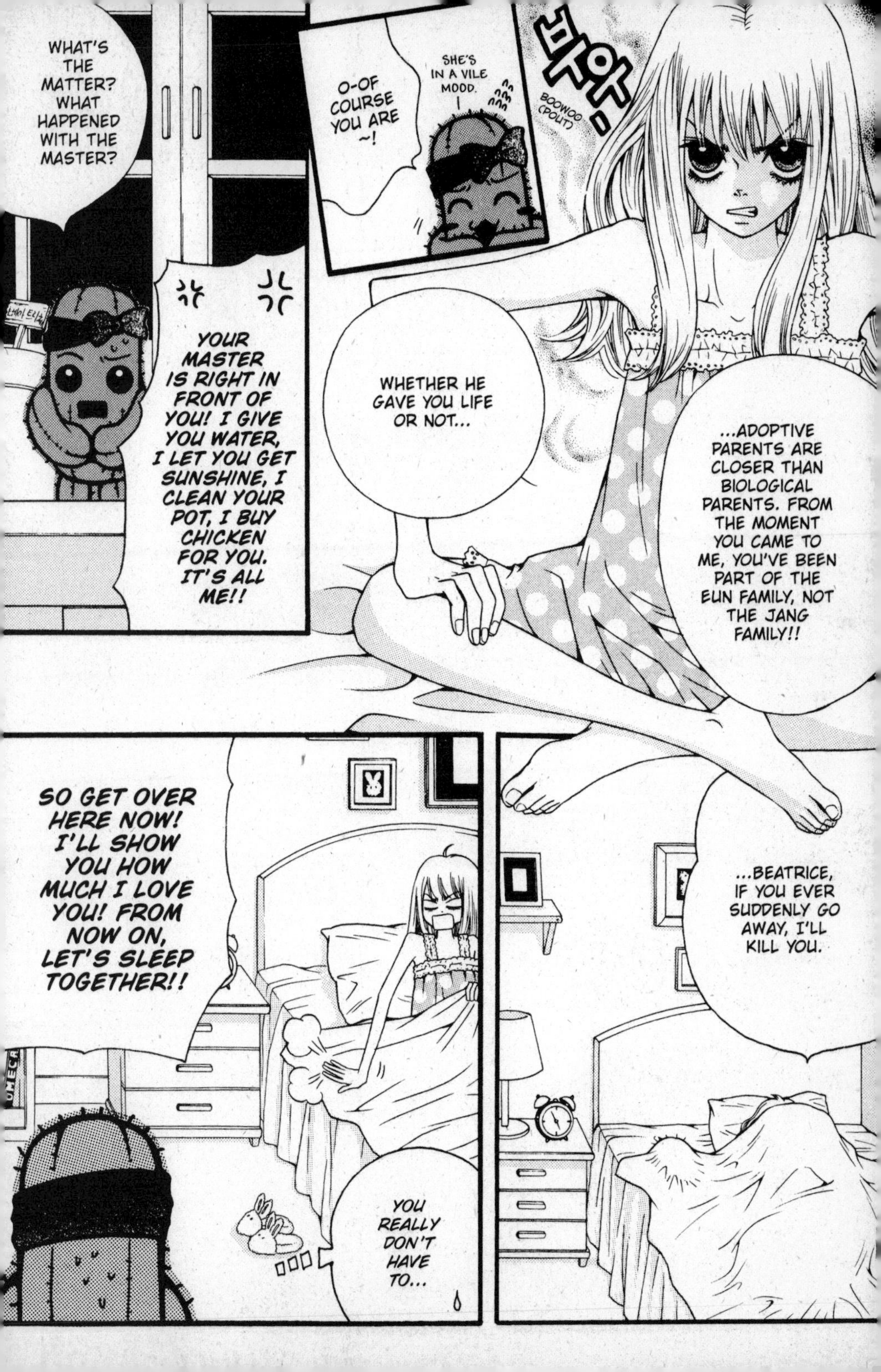
WHAT'S THE MATTER? WHAT HAPPENED WITH THE MASTER?
YOUR MASTER IS RIGHT IN FRONT OF YOU! I GIVE YOU WATER, I LET YOU GET SUNSHINE, I CLEAN YOUR POT, I BUY CHICKEN FOR YOU. IT'S ALL ME!!
O-OF COURSE YOU ARE ~!
SHE'S IN A VILE MOOD.
BOOWOO (POUT)
WHETHER HE GAVE YOU LIFE OR NOT...
...ADOPTIVE PARENTS ARE CLOSER THAN BIOLOGICAL PARENTS. FROM THE MOMENT YOU CAME TO ME, YOU'VE BEEN PART OF THE EUN FAMILY, NOT THE JANG FAMILY!!
SO GET OVER HERE NOW! I'LL SHOW YOU HOW MUCH I LOVE YOU! FROM NOW ON, LET'S SLEEP TOGETHER!!
YOU REALLY DON'T HAVE TO...
...BEATRICE, IF YOU EVER SUDDENLY GO AWAY, I'LL KILL YOU.

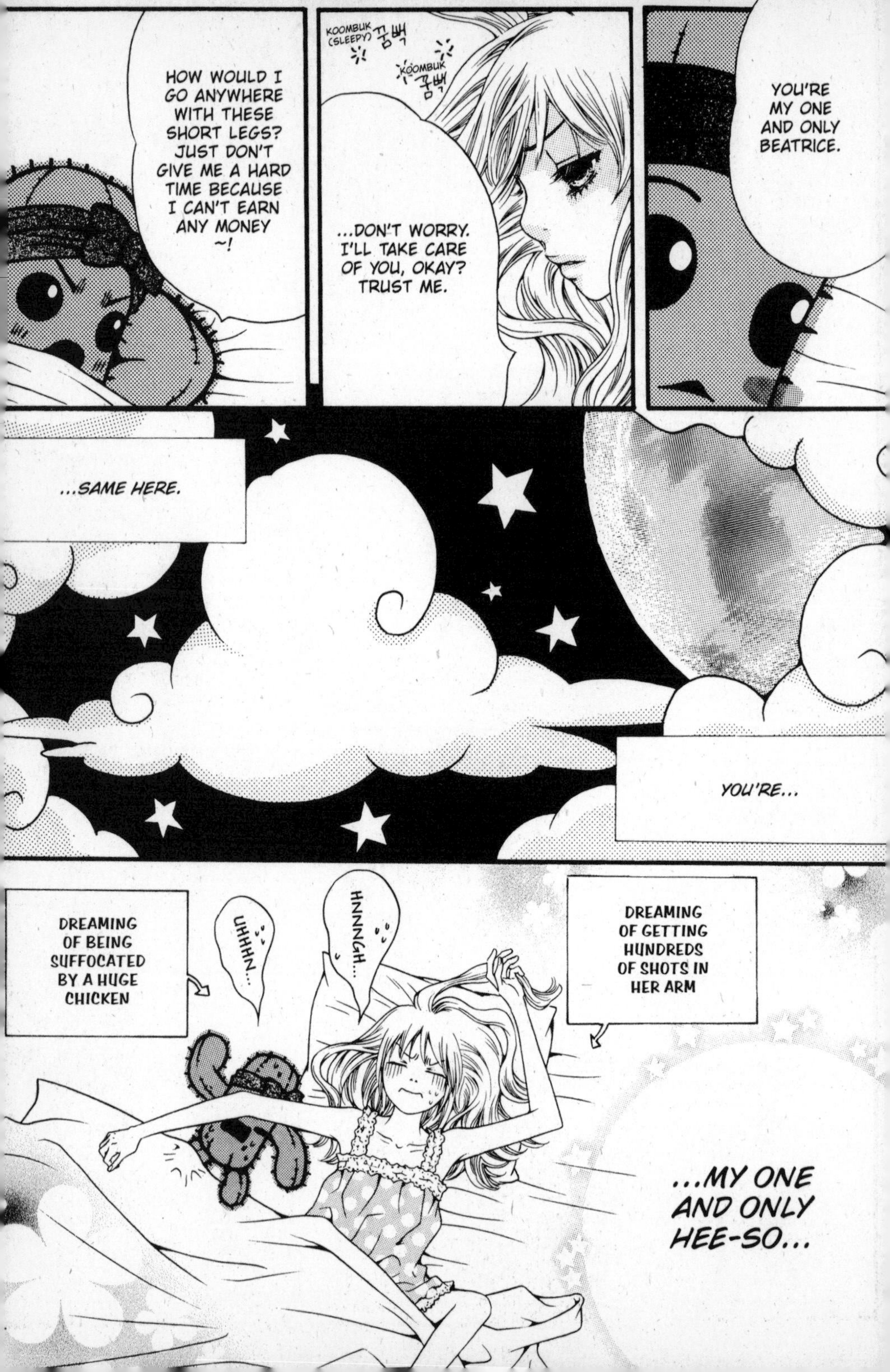
HOW WOULD I GO ANYWHERE WITH THESE SHORT LEGS? JUST DON'T GIVE ME A HARD TIME BECAUSE I CAN'T EARN ANY MONEY ~!
KOOMBUK (SLEEPY) 꿈뻑
KOOMBUK 꿈뻑
...DON'T WORRY. I'LL TAKE CARE OF YOU, OKAY? TRUST ME.
YOU'RE MY ONE AND ONLY BEATRICE.
...SAME HERE.
YOU'RE...
DREAMING OF BEING SUFFOCATED BY A HUGE CHICKEN
UHHHN...
HNNNGH...
DREAMING OF GETTING HUNDREDS OF SHOTS IN HER ARM
...MY ONE AND ONLY HEE-SO...

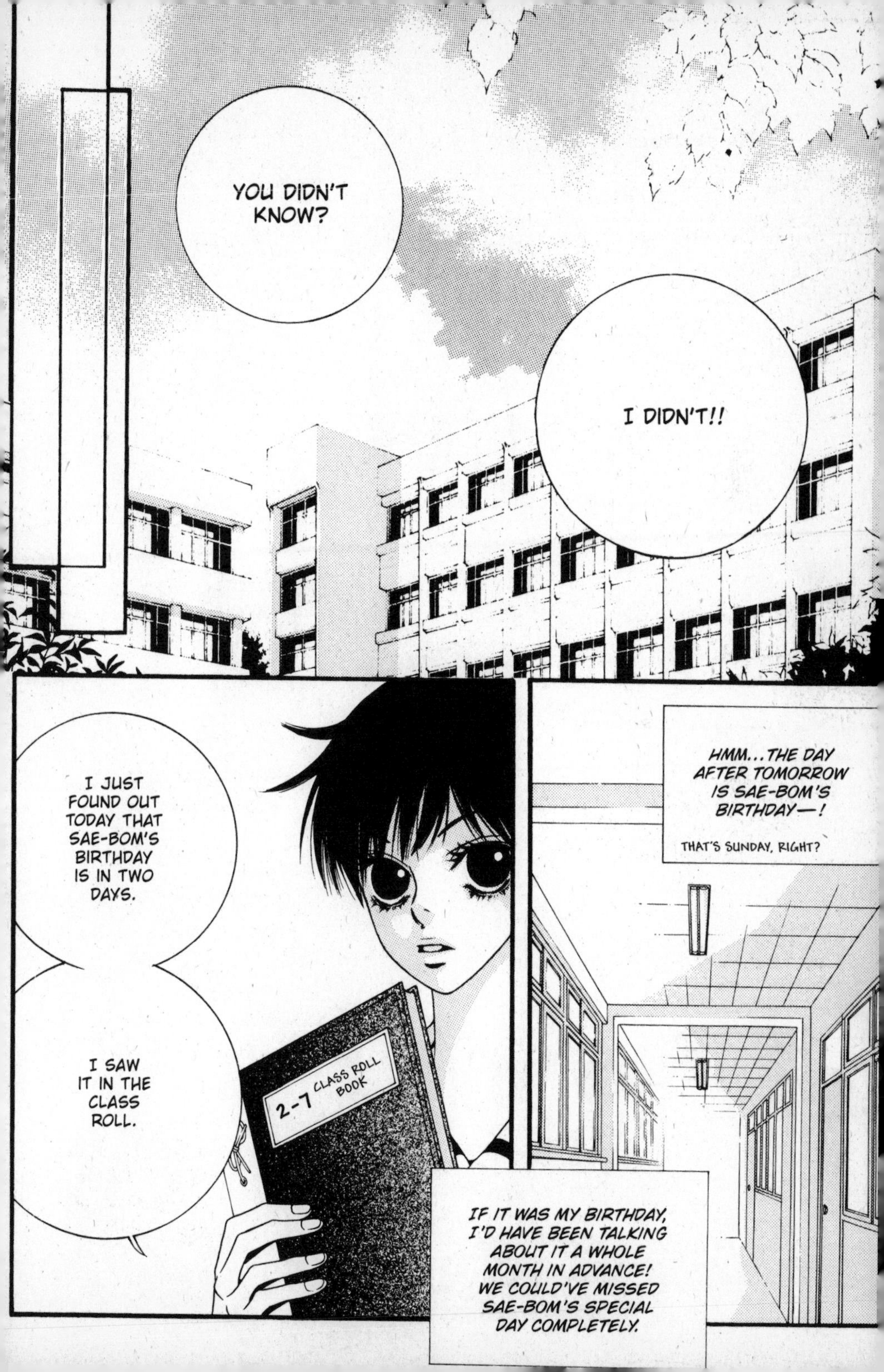
YOU DIDN'T KNOW?
I DIDN'T!!
I JUST FOUND OUT TODAY THAT SAE-BOM'S BIRTHDAY IS IN TWO DAYS.
I SAW IT IN THE CLASS ROLL.
2-7 CLASS ROLL BOOK
HMM...THE DAY AFTER TOMORROW IS SAE-BOM'S BIRTHDAY—!
THAT'S SUNDAY, RIGHT?
IF IT WAS MY BIRTHDAY, I'D HAVE BEEN TALKING ABOUT IT A WHOLE MONTH IN ADVANCE! WE COULD'VE MISSED SAE-BOM'S SPECIAL DAY COMPLETELY.

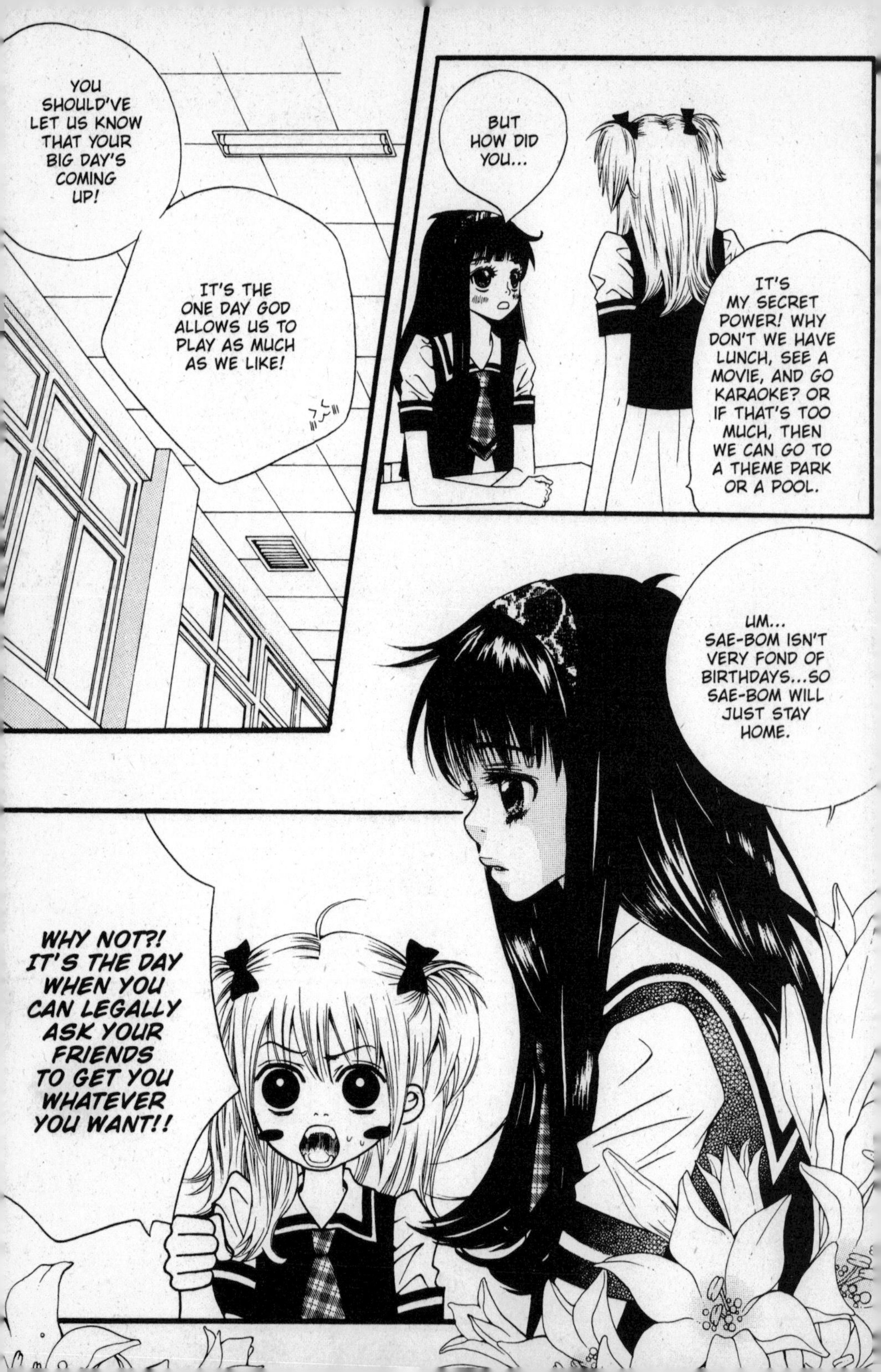
YOU SHOULD'VE LET US KNOW THAT YOUR BIG DAY'S COMING UP!
IT'S THE ONE DAY GOD ALLOWS US TO PLAY AS MUCH AS WE LIKE!
BUT HOW DID YOU...
IT'S MY SECRET POWER! WHY DON'T WE HAVE LUNCH, SEE A MOVIE, AND GO KARAOKE? OR IF THAT'S TOO MUCH, THEN WE CAN GO TO A THEME PARK OR A POOL.
UM... SAE-BOM ISN'T VERY FOND OF BIRTHDAYS...SO SAE-BOM WILL JUST STAY HOME.
WHY NOT?! IT'S THE DAY WHEN YOU CAN LEGALLY ASK YOUR FRIENDS TO GET YOU WHATEVER YOU WANT!!

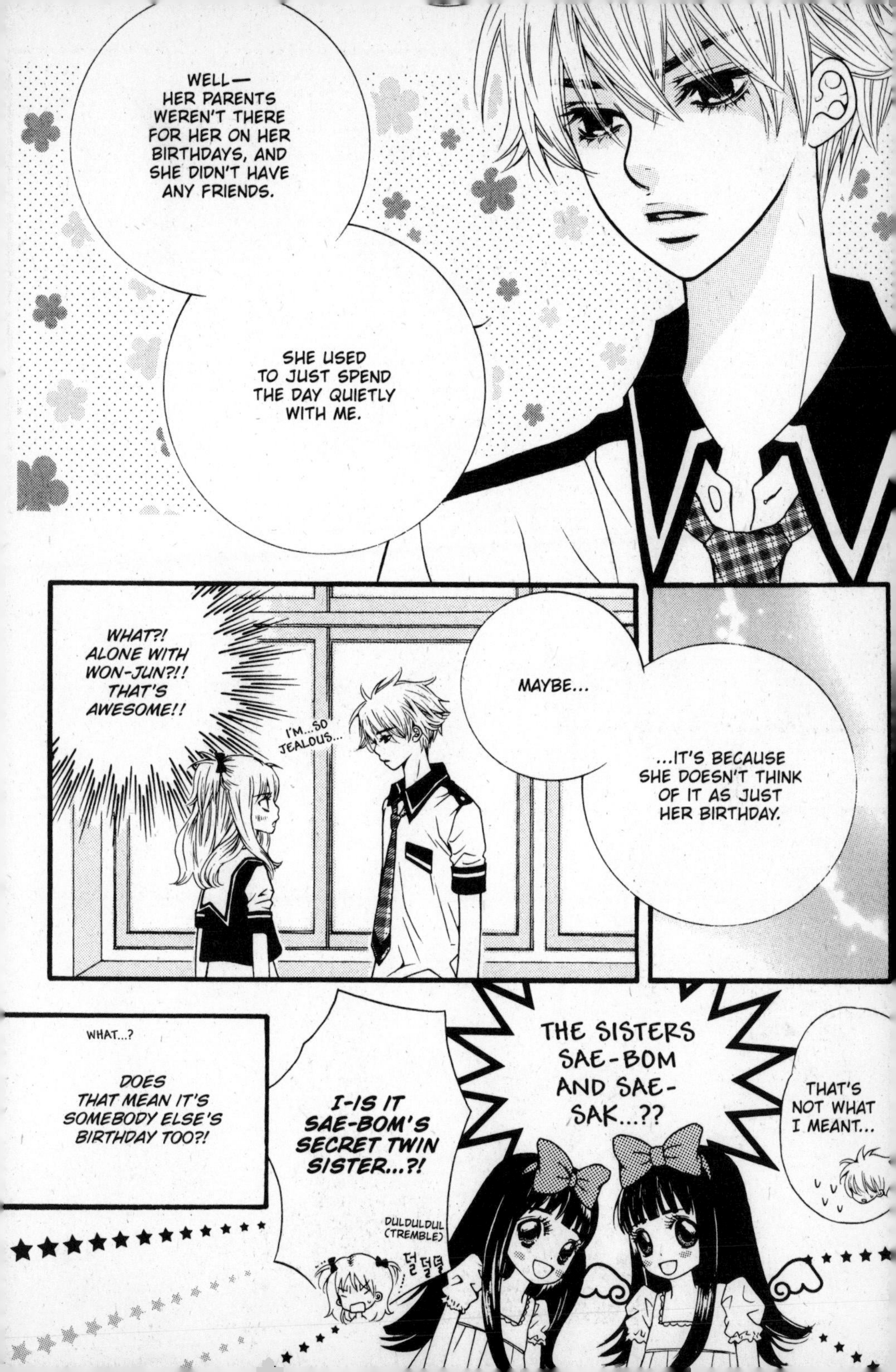
WELL— HER PARENTS WEREN'T THERE FOR HER ON HER BIRTHDAYS, AND SHE DIDN'T HAVE ANY FRIENDS.
SHE USED TO JUST SPEND THE DAY QUIETLY WITH ME.
WHAT?! ALONE WITH WON-JUN?!! THAT'S AWESOME!!
I'M...SO JEALOUS...
MAYBE...
...IT'S BECAUSE SHE DOESN'T THINK OF IT AS JUST HER BIRTHDAY.
WHAT...?
DOES THAT MEAN IT'S SOMEBODY ELSE'S BIRTHDAY TOO?!
I-IS IT SAE-BOM'S SECRET TWIN SISTER...?!
THE SISTERS SAE-BOM AND SAE-SAK...??
DULDULDUL (TREMBLE)
덜덜덜
THAT'S NOT WHAT I MEANT...

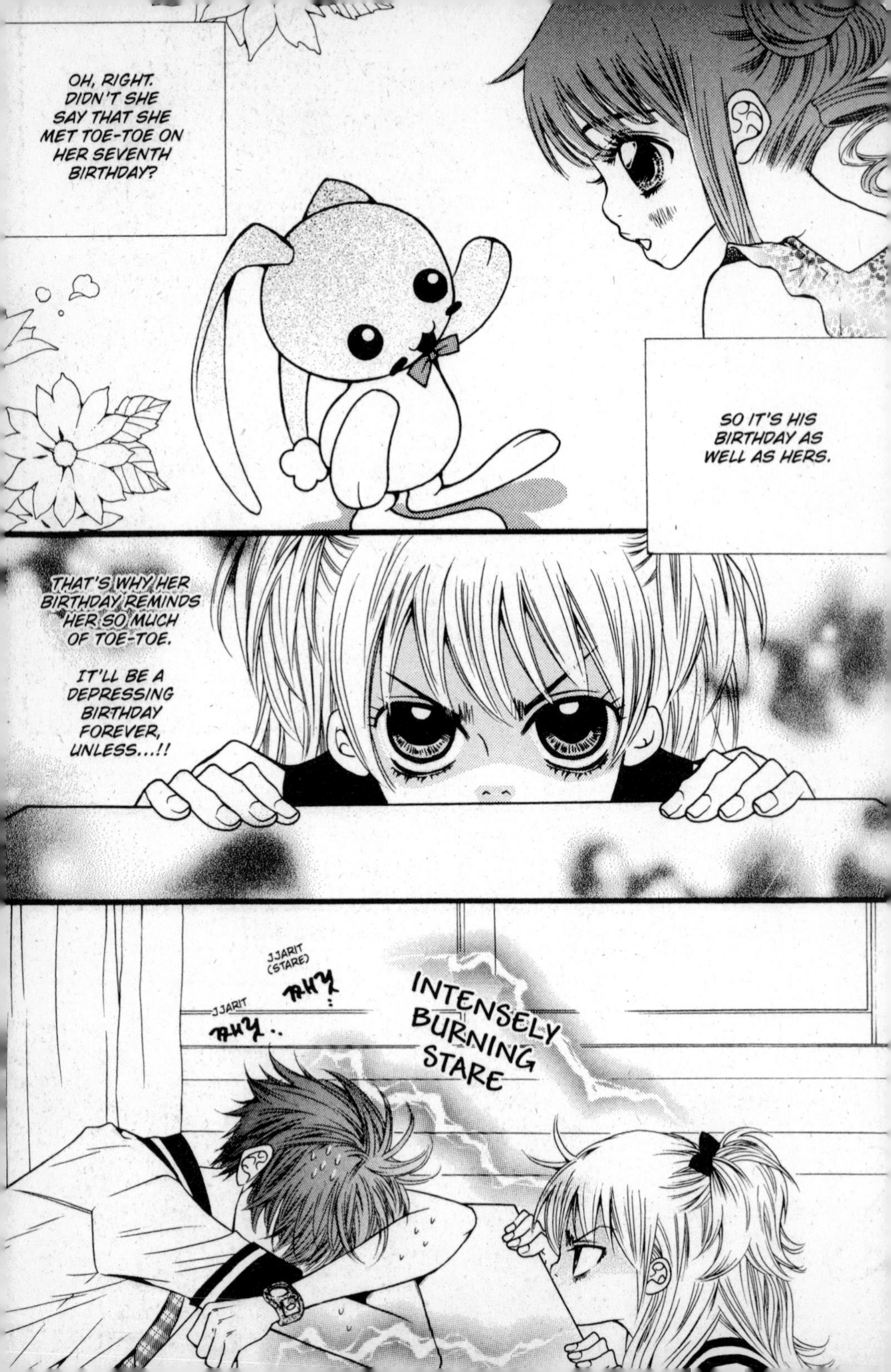
OH, RIGHT. DIDN'T SHE SAY THAT SHE MET TOE-TOE ON HER SEVENTH BIRTHDAY?
SO IT'S HIS BIRTHDAY AS WELL AS HERS.
THAT'S WHY HER BIRTHDAY REMINDS HER SO MUCH OF TOE-TOE.
IT'LL BE A DEPRESSING BIRTHDAY FOREVER, UNLESS...!!
JJARIT (STARE)
JJARIT
INTENSELY BURNING STARE

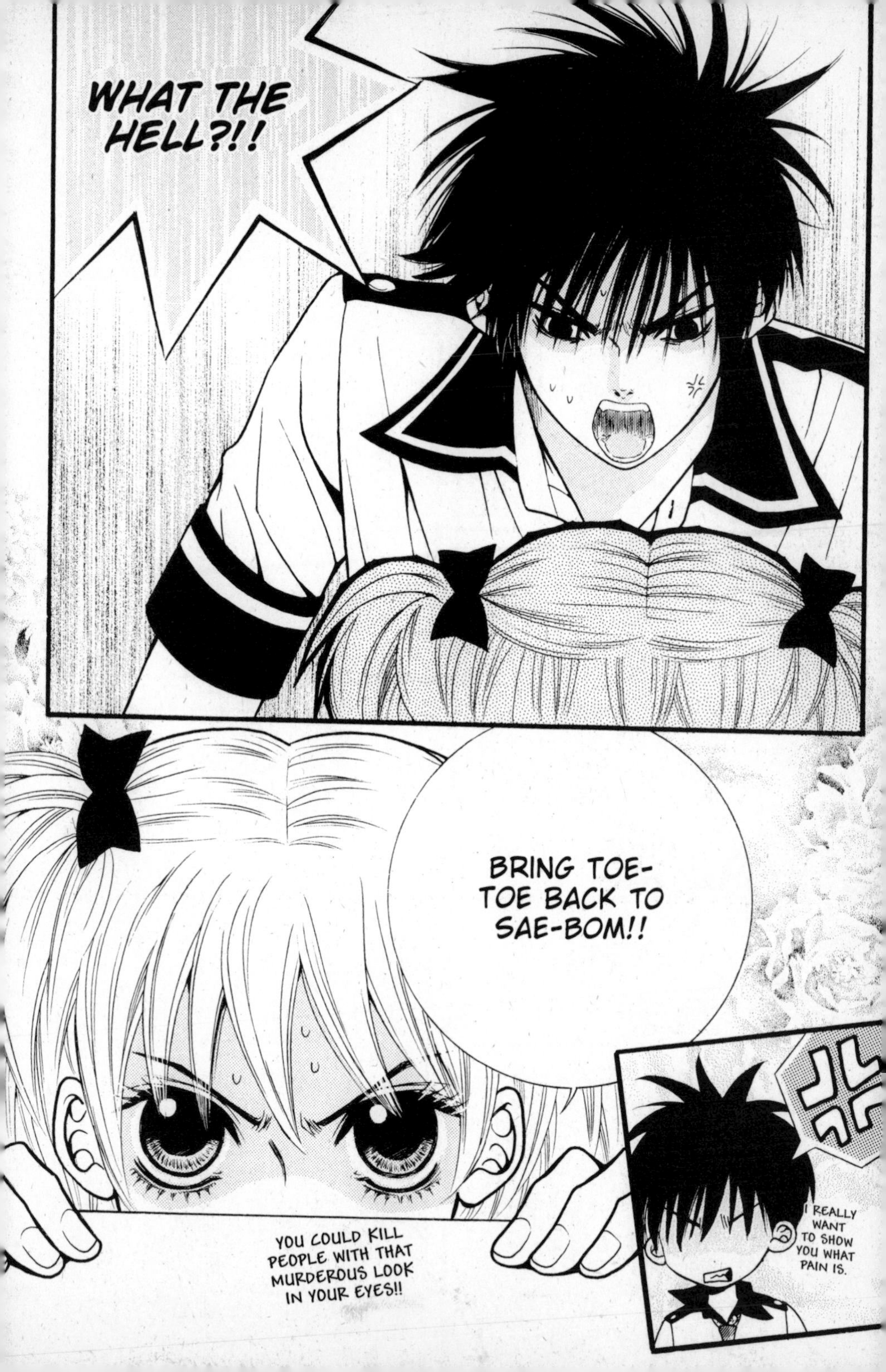
WHAT THE HELL?!!
BRING TOE-TOE BACK TO SAE-BOM!!
YOU COULD KILL PEOPLE WITH THAT MURDEROUS LOOK IN YOUR EYES!!
I REALLY WANT TO SHOW YOU WHAT PAIN IS.

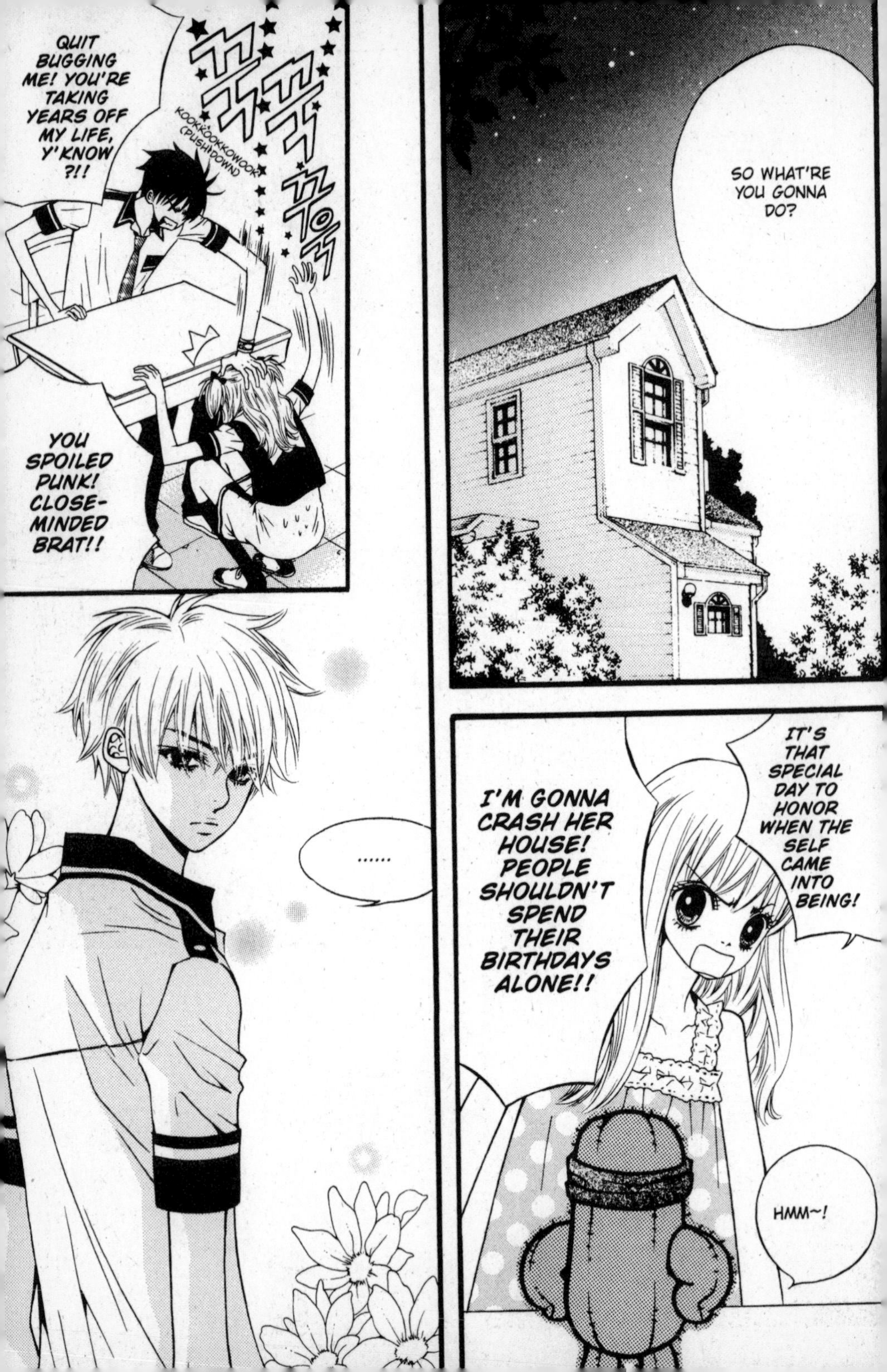
QUIT BUGGING ME! YOU'RE TAKING YEARS OFF MY LIFE, Y'KNOW ?!!
KOOKKOOKKOWOOK (PUSH DOWN)
YOU SPOILED PUNK! CLOSE-MINDED BRAT!!
......
SO WHAT'RE YOU GONNA DO?
I'M GONNA CRASH HER HOUSE! PEOPLE SHOULDN'T SPEND THEIR BIRTHDAYS ALONE!!
IT'S THAT SPECIAL DAY TO HONOR WHEN THE SELF CAME INTO BEING!
HMM~!

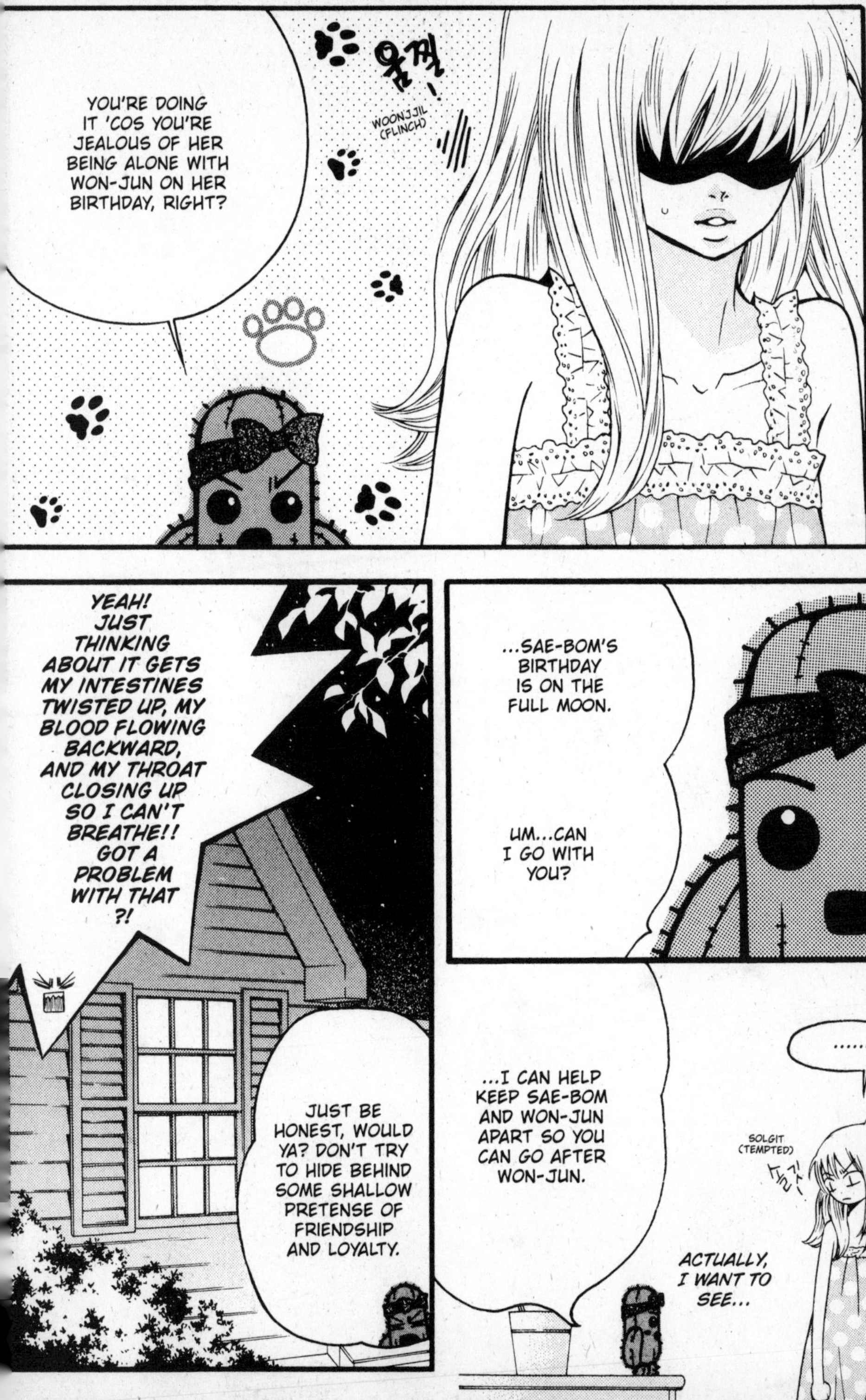
YOU'RE DOING IT 'COS YOU'RE JEALOUS OF HER BEING ALONE WITH WON-JUN ON HER BIRTHDAY, RIGHT?
WOONJJIL (FLINCH)
YEAH! JUST THINKING ABOUT IT GETS MY INTESTINES TWISTED UP, MY BLOOD FLOWING BACKWARD, AND MY THROAT CLOSING UP SO I CAN'T BREATHE!! GOT A PROBLEM WITH THAT ?!
JUST BE HONEST, WOULD YA? DON'T TRY TO HIDE BEHIND SOME SHALLOW PRETENSE OF FRIENDSHIP AND LOYALTY.
...SAE-BOM'S BIRTHDAY IS ON THE FULL MOON.
UM...CAN I GO WITH YOU?
...I CAN HELP KEEP SAE-BOM AND WON-JUN APART SO YOU CAN GO AFTER WON-JUN.
......
SOLGIT (TEMPTED)
ACTUALLY, I WANT TO SEE...

STEP 18. YOU CAN'T HAVE A BIRTHDAY WITHOUT SEAWEED SOUP!

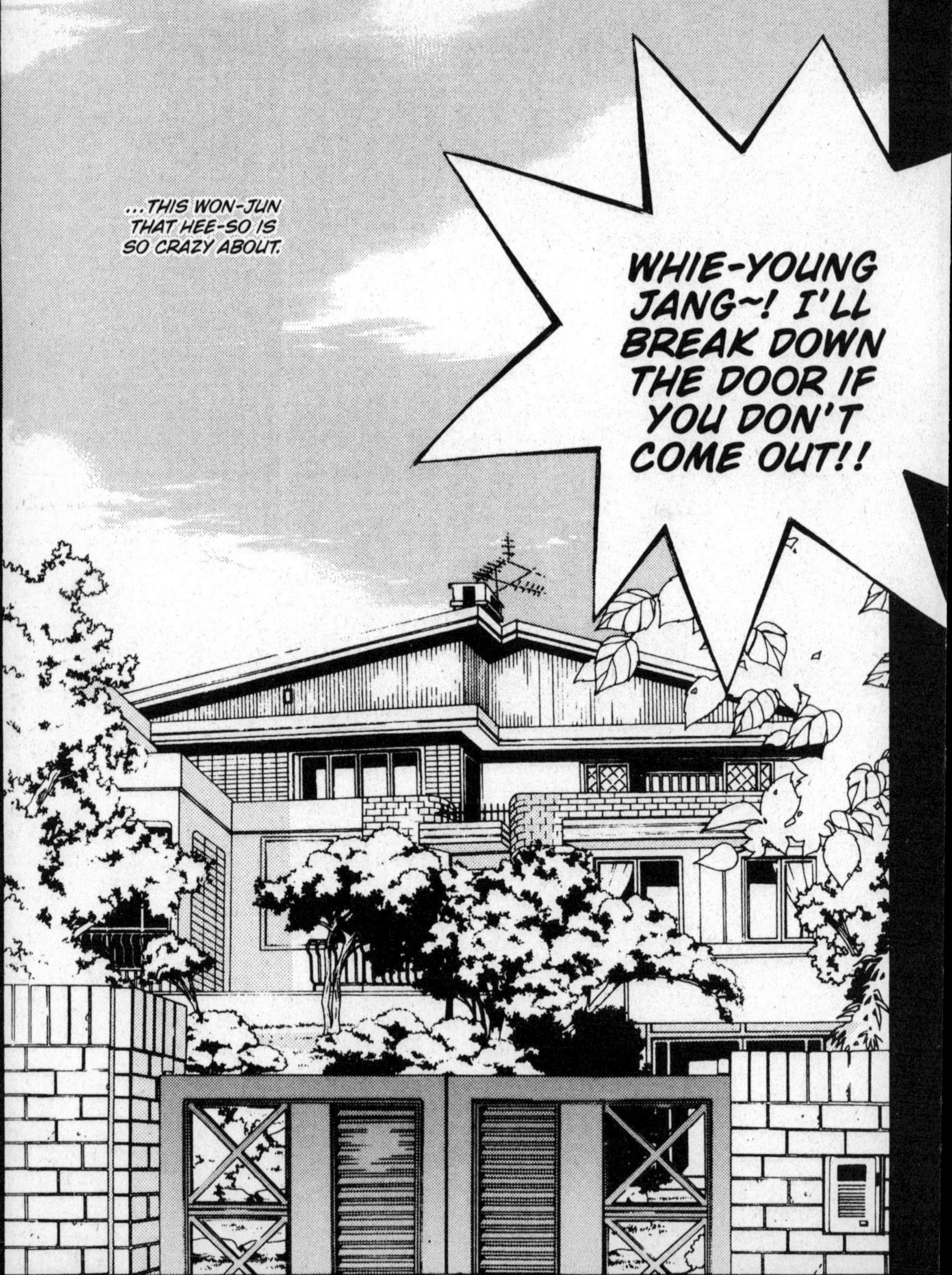
...THIS WON-JUN THAT HEE-SO IS SO CRAZY ABOUT.
WHIE-YOUNG JANG~! I'LL BREAK DOWN THE DOOR IF YOU DON'T COME OUT!!

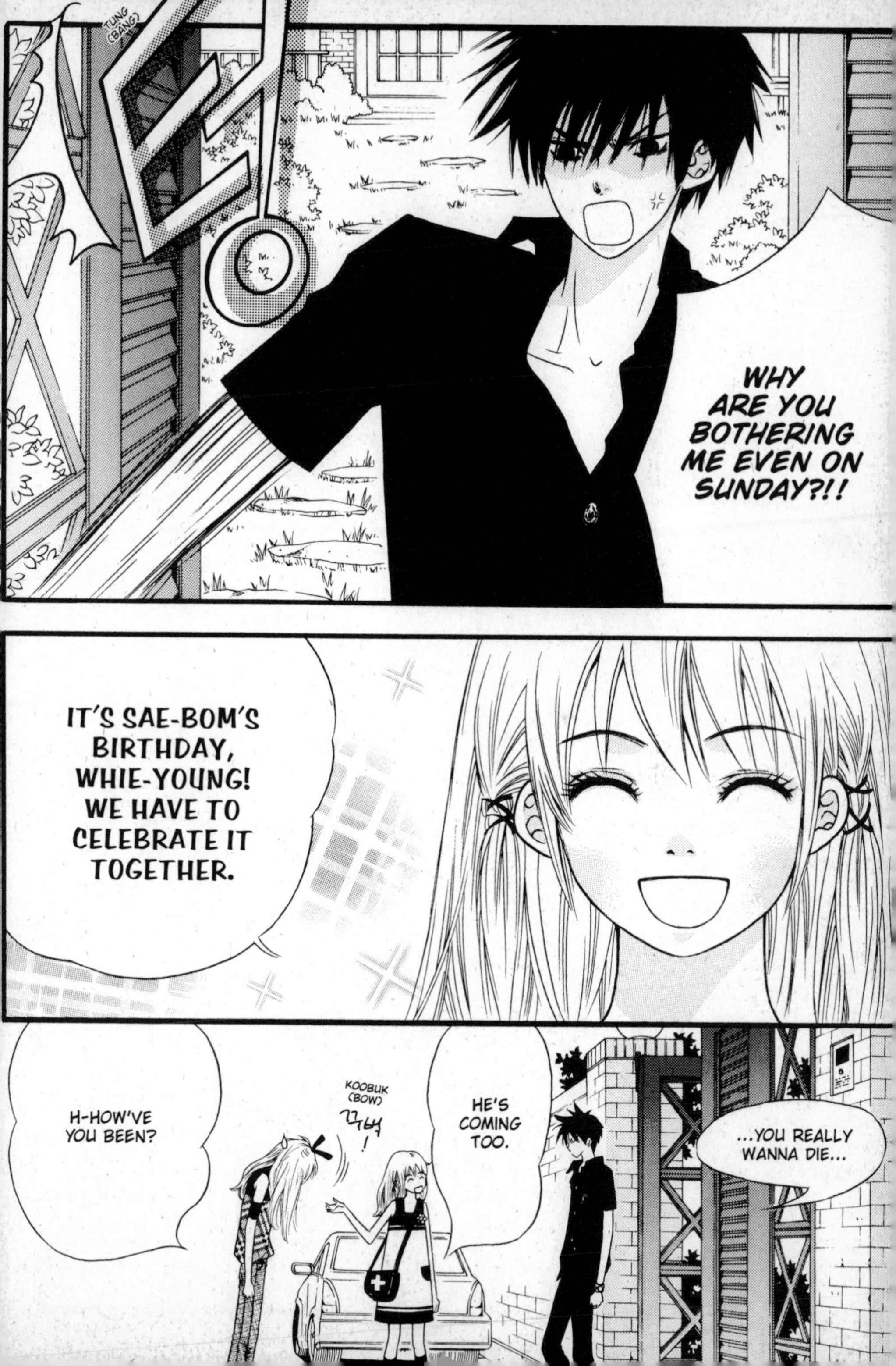
TLING (BANG)
WHY ARE YOU BOTHERING ME EVEN ON SUNDAY?!!
IT'S SAE-BOM'S BIRTHDAY, WHIE-YOUNG! WE HAVE TO CELEBRATE IT TOGETHER.
H-HOW'VE YOU BEEN?
KOOBUK (BOW)
꾸벅!
HE'S COMING TOO.
...YOU REALLY WANNA DIE...

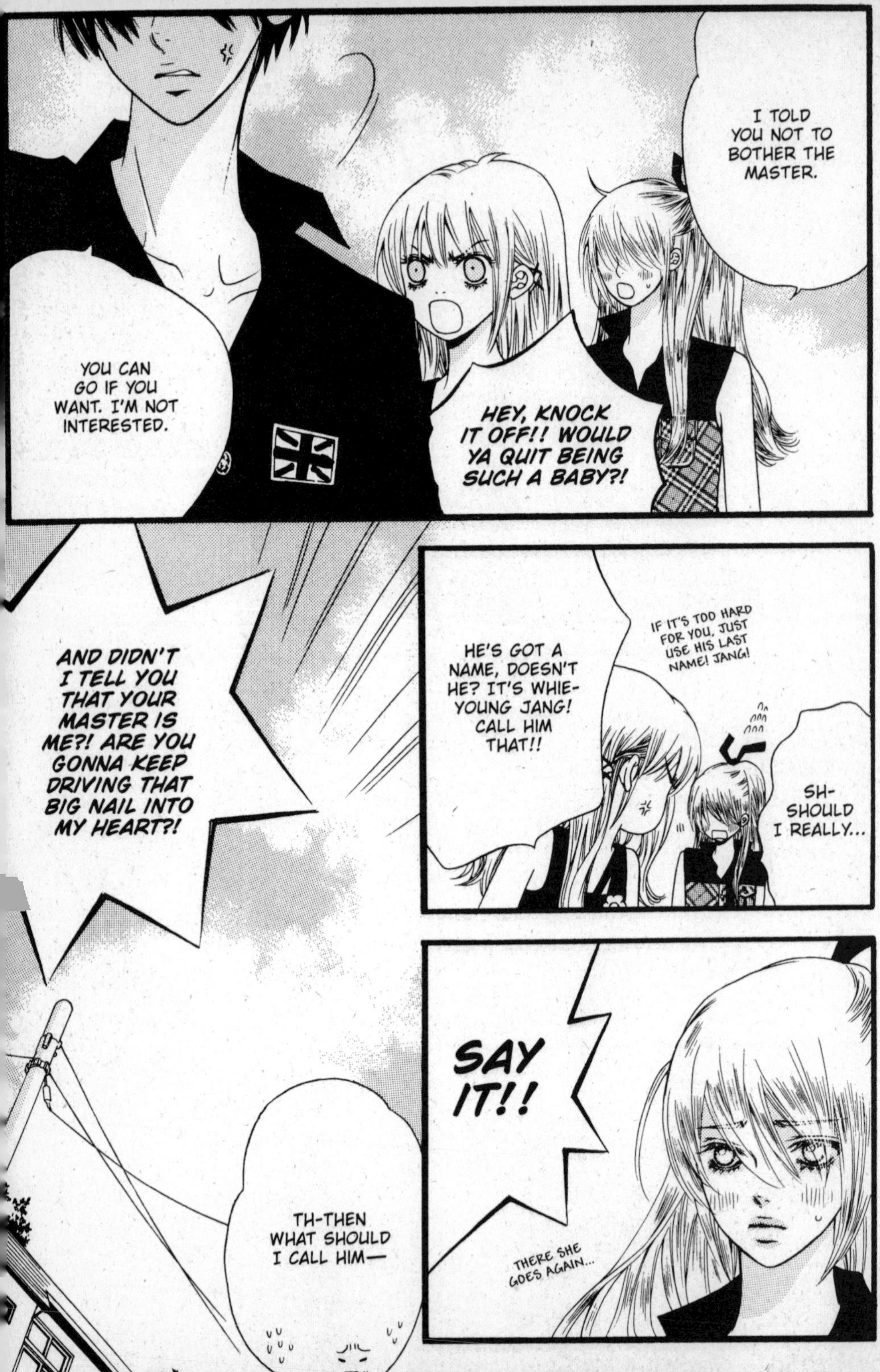
YOU CAN GO IF YOU WANT. I'M NOT INTERESTED.
HEY, KNOCK IT OFF!! WOULD YA QUIT BEING SUCH A BABY?!
I TOLD YOU NOT TO BOTHER THE MASTER.
AND DIDN'T I TELL YOU THAT YOUR MASTER IS ME?! ARE YOU GONNA KEEP DRIVING THAT BIG NAIL INTO MY HEART?!
TH-THEN WHAT SHOULD I CALL HIM—
HE'S GOT A NAME, DOESN'T HE? IT'S WHIE-YOUNG JANG! CALL HIM THAT!!
IF IT'S TOO HARD FOR YOU, JUST USE HIS LAST NAME! JANG!
SH-SHOULD I REALLY...
SAY IT!!
THERE SHE GOES AGAIN...

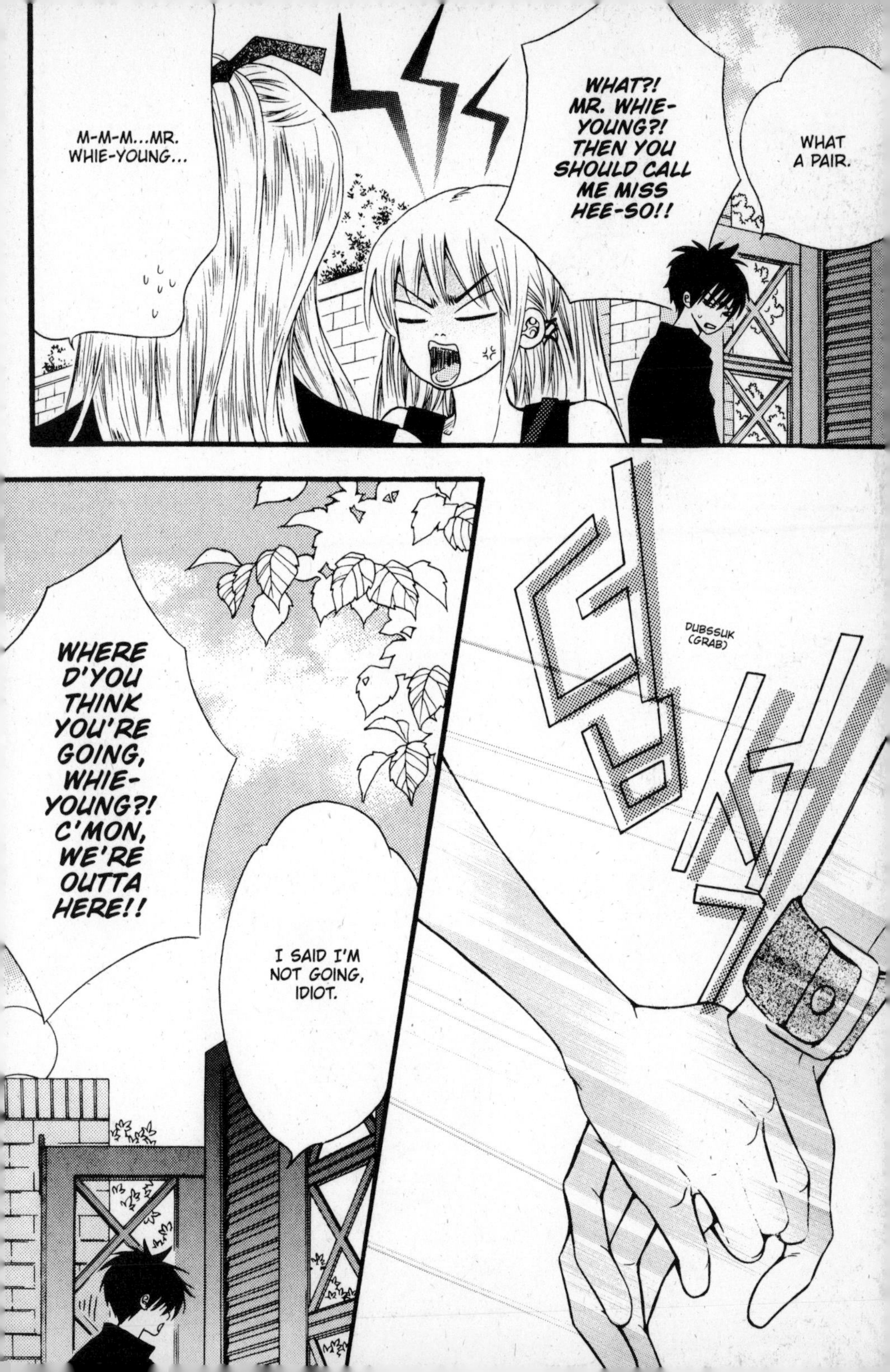
M-M-M...MR. WHIE-YOUNG...
WHAT?! MR. WHIE-YOUNG?! THEN YOU SHOULD CALL ME MISS HEE-SO!!
WHAT A PAIR.
WHERE D'YOU THINK YOU'RE GOING, WHIE-YOUNG?! C'MON, WE'RE OUTTA HERE!!
I SAID I'M NOT GOING, IDIOT.
DUBSSUK (GRAB)

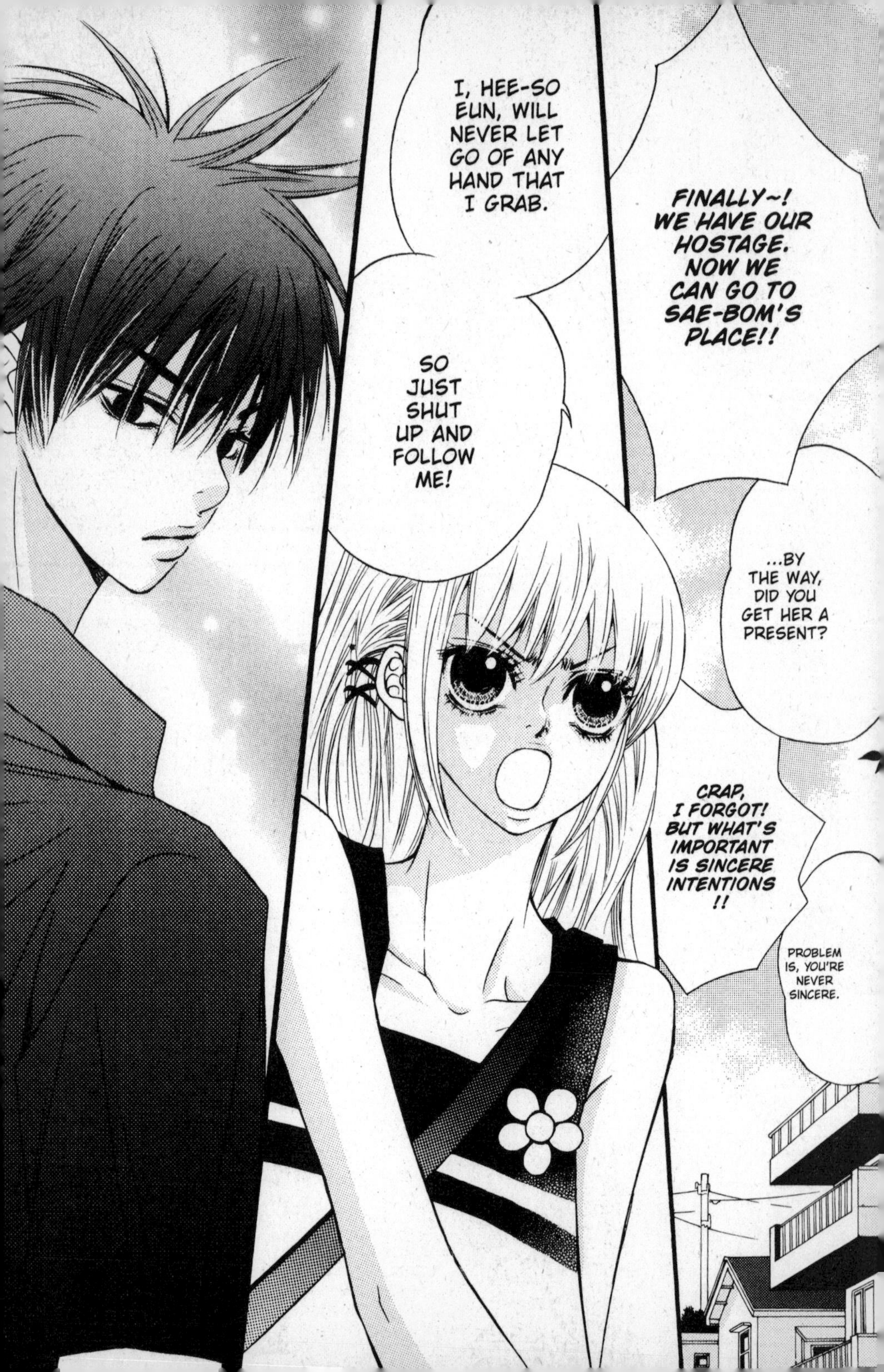
I, HEE-SO EUN, WILL NEVER LET GO OF ANY HAND THAT I GRAB.
SO JUST SHUT UP AND FOLLOW ME!
FINALLY~! WE HAVE OUR HOSTAGE. NOW WE CAN GO TO SAE-BOM'S PLACE!!
...BY THE WAY, DID YOU GET HER A PRESENT?
CRAP, I FORGOT! BUT WHAT'S IMPORTANT IS SINCERE INTENTIONS !!
PROBLEM IS, YOU'RE NEVER SINCERE.

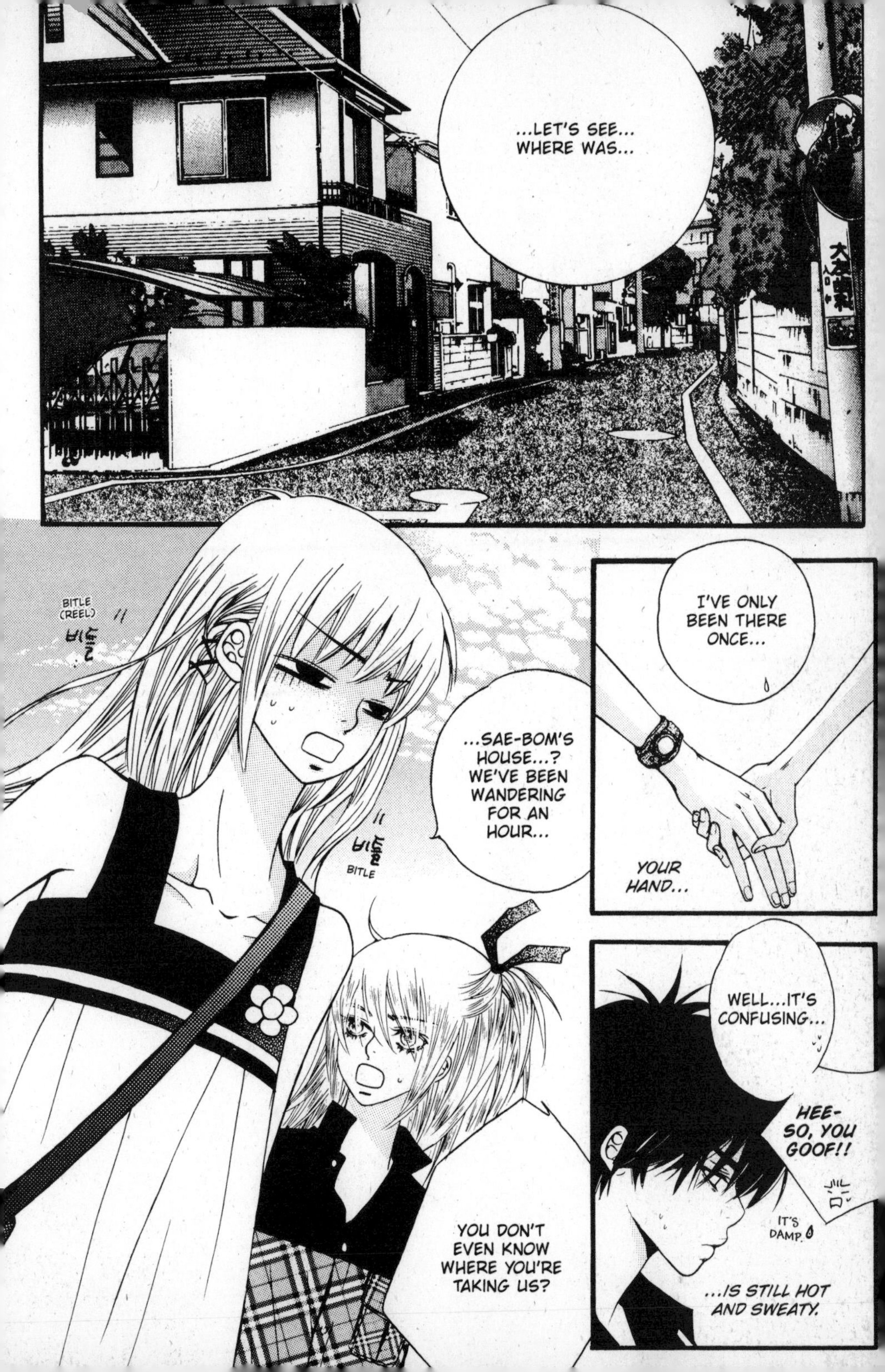
...LET'S SEE... WHERE WAS...
BITLE (REEL)
비틀
...SAE-BOM'S HOUSE...? WE'VE BEEN WANDERING FOR AN HOUR...
비틀
BITLE
YOU DON'T EVEN KNOW WHERE YOU'RE TAKING US?
I'VE ONLY BEEN THERE ONCE...
YOUR HAND...
WELL...IT'S CONFUSING...
HEE-SO, YOU GOOF!!
IT'S DAMP.
...IS STILL HOT AND SWEATY.

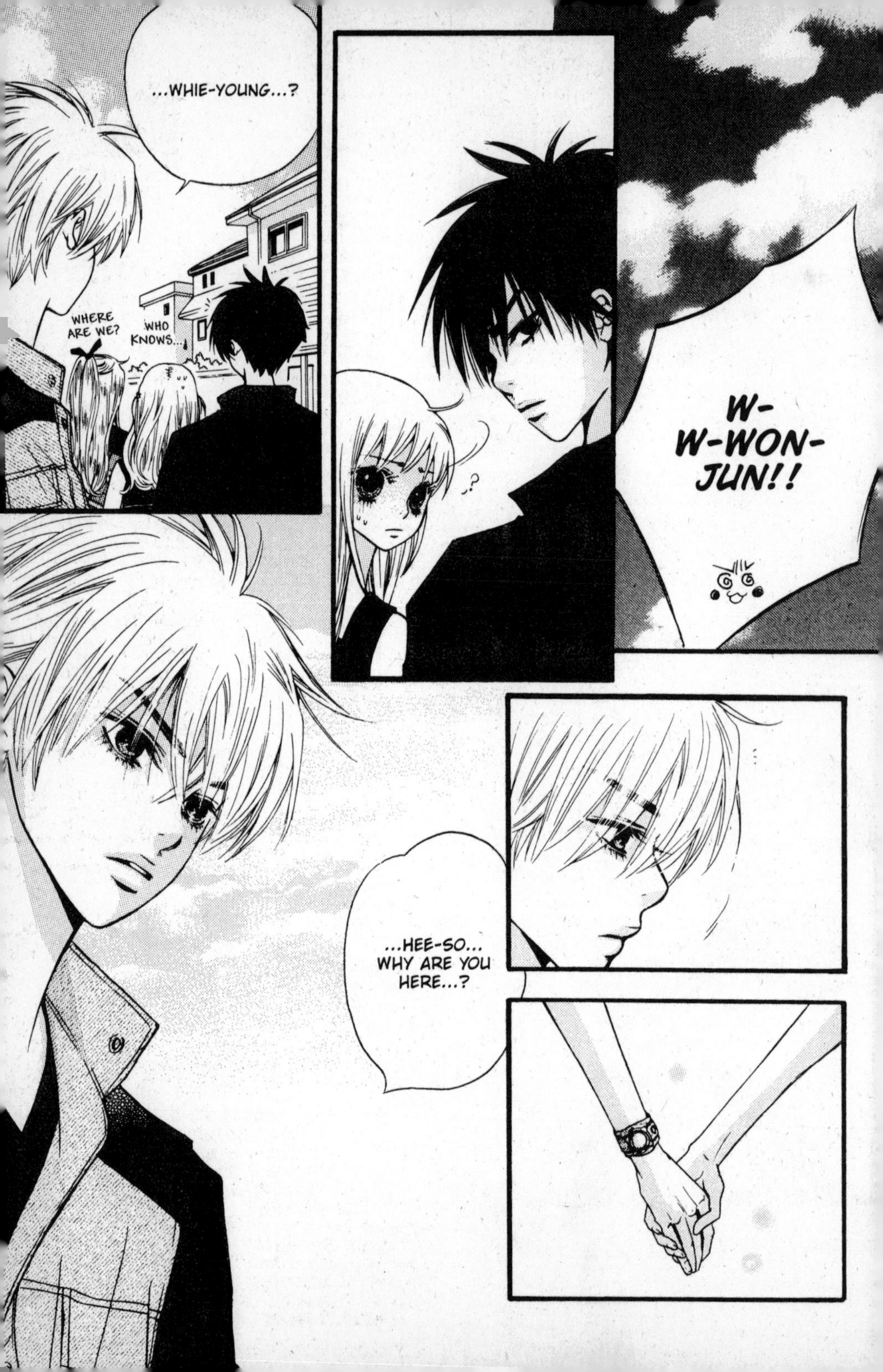
...WHIE-YOUNG...?
WHERE ARE WE?
WHO KNOWS...
W- W-WON-JUN!!
...HEE-SO... WHY ARE YOU HERE...?

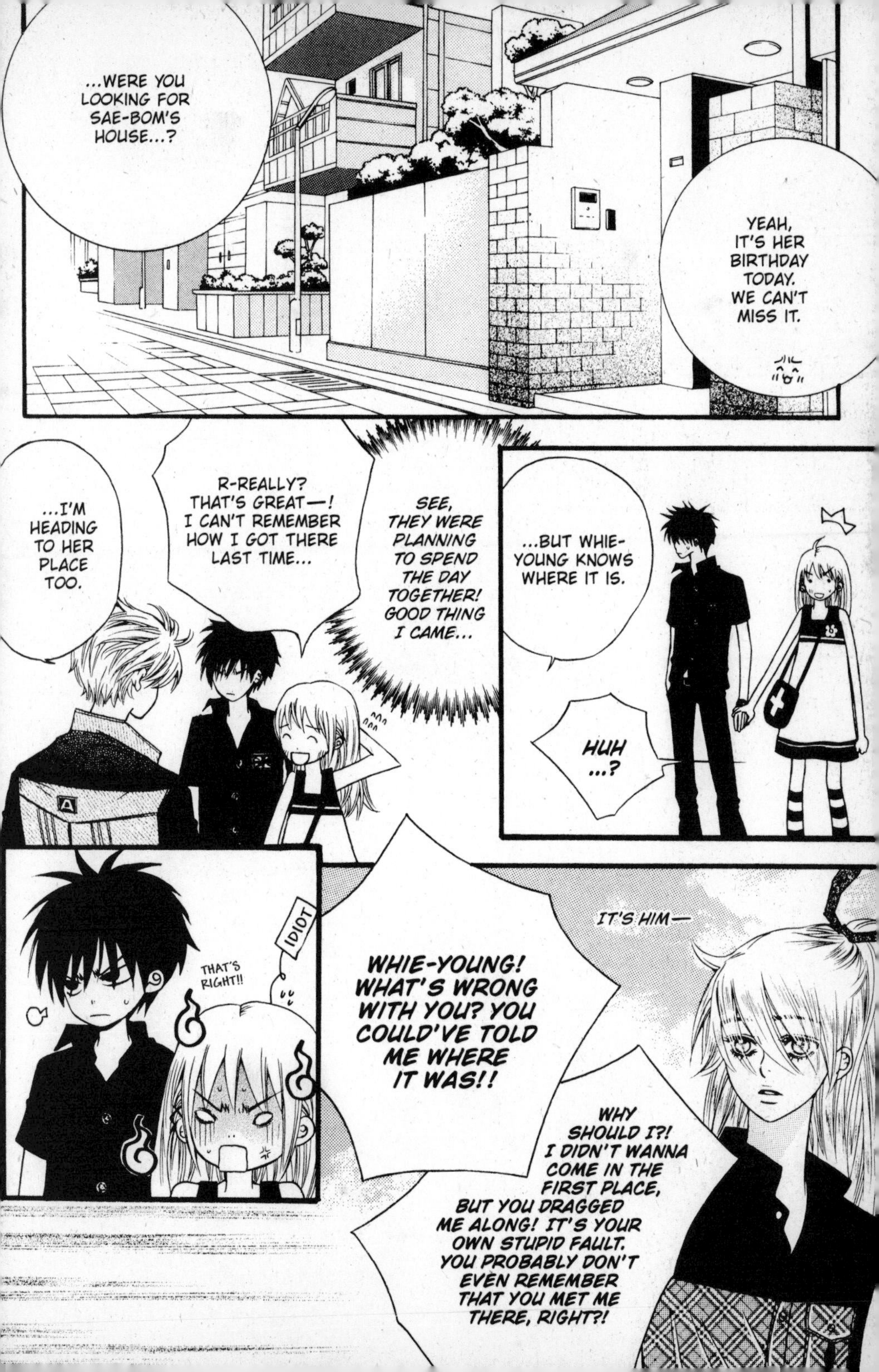

YEAH, IT'S HER BIRTHDAY TODAY. WE CAN'T MISS IT.
...WERE YOU LOOKING FOR SAE-BOM'S HOUSE...?
...BUT WHIE-YOUNG KNOWS WHERE IT IS.
HUH ...?
SEE, THEY WERE PLANNING TO SPEND THE DAY TOGETHER! GOOD THING I CAME...
R-REALLY? THAT'S GREAT—! I CAN'T REMEMBER HOW I GOT THERE LAST TIME...
...I'M HEADING TO HER PLACE TOO.
IT'S HIM—
WHY SHOULD I?! I DIDN'T WANNA COME IN THE FIRST PLACE, BUT YOU DRAGGED ME ALONG! IT'S YOUR OWN STUPID FAULT. YOU PROBABLY DON'T EVEN REMEMBER THAT YOU MET ME THERE, RIGHT?!
WHIE-YOUNG! WHAT'S WRONG WITH YOU? YOU COULD'VE TOLD ME WHERE IT WAS!!
IDIOT
THAT'S RIGHT!!

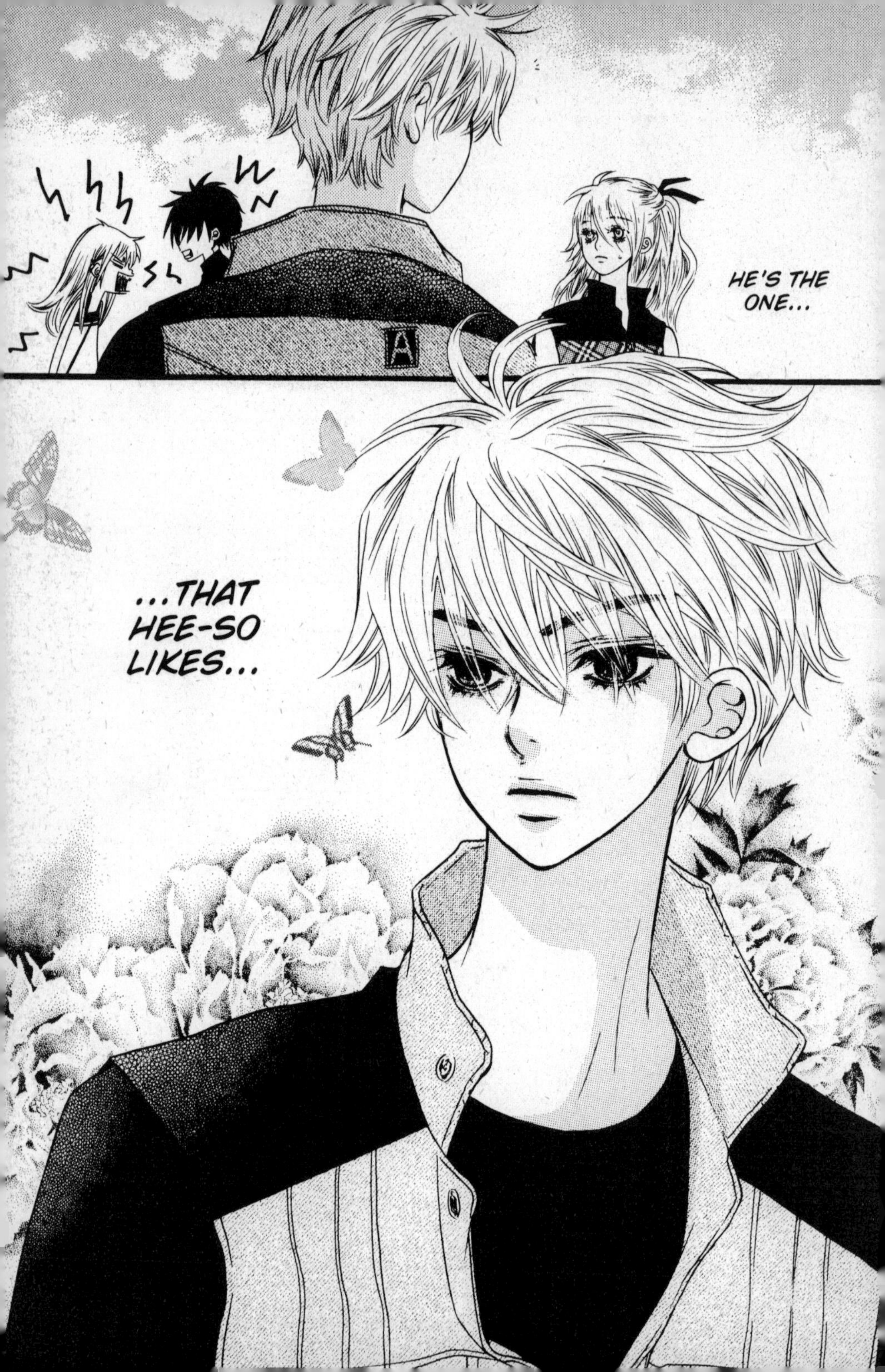
HE'S THE ONE...
...THAT HEE-SO LIKES...

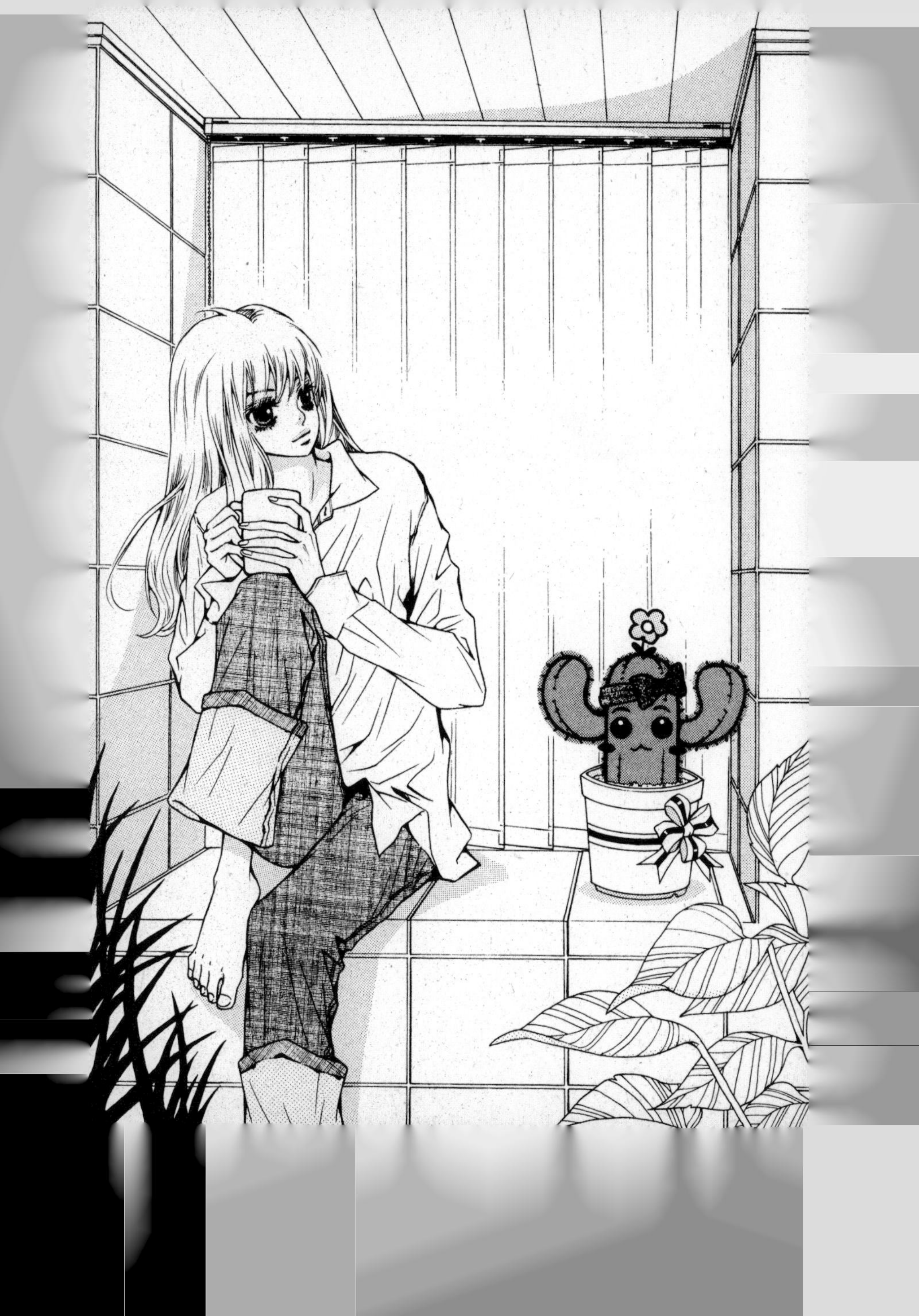

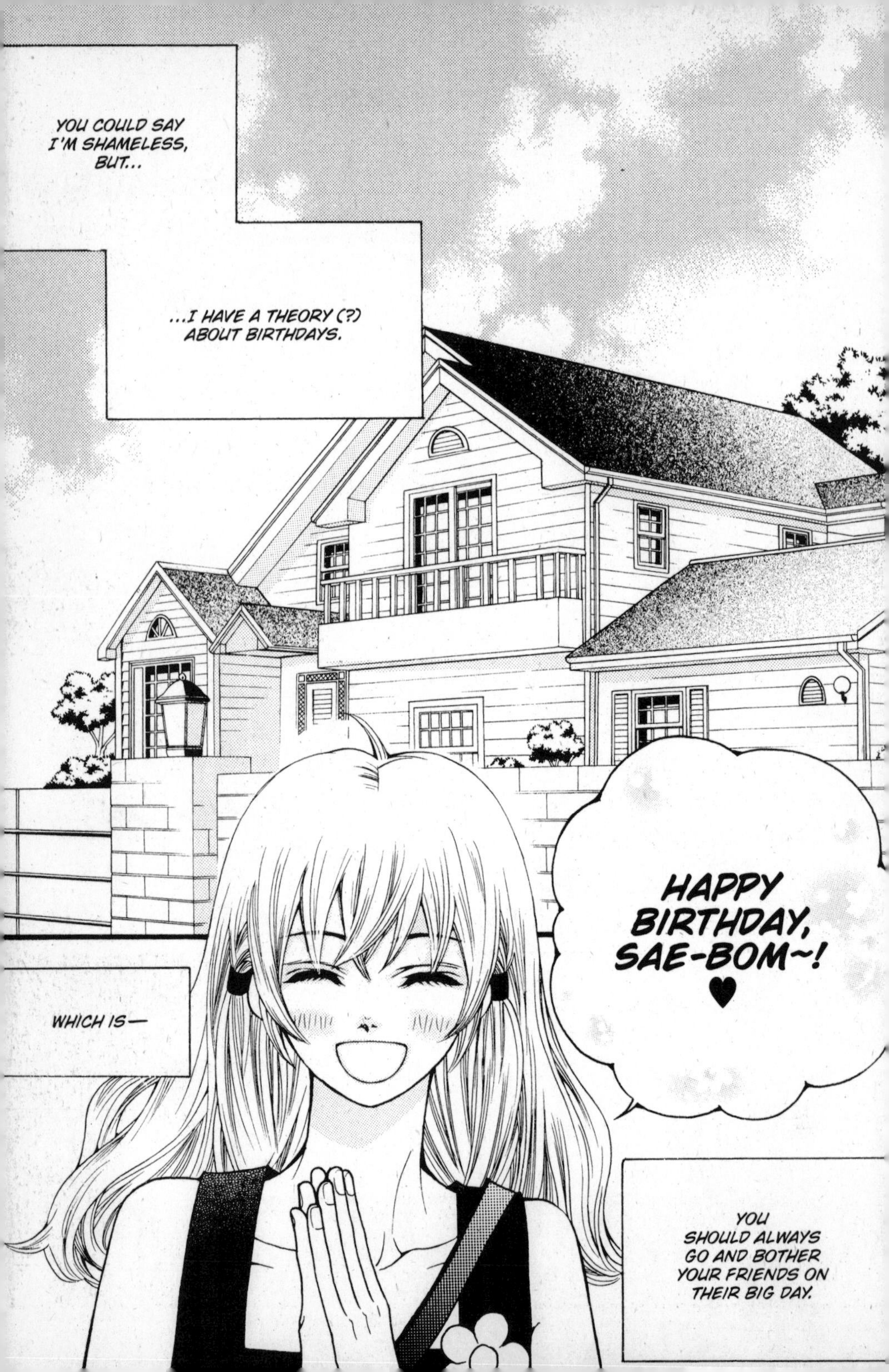
YOU COULD SAY I'M SHAMELESS, BUT...
...I HAVE A THEORY (?) ABOUT BIRTHDAYS.
WHICH IS—
HAPPY BIRTHDAY, SAE-BOM~! ♥
YOU SHOULD ALWAYS GO AND BOTHER YOUR FRIENDS ON THEIR BIG DAY.

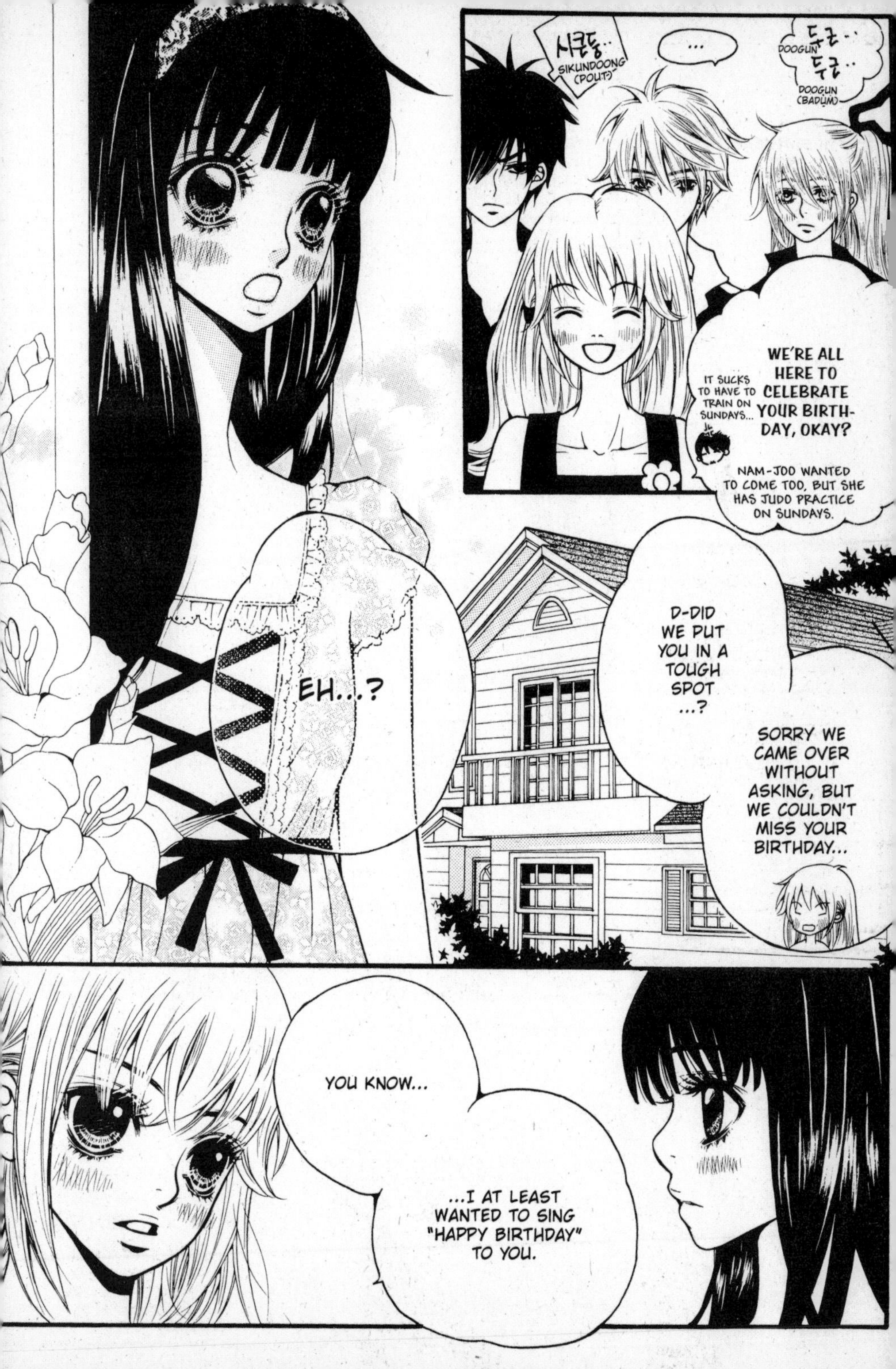
EH...?
시쿤둥..
SIKUNDOONG (POUT)
...
두군..
DOOGUN
두군..
DOOGUN (BADUM)
WE'RE ALL HERE TO CELEBRATE YOUR BIRTHDAY, OKAY?
IT SUCKS TO HAVE TO TRAIN ON SUNDAYS...
NAM-JOO WANTED TO COME TOO, BUT SHE HAS JUDO PRACTICE ON SUNDAYS.
D-DID WE PUT YOU IN A TOUGH SPOT ...?
SORRY WE CAME OVER WITHOUT ASKING, BUT WE COULDN'T MISS YOUR BIRTHDAY...
YOU KNOW...
...I AT LEAST WANTED TO SING "HAPPY BIRTHDAY" TO YOU.

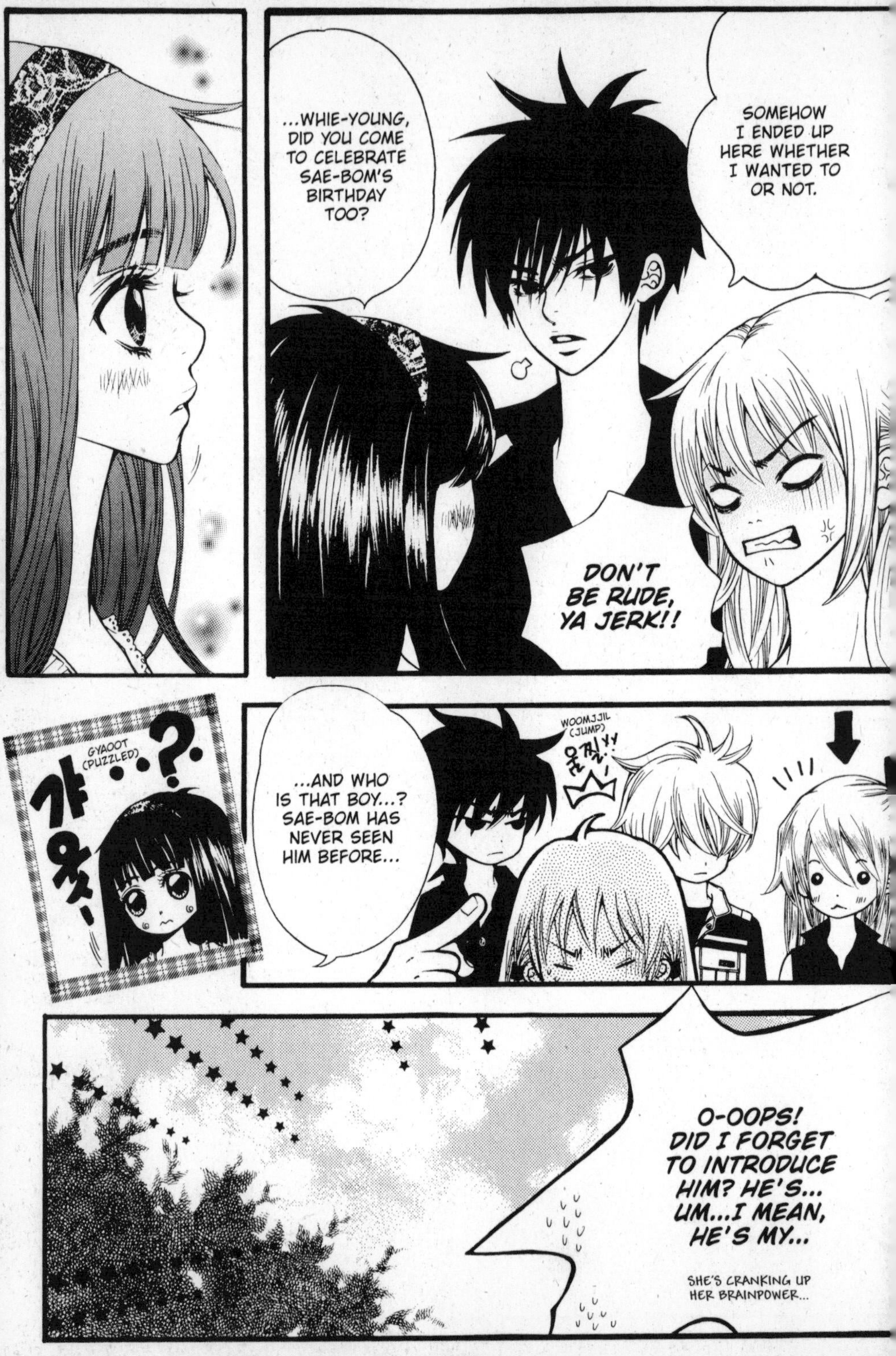
...WHIE-YOUNG, DID YOU COME TO CELEBRATE SAE-BOM'S BIRTHDAY TOO?
SOMEHOW I ENDED UP HERE WHETHER I WANTED TO OR NOT.
DON'T BE RUDE, YA JERK!!
GYAOOT (PUZZLED)
갸웃
...AND WHO IS THAT BOY...? SAE-BOM HAS NEVER SEEN HIM BEFORE...
WOOMJJIL (JUMP)
움찔
O-OOPS! DID I FORGET TO INTRODUCE HIM? HE'S... UM...I MEAN, HE'S MY...
SHE'S CRANKING UP HER BRAINPOWER...

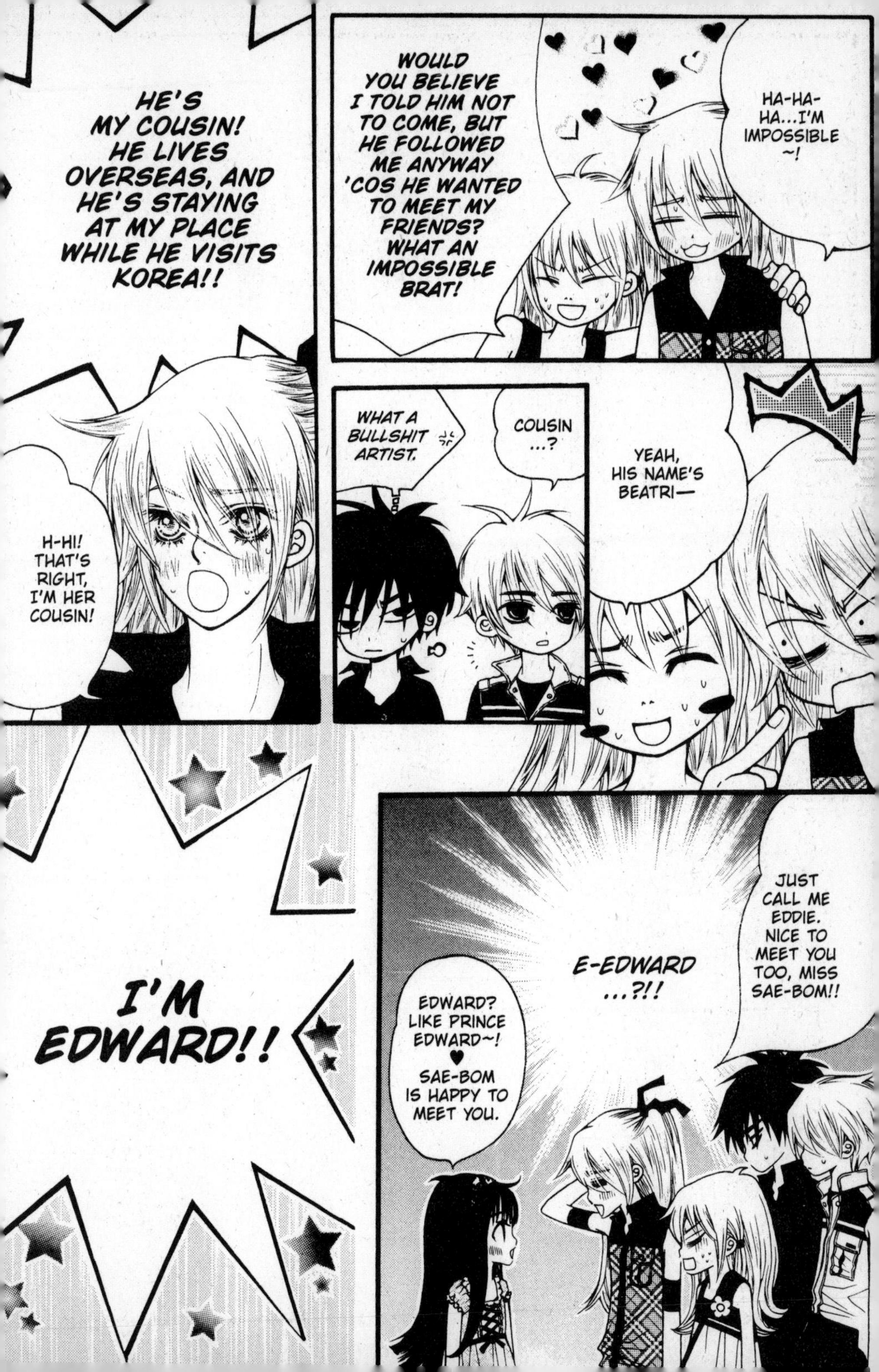

HE'S MY COUSIN! HE LIVES OVERSEAS, AND HE'S STAYING AT MY PLACE WHILE HE VISITS KOREA!!
WOULD YOU BELIEVE I TOLD HIM NOT TO COME, BUT HE FOLLOWED ME ANYWAY 'COS HE WANTED TO MEET MY FRIENDS? WHAT AN IMPOSSIBLE BRAT!
HA-HA-HA...I'M IMPOSSIBLE ~!
H-HI! THAT'S RIGHT, I'M HER COUSIN!
WHAT A BULLSHIT ARTIST.
COUSIN ...?
YEAH, HIS NAME'S BEATRI—
I'M EDWARD!!
E-EDWARD ...?!!
JUST CALL ME EDDIE. NICE TO MEET YOU TOO, MISS SAE-BOM!!
EDWARD? LIKE PRINCE EDWARD~! ♥ SAE-BOM IS HAPPY TO MEET YOU.

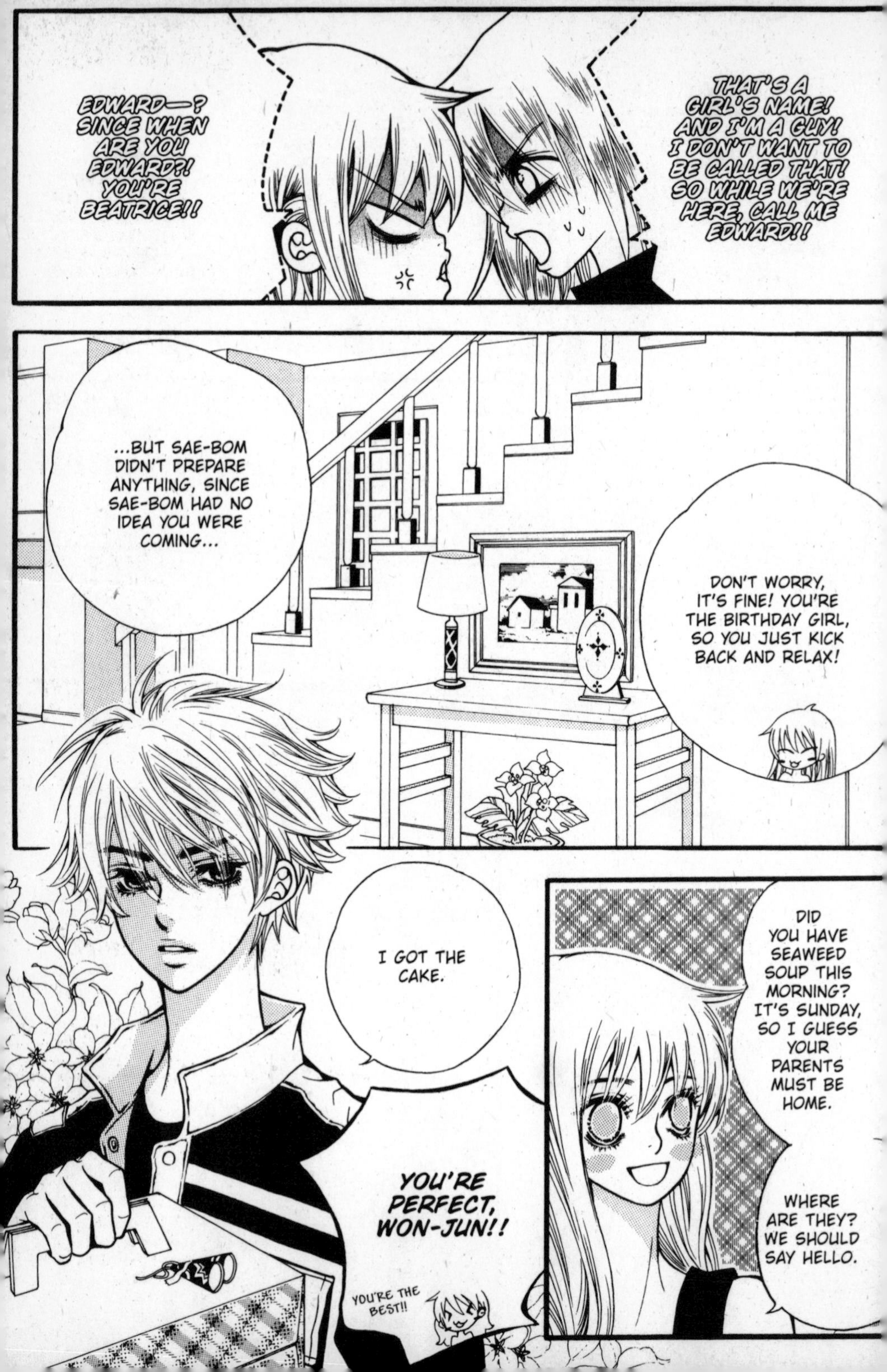
EDWARD—? SINCE WHEN ARE YOU EDWARD?! YOU'RE BEATRICE!!
THAT'S A GIRL'S NAME! AND I'M A GUY! I DON'T WANT TO BE CALLED THAT! SO WHILE WE'RE HERE, CALL ME EDWARD!!
...BUT SAE-BOM DIDN'T PREPARE ANYTHING, SINCE SAE-BOM HAD NO IDEA YOU WERE COMING...
DON'T WORRY, IT'S FINE! YOU'RE THE BIRTHDAY GIRL, SO YOU JUST KICK BACK AND RELAX!
I GOT THE CAKE.
YOU'RE PERFECT, WON-JUN!!
YOU'RE THE BEST!!
DID YOU HAVE SEAWEED SOUP THIS MORNING? IT'S SUNDAY, SO I GUESS YOUR PARENTS MUST BE HOME.
WHERE ARE THEY? WE SHOULD SAY HELLO.

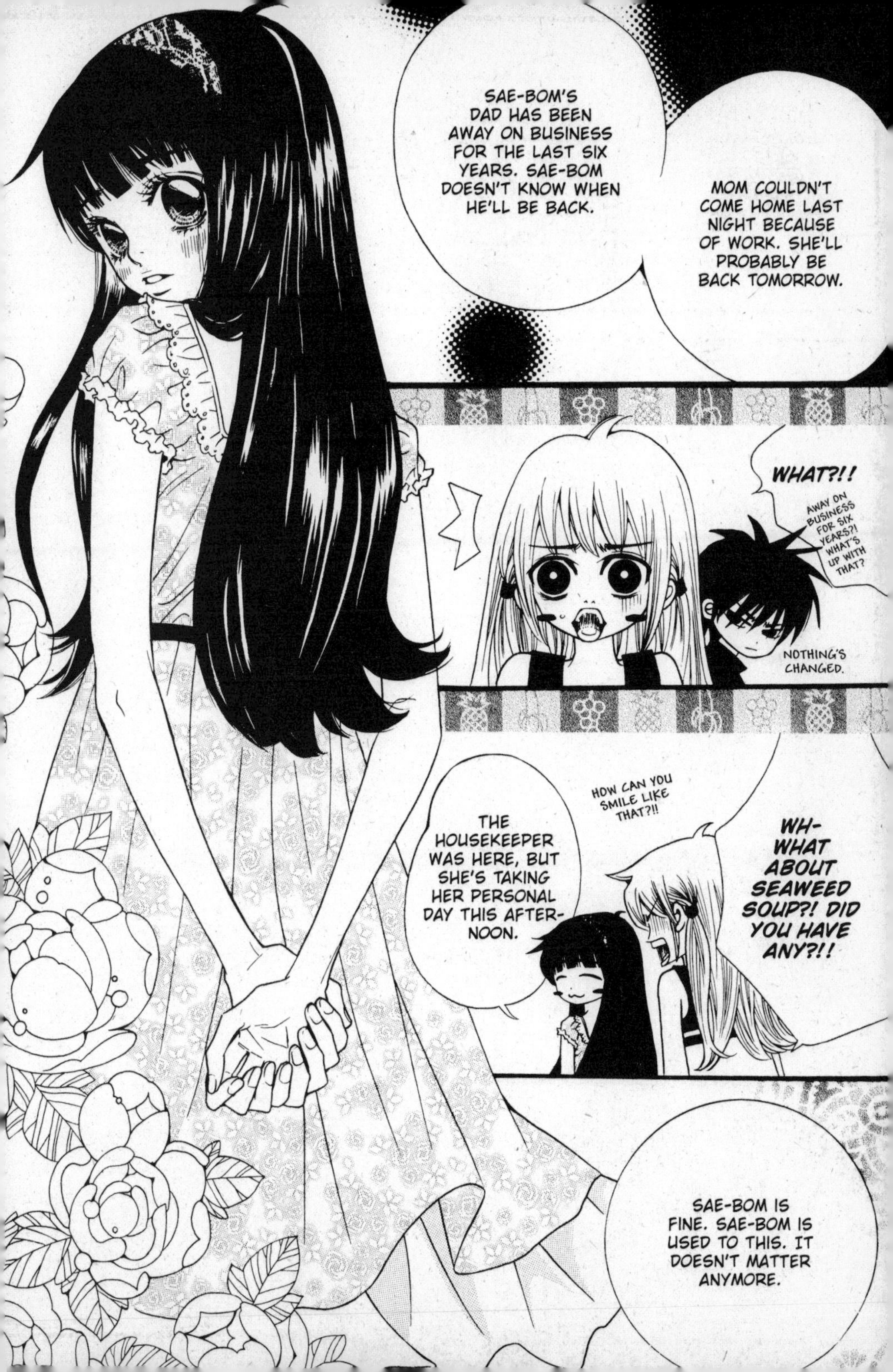
SAE-BOM'S DAD HAS BEEN AWAY ON BUSINESS FOR THE LAST SIX YEARS. SAE-BOM DOESN'T KNOW WHEN HE'LL BE BACK.
MOM COULDN'T COME HOME LAST NIGHT BECAUSE OF WORK. SHE'LL PROBABLY BE BACK TOMORROW.
WHAT?!!
AWAY ON BUSINESS FOR SIX YEARS?! WHAT'S UP WITH THAT?
NOTHING'S CHANGED.
THE HOUSEKEEPER WAS HERE, BUT SHE'S TAKING HER PERSONAL DAY THIS AFTER-NOON.
HOW CAN YOU SMILE LIKE THAT?!!
WH-WHAT ABOUT SEAWEED SOUP?! DID YOU HAVE ANY?!!
SAE-BOM IS FINE. SAE-BOM IS USED TO THIS. IT DOESN'T MATTER ANYMORE.

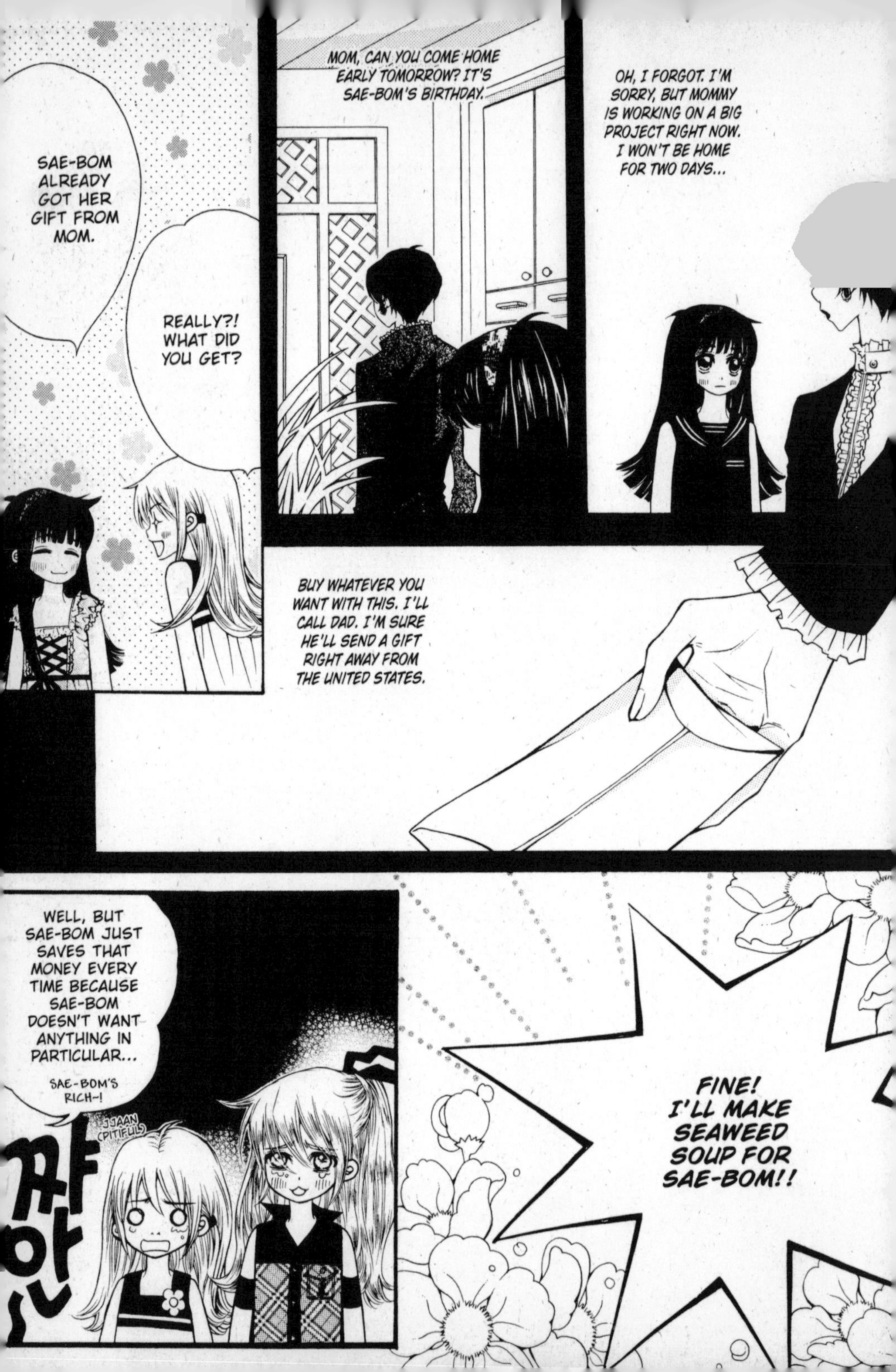

SAE-BOM ALREADY GOT HER GIFT FROM MOM.
REALLY?! WHAT DID YOU GET?
MOM, CAN YOU COME HOME EARLY TOMORROW? IT'S SAE-BOM'S BIRTHDAY.
OH, I FORGOT. I'M SORRY, BUT MOMMY IS WORKING ON A BIG PROJECT RIGHT NOW. I WON'T BE HOME FOR TWO DAYS...
BUY WHATEVER YOU WANT WITH THIS. I'LL CALL DAD. I'M SURE HE'LL SEND A GIFT RIGHT AWAY FROM THE UNITED STATES.
WELL, BUT SAE-BOM JUST SAVES THAT MONEY EVERY TIME BECAUSE SAE-BOM DOESN'T WANT ANYTHING IN PARTICULAR...
SAE-BOM'S RICH-!
JJAAN (PITIFUL)
FINE! I'LL MAKE SEAWEED SOUP FOR SAE-BOM!!

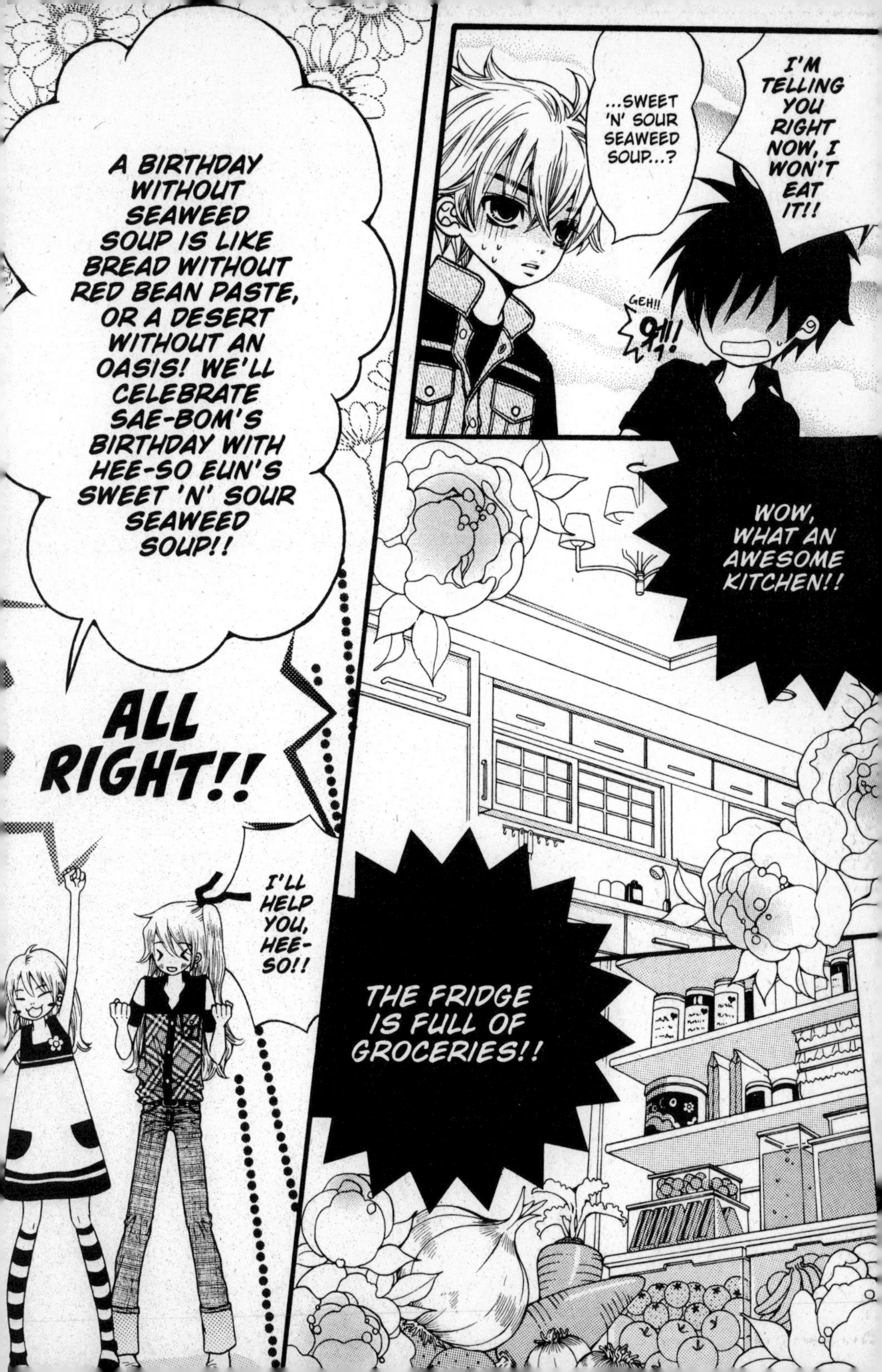
A BIRTHDAY WITHOUT SEAWEED SOUP IS LIKE BREAD WITHOUT RED BEAN PASTE, OR A DESERT WITHOUT AN OASIS! WE'LL CELEBRATE SAE-BOM'S BIRTHDAY WITH HEE-SO EUN'S SWEET 'N' SOUR SEAWEED SOUP!!
ALL RIGHT!!
I'LL HELP YOU, HEE-SO!!
...SWEET 'N' SOUR SEAWEED SOUP...?
I'M TELLING YOU RIGHT NOW, I WON'T EAT IT!!
GEH!!
WOW, WHAT AN AWESOME KITCHEN!!
THE FRIDGE IS FULL OF GROCERIES!!

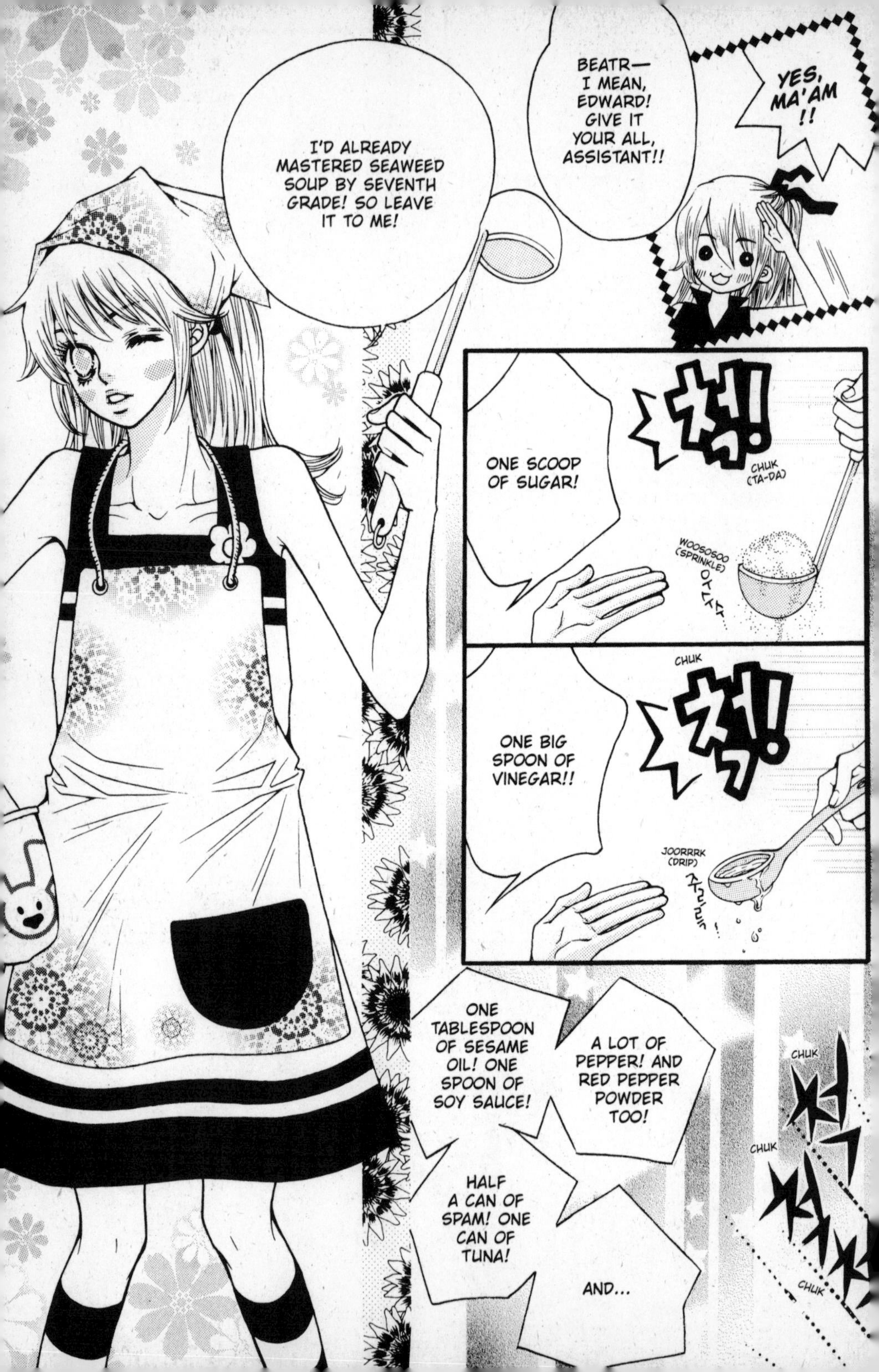
I'D ALREADY MASTERED SEAWEED SOUP BY SEVENTH GRADE! SO LEAVE IT TO ME!
BEATR— I MEAN, EDWARD! GIVE IT YOUR ALL, ASSISTANT!!
YES, MA'AM!!
ONE SCOOP OF SUGAR!
CHUK (TA-DA)
WOOSOSOO (SPRINKLE)
CHUK
ONE BIG SPOON OF VINEGAR!!
JOORRRK (DRIP)
ONE TABLESPOON OF SESAME OIL! ONE SPOON OF SOY SAUCE!
A LOT OF PEPPER! AND RED PEPPER POWDER TOO!
HALF A CAN OF SPAM! ONE CAN OF TUNA!
AND...
CHUK
CHUK
CHUK

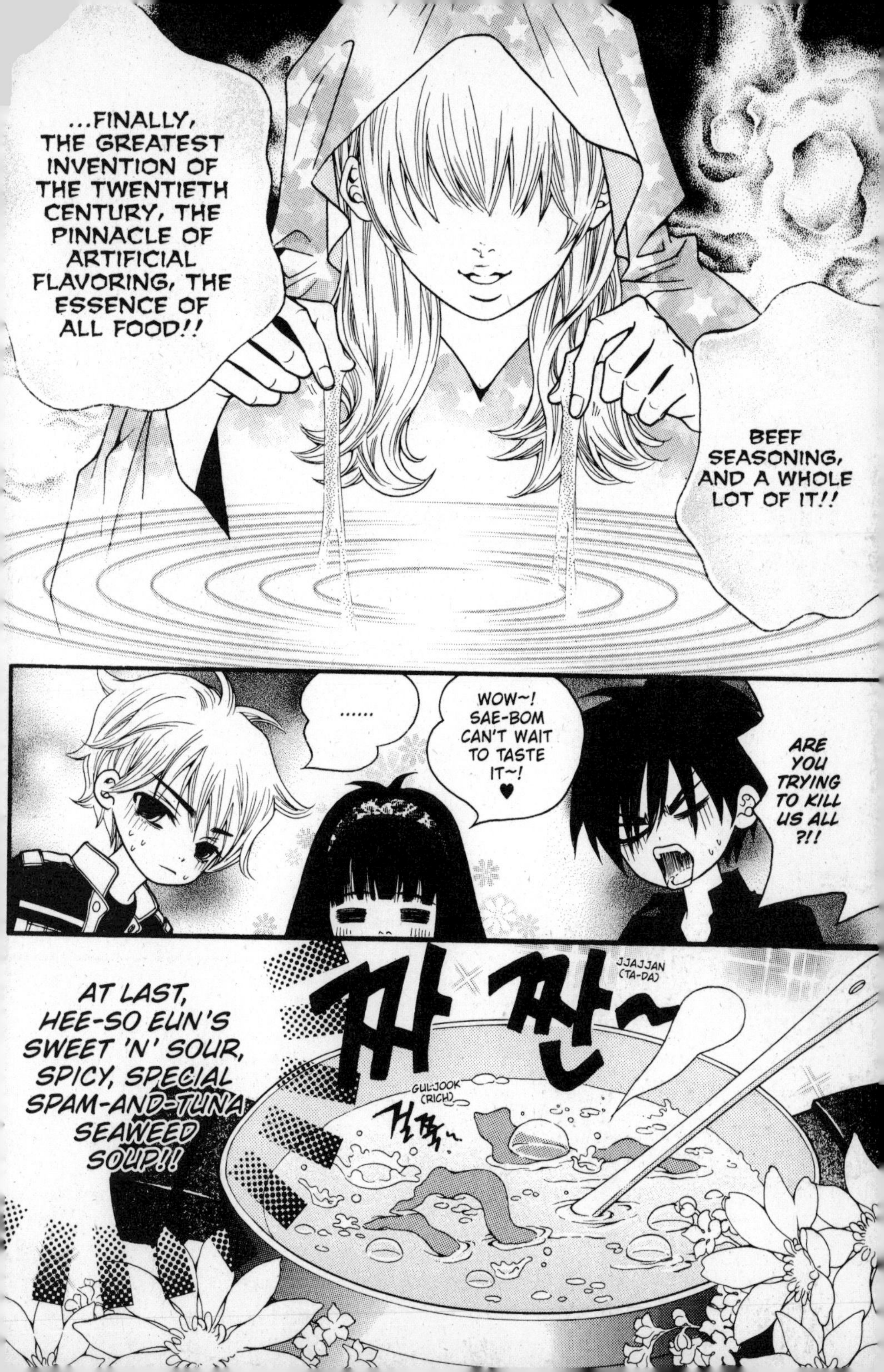

...FINALLY, THE GREATEST INVENTION OF THE TWENTIETH CENTURY, THE PINNACLE OF ARTIFICIAL FLAVORING, THE ESSENCE OF ALL FOOD!!
BEEF SEASONING, AND A WHOLE LOT OF IT!!
......
WOW~! SAE-BOM CAN'T WAIT TO TASTE IT~! ♥
ARE YOU TRYING TO KILL US ALL ?!!
AT LAST, HEE-SO EUN'S SWEET 'N' SOUR, SPICY, SPECIAL SPAM-AND-TUNA SEAWEED SOUP!!
짜잔~
JJAJJAN (TA-DA)
걸쭉..
GUL-JOOK (RICH)

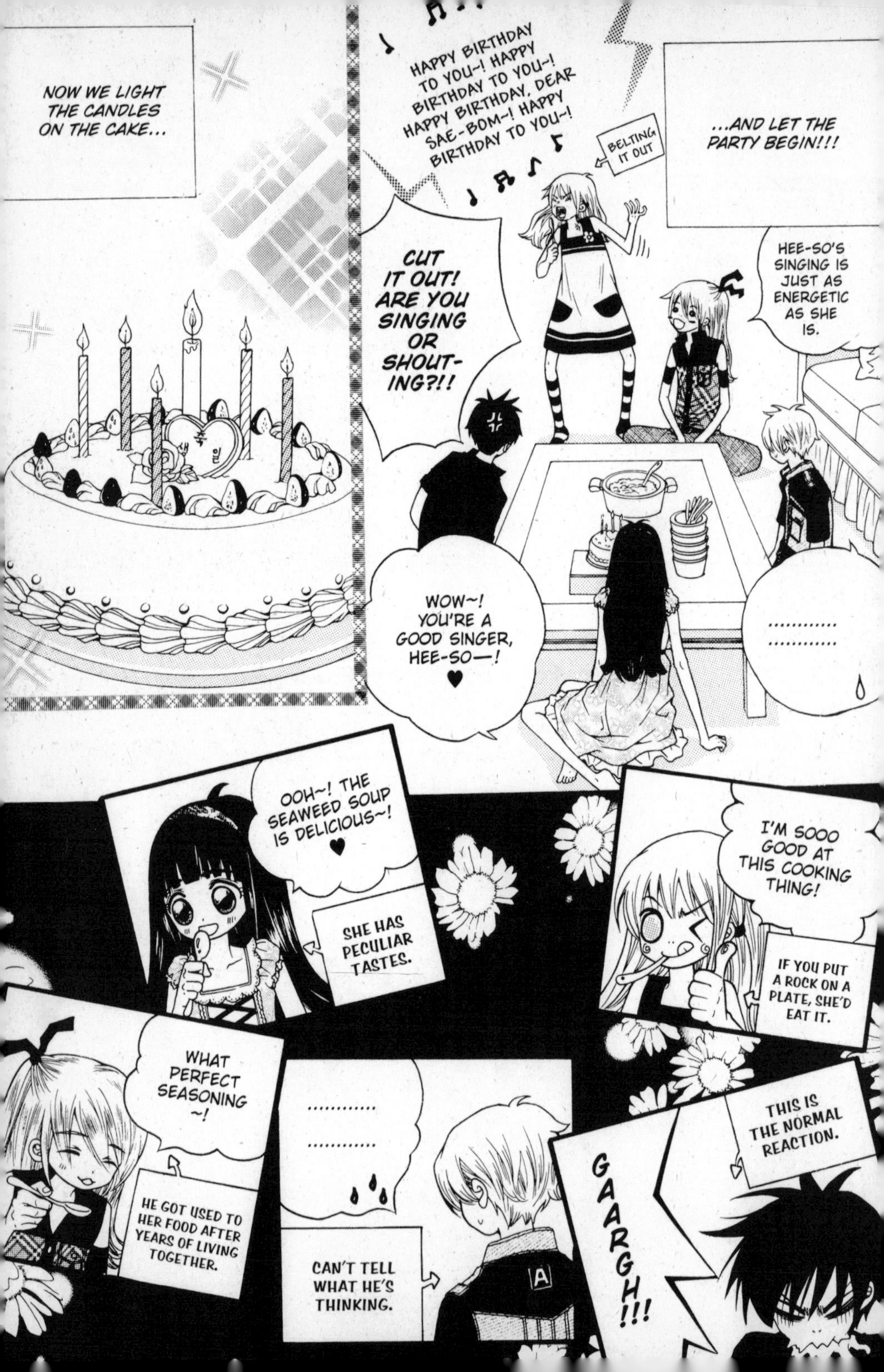
NOW WE LIGHT THE CANDLES ON THE CAKE...
HAPPY BIRTHDAY TO YOU~! HAPPY BIRTHDAY TO YOU~! HAPPY BIRTHDAY, DEAR SAE-BOM~! HAPPY BIRTHDAY TO YOU~!
BELTING IT OUT
...AND LET THE PARTY BEGIN!!!
CUT IT OUT! ARE YOU SINGING OR SHOUT-ING?!!
HEE-SO'S SINGING IS JUST AS ENERGETIC AS SHE IS.
WOW~! YOU'RE A GOOD SINGER, HEE-SO—! ♥
....
....
OOH~! THE SEAWEED SOUP IS DELICIOUS~! ♥
SHE HAS PECULIAR TASTES.
I'M SOOO GOOD AT THIS COOKING THING!
IF YOU PUT A ROCK ON A PLATE, SHE'D EAT IT.
WHAT PERFECT SEASONING ~!
HE GOT USED TO HER FOOD AFTER YEARS OF LIVING TOGETHER.
....
....
CAN'T TELL WHAT HE'S THINKING.
GAARGH!!!
THIS IS THE NORMAL REACTION.

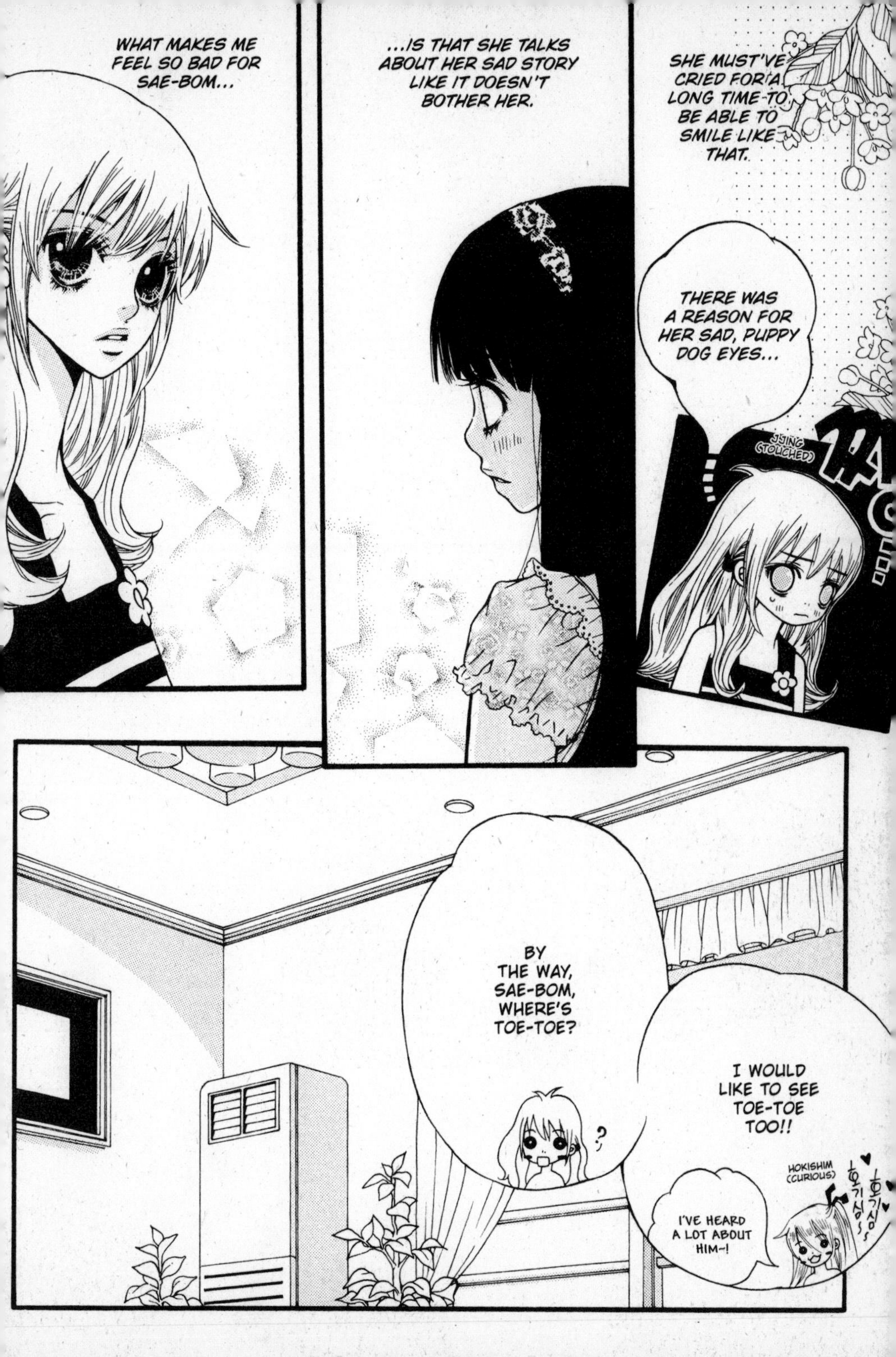
WHAT MAKES ME FEEL SO BAD FOR SAE-BOM...
...IS THAT SHE TALKS ABOUT HER SAD STORY LIKE IT DOESN'T BOTHER HER.
SHE MUST'VE CRIED FOR A LONG TIME TO BE ABLE TO SMILE LIKE THAT.
THERE WAS A REASON FOR HER SAD, PUPPY DOG EYES...
JJING (TOUCHED)
BY THE WAY, SAE-BOM, WHERE'S TOE-TOE?
I WOULD LIKE TO SEE TOE-TOE TOO!!
HOKISHIM (CURIOUS)
I'VE HEARD A LOT ABOUT HIM~!

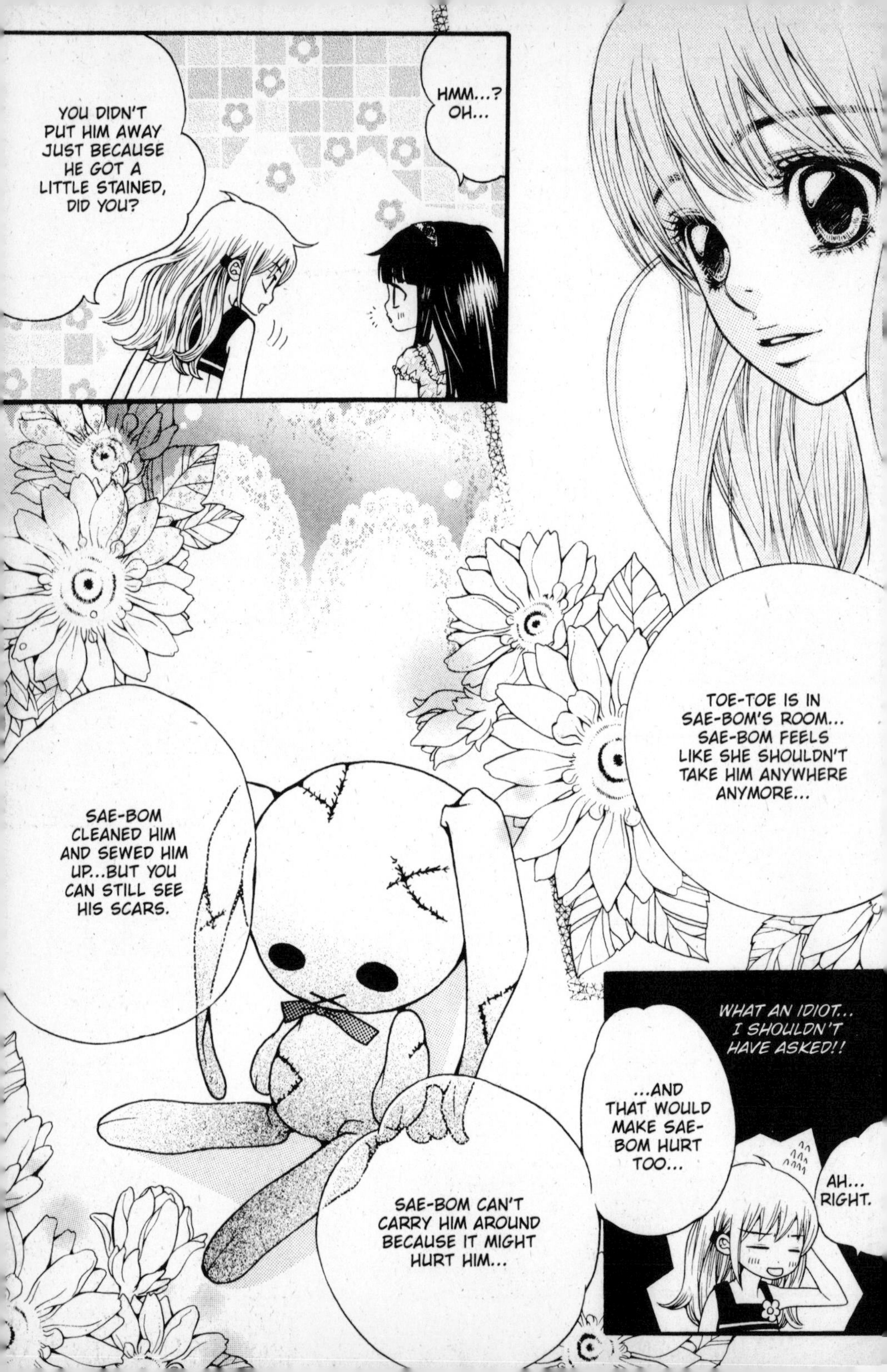
YOU DIDN'T PUT HIM AWAY JUST BECAUSE HE GOT A LITTLE STAINED, DID YOU?
HMM...? OH...
SAE-BOM CLEANED HIM AND SEWED HIM UP...BUT YOU CAN STILL SEE HIS SCARS.
TOE-TOE IS IN SAE-BOM'S ROOM... SAE-BOM FEELS LIKE SHE SHOULDN'T TAKE HIM ANYWHERE ANYMORE...
SAE-BOM CAN'T CARRY HIM AROUND BECAUSE IT MIGHT HURT HIM...
...AND THAT WOULD MAKE SAE-BOM HURT TOO...
WHAT AN IDIOT... I SHOULDN'T HAVE ASKED!!
AH... RIGHT.

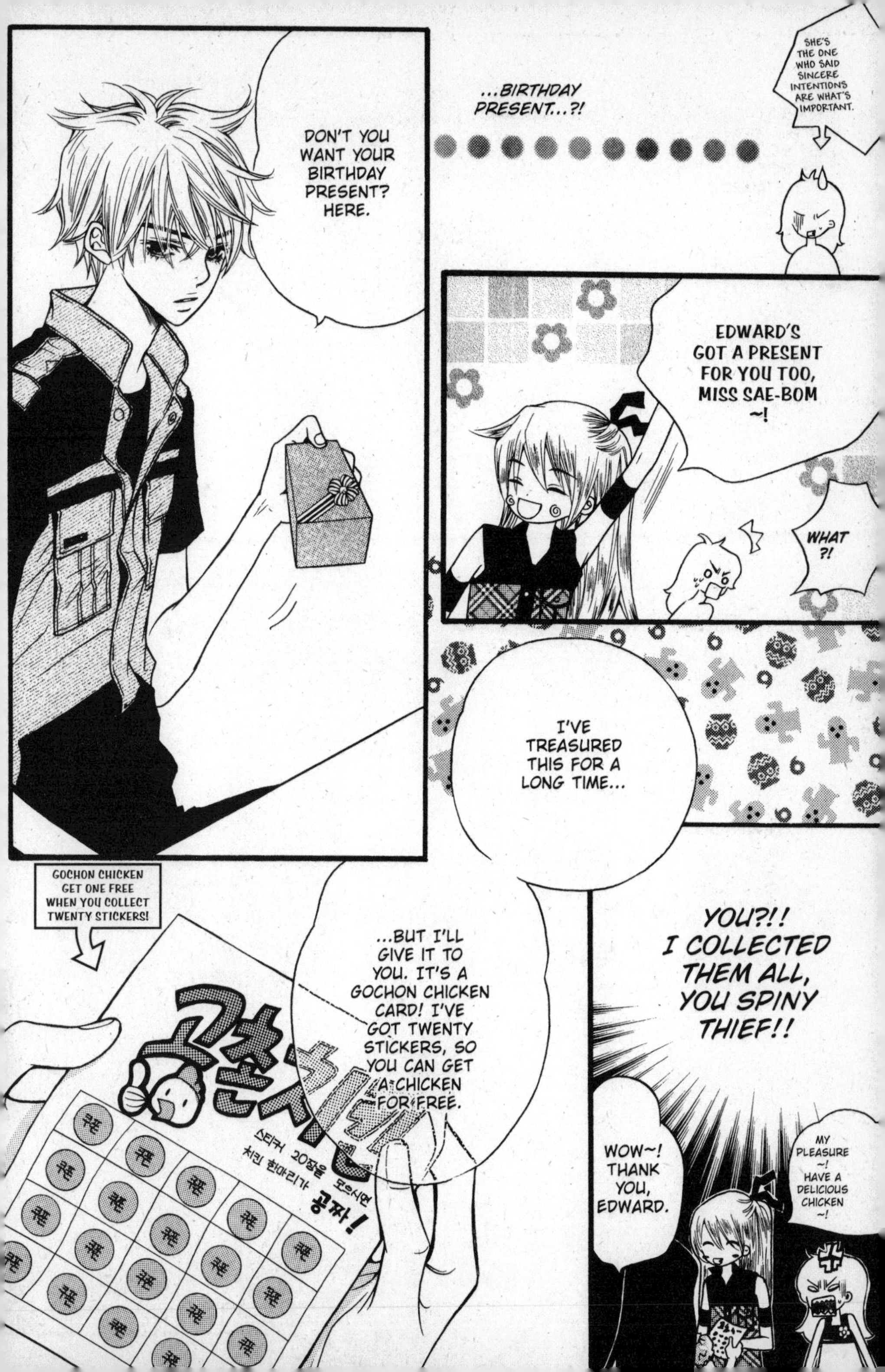
DON'T YOU WANT YOUR BIRTHDAY PRESENT? HERE.
...BIRTHDAY PRESENT...?!
SHE'S THE ONE WHO SAID SINCERE INTENTIONS ARE WHAT'S IMPORTANT.
EDWARD'S GOT A PRESENT FOR YOU TOO, MISS SAE-BOM ~!
WHAT ?!
I'VE TREASURED THIS FOR A LONG TIME...
GOCHON CHICKEN GET ONE FREE WHEN YOU COLLECT TWENTY STICKERS!
스티커 20장을 모으시면 치킨 한마리가 공짜!
...BUT I'LL GIVE IT TO YOU. IT'S A GOCHON CHICKEN CARD! I'VE GOT TWENTY STICKERS, SO YOU CAN GET A CHICKEN FOR FREE.
YOU?!! I COLLECTED THEM ALL, YOU SPINY THIEF!!
WOW~! THANK YOU, EDWARD.
MY PLEASURE ~! HAVE A DELICIOUS CHICKEN ~!

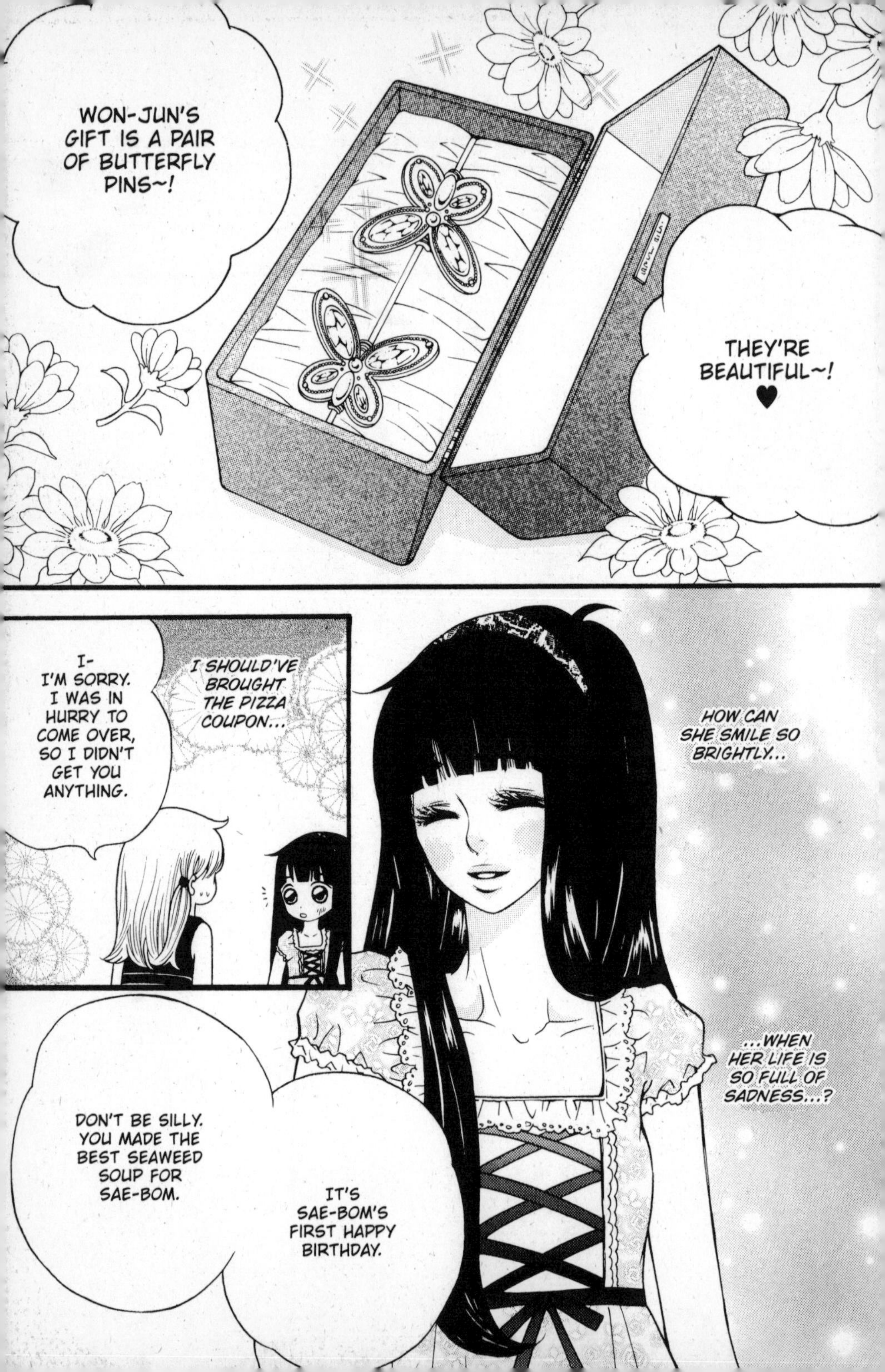
WON-JUN'S GIFT IS A PAIR OF BUTTERFLY PINS~!
THEY'RE BEAUTIFUL~! ♥
I- I'M SORRY. I WAS IN HURRY TO COME OVER, SO I DIDN'T GET YOU ANYTHING.
I SHOULD'VE BROUGHT THE PIZZA COUPON...
HOW CAN SHE SMILE SO BRIGHTLY...
...WHEN HER LIFE IS SO FULL OF SADNESS...?
DON'T BE SILLY. YOU MADE THE BEST SEAWEED SOUP FOR SAE-BOM.
IT'S SAE-BOM'S FIRST HAPPY BIRTHDAY.

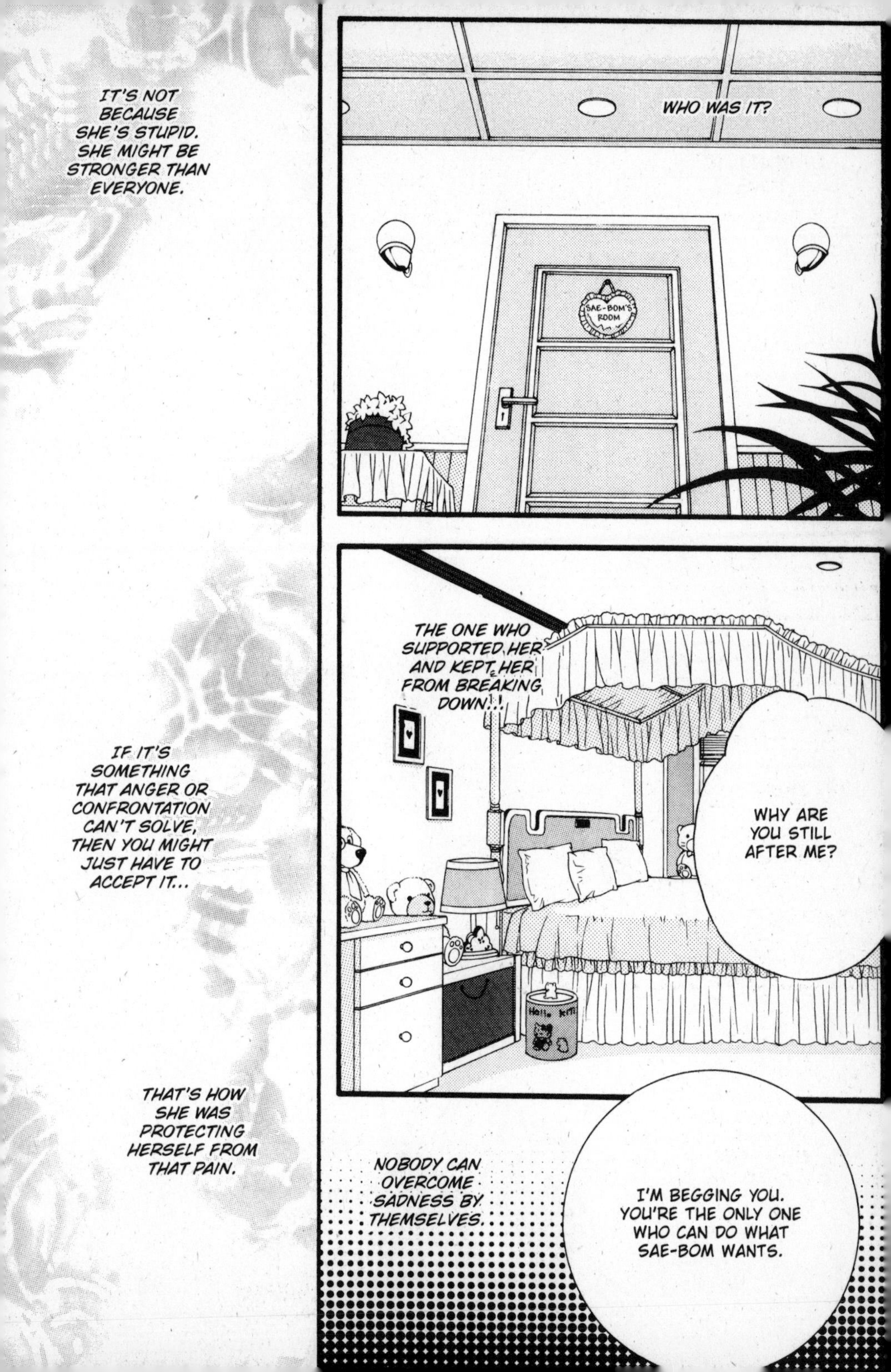
IT'S NOT BECAUSE SHE'S STUPID. SHE MIGHT BE STRONGER THAN EVERYONE.
IF IT'S SOMETHING THAT ANGER OR CONFRONTATION CAN'T SOLVE, THEN YOU MIGHT JUST HAVE TO ACCEPT IT...
THAT'S HOW SHE WAS PROTECTING HERSELF FROM THAT PAIN.
WHO WAS IT?
SAE-BOM'S ROOM
THE ONE WHO SUPPORTED HER AND KEPT HER FROM BREAKING DOWN...!
WHY ARE YOU STILL AFTER ME?
NOBODY CAN OVERCOME SADNESS BY THEMSELVES.
I'M BEGGING YOU. YOU'RE THE ONLY ONE WHO CAN DO WHAT SAE-BOM WANTS.

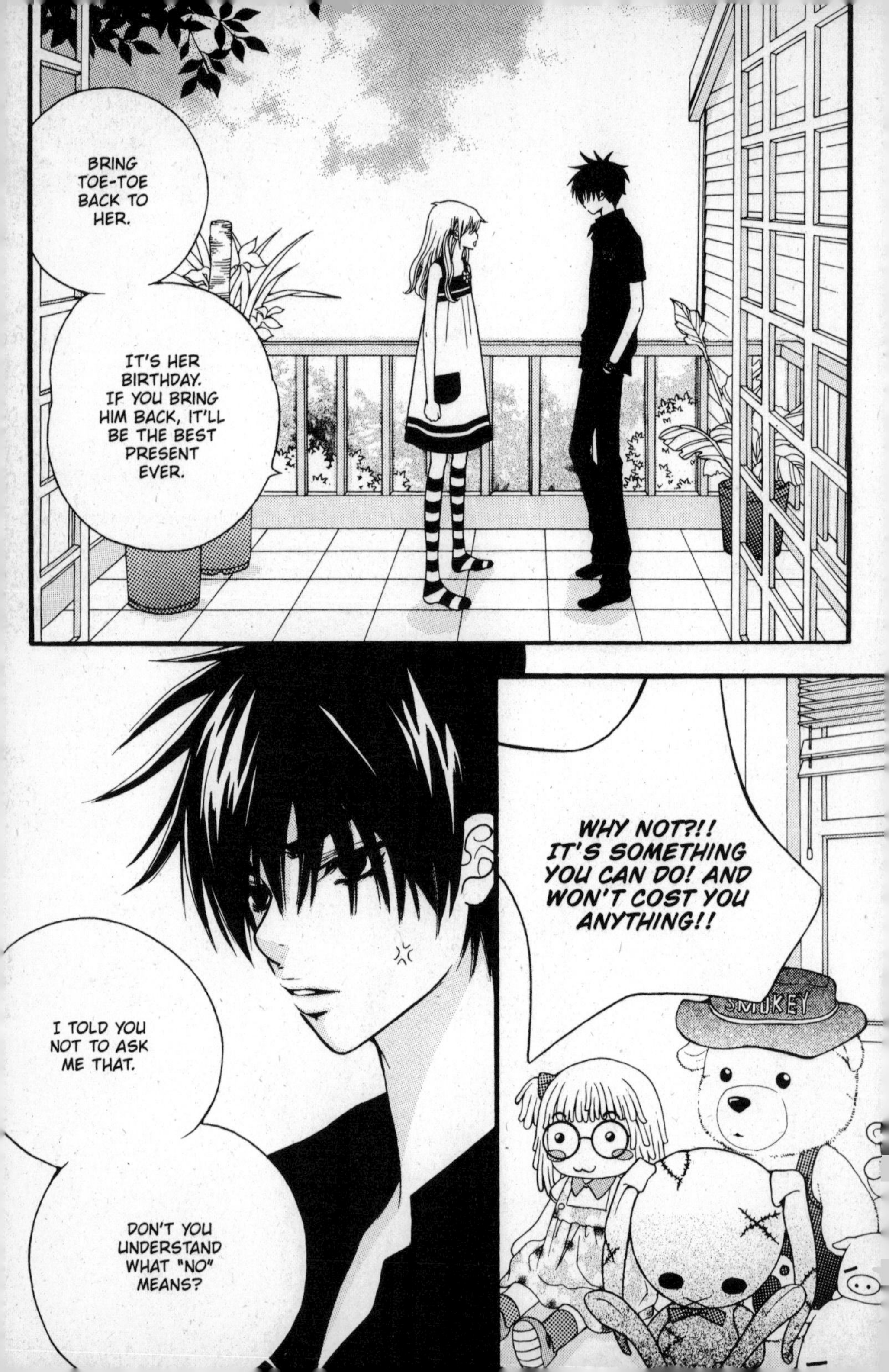
BRING TOE-TOE BACK TO HER.
IT'S HER BIRTHDAY. IF YOU BRING HIM BACK, IT'LL BE THE BEST PRESENT EVER.
I TOLD YOU NOT TO ASK ME THAT.
DON'T YOU UNDERSTAND WHAT "NO" MEANS?
WHY NOT?!! IT'S SOMETHING YOU CAN DO! AND WON'T COST YOU ANYTHING!!
SMOKEY

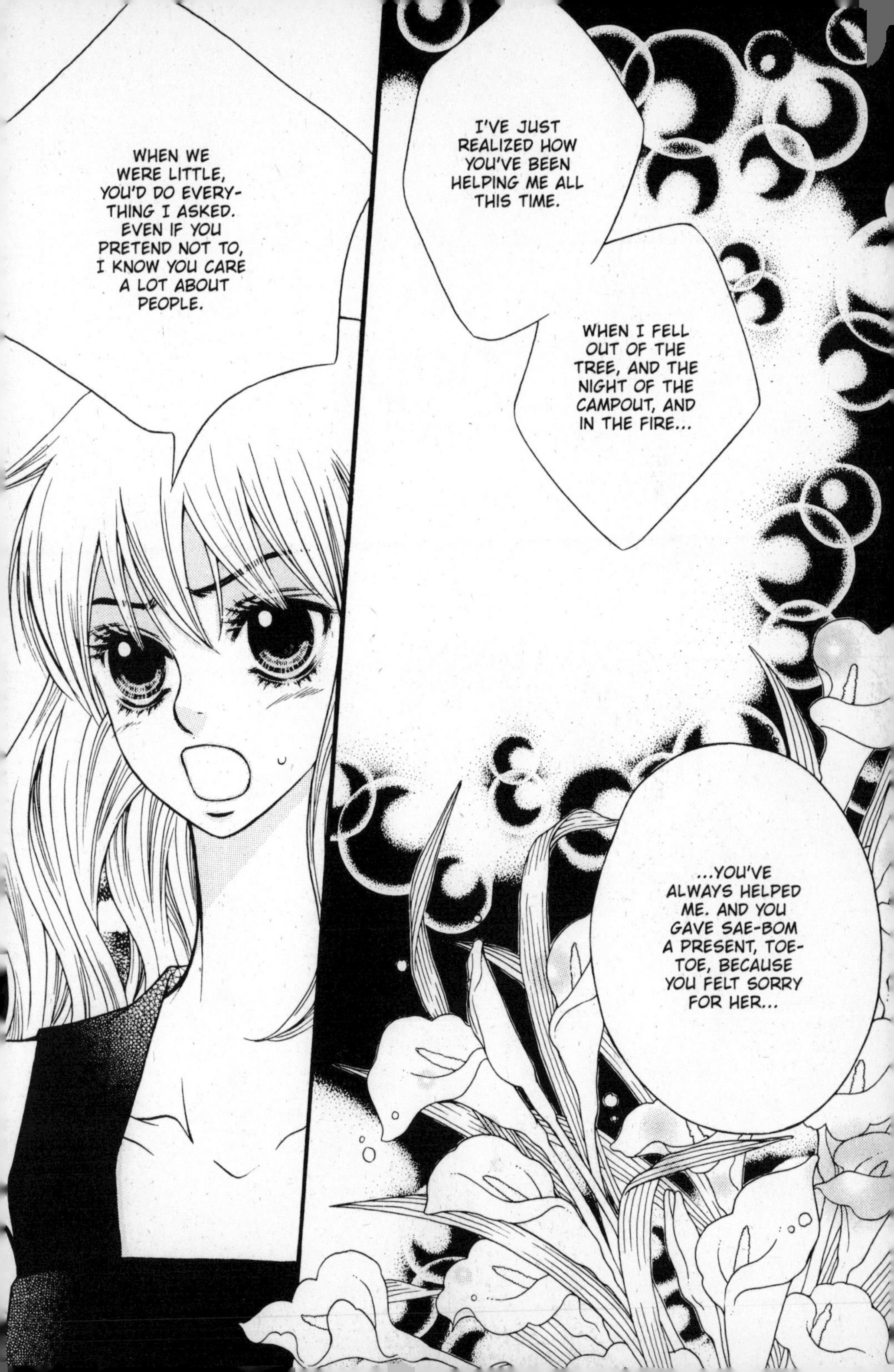
WHEN WE WERE LITTLE, YOU'D DO EVERY-THING I ASKED. EVEN IF YOU PRETEND NOT TO, I KNOW YOU CARE A LOT ABOUT PEOPLE.
I'VE JUST REALIZED HOW YOU'VE BEEN HELPING ME ALL THIS TIME.
WHEN I FELL OUT OF THE TREE, AND THE NIGHT OF THE CAMPOUT, AND IN THE FIRE...
...YOU'VE ALWAYS HELPED ME. AND YOU GAVE SAE-BOM A PRESENT, TOE-TOE, BECAUSE YOU FELT SORRY FOR HER...

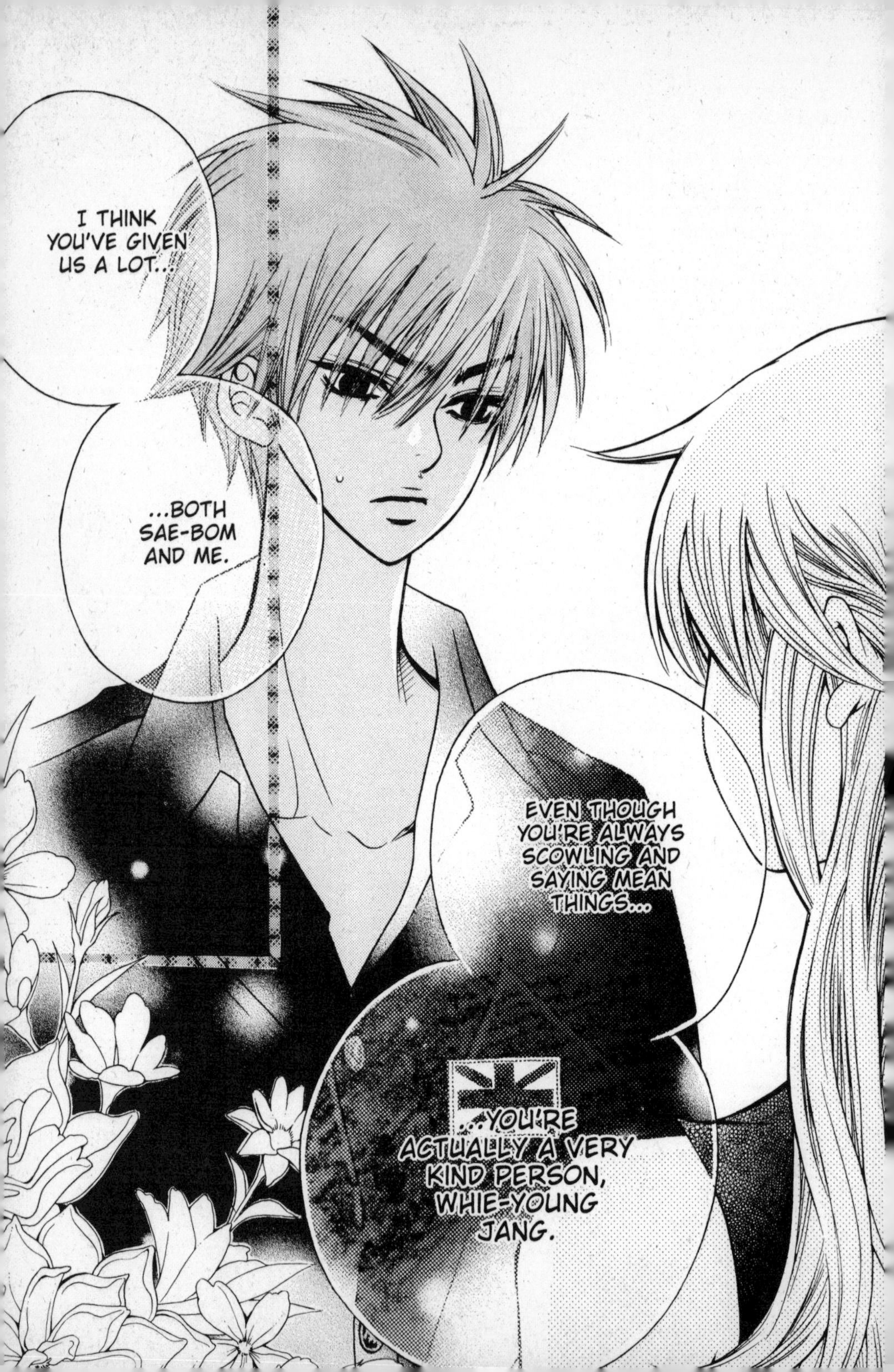
I THINK YOU'VE GIVEN US A LOT...
...BOTH SAE-BOM AND ME.
EVEN THOUGH YOU'RE ALWAYS SCOWLING AND SAYING MEAN THINGS...
...YOU'RE ACTUALLY A VERY KIND PERSON, WHIE-YOUNG JANG.

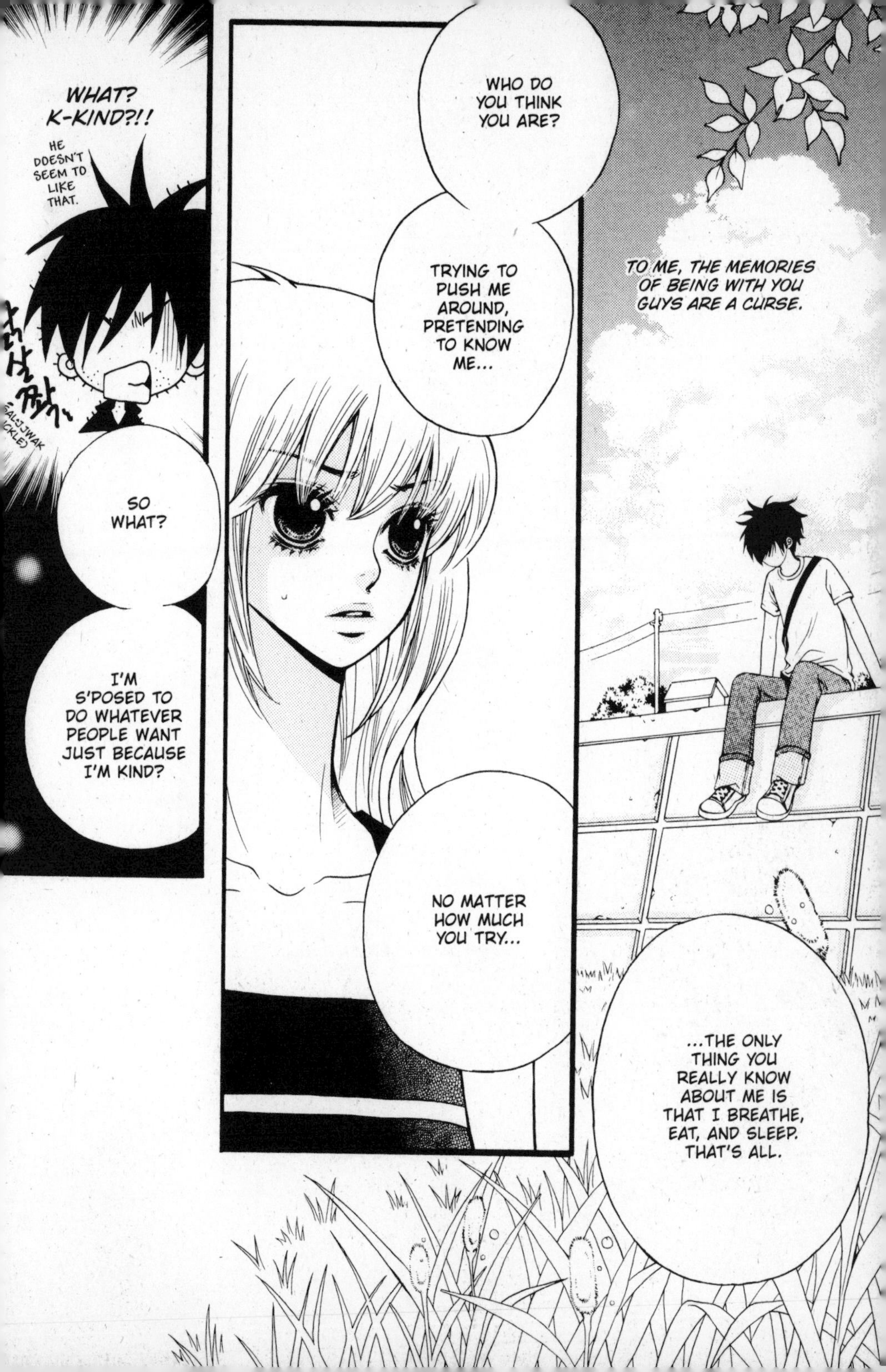
WHAT? K-KIND?!!
HE DOESN'T SEEM TO LIKE THAT.
SALJJWAK
SO WHAT?
I'M S'POSED TO DO WHATEVER PEOPLE WANT JUST BECAUSE I'M KIND?
WHO DO YOU THINK YOU ARE?
TRYING TO PUSH ME AROUND, PRETENDING TO KNOW ME...
NO MATTER HOW MUCH YOU TRY...
TO ME, THE MEMORIES OF BEING WITH YOU GUYS ARE A CURSE.
...THE ONLY THING YOU REALLY KNOW ABOUT ME IS THAT I BREATHE, EAT, AND SLEEP. THAT'S ALL.

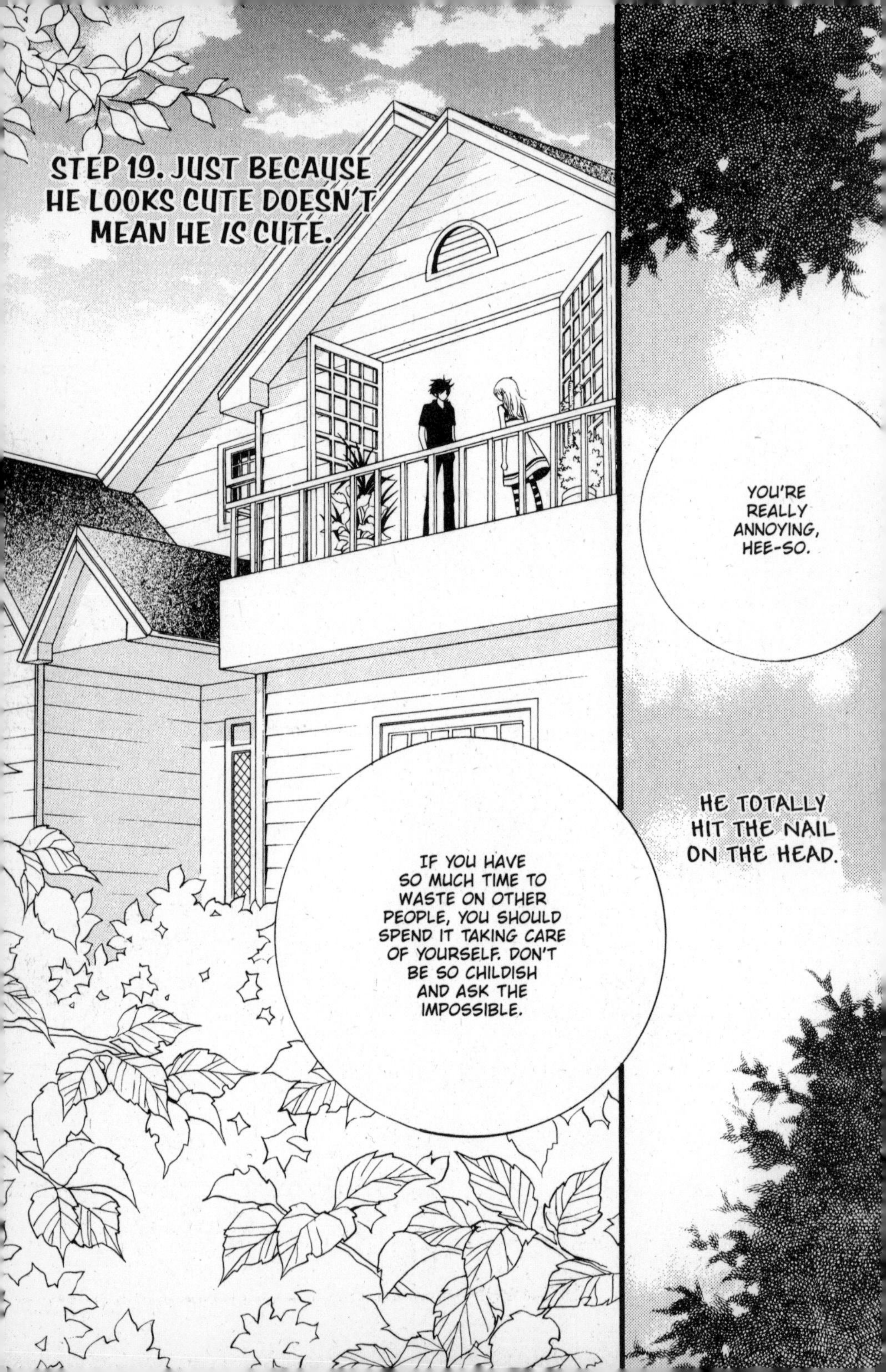
STEP 19. JUST BECAUSE HE LOOKS CUTE DOESN'T MEAN HE *IS* CUTE.
IF YOU HAVE SO MUCH TIME TO WASTE ON OTHER PEOPLE, YOU SHOULD SPEND IT TAKING CARE OF YOURSELF. DON'T BE SO CHILDISH AND ASK THE IMPOSSIBLE.
YOU'RE REALLY ANNOYING, HEE-SO.
HE TOTALLY HIT THE NAIL ON THE HEAD.

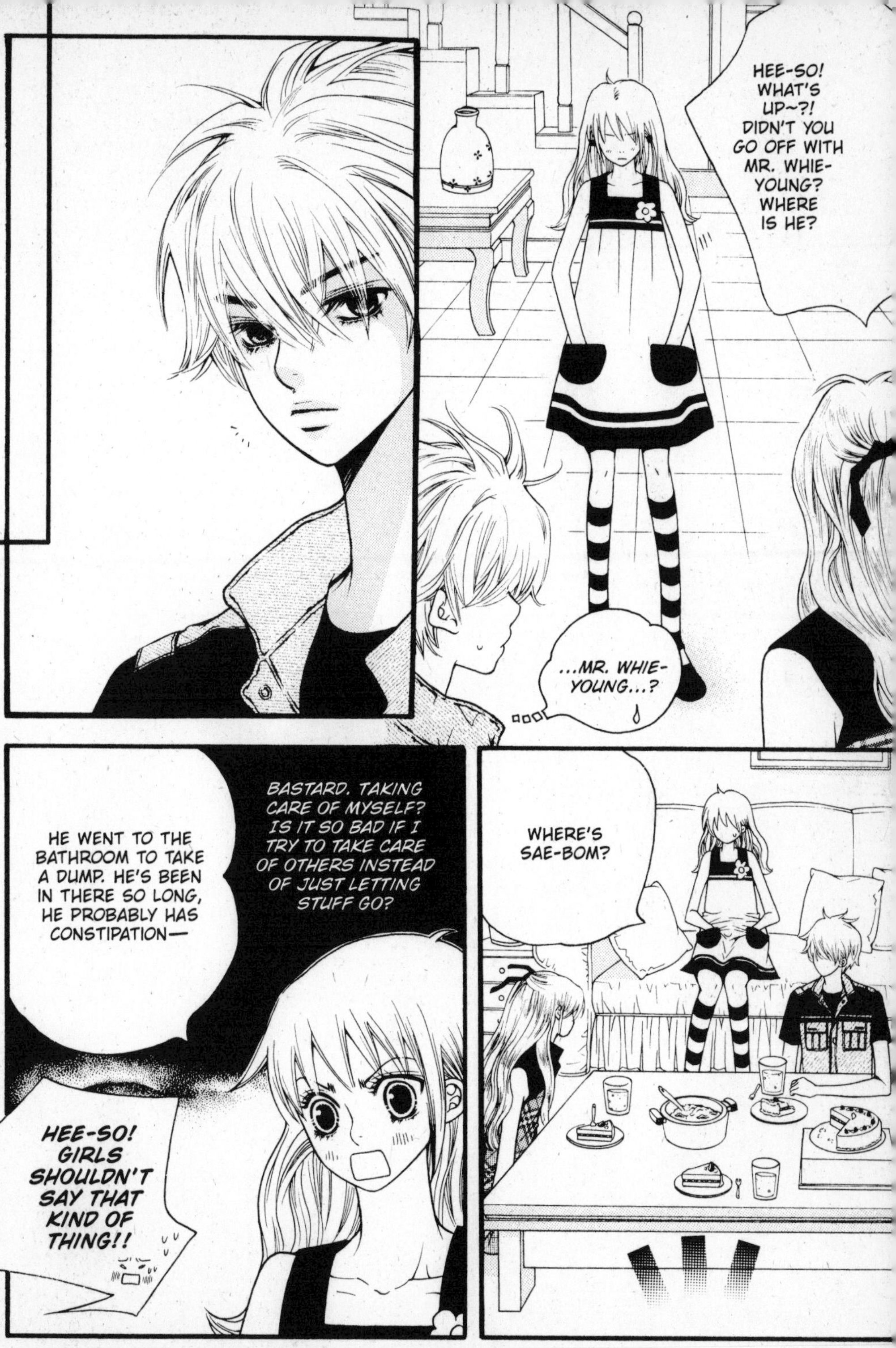
HEE-SO! WHAT'S UP~?! DIDN'T YOU GO OFF WITH MR. WHIE-YOUNG? WHERE IS HE?
...MR. WHIE-YOUNG...?
HE WENT TO THE BATHROOM TO TAKE A DUMP. HE'S BEEN IN THERE SO LONG, HE PROBABLY HAS CONSTIPATION—
BASTARD. TAKING CARE OF MYSELF? IS IT SO BAD IF I TRY TO TAKE CARE OF OTHERS INSTEAD OF JUST LETTING STUFF GO?
HEE-SO! GIRLS SHOULDN'T SAY THAT KIND OF THING!!
WHERE'S SAE-BOM?

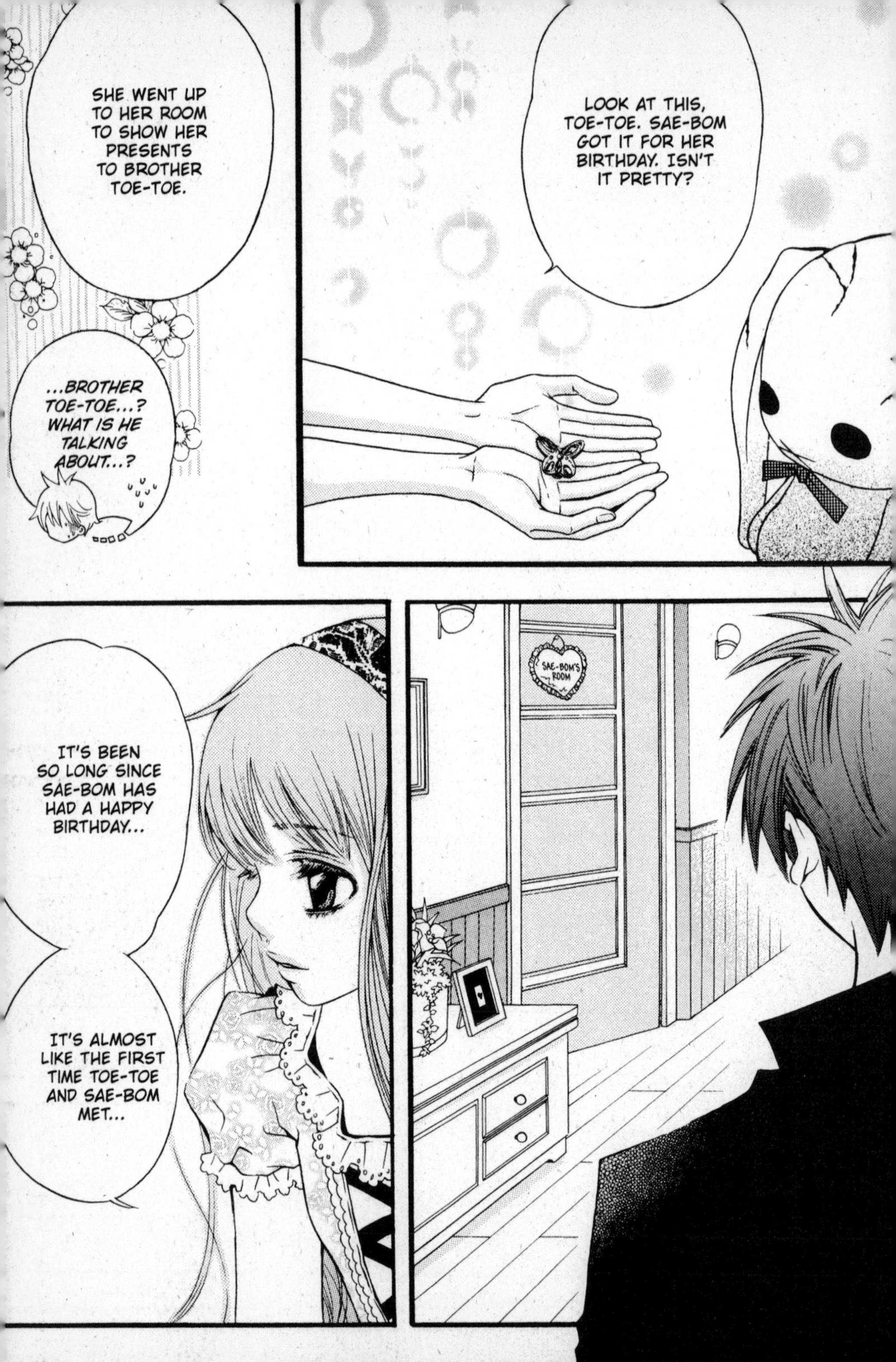

SHE WENT UP TO HER ROOM TO SHOW HER PRESENTS TO BROTHER TOE-TOE.
...BROTHER TOE-TOE...? WHAT IS HE TALKING ABOUT...?
LOOK AT THIS, TOE-TOE. SAE-BOM GOT IT FOR HER BIRTHDAY. ISN'T IT PRETTY?
IT'S BEEN SO LONG SINCE SAE-BOM HAS HAD A HAPPY BIRTHDAY...
IT'S ALMOST LIKE THE FIRST TIME TOE-TOE AND SAE-BOM MET...
SAE-BOM'S ROOM

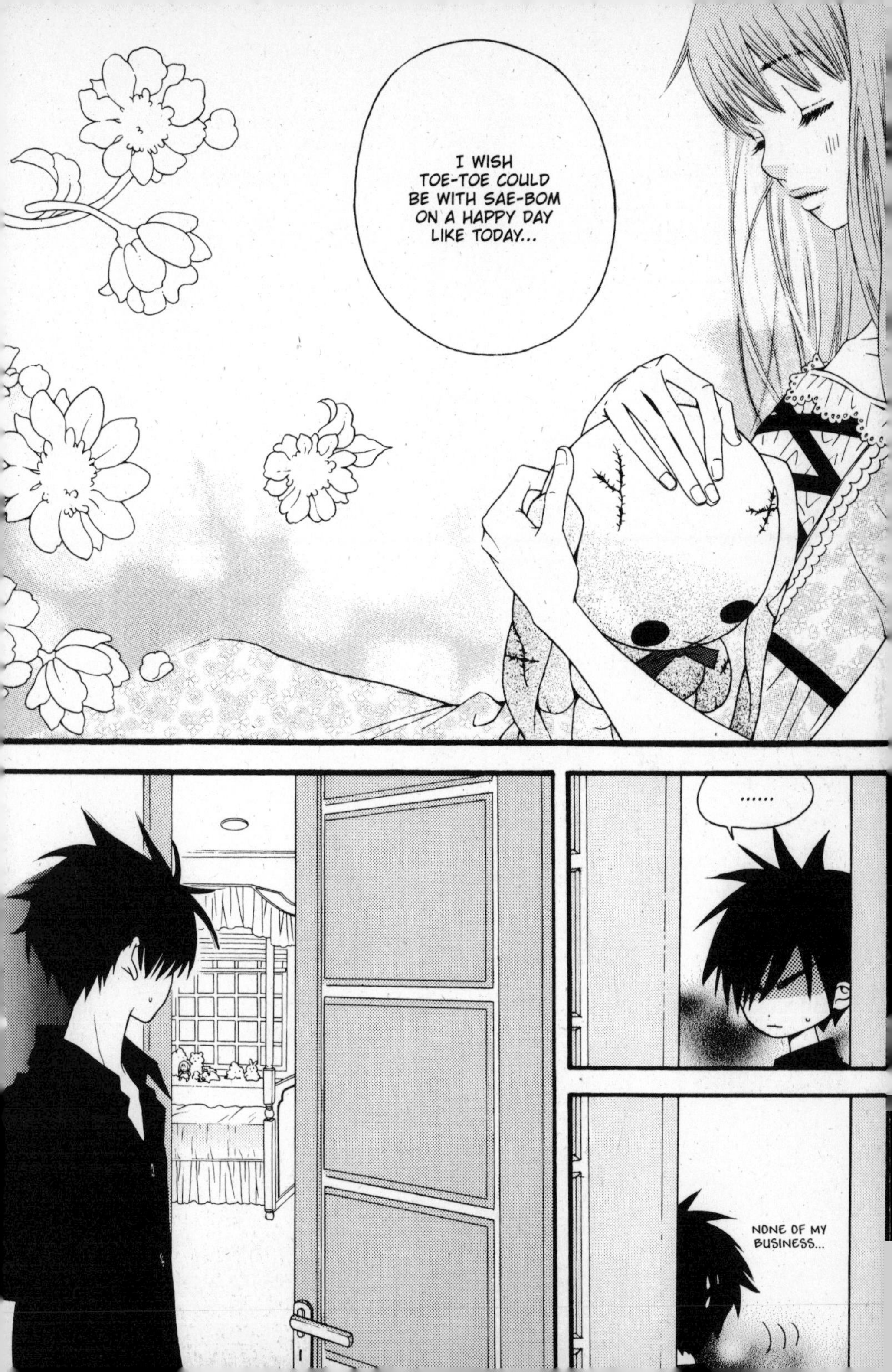
I WISH TOE-TOE COULD BE WITH SAE-BOM ON A HAPPY DAY LIKE TODAY...
......
NONE OF MY BUSINESS...

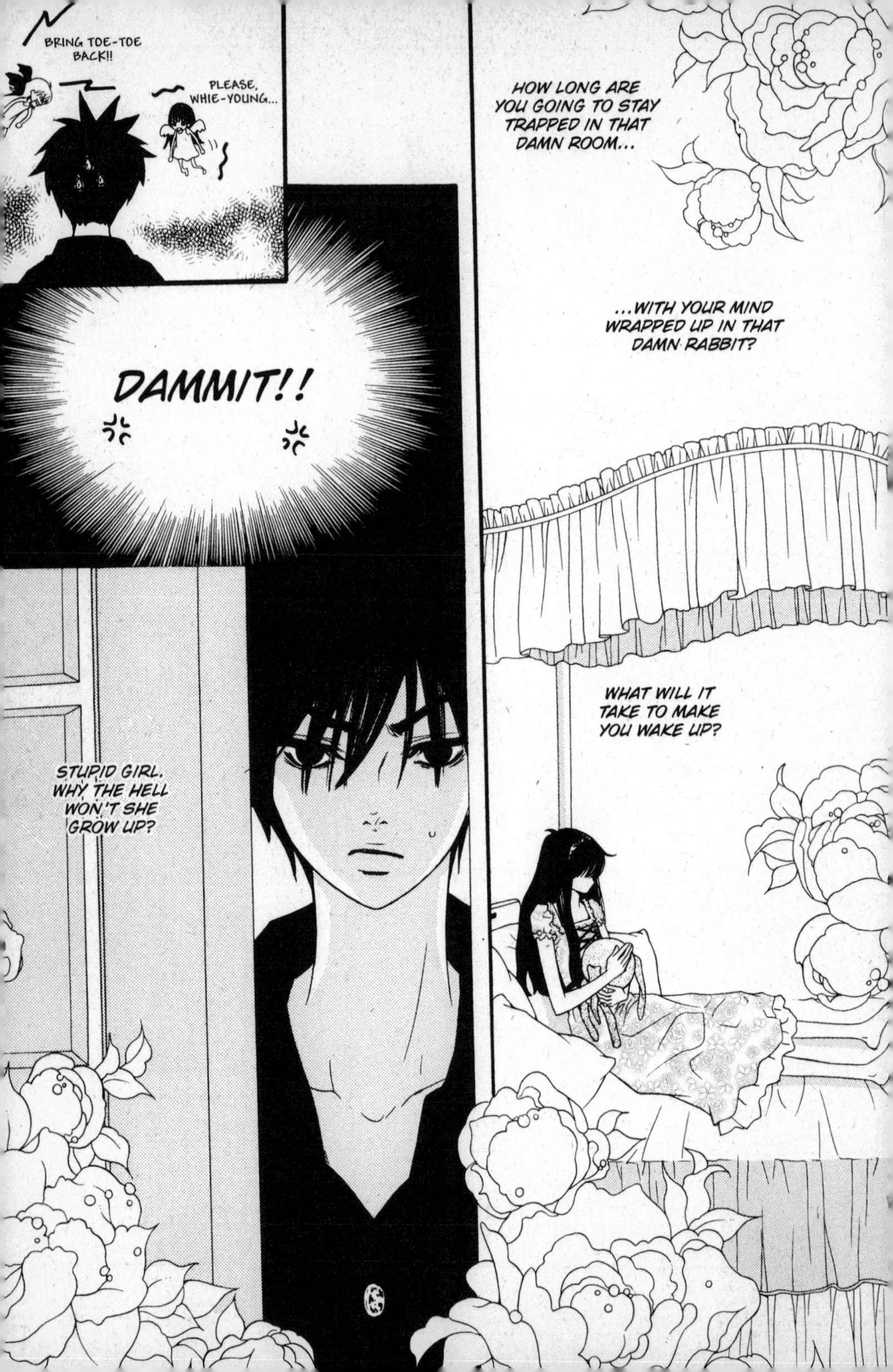
BRING TOE-TOE BACK!!
PLEASE, WHIE-YOUNG...
DAMMIT!!
STUPID GIRL. WHY THE HELL WON'T SHE GROW UP?
HOW LONG ARE YOU GOING TO STAY TRAPPED IN THAT DAMN ROOM...
...WITH YOUR MIND WRAPPED UP IN THAT DAMN RABBIT?
WHAT WILL IT TAKE TO MAKE YOU WAKE UP?

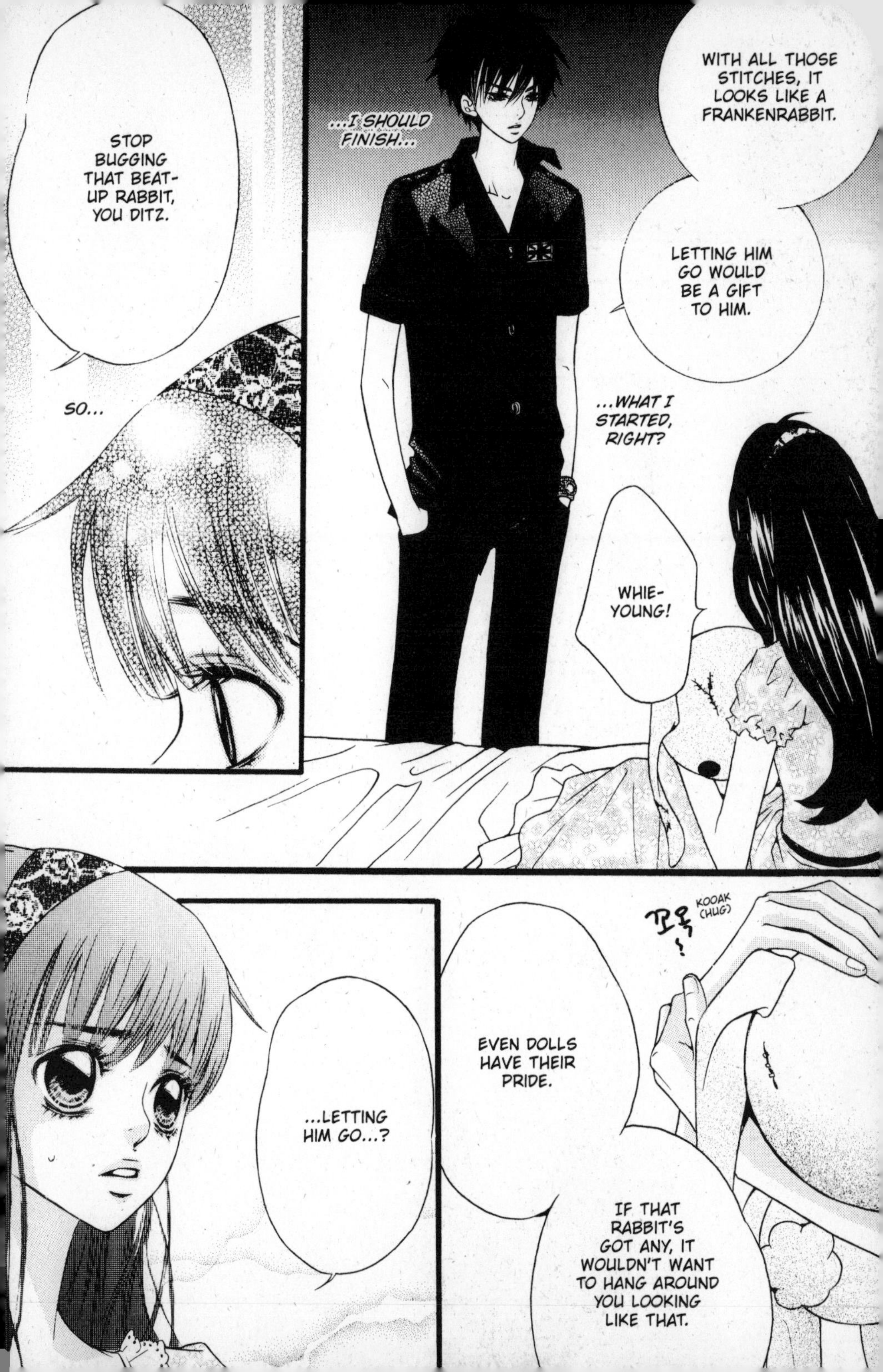
STOP BUGGING THAT BEAT-UP RABBIT, YOU DITZ.
SO...
...I SHOULD FINISH...
...WHAT I STARTED, RIGHT?
WITH ALL THOSE STITCHES, IT LOOKS LIKE A FRANKENRABBIT.
LETTING HIM GO WOULD BE A GIFT TO HIM.
WHIE-YOUNG!
...LETTING HIM GO...?
꼬옥
KOOAK (HUG)
EVEN DOLLS HAVE THEIR PRIDE.
IF THAT RABBIT'S GOT ANY, IT WOULDN'T WANT TO HANG AROUND YOU LOOKING LIKE THAT.

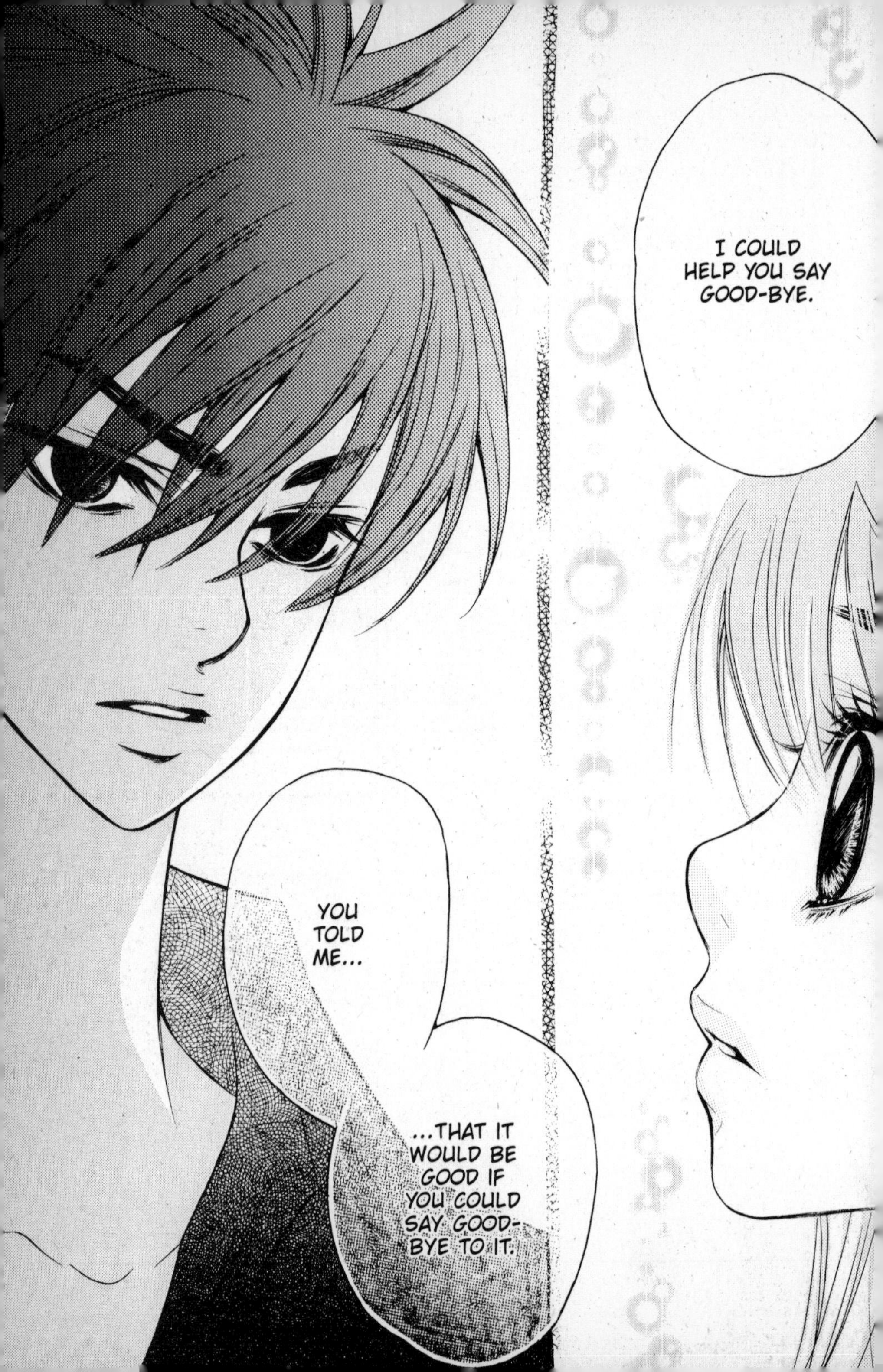
YOU TOLD ME...
...THAT IT WOULD BE GOOD IF YOU COULD SAY GOOD-BYE TO IT.
I COULD HELP YOU SAY GOOD-BYE.

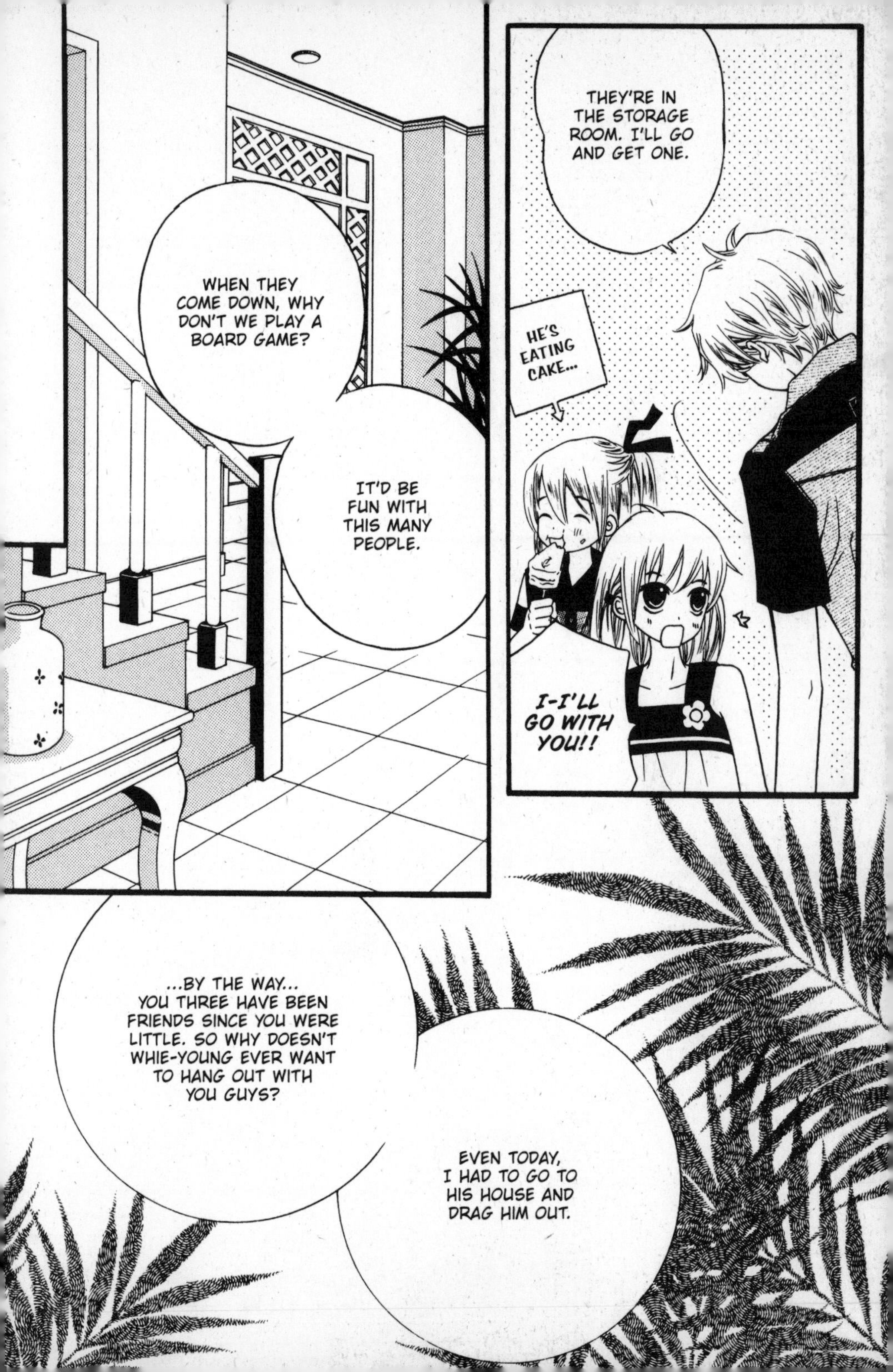
WHEN THEY COME DOWN, WHY DON'T WE PLAY A BOARD GAME?
IT'D BE FUN WITH THIS MANY PEOPLE.
THEY'RE IN THE STORAGE ROOM. I'LL GO AND GET ONE.
HE'S EATING CAKE...
I-I'LL GO WITH YOU!!
...BY THE WAY... YOU THREE HAVE BEEN FRIENDS SINCE YOU WERE LITTLE. SO WHY DOESN'T WHIE-YOUNG EVER WANT TO HANG OUT WITH YOU GUYS?
EVEN TODAY, I HAD TO GO TO HIS HOUSE AND DRAG HIM OUT.

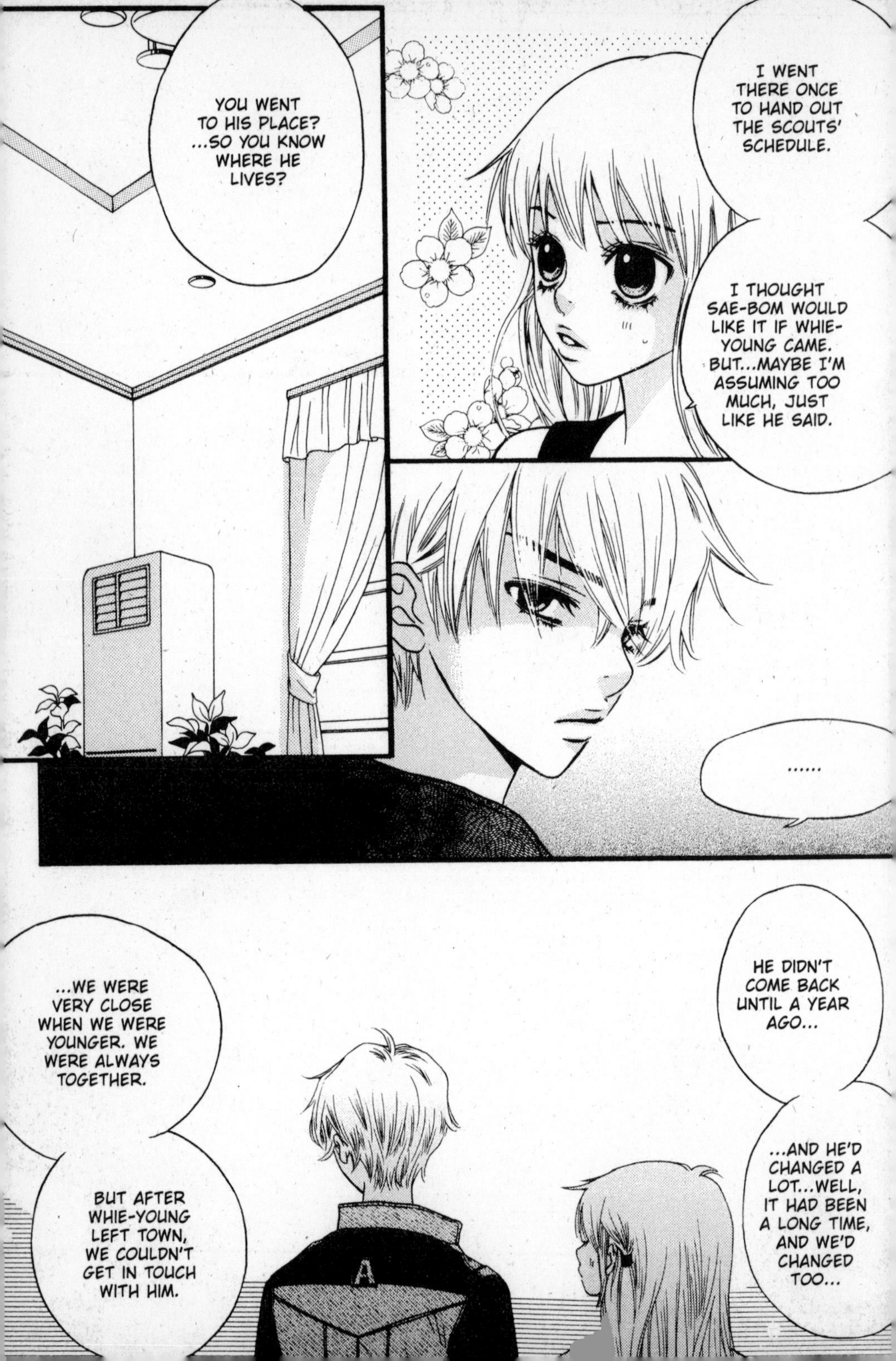
YOU WENT TO HIS PLACE? ...SO YOU KNOW WHERE HE LIVES?
I WENT THERE ONCE TO HAND OUT THE SCOUTS' SCHEDULE.
I THOUGHT SAE-BOM WOULD LIKE IT IF WHIE-YOUNG CAME. BUT...MAYBE I'M ASSUMING TOO MUCH, JUST LIKE HE SAID.
......
...WE WERE VERY CLOSE WHEN WE WERE YOUNGER. WE WERE ALWAYS TOGETHER.
BUT AFTER WHIE-YOUNG LEFT TOWN, WE COULDN'T GET IN TOUCH WITH HIM.
HE DIDN'T COME BACK UNTIL A YEAR AGO...
...AND HE'D CHANGED A LOT...WELL, IT HAD BEEN A LONG TIME, AND WE'D CHANGED TOO...
A

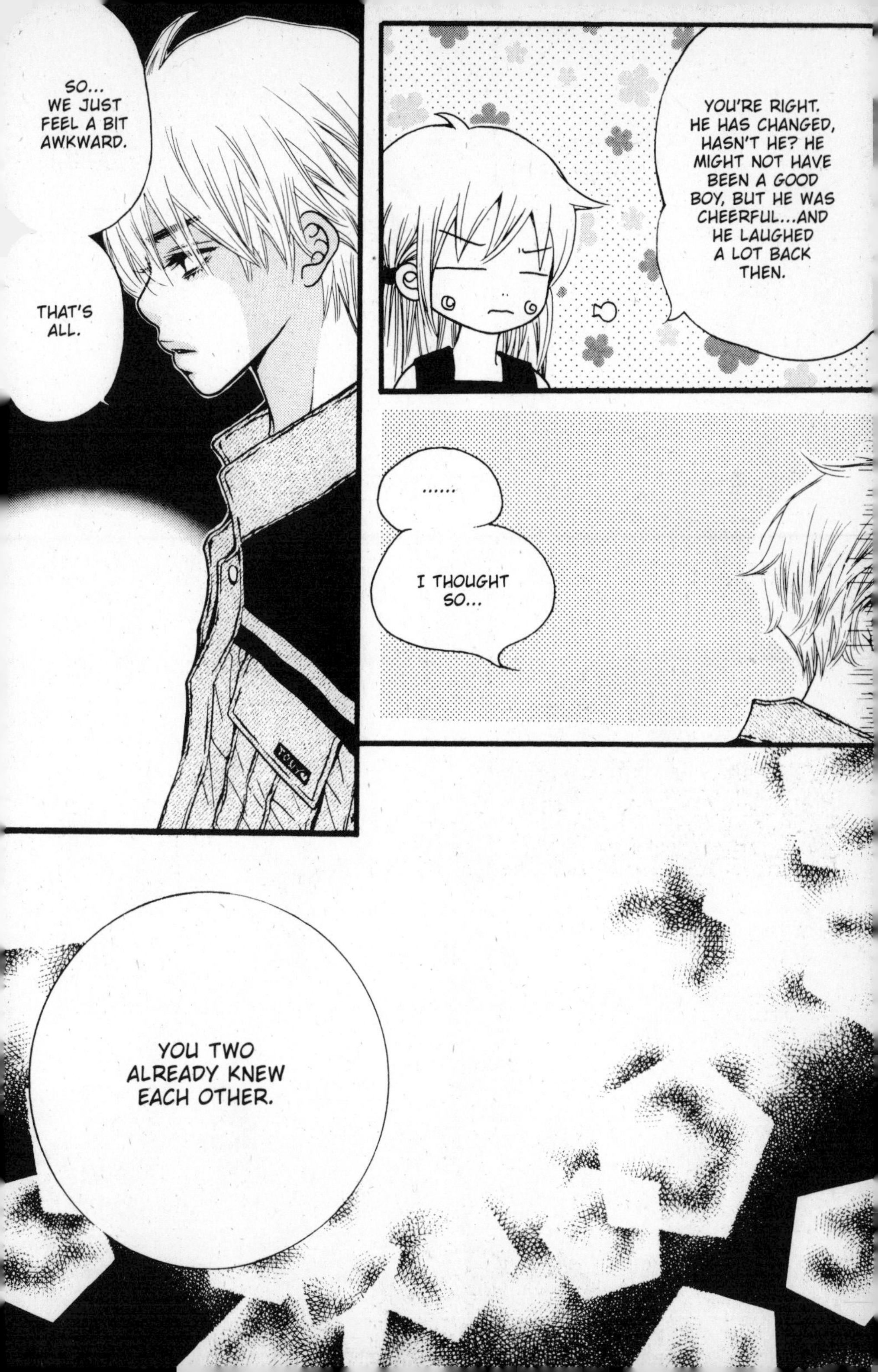
SO... WE JUST FEEL A BIT AWKWARD.
THAT'S ALL.
YOU'RE RIGHT. HE HAS CHANGED, HASN'T HE? HE MIGHT NOT HAVE BEEN A GOOD BOY, BUT HE WAS CHEERFUL...AND HE LAUGHED A LOT BACK THEN.
......
I THOUGHT SO...
YOU TWO ALREADY KNEW EACH OTHER.

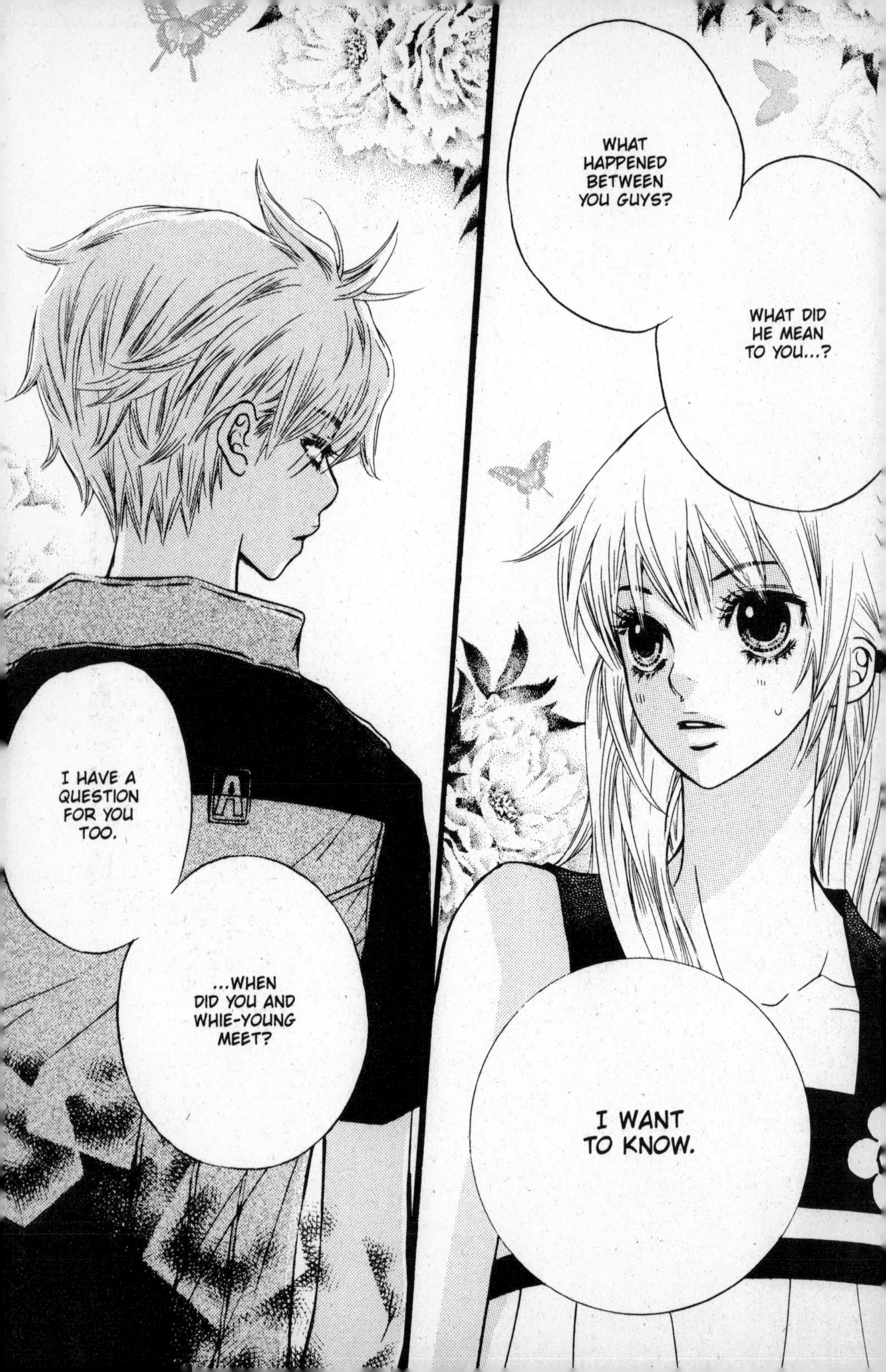
I HAVE A QUESTION FOR YOU TOO.
...WHEN DID YOU AND WHIE-YOUNG MEET?
WHAT HAPPENED BETWEEN YOU GUYS?
WHAT DID HE MEAN TO YOU...?
I WANT TO KNOW.

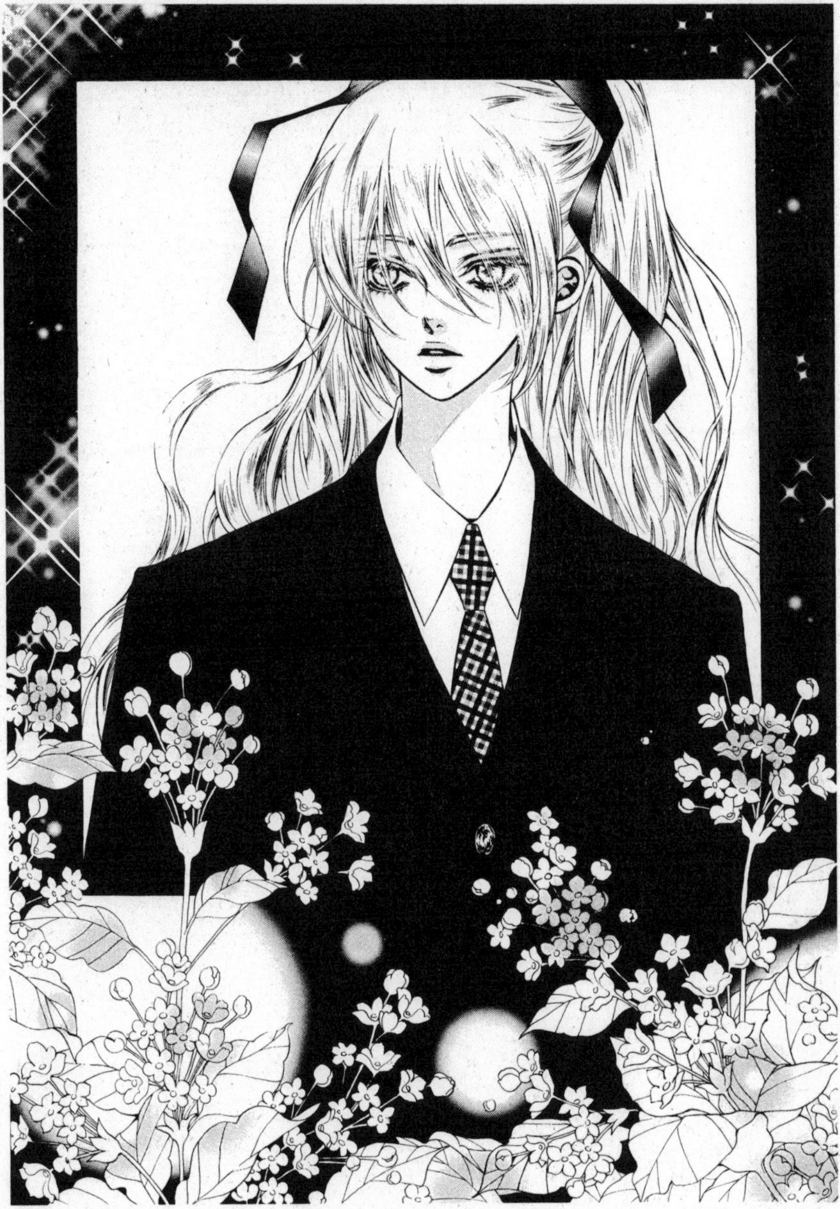

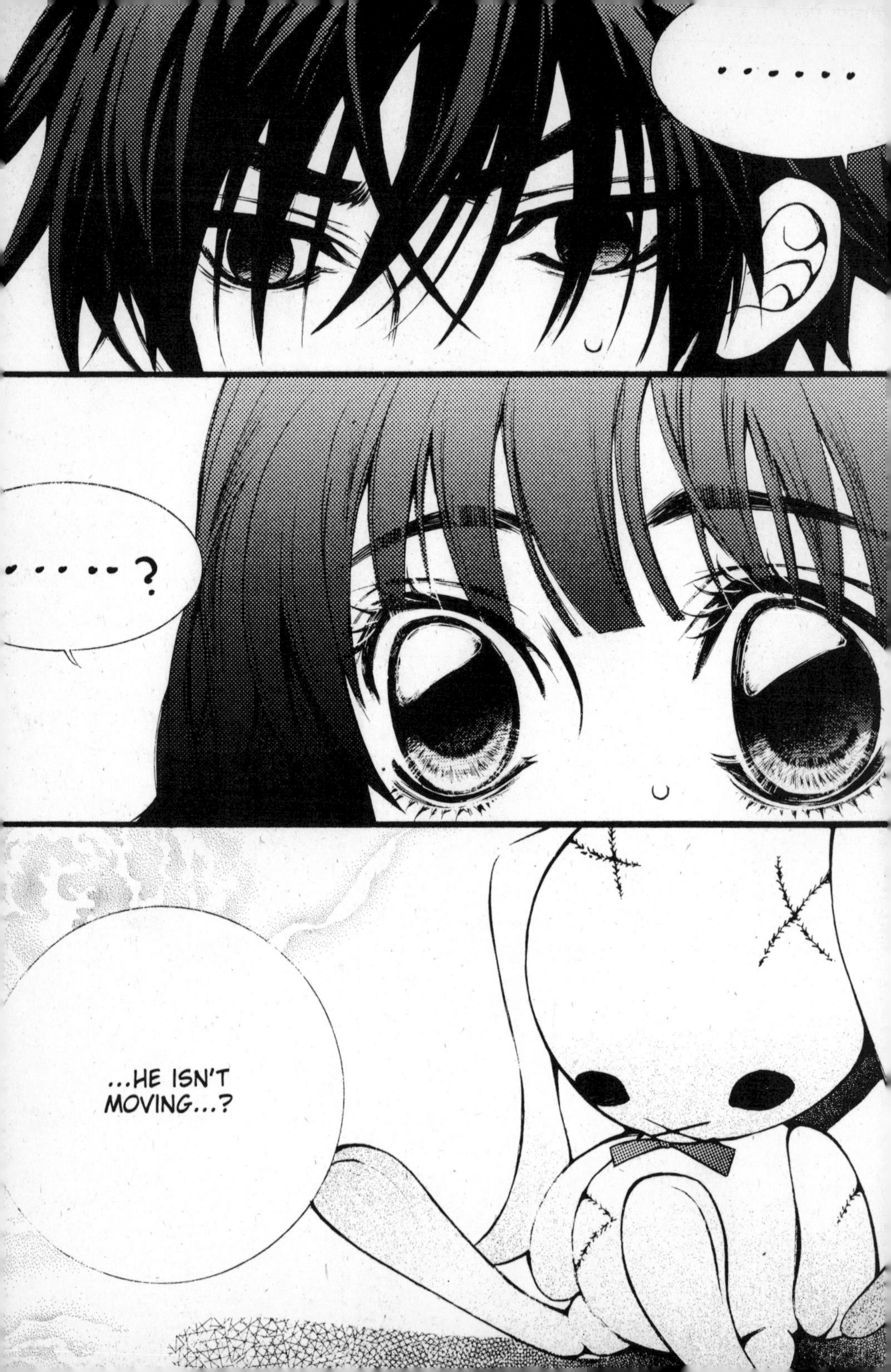
......
......?
...HE ISN'T MOVING...?

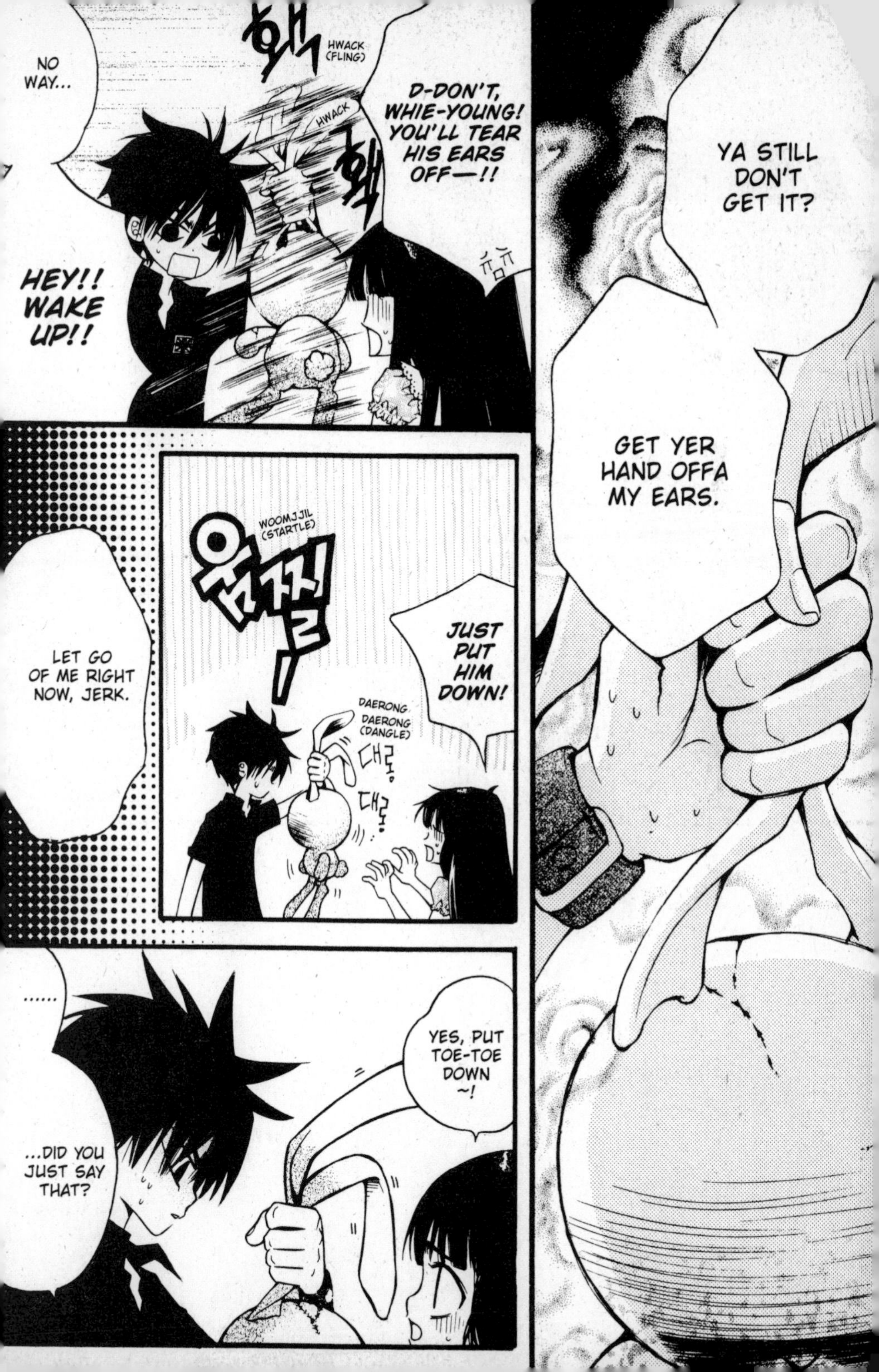
NO WAY...
홱
HWACK (FLING)
D-DON'T, WHIE-YOUNG! YOU'LL TEAR HIS EARS OFF—!!
HWACK
홱
HEY!! WAKE UP!!
LET GO OF ME RIGHT NOW, JERK.
움찔
WOOMJJIL (STARTLE)
JUST PUT HIM DOWN!
DAERONG DAERONG (DANGLE)
대롱
대롱
......
YES, PUT TOE-TOE DOWN ~!
...DID YOU JUST SAY THAT?
YA STILL DON'T GET IT?
GET YER HAND OFFA MY EARS.

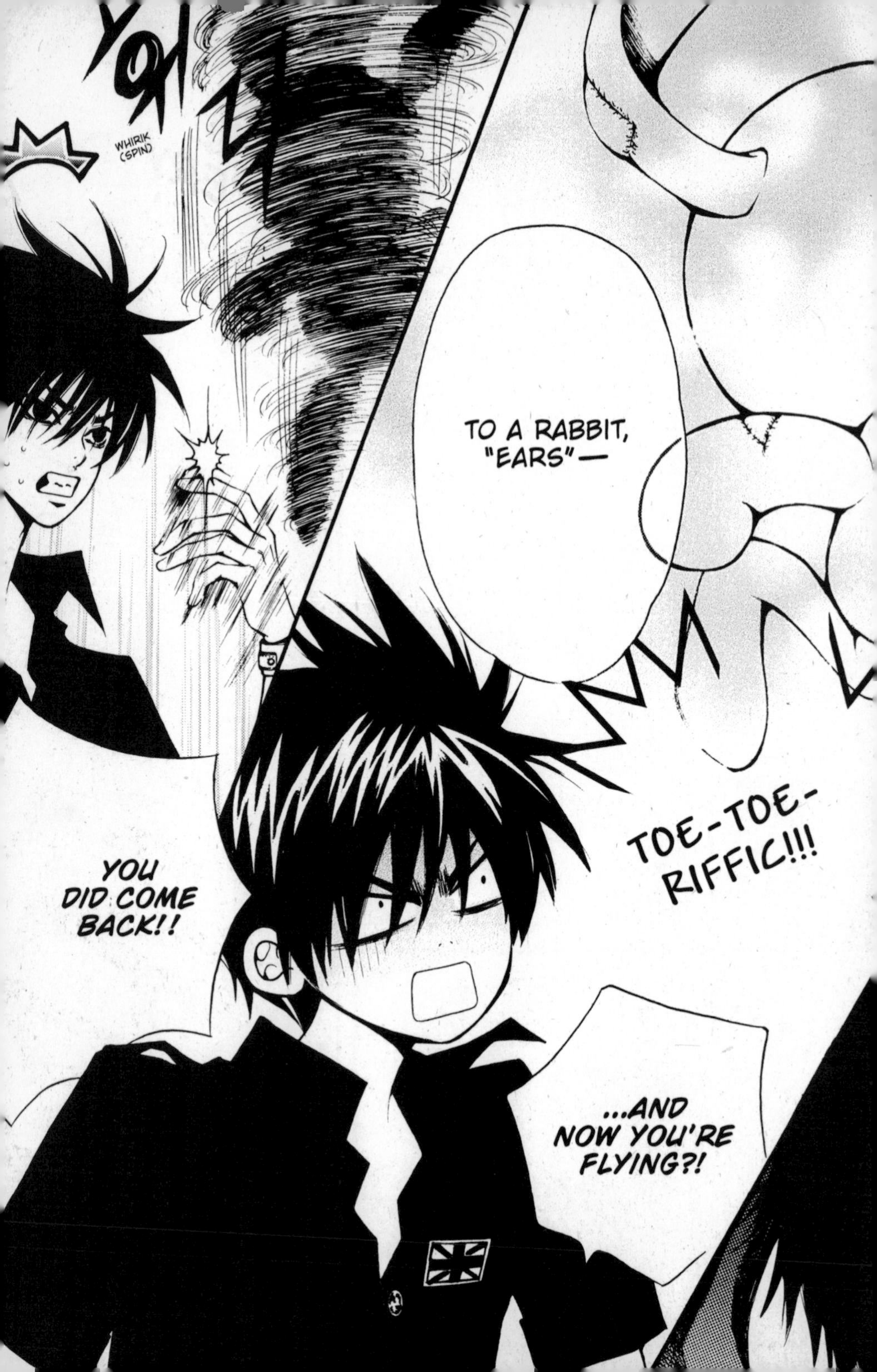
WHIRIK (SPIN)
TO A RABBIT, "EARS"—
YOU DID COME BACK!!
TOE-TOE-RIFFIC!!!
...AND NOW YOU'RE FLYING?!

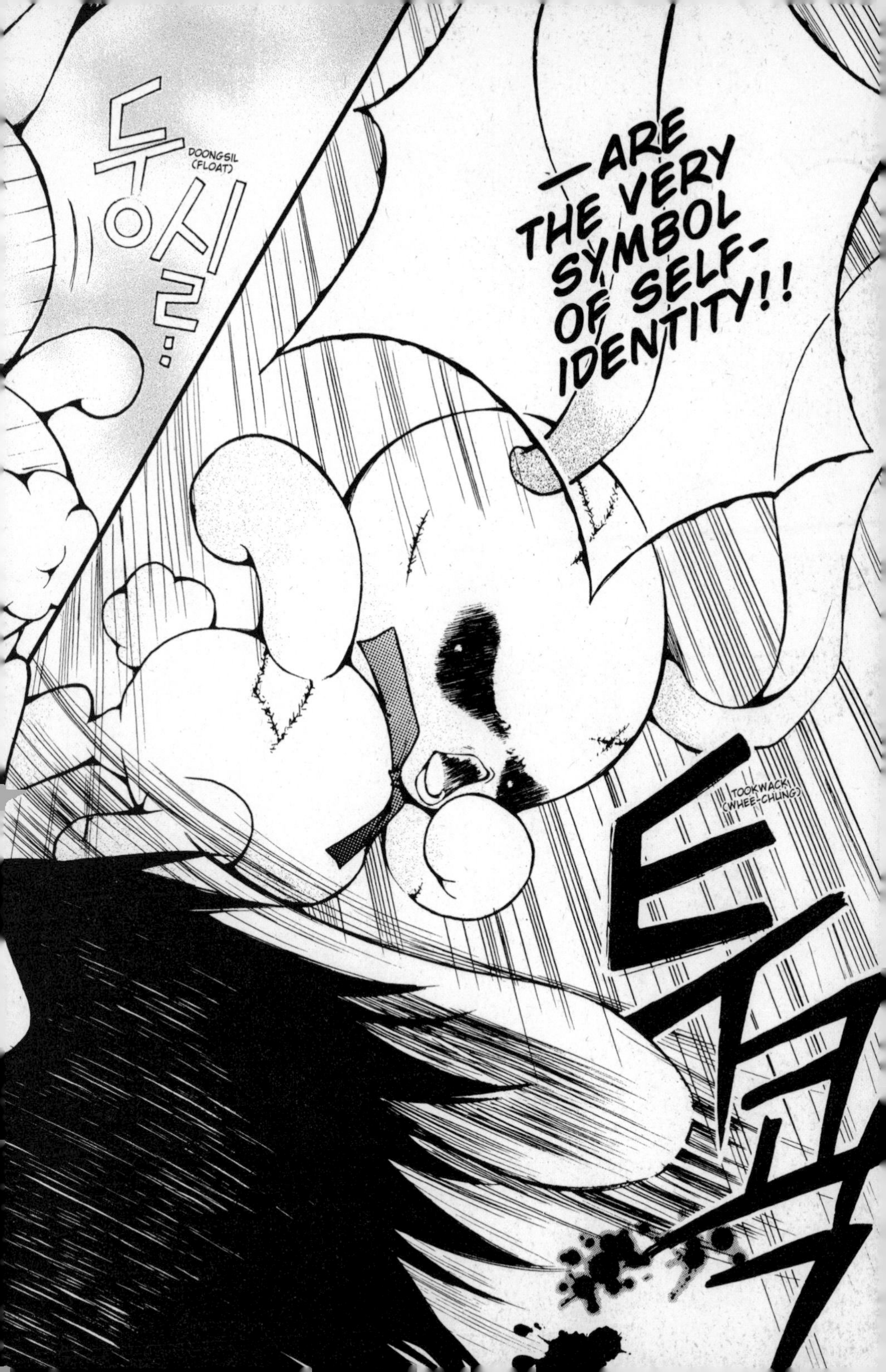
둥실..
DOONGSIL (FLOAT)
—ARE THE VERY SYMBOL OF SELF-IDENTITY!!
TOOKWACK (WHEE-CHUNG)

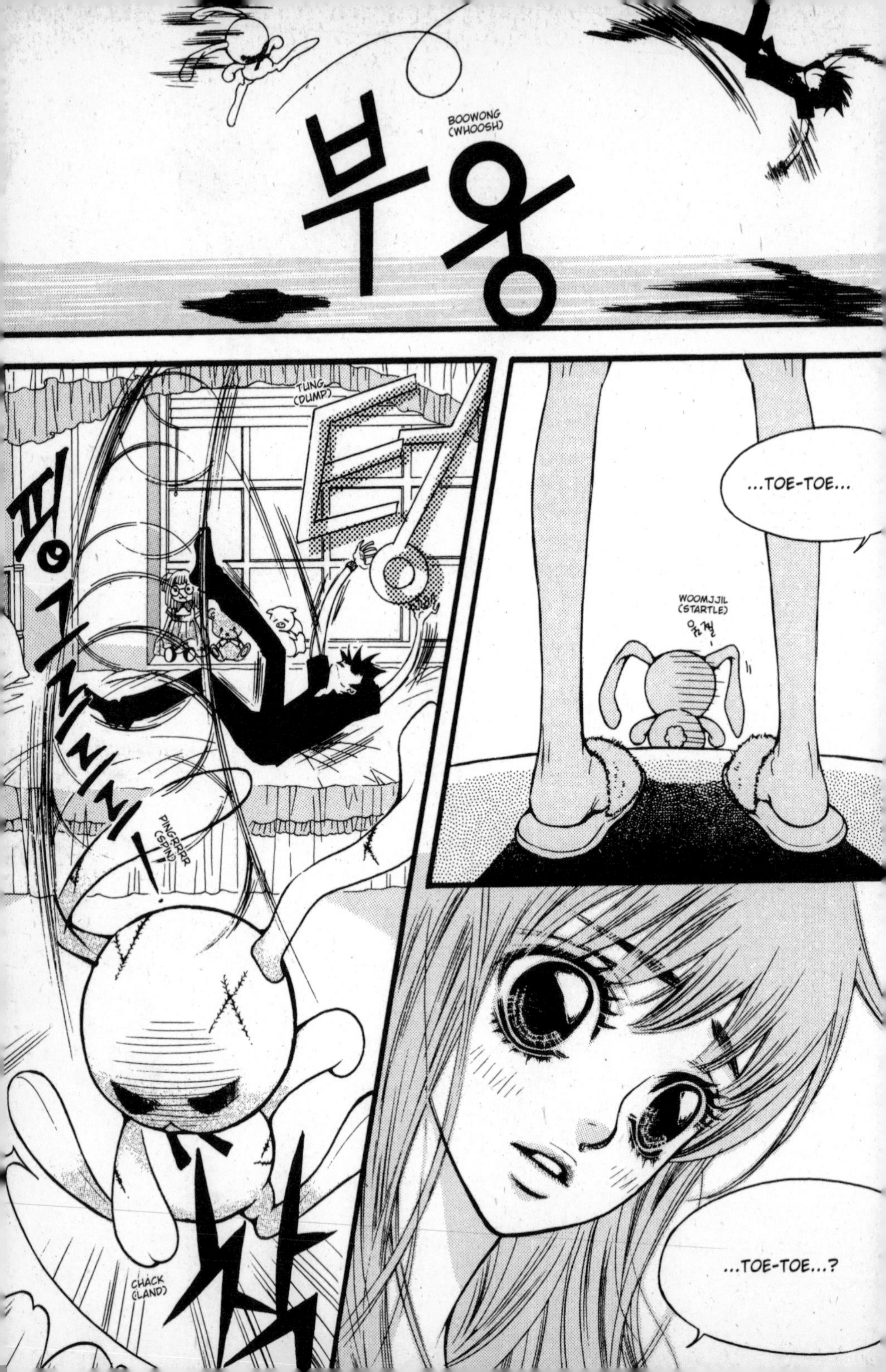
부웅
BOOWONG (WHOOSH)
TUNG (DUMP)
PINGRRRR (SPIN)
CHACK (LAND)
...TOE-TOE...
WOOMJJIL (STARTLE)
...TOE-TOE...?

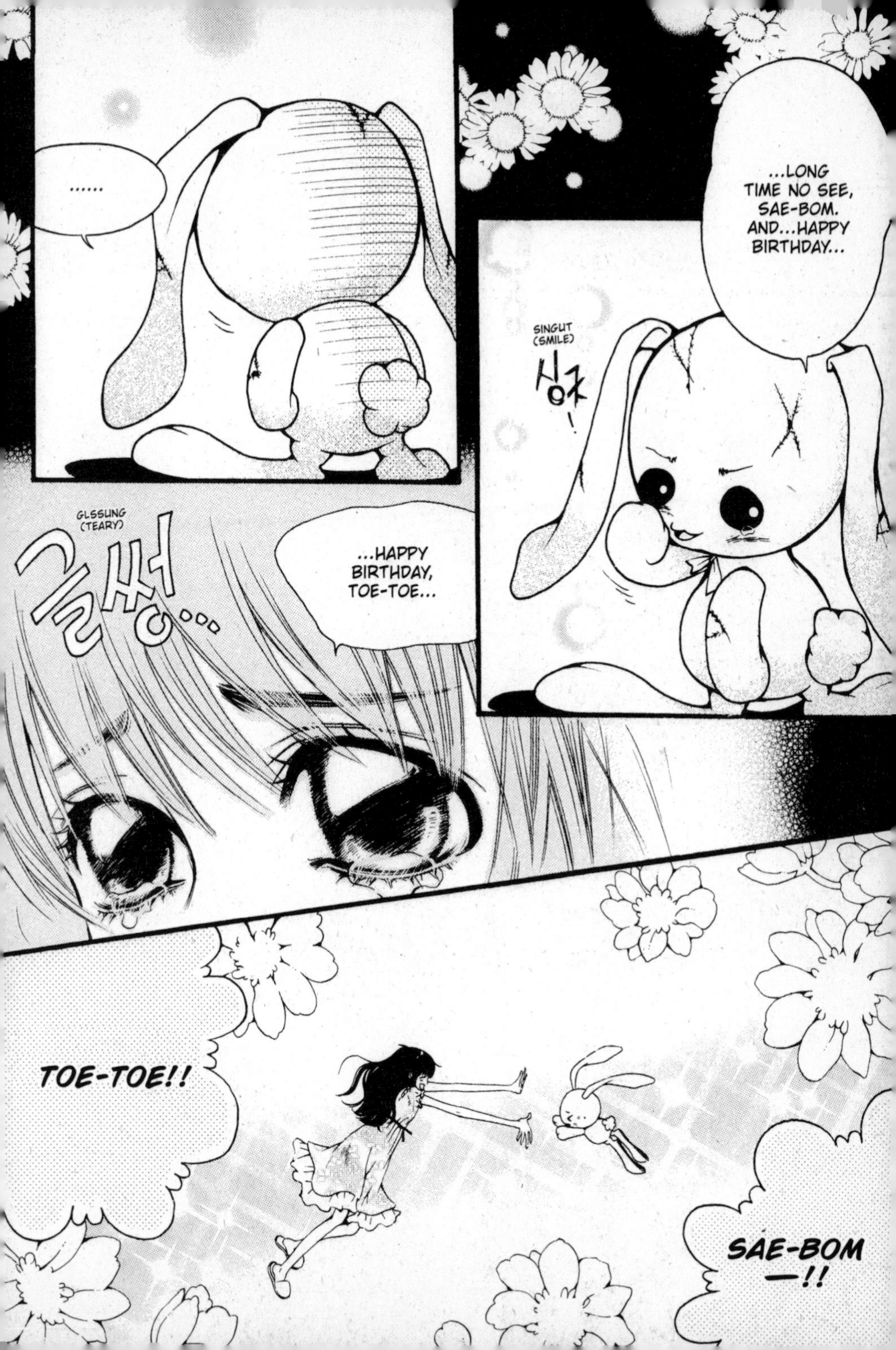
......
...LONG TIME NO SEE, SAE-BOM. AND...HAPPY BIRTHDAY...
SINGUT (SMILE)
싱긋!
GLSSUNG (TEARY)
글썽...
...HAPPY BIRTHDAY, TOE-TOE...
TOE-TOE!!
SAE-BOM—!!

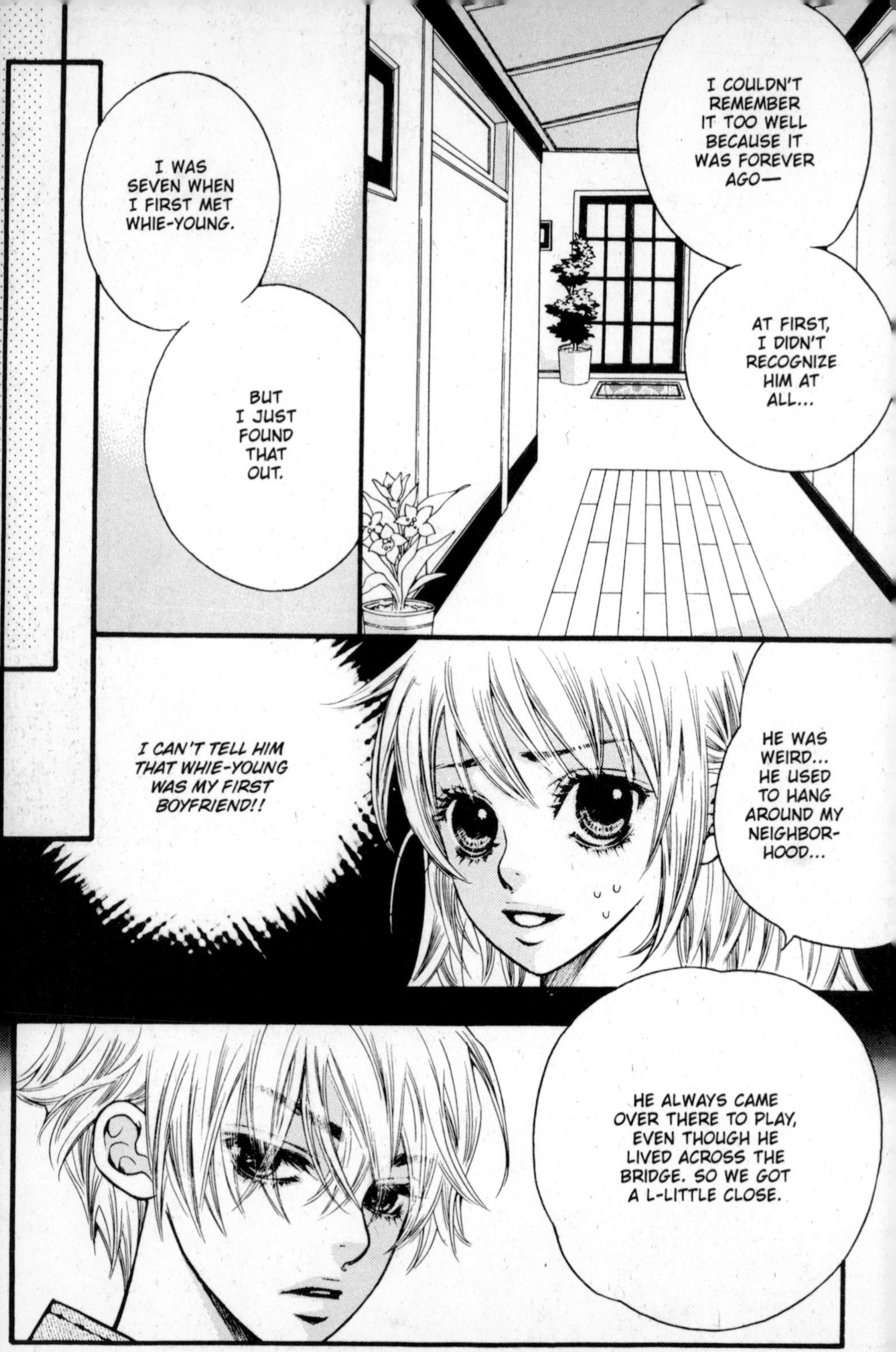
I WAS SEVEN WHEN I FIRST MET WHIE-YOUNG.
BUT I JUST FOUND THAT OUT.
I COULDN'T REMEMBER IT TOO WELL BECAUSE IT WAS FOREVER AGO—
AT FIRST, I DIDN'T RECOGNIZE HIM AT ALL...
I CAN'T TELL HIM THAT WHIE-YOUNG WAS MY FIRST BOYFRIEND!!
HE WAS WEIRD... HE USED TO HANG AROUND MY NEIGHBOR-HOOD...
HE ALWAYS CAME OVER THERE TO PLAY, EVEN THOUGH HE LIVED ACROSS THE BRIDGE. SO WE GOT A L-LITTLE CLOSE.

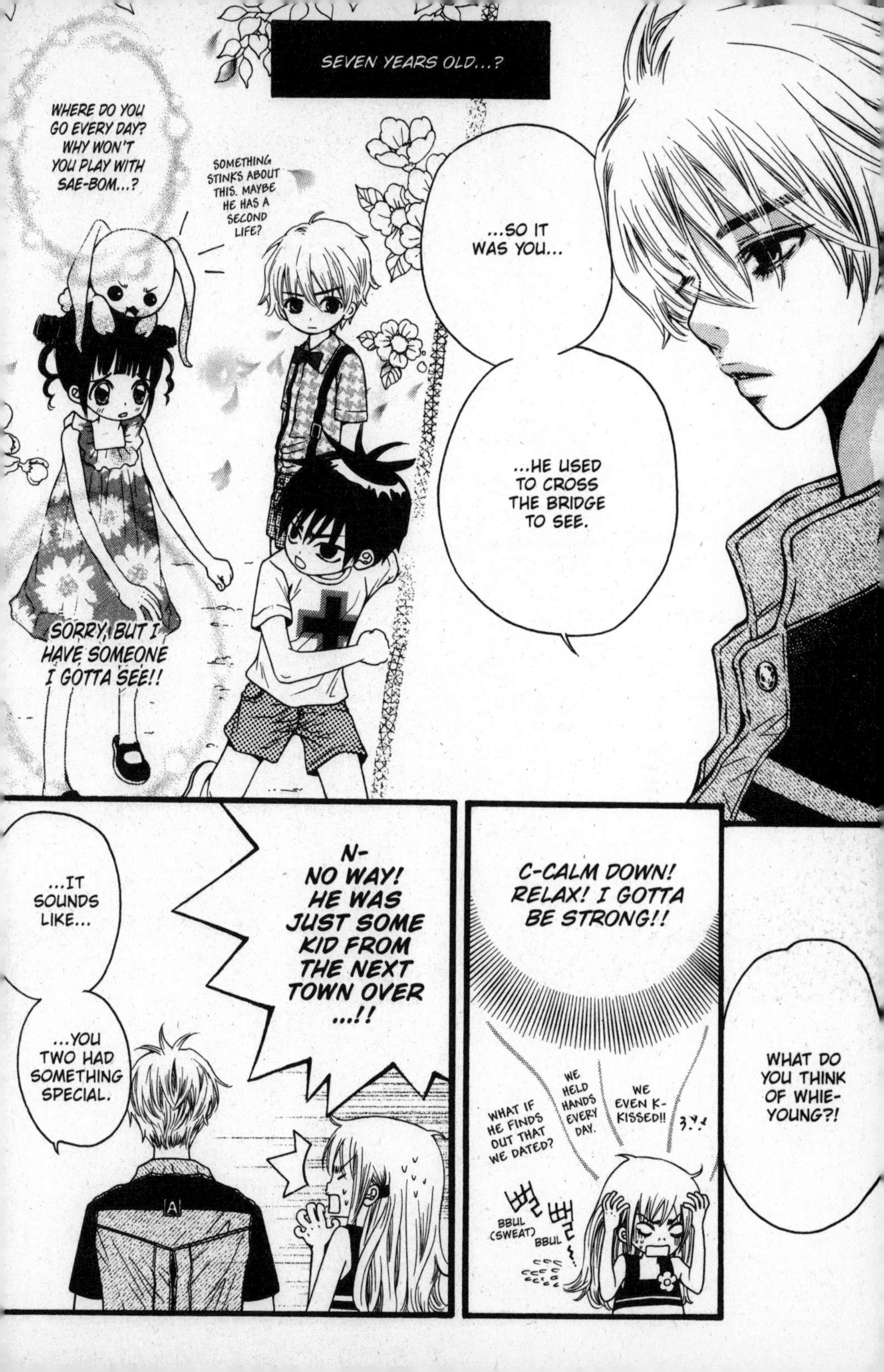
SEVEN YEARS OLD...?
WHERE DO YOU GO EVERY DAY? WHY WON'T YOU PLAY WITH SAE-BOM...?
SOMETHING STINKS ABOUT THIS. MAYBE HE HAS A SECOND LIFE?
SORRY, BUT I HAVE SOMEONE I GOTTA SEE!!
...SO IT WAS YOU...
...HE USED TO CROSS THE BRIDGE TO SEE.
...IT SOUNDS LIKE...
...YOU TWO HAD SOMETHING SPECIAL.
N- NO WAY! HE WAS JUST SOME KID FROM THE NEXT TOWN OVER ...!!
C-CALM DOWN! RELAX! I GOTTA BE STRONG!!
WHAT IF HE FINDS OUT THAT WE DATED?
WE HELD HANDS EVERY DAY.
WE EVEN K-KISSED!!
BBUL (SWEAT) BBUL
WHAT DO YOU THINK OF WHIE-YOUNG?!

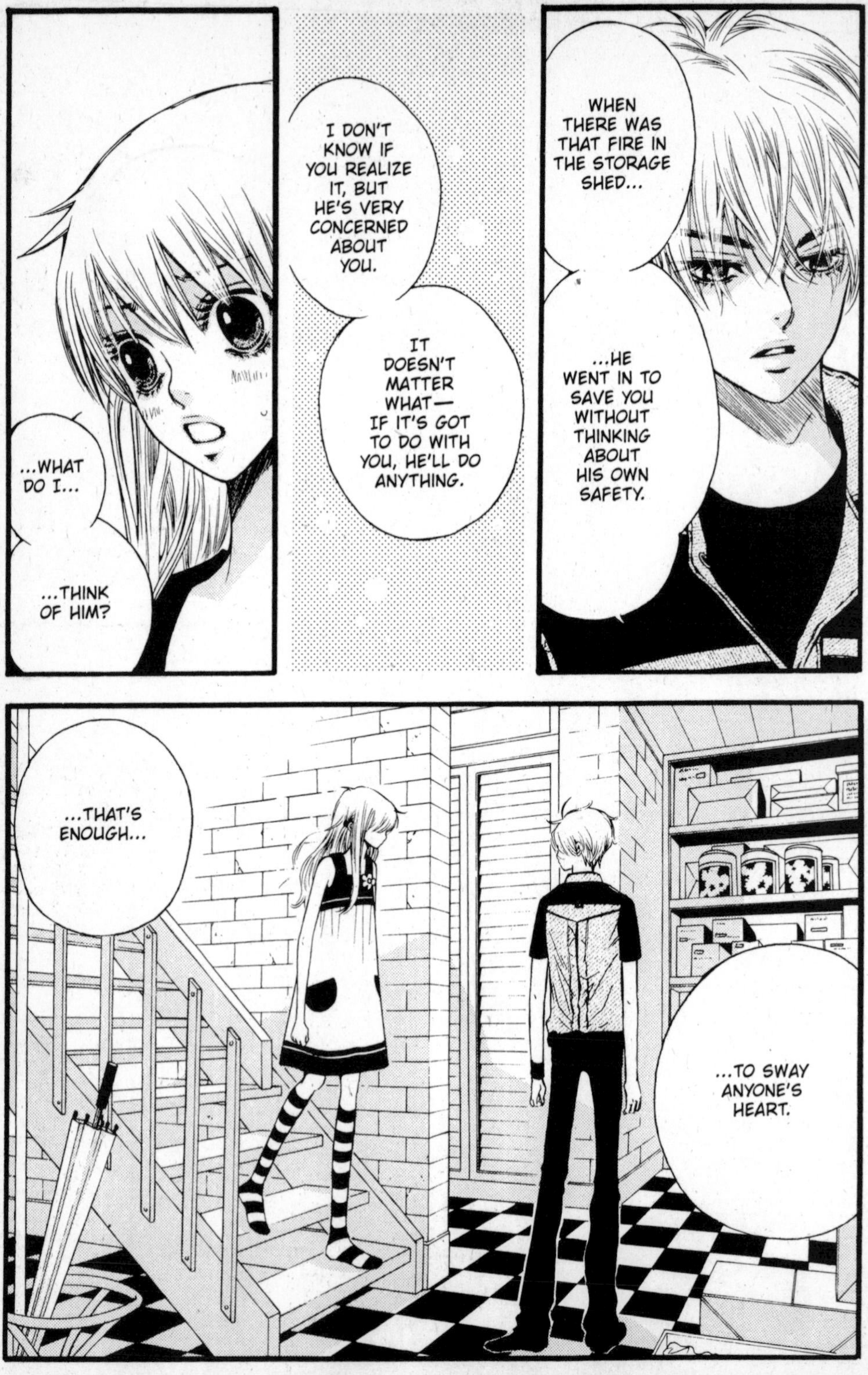
...WHAT DO I...
...THINK OF HIM?
I DON'T KNOW IF YOU REALIZE IT, BUT HE'S VERY CONCERNED ABOUT YOU.
IT DOESN'T MATTER WHAT— IF IT'S GOT TO DO WITH YOU, HE'LL DO ANYTHING.
WHEN THERE WAS THAT FIRE IN THE STORAGE SHED...
...HE WENT IN TO SAVE YOU WITHOUT THINKING ABOUT HIS OWN SAFETY.
...THAT'S ENOUGH...
...TO SWAY ANYONE'S HEART.

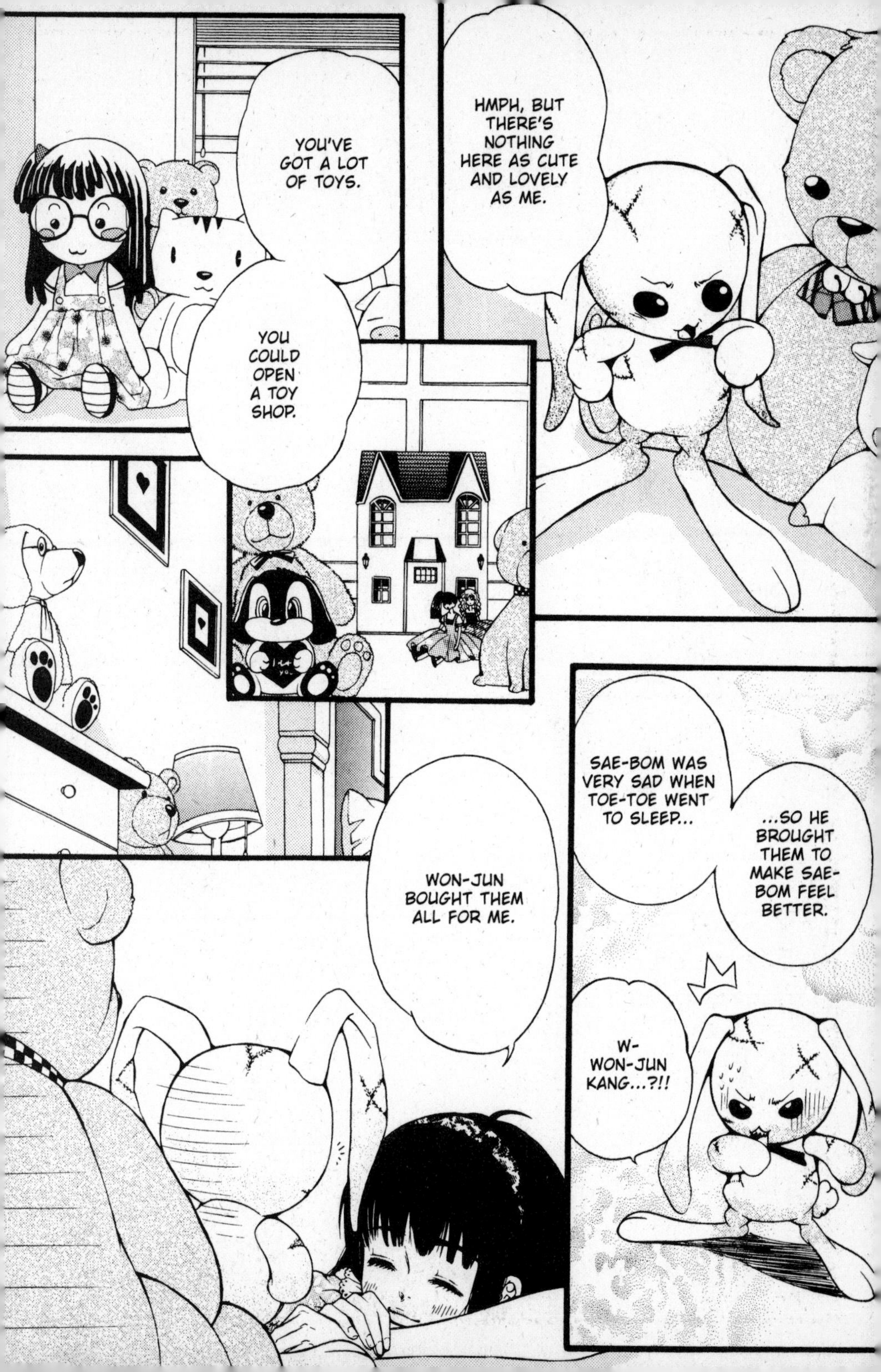
YOU'VE GOT A LOT OF TOYS.
YOU COULD OPEN A TOY SHOP.
HMPH, BUT THERE'S NOTHING HERE AS CUTE AND LOVELY AS ME.
WON-JUN BOUGHT THEM ALL FOR ME.
SAE-BOM WAS VERY SAD WHEN TOE-TOE WENT TO SLEEP...
...SO HE BROUGHT THEM TO MAKE SAE-BOM FEEL BETTER.
W-WON-JUN KANG...?!!

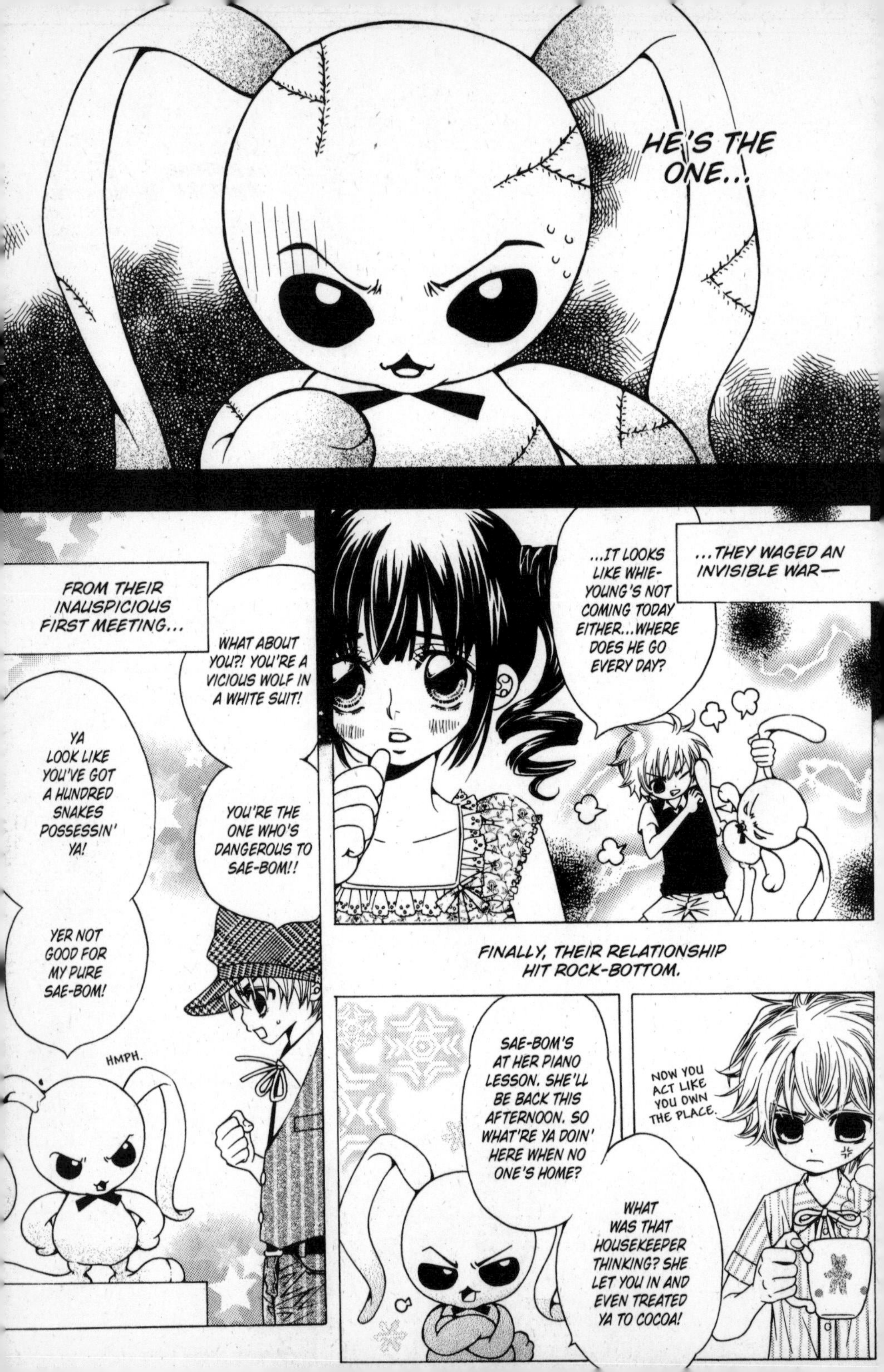
HE'S THE ONE...
FROM THEIR INAUSPICIOUS FIRST MEETING...
WHAT ABOUT YOU?! YOU'RE A VICIOUS WOLF IN A WHITE SUIT!
YA LOOK LIKE YOU'VE GOT A HUNDRED SNAKES POSSESSIN' YA!
YOU'RE THE ONE WHO'S DANGEROUS TO SAE-BOM!!
YER NOT GOOD FOR MY PURE SAE-BOM!
HMPH.
...IT LOOKS LIKE WHIE-YOUNG'S NOT COMING TODAY EITHER...WHERE DOES HE GO EVERY DAY?
...THEY WAGED AN INVISIBLE WAR—
FINALLY, THEIR RELATIONSHIP HIT ROCK-BOTTOM.
SAE-BOM'S AT HER PIANO LESSON. SHE'LL BE BACK THIS AFTERNOON. SO WHAT'RE YA DOIN' HERE WHEN NO ONE'S HOME?
WHAT WAS THAT HOUSEKEEPER THINKING? SHE LET YOU IN AND EVEN TREATED YA TO COCOA!
NOW YOU ACT LIKE YOU OWN THE PLACE.

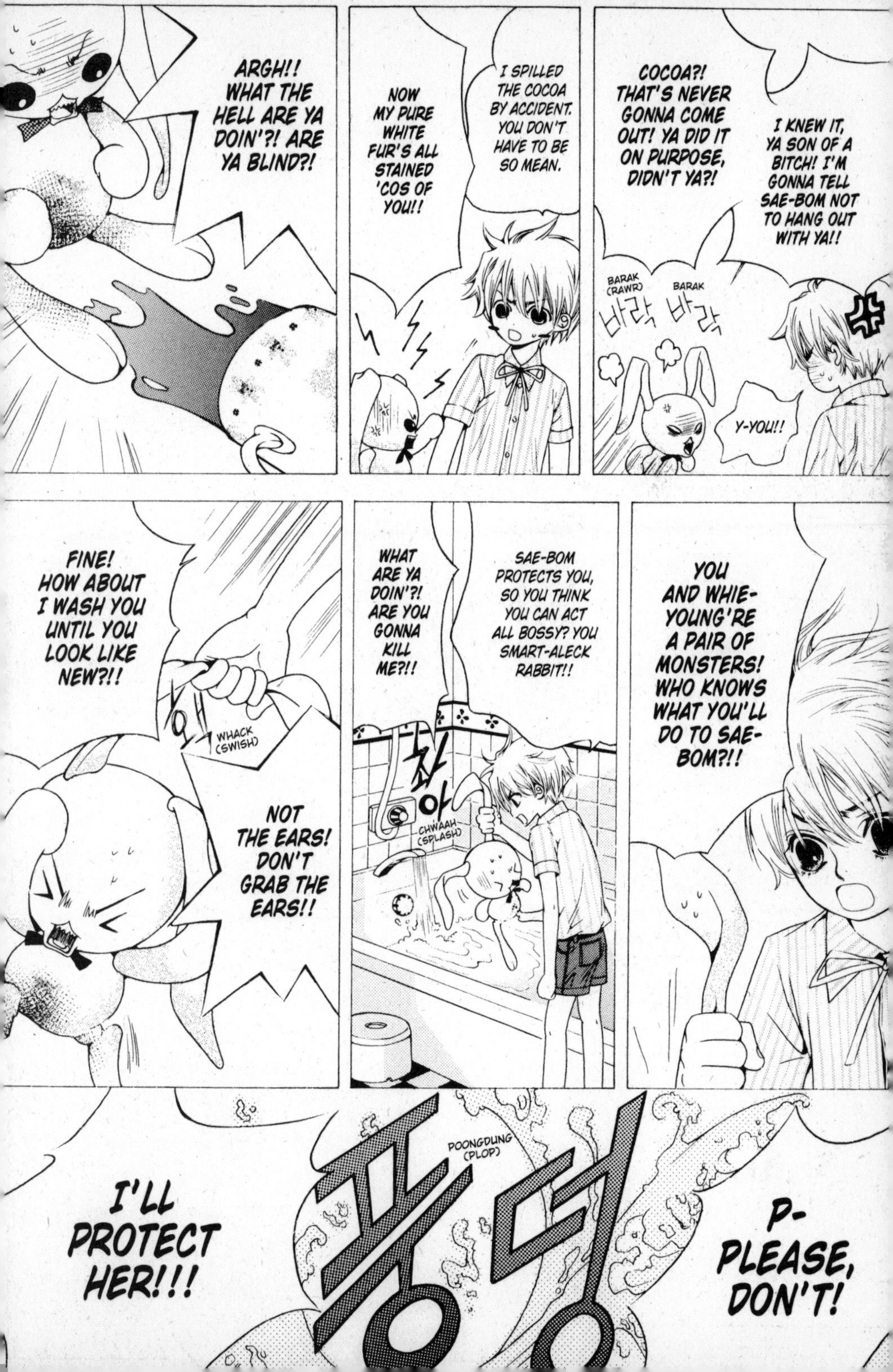
ARGH!! WHAT THE HELL ARE YA DOIN'?! ARE YA BLIND?!
NOW MY PURE WHITE FUR'S ALL STAINED 'COS OF YOU!!
I SPILLED THE COCOA BY ACCIDENT. YOU DON'T HAVE TO BE SO MEAN.
COCOA?! THAT'S NEVER GONNA COME OUT! YA DID IT ON PURPOSE, DIDN'T YA?!
I KNEW IT, YA SON OF A BITCH! I'M GONNA TELL SAE-BOM NOT TO HANG OUT WITH YA!!
바락 바락
BARAK (RAWR) BARAK
Y-YOU!!
FINE! HOW ABOUT I WASH YOU UNTIL YOU LOOK LIKE NEW?!!
WHACK (SWISH)
NOT THE EARS! DON'T GRAB THE EARS!!
WHAT ARE YA DOIN'?! ARE YOU GONNA KILL ME?!!
SAE-BOM PROTECTS YOU, SO YOU THINK YOU CAN ACT ALL BOSSY? YOU SMART-ALECK RABBIT!!
좌아
CHWAAH (SPLASH)
YOU AND WHIE-YOUNG'RE A PAIR OF MONSTERS! WHO KNOWS WHAT YOU'LL DO TO SAE-BOM?!!
I'LL PROTECT HER!!!
풍덩
POONGDUNG (PLOP)
P-PLEASE, DON'T!

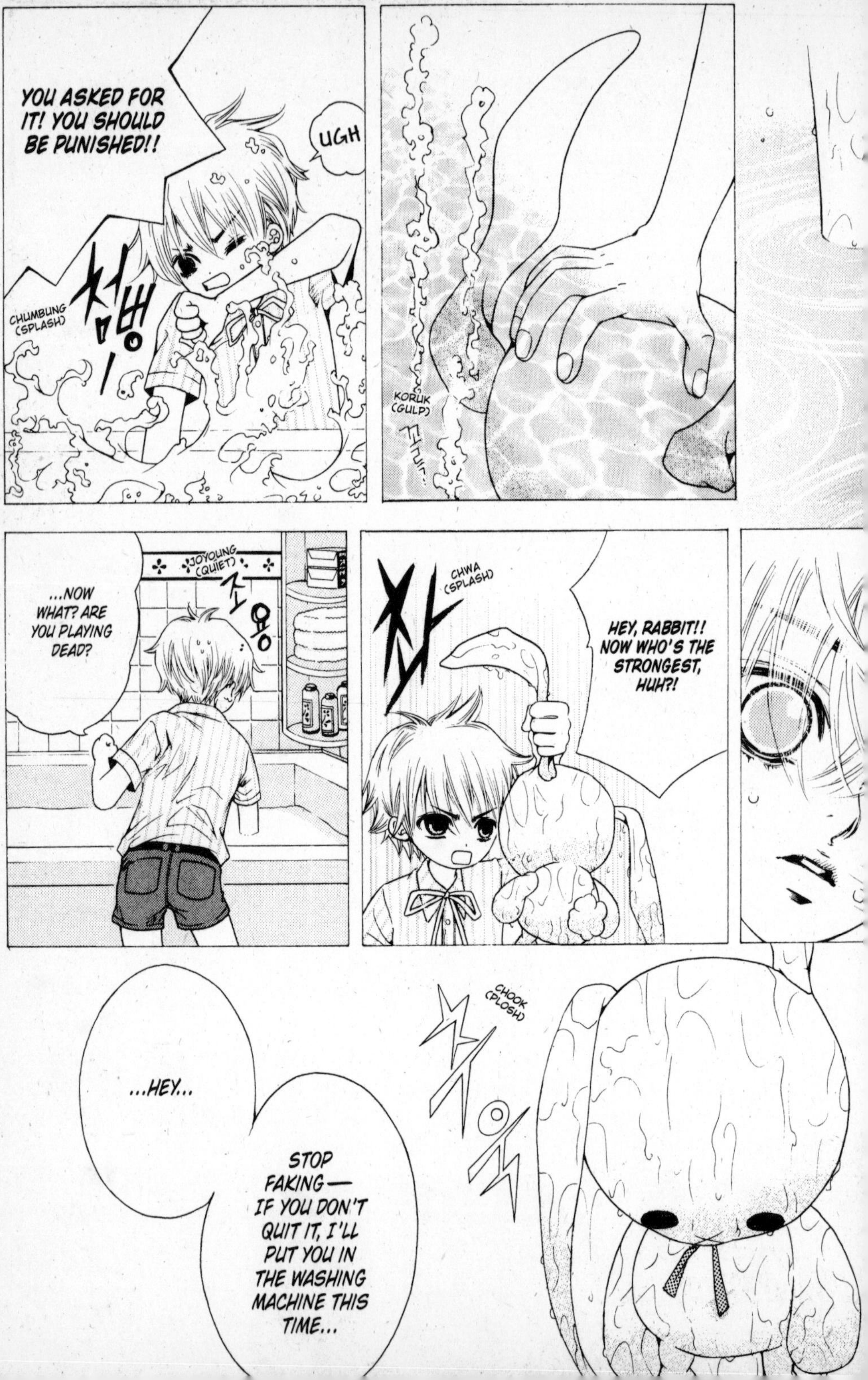
YOU ASKED FOR IT! YOU SHOULD BE PUNISHED!!
UGH
CHUMBUNG (SPLASH)
KORUK (GULP)
...NOW WHAT? ARE YOU PLAYING DEAD?
JOYOUNG (QUIET)
CHWA (SPLASH)
HEY, RABBIT!! NOW WHO'S THE STRONGEST, HUH?!
...HEY...
STOP FAKING— IF YOU DON'T QUIT IT, I'LL PUT YOU IN THE WASHING MACHINE THIS TIME...
CHOOK (PLOSH)

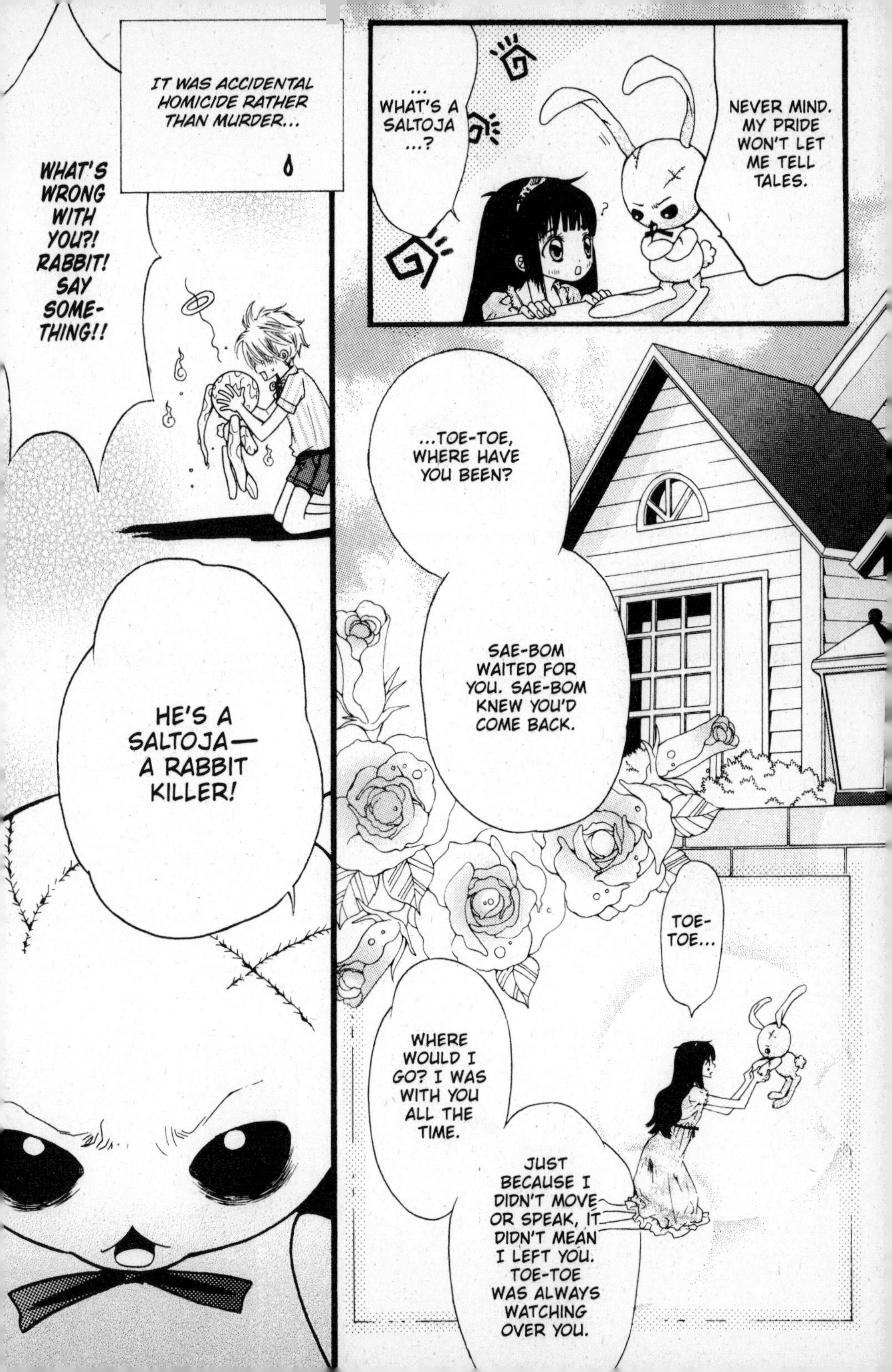

IT WAS ACCIDENTAL HOMICIDE RATHER THAN MURDER...
WHAT'S WRONG WITH YOU?! RABBIT! SAY SOME-THING!!
HE'S A SALTOJA—A RABBIT KILLER!
... WHAT'S A SALTOJA ...?
NEVER MIND. MY PRIDE WON'T LET ME TELL TALES.
...TOE-TOE, WHERE HAVE YOU BEEN?
SAE-BOM WAITED FOR YOU. SAE-BOM KNEW YOU'D COME BACK.
TOE-TOE...
WHERE WOULD I GO? I WAS WITH YOU ALL THE TIME.
JUST BECAUSE I DIDN'T MOVE OR SPEAK, IT DIDN'T MEAN I LEFT YOU. TOE-TOE WAS ALWAYS WATCHING OVER YOU.

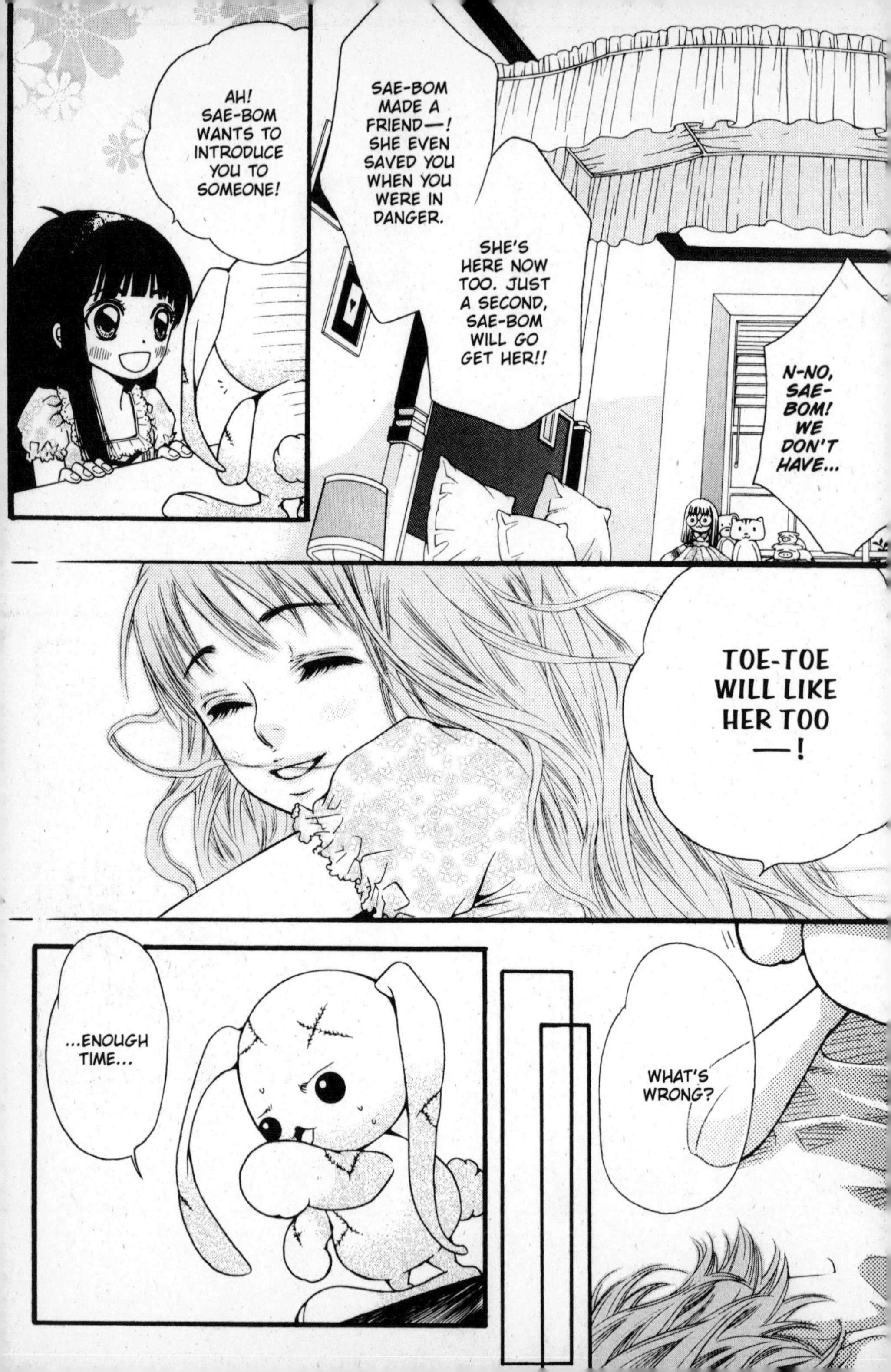
AH! SAE-BOM WANTS TO INTRODUCE YOU TO SOMEONE!
SAE-BOM MADE A FRIEND—! SHE EVEN SAVED YOU WHEN YOU WERE IN DANGER.
SHE'S HERE NOW TOO. JUST A SECOND, SAE-BOM WILL GO GET HER!!
N-NO, SAE-BOM! WE DON'T HAVE...
TOE-TOE WILL LIKE HER TOO—!
...ENOUGH TIME...
WHAT'S WRONG?

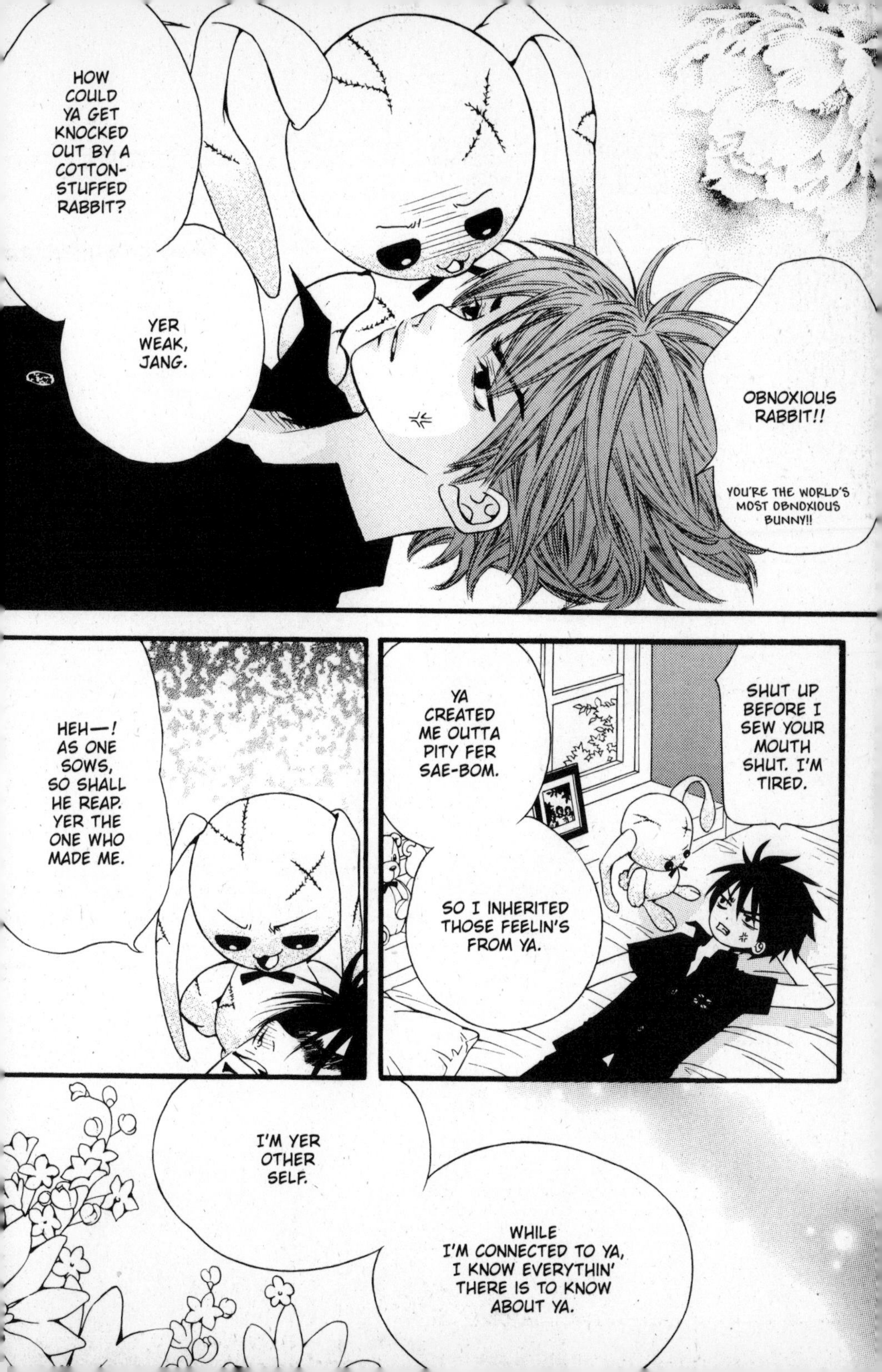
HOW COULD YA GET KNOCKED OUT BY A COTTON-STUFFED RABBIT?
YER WEAK, JANG.
OBNOXIOUS RABBIT!!
YOU'RE THE WORLD'S MOST OBNOXIOUS BUNNY!!
HEH—! AS ONE SOWS, SO SHALL HE REAP. YER THE ONE WHO MADE ME.
YA CREATED ME OUTTA PITY FER SAE-BOM.
SO I INHERITED THOSE FEELIN'S FROM YA.
SHUT UP BEFORE I SEW YOUR MOUTH SHUT. I'M TIRED.
I'M YER OTHER SELF.
WHILE I'M CONNECTED TO YA, I KNOW EVERYTHIN' THERE IS TO KNOW ABOUT YA.

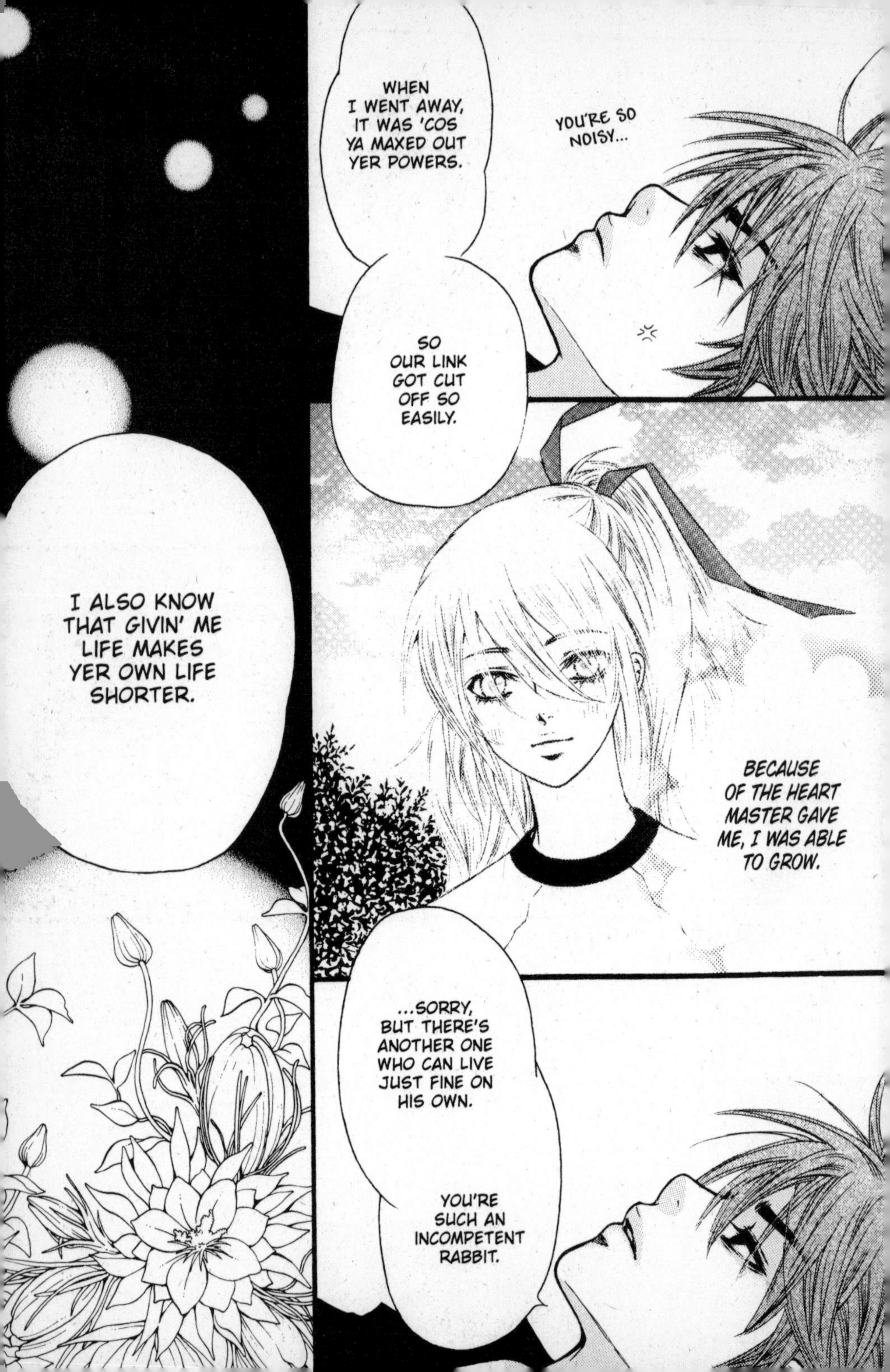

I ALSO KNOW THAT GIVIN' ME LIFE MAKES YER OWN LIFE SHORTER.
WHEN I WENT AWAY, IT WAS 'COS YA MAXED OUT YER POWERS.
SO OUR LINK GOT CUT OFF SO EASILY.
YOU'RE SO NOISY...
BECAUSE OF THE HEART MASTER GAVE ME, I WAS ABLE TO GROW.
...SORRY, BUT THERE'S ANOTHER ONE WHO CAN LIVE JUST FINE ON HIS OWN.
YOU'RE SUCH AN INCOMPETENT RABBIT.

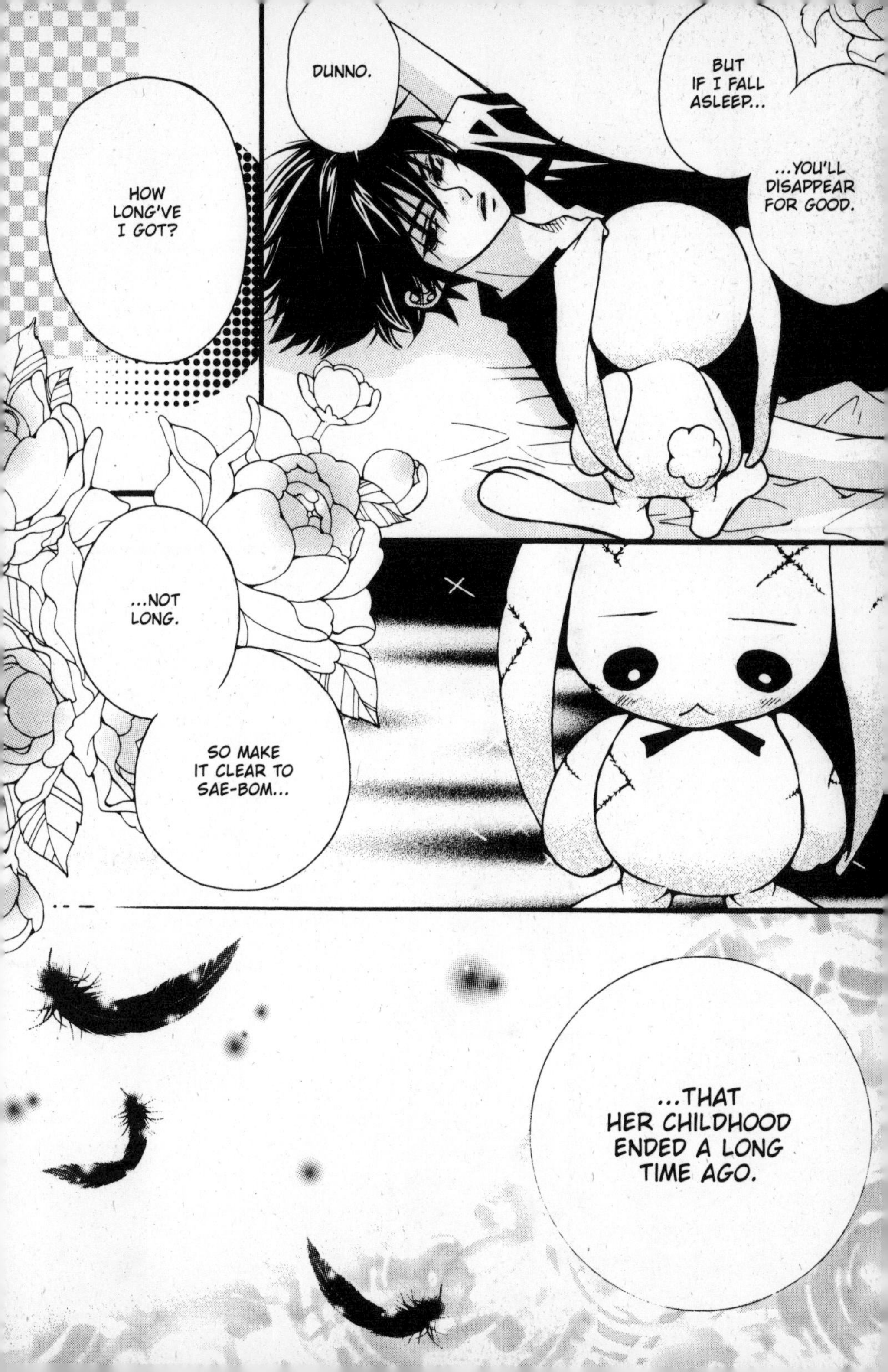
HOW LONG'VE I GOT?
DUNNO.
BUT IF I FALL ASLEEP...
...YOU'LL DISAPPEAR FOR GOOD.
...NOT LONG.
SO MAKE IT CLEAR TO SAE-BOM...
...THAT HER CHILDHOOD ENDED A LONG TIME AGO.

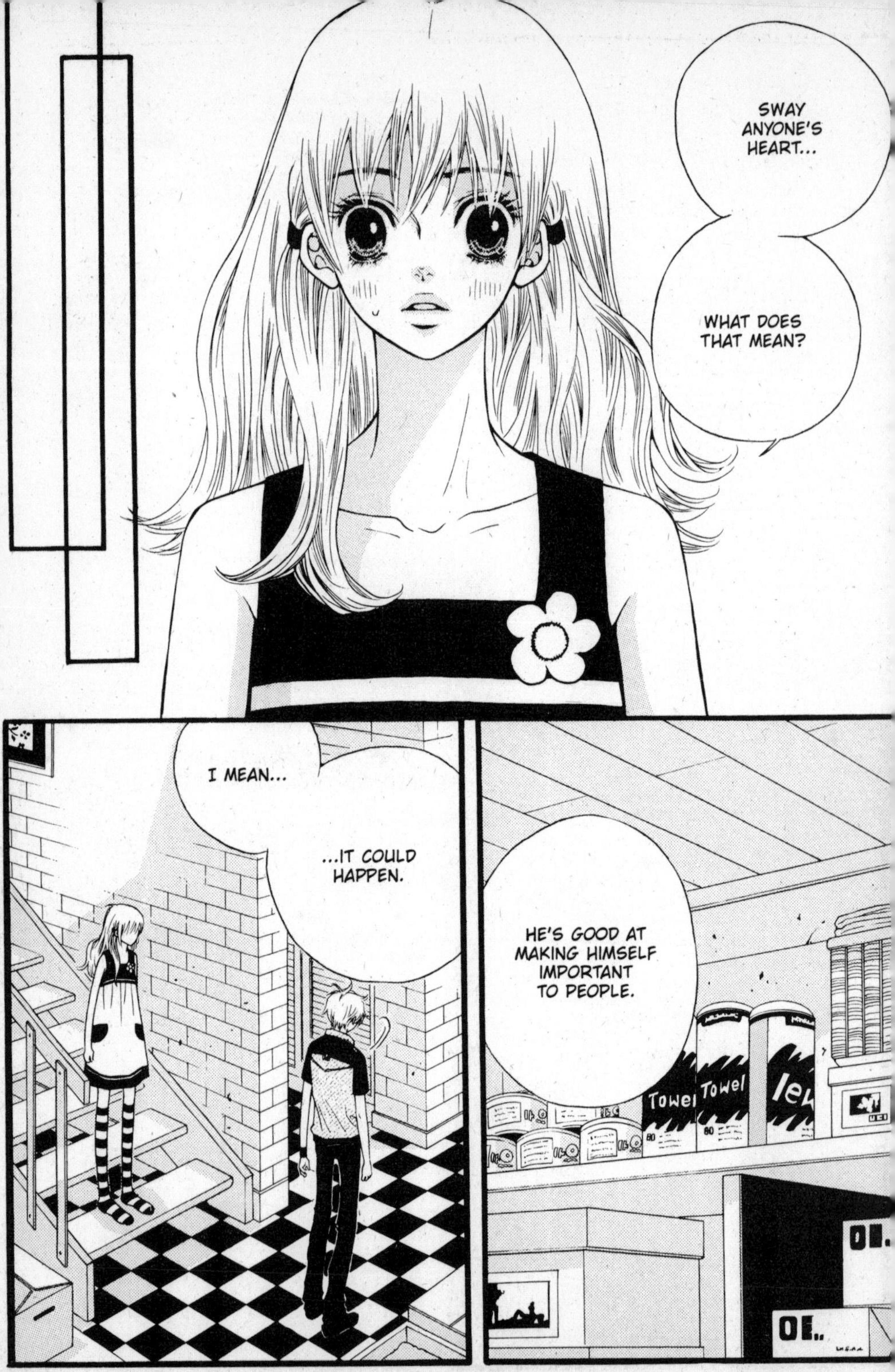
SWAY ANYONE'S HEART...
WHAT DOES THAT MEAN?
I MEAN...
...IT COULD HAPPEN.
HE'S GOOD AT MAKING HIMSELF IMPORTANT TO PEOPLE.
Towel
Towel

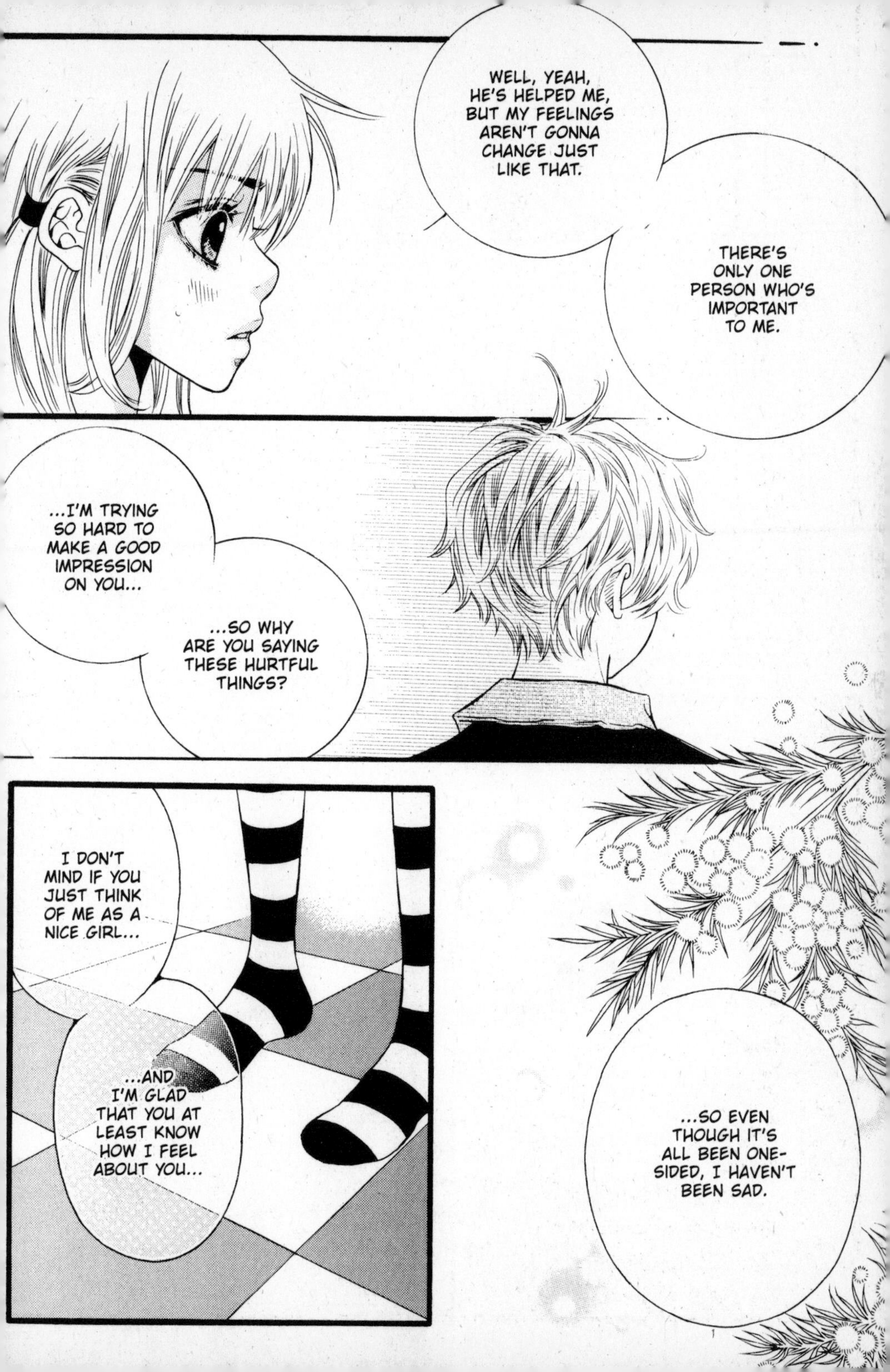
WELL, YEAH, HE'S HELPED ME, BUT MY FEELINGS AREN'T GONNA CHANGE JUST LIKE THAT.
THERE'S ONLY ONE PERSON WHO'S IMPORTANT TO ME.
...I'M TRYING SO HARD TO MAKE A GOOD IMPRESSION ON YOU...
...SO WHY ARE YOU SAYING THESE HURTFUL THINGS?
I DON'T MIND IF YOU JUST THINK OF ME AS A NICE GIRL...
...AND I'M GLAD THAT YOU AT LEAST KNOW HOW I FEEL ABOUT YOU...
...SO EVEN THOUGH IT'S ALL BEEN ONE-SIDED, I HAVEN'T BEEN SAD.

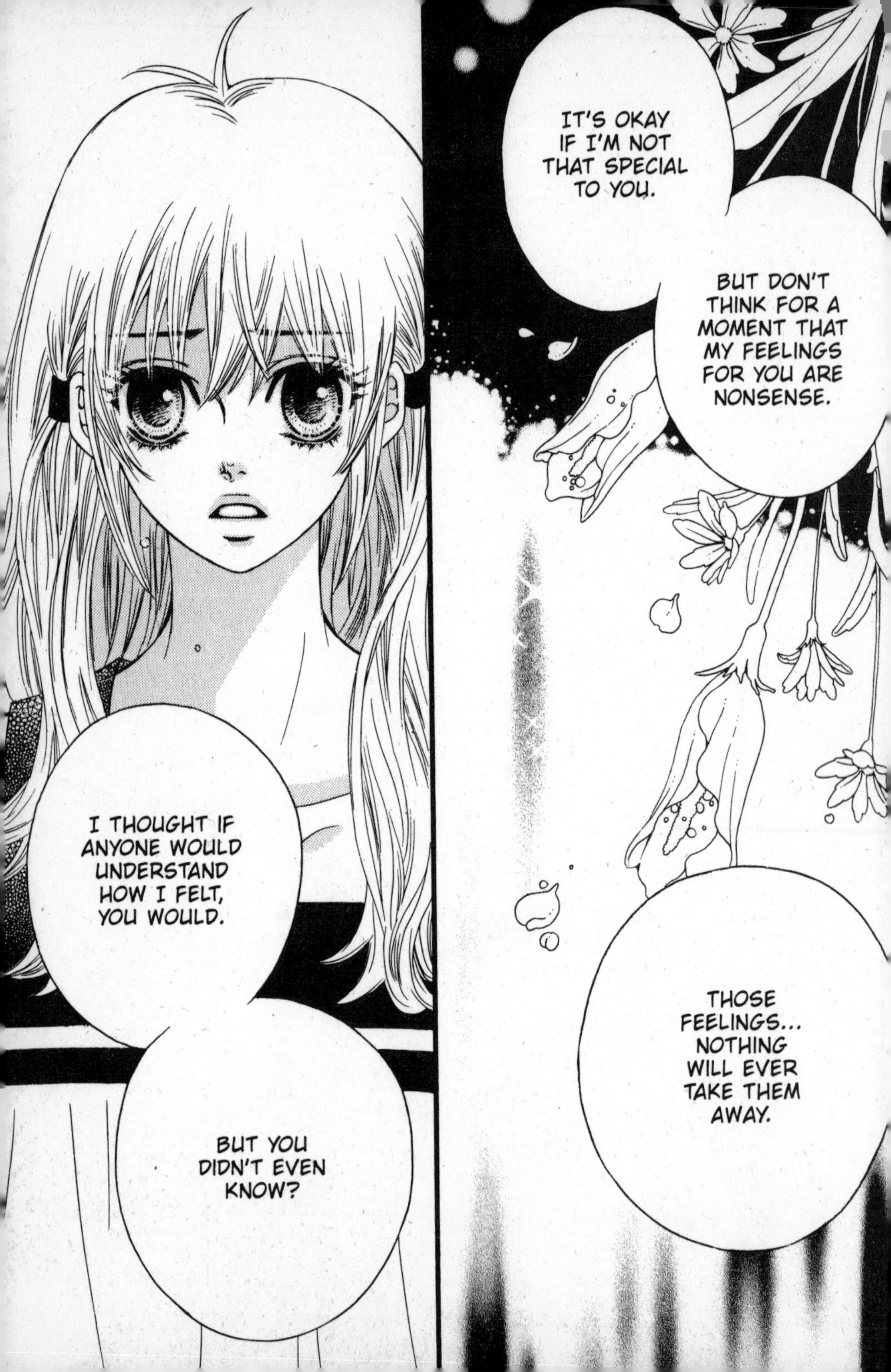
I THOUGHT IF ANYONE WOULD UNDERSTAND HOW I FELT, YOU WOULD.
BUT YOU DIDN'T EVEN KNOW?
IT'S OKAY IF I'M NOT THAT SPECIAL TO YOU.
BUT DON'T THINK FOR A MOMENT THAT MY FEELINGS FOR YOU ARE NONSENSE.
THOSE FEELINGS... NOTHING WILL EVER TAKE THEM AWAY.

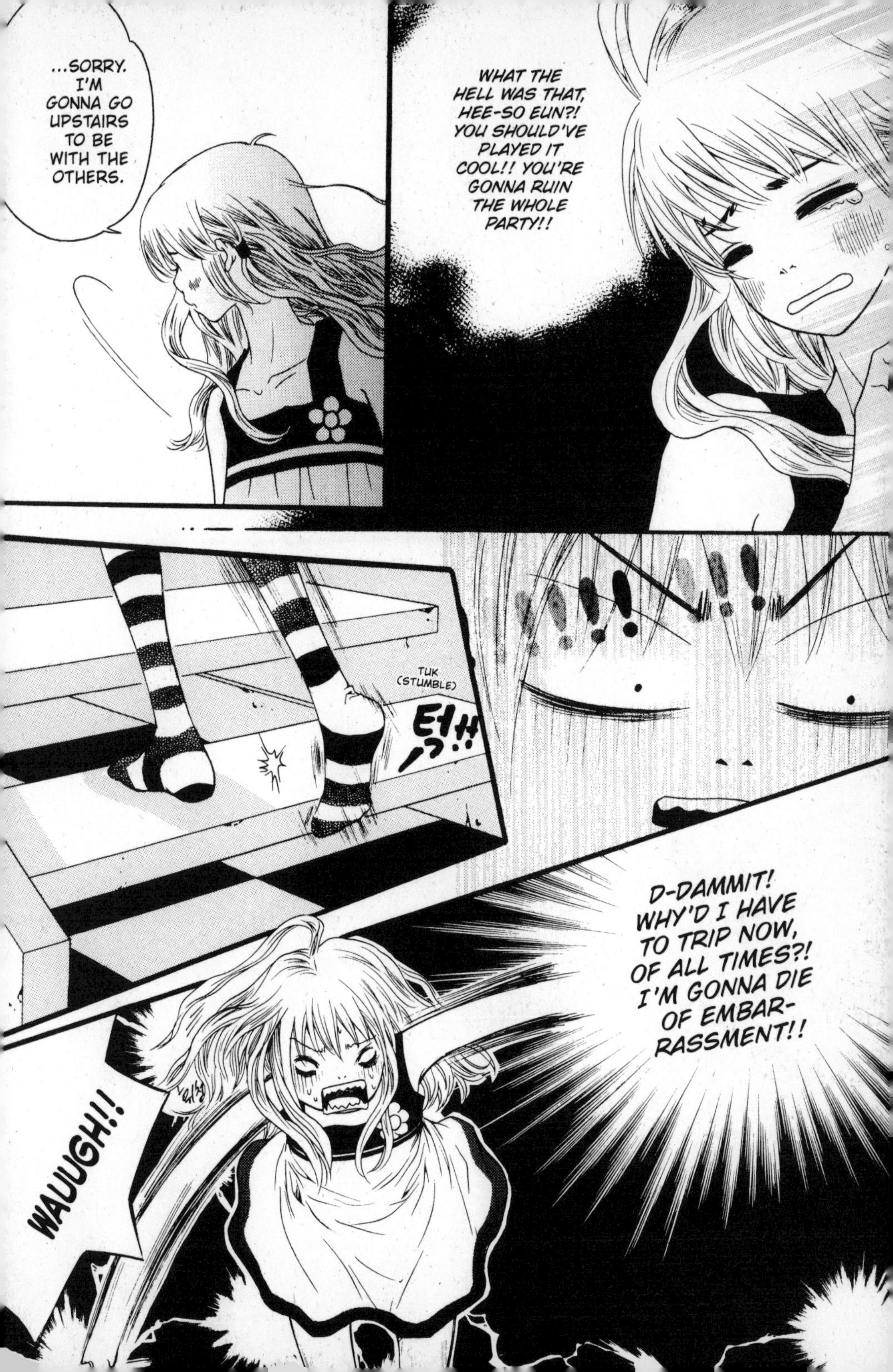
...SORRY. I'M GONNA GO UPSTAIRS TO BE WITH THE OTHERS.
WHAT THE HELL WAS THAT, HEE-SO EUN?! YOU SHOULD'VE PLAYED IT COOL!! YOU'RE GONNA RUIN THE WHOLE PARTY!!
TUK (STUMBLE)
D-DAMMIT! WHY'D I HAVE TO TRIP NOW, OF ALL TIMES?! I'M GONNA DIE OF EMBAR-RASSMENT!!
WAUUGH!!

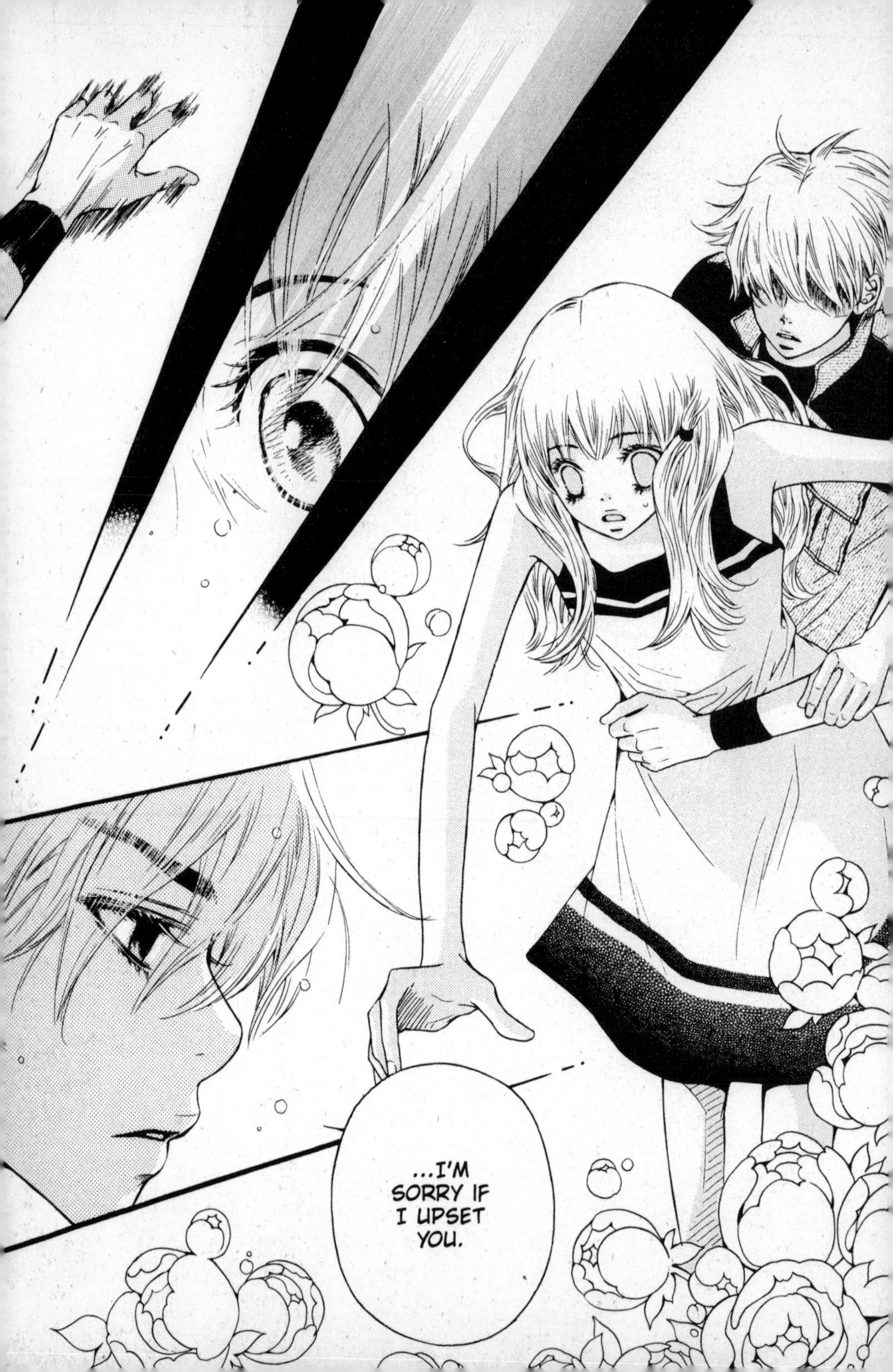
...I'M SORRY IF I UPSET YOU.

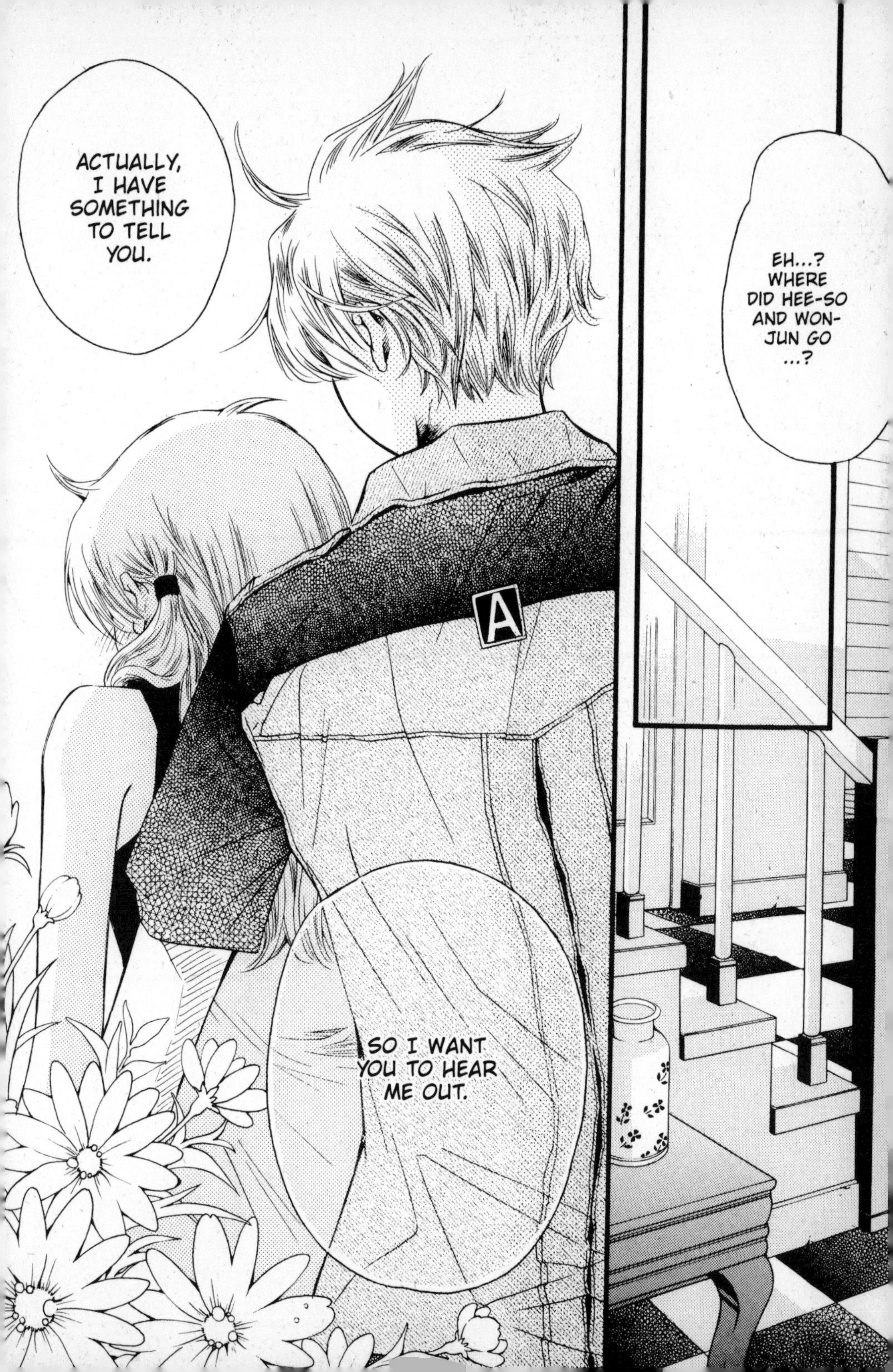
ACTUALLY, I HAVE SOMETHING TO TELL YOU.
SO I WANT YOU TO HEAR ME OUT.
EH...? WHERE DID HEE-SO AND WON-JUN GO ...?

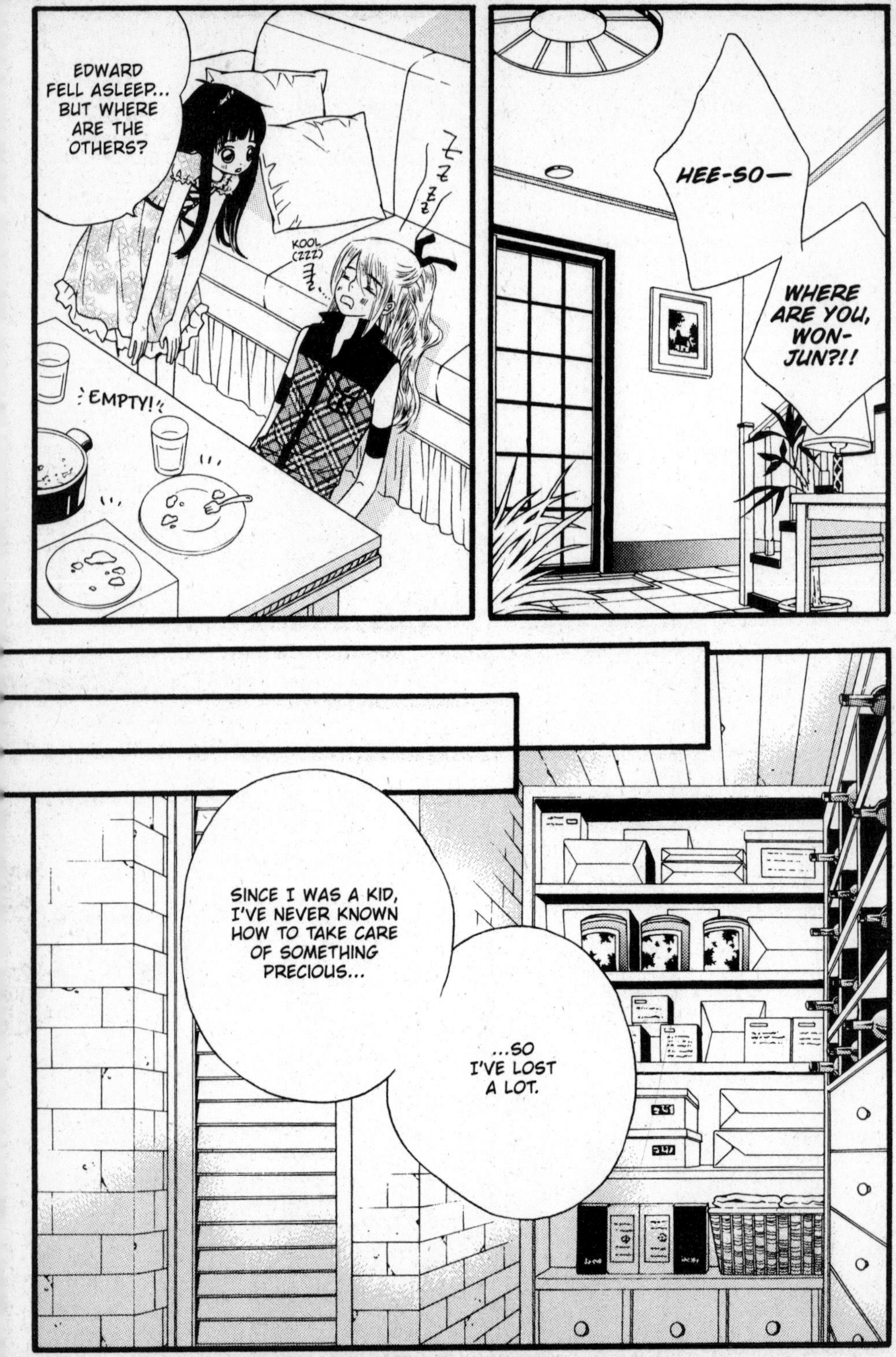
EDWARD FELL ASLEEP... BUT WHERE ARE THE OTHERS?
KOOL (ZZZ)
EMPTY!!
HEE-SO—
WHERE ARE YOU, WON-JUN?!!
SINCE I WAS A KID, I'VE NEVER KNOWN HOW TO TAKE CARE OF SOMETHING PRECIOUS...
...SO I'VE LOST A LOT.

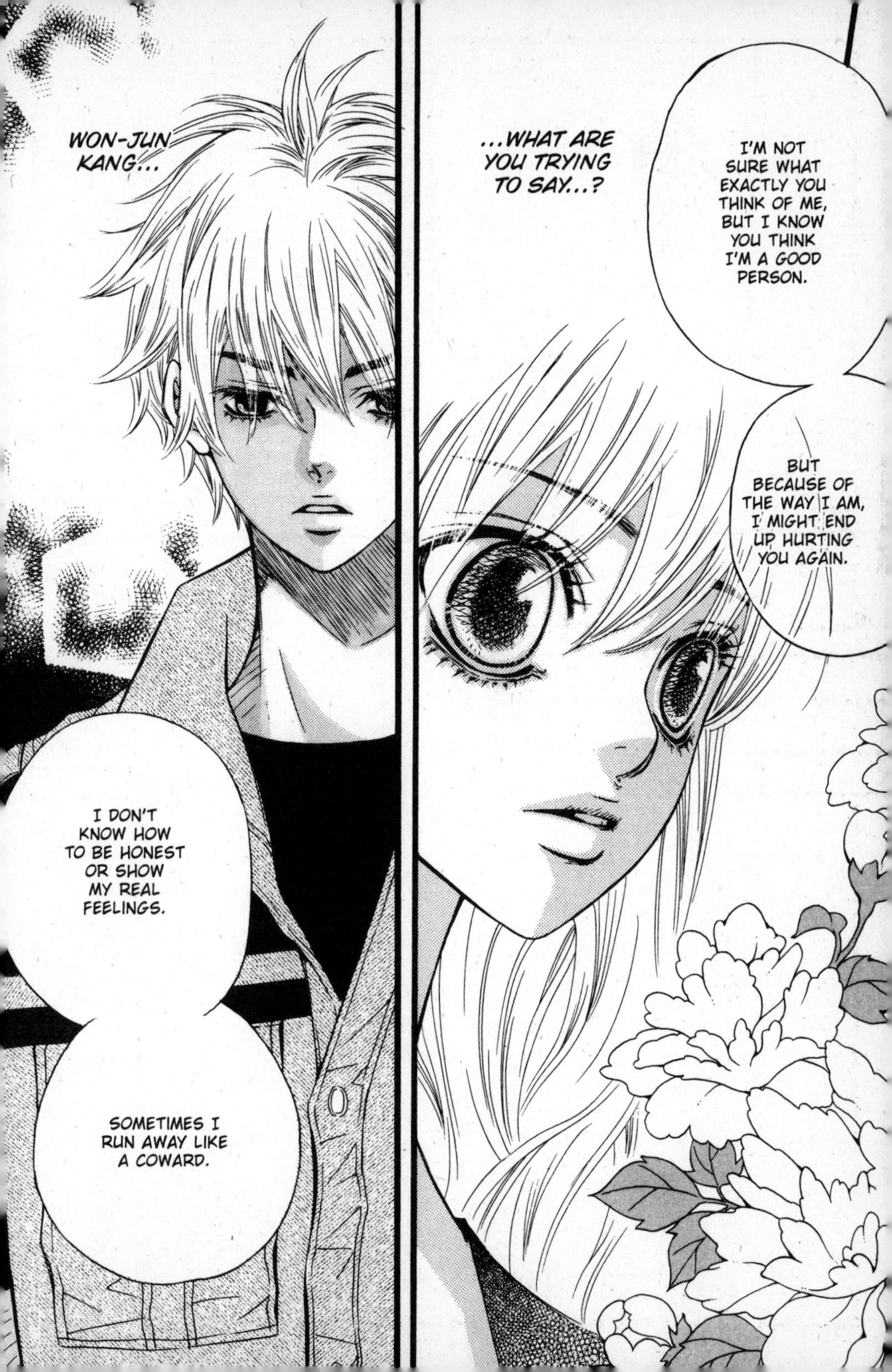
WON-JUN KANG...
I DON'T KNOW HOW TO BE HONEST OR SHOW MY REAL FEELINGS.
SOMETIMES I RUN AWAY LIKE A COWARD.
...WHAT ARE YOU TRYING TO SAY...?
I'M NOT SURE WHAT EXACTLY YOU THINK OF ME, BUT I KNOW YOU THINK I'M A GOOD PERSON.
BUT BECAUSE OF THE WAY I AM, I MIGHT END UP HURTING YOU AGAIN.

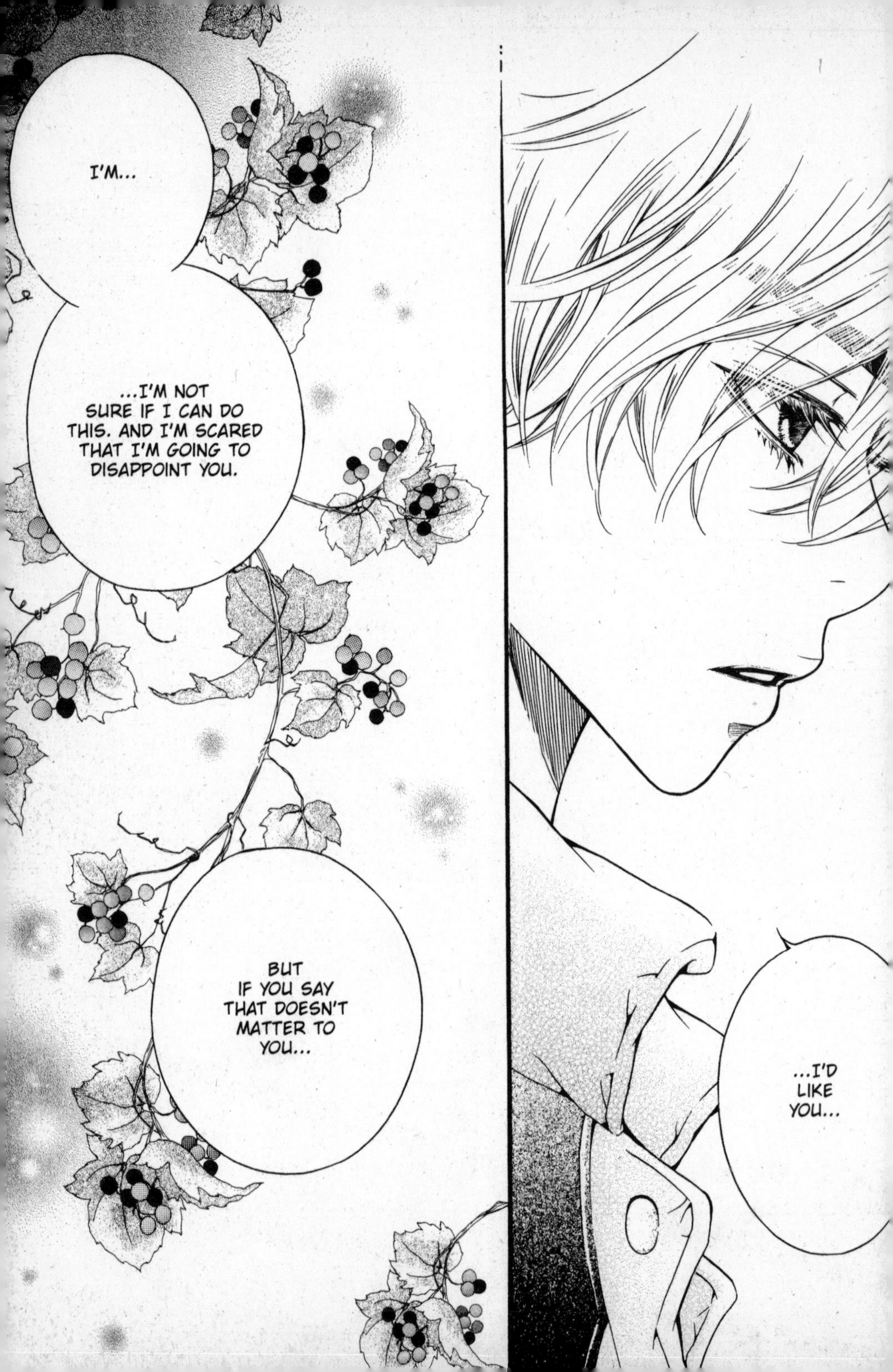
I'M...
...I'M NOT SURE IF I CAN DO THIS. AND I'M SCARED THAT I'M GOING TO DISAPPOINT YOU.
BUT IF YOU SAY THAT DOESN'T MATTER TO YOU...
...I'D LIKE YOU...

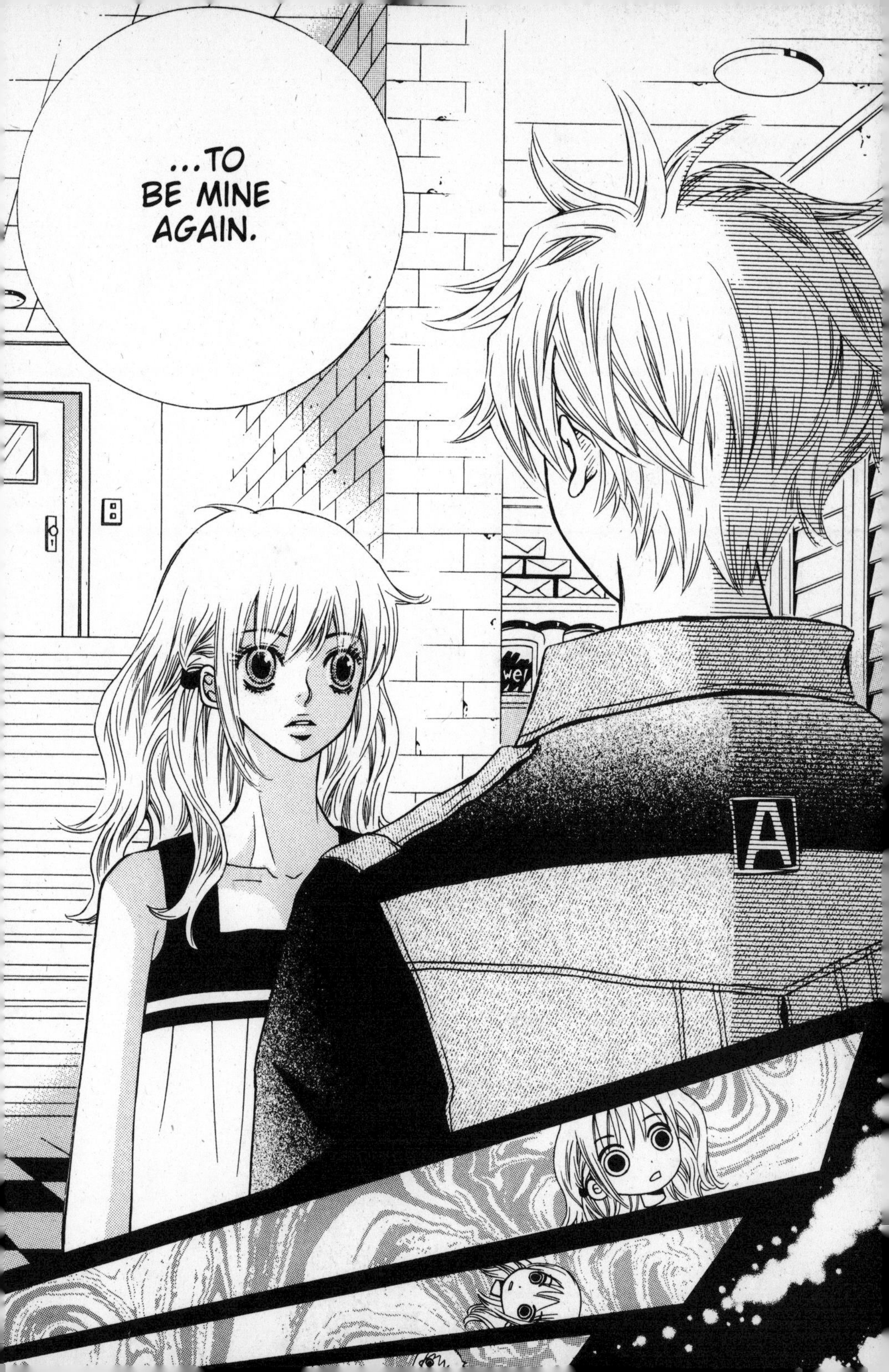
...TO BE MINE AGAIN.

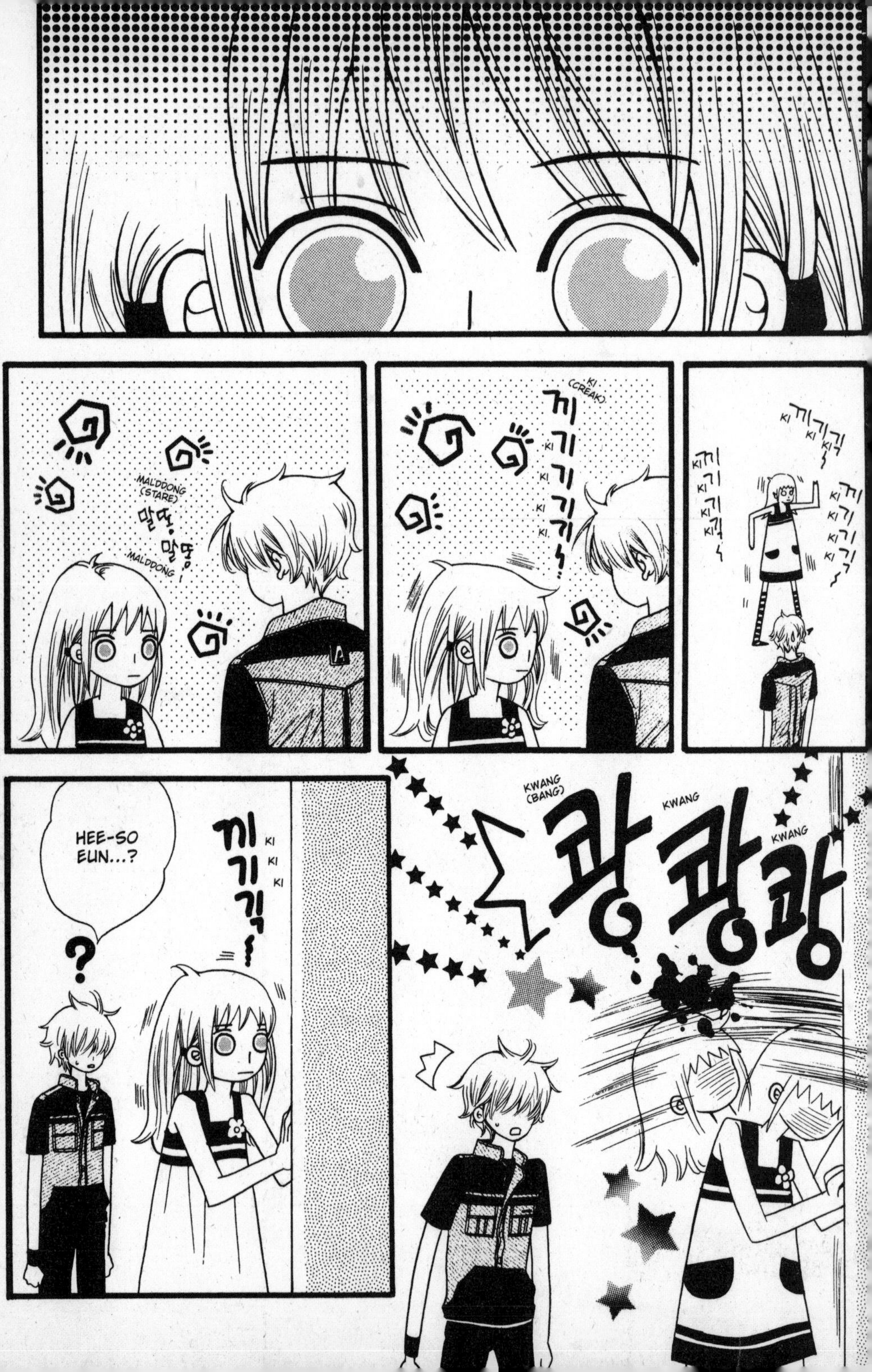
MALDDONG (STARE)
말똥 말똥
MALDDONG
KI (CREAK)
끼기기기긱~!
KI KI KI KI
KI KI KI KI
끼기기긱
끼기긱
KI KI KI
HEE-SO EUN...?
?
끼기긱~!
KI KI KI
KWANG (BANG)
KWANG
KWANG
쾅 쾅 쾅

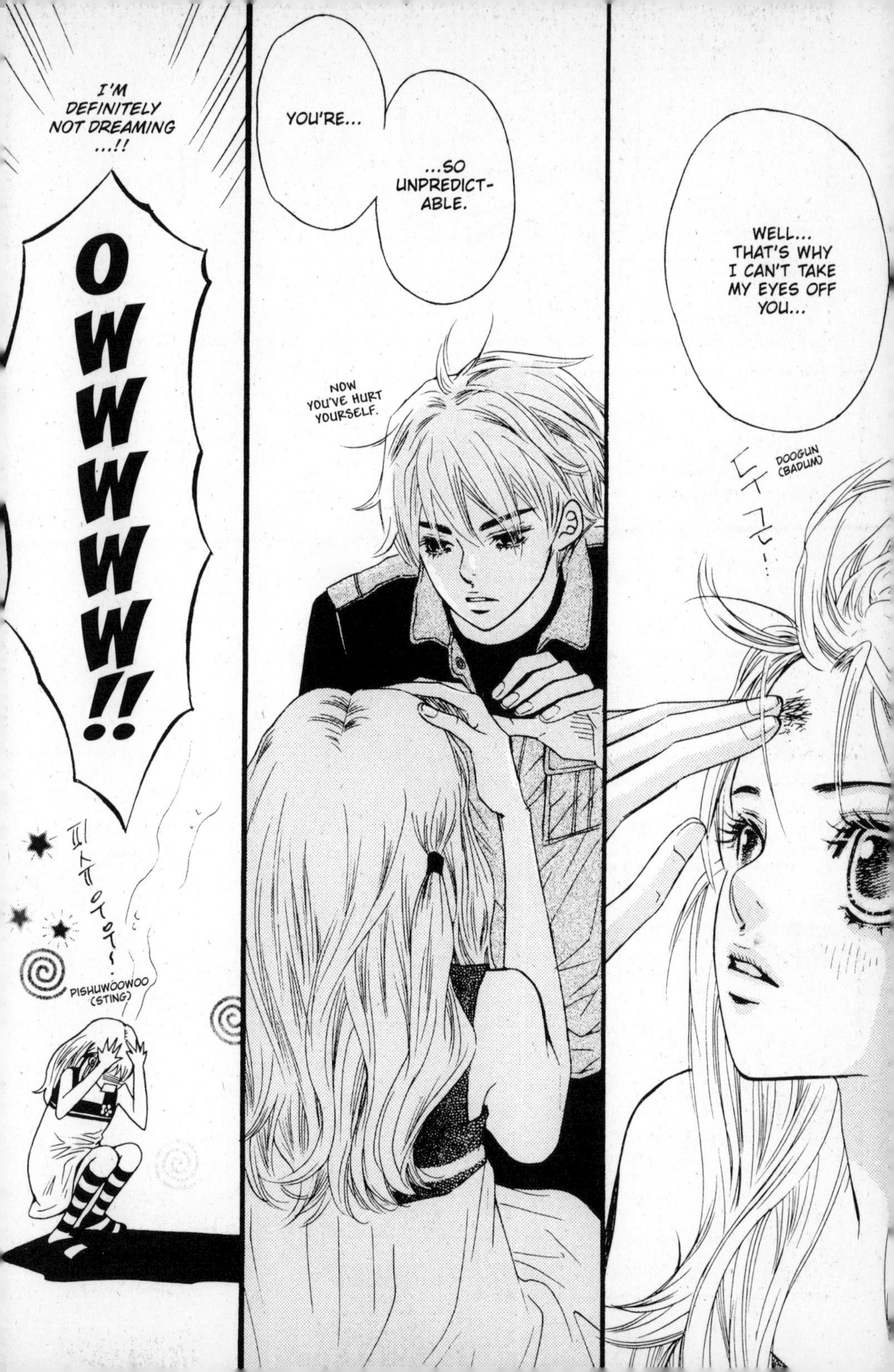
I'M DEFINITELY NOT DREAMING ...!!
OWWWWW!!
PISHUWOOWOO (STING)
YOU'RE...
...SO UNPREDICT-ABLE.
NOW YOU'VE HURT YOURSELF.
WELL... THAT'S WHY I CAN'T TAKE MY EYES OFF YOU...
DOOGUN (BADUM)

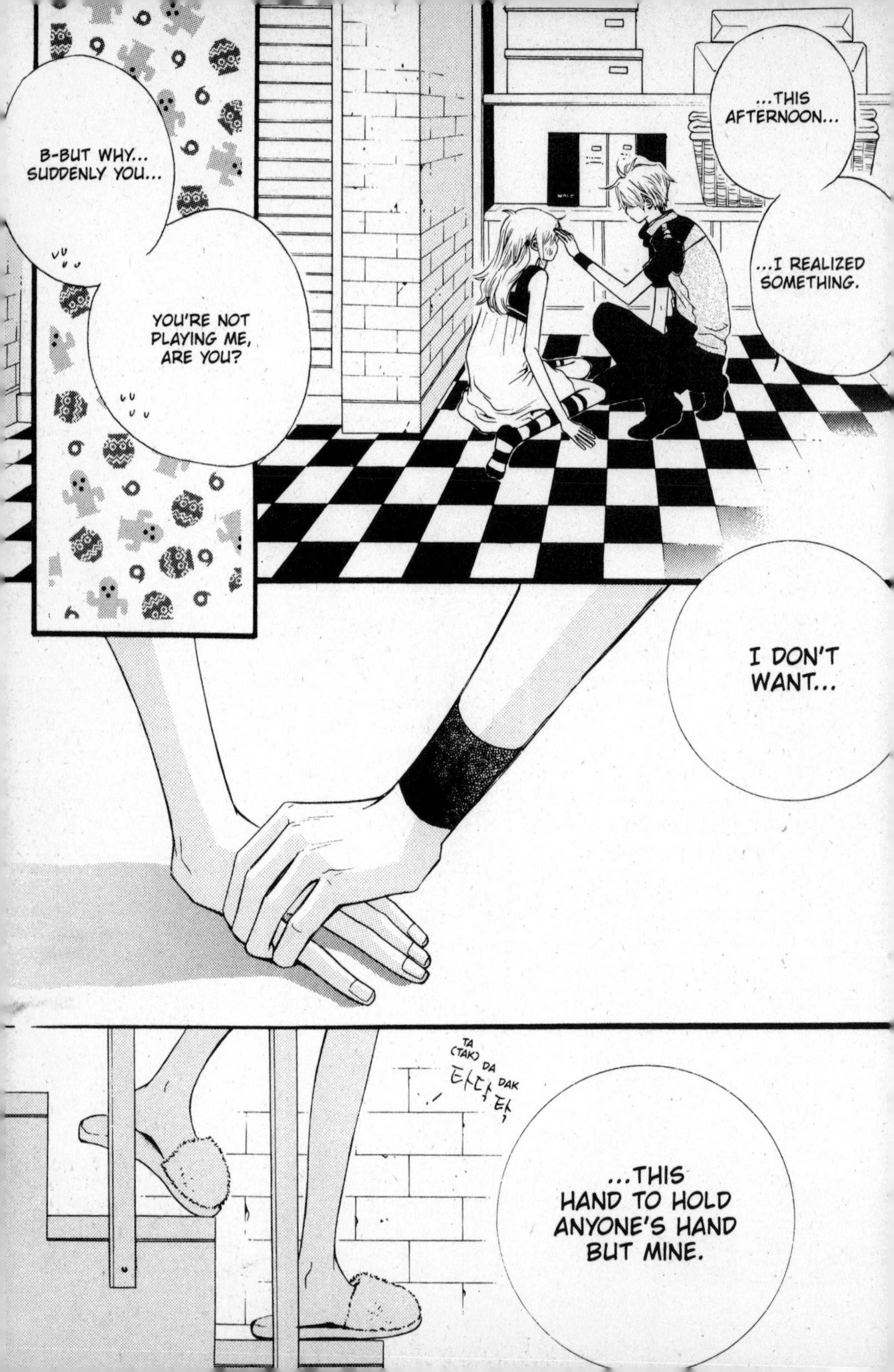
B-BUT WHY... SUDDENLY YOU...
YOU'RE NOT PLAYING ME, ARE YOU?
...THIS AFTERNOON...
...I REALIZED SOMETHING.
I DON'T WANT...
TA (TAK) DA DAK
타다닥 탁
...THIS HAND TO HOLD ANYONE'S HAND BUT MINE.

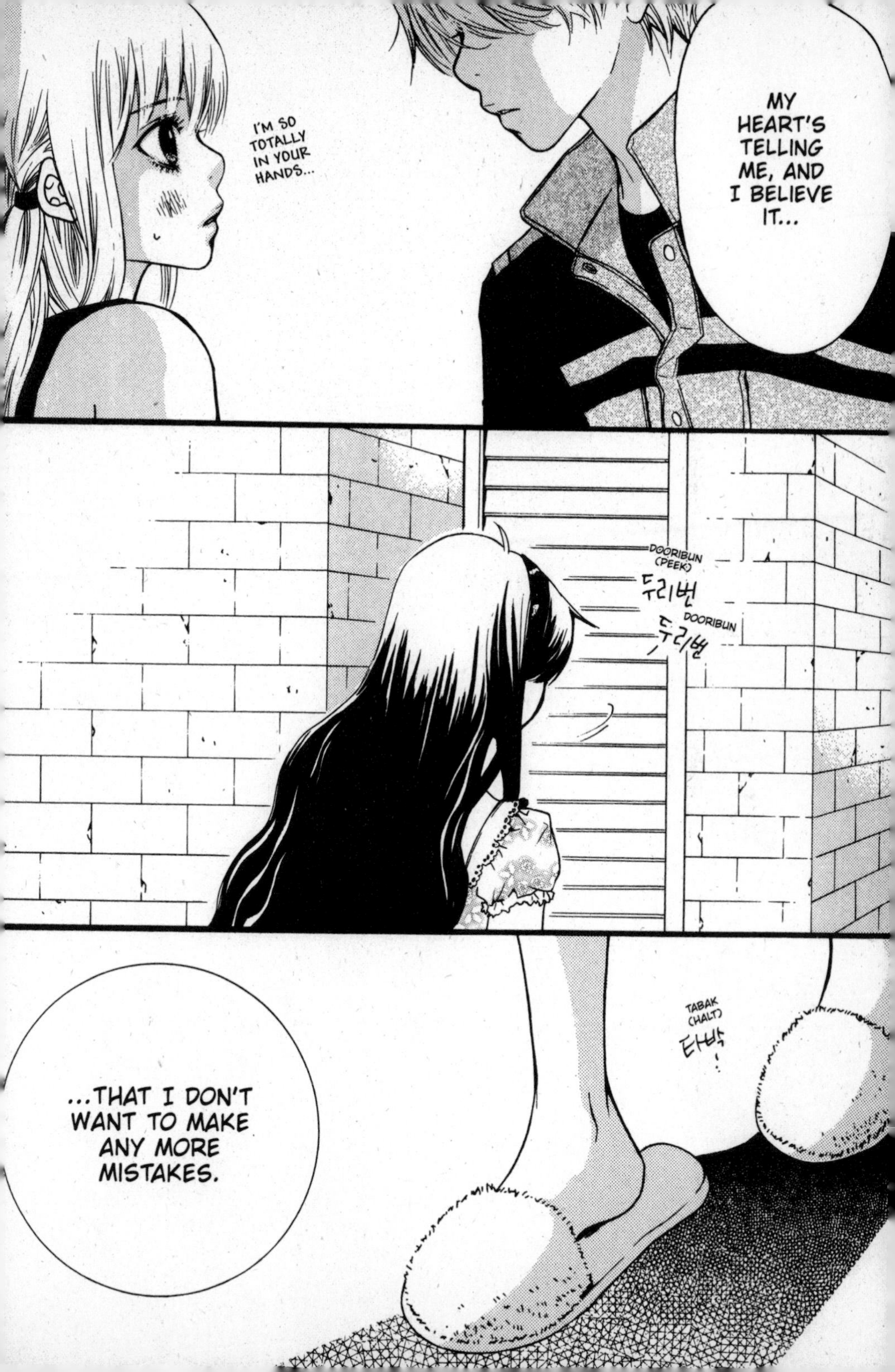
I'M SO TOTALLY IN YOUR HANDS...
MY HEART'S TELLING ME, AND I BELIEVE IT...
DOORIBUN (PEEK)
두리번
DOORIBUN
두리번
...THAT I DON'T WANT TO MAKE ANY MORE MISTAKES.
TABAK (HALT)
타박!

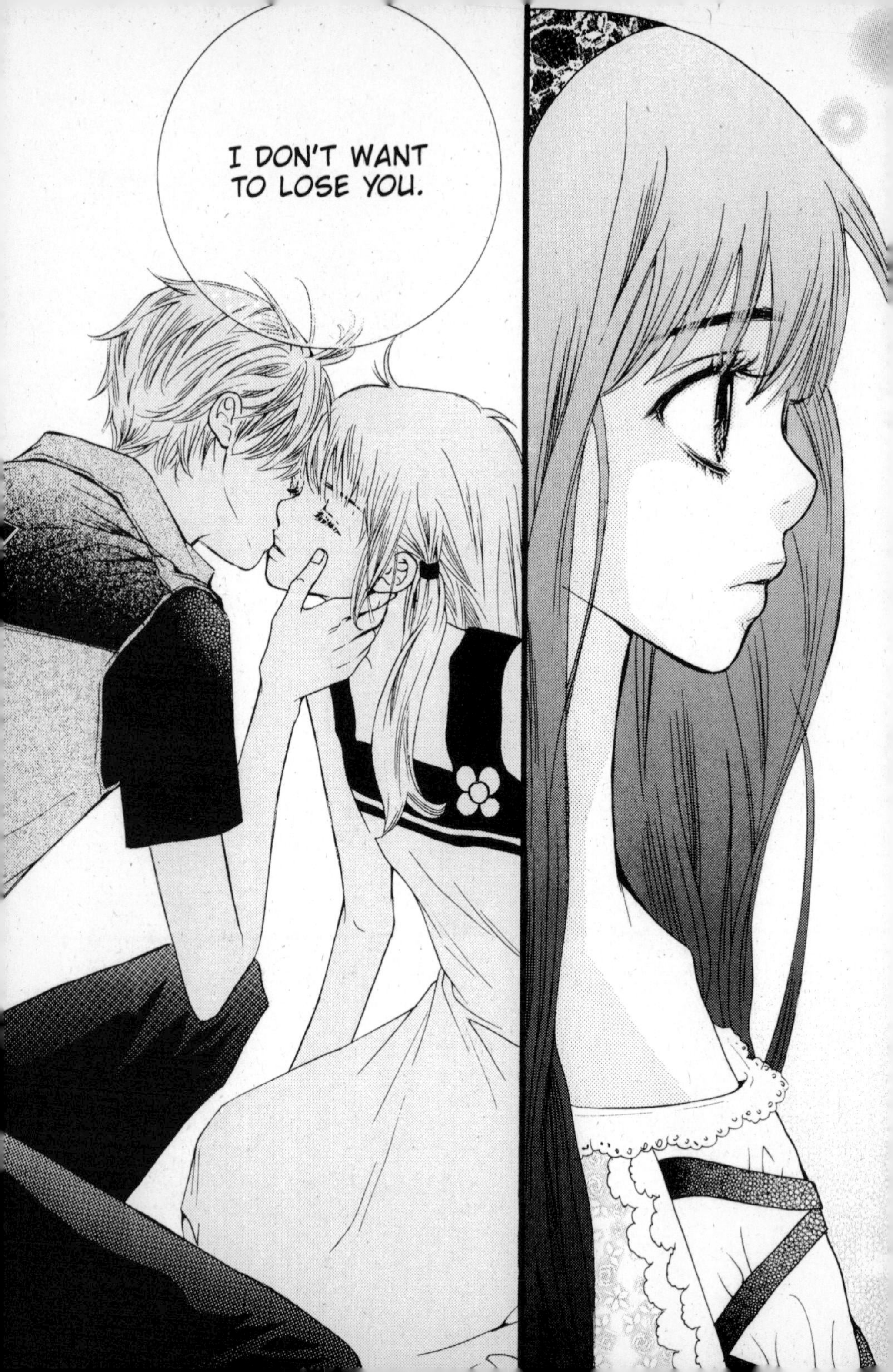
I DON'T WANT TO LOSE YOU.

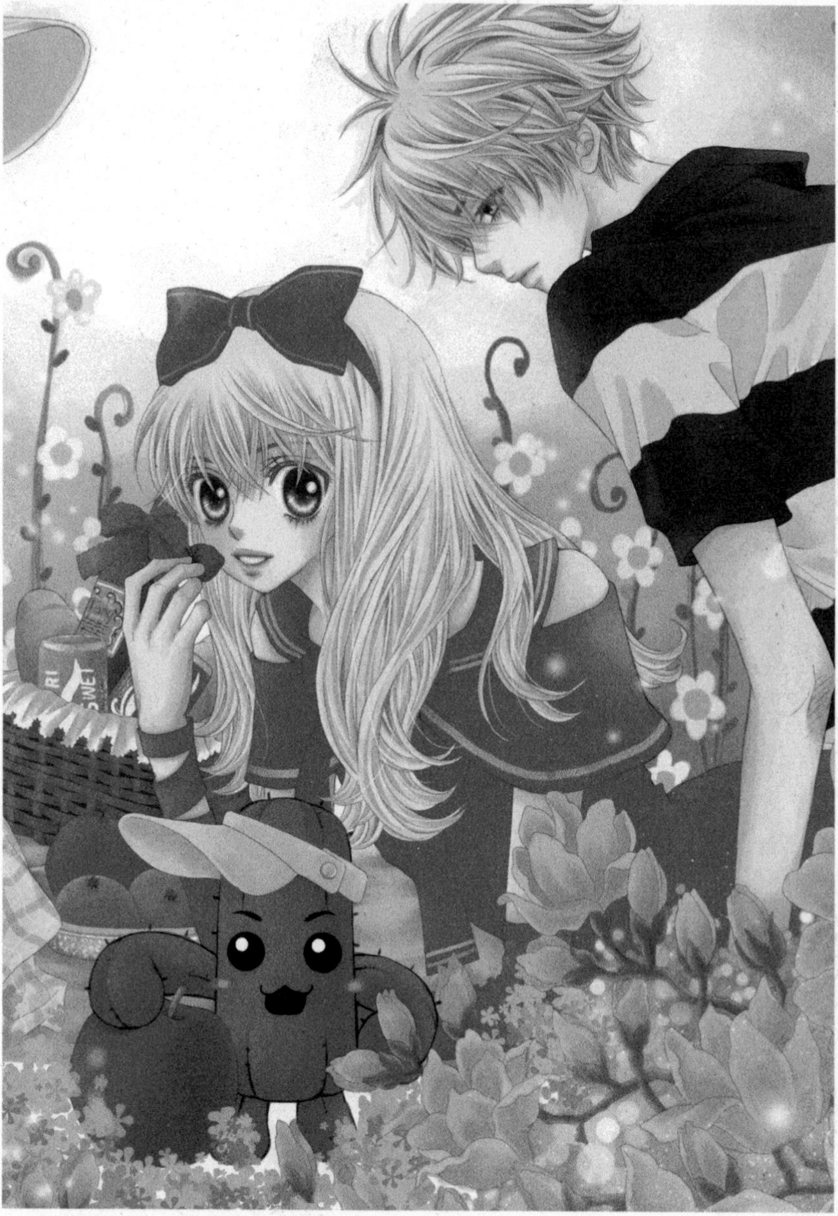

13th BOY

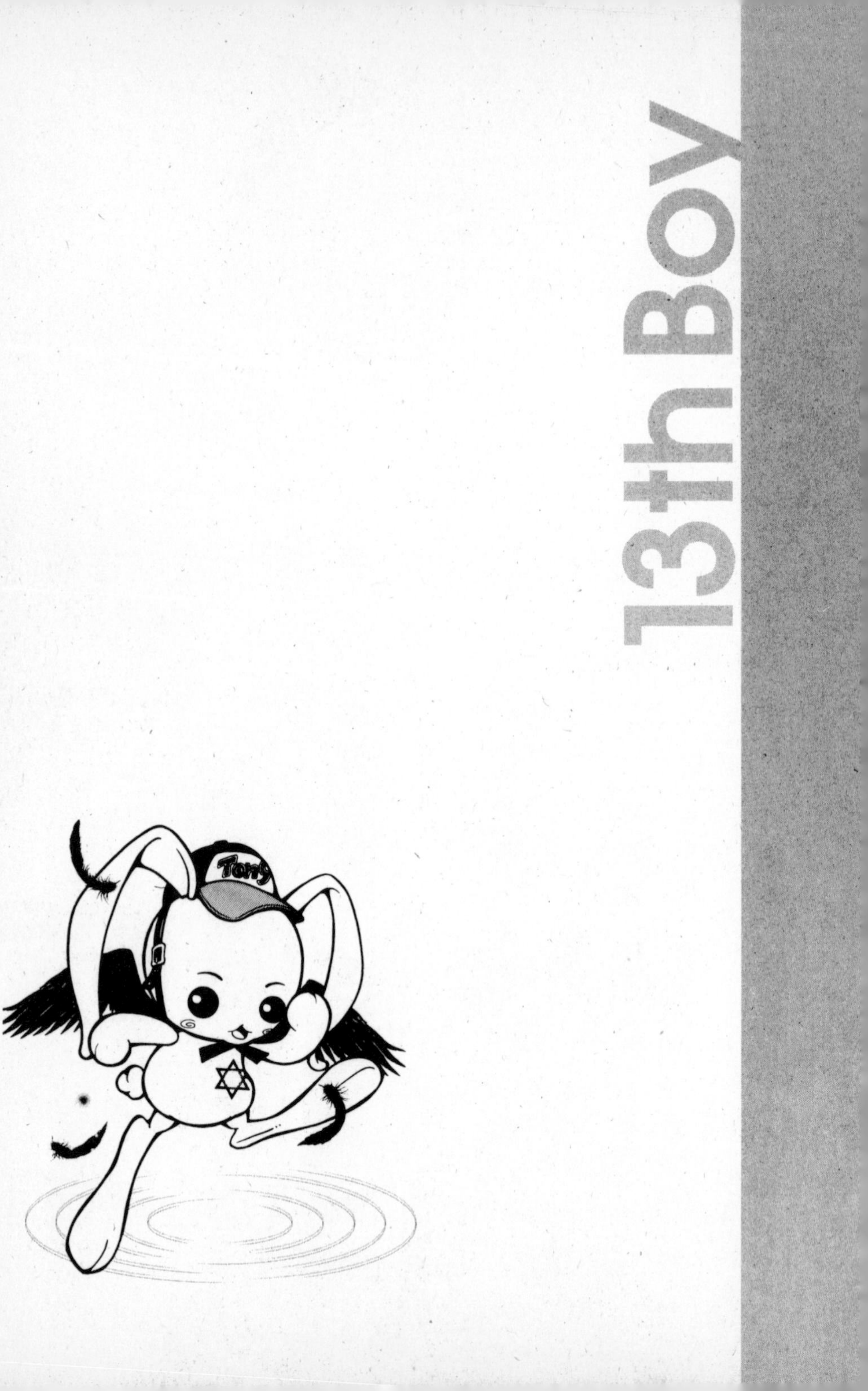
Tony

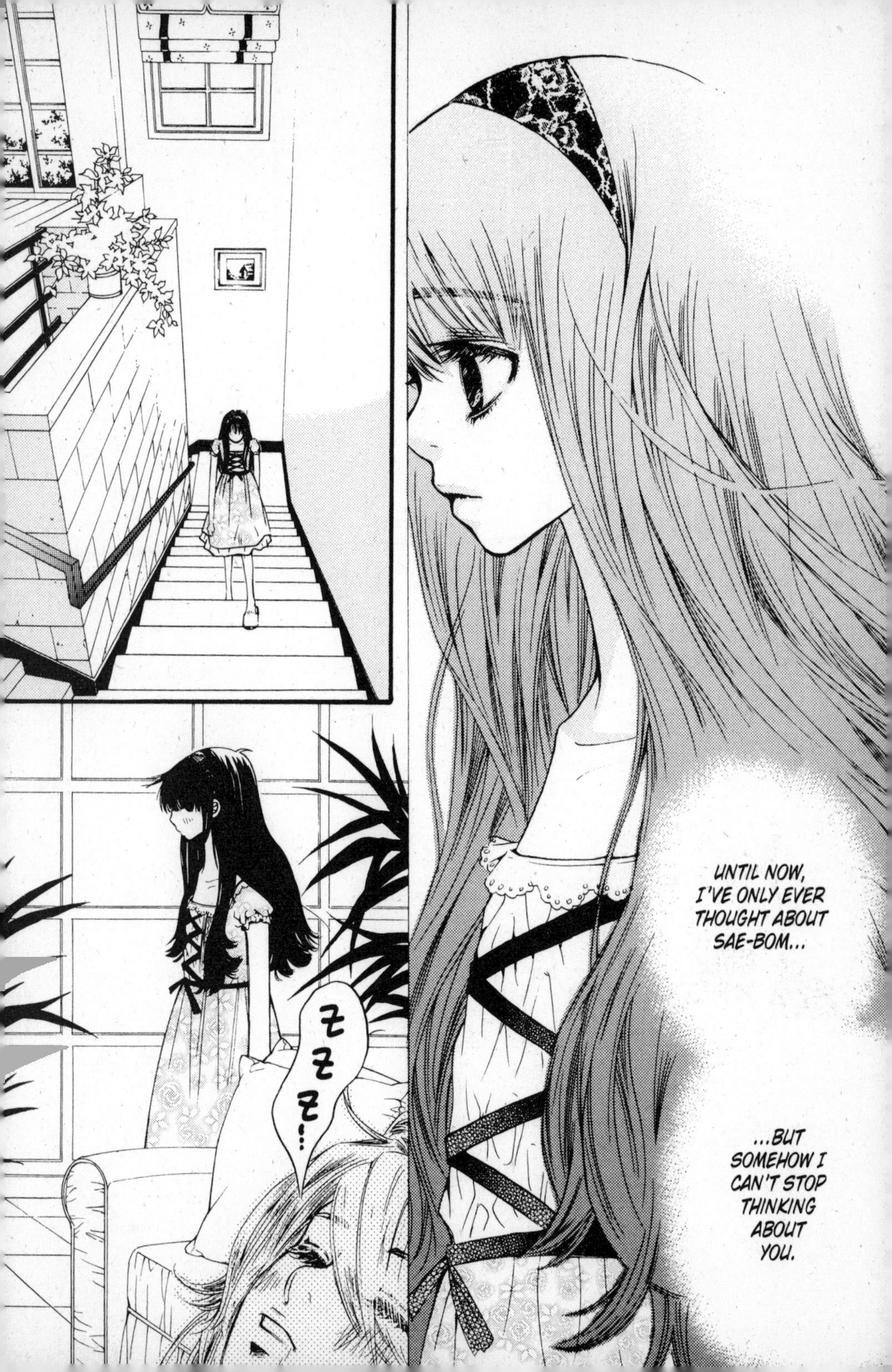

Z Z Z...
UNTIL NOW, I'VE ONLY EVER THOUGHT ABOUT SAE-BOM...
...BUT SOMEHOW I CAN'T STOP THINKING ABOUT YOU.

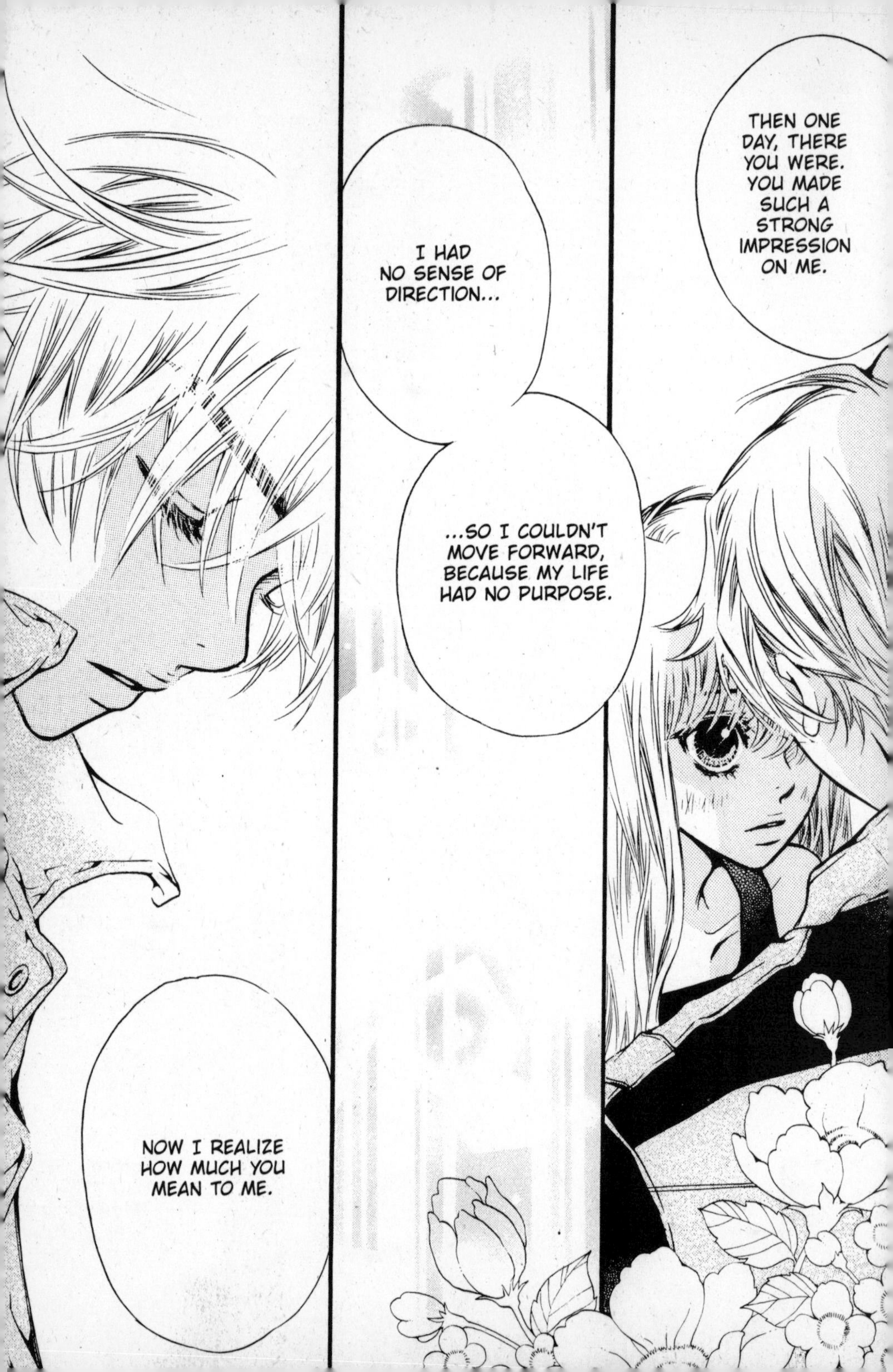
NOW I REALIZE HOW MUCH YOU MEAN TO ME.
I HAD NO SENSE OF DIRECTION...
...SO I COULDN'T MOVE FORWARD, BECAUSE MY LIFE HAD NO PURPOSE.
THEN ONE DAY, THERE YOU WERE. YOU MADE SUCH A STRONG IMPRESSION ON ME.

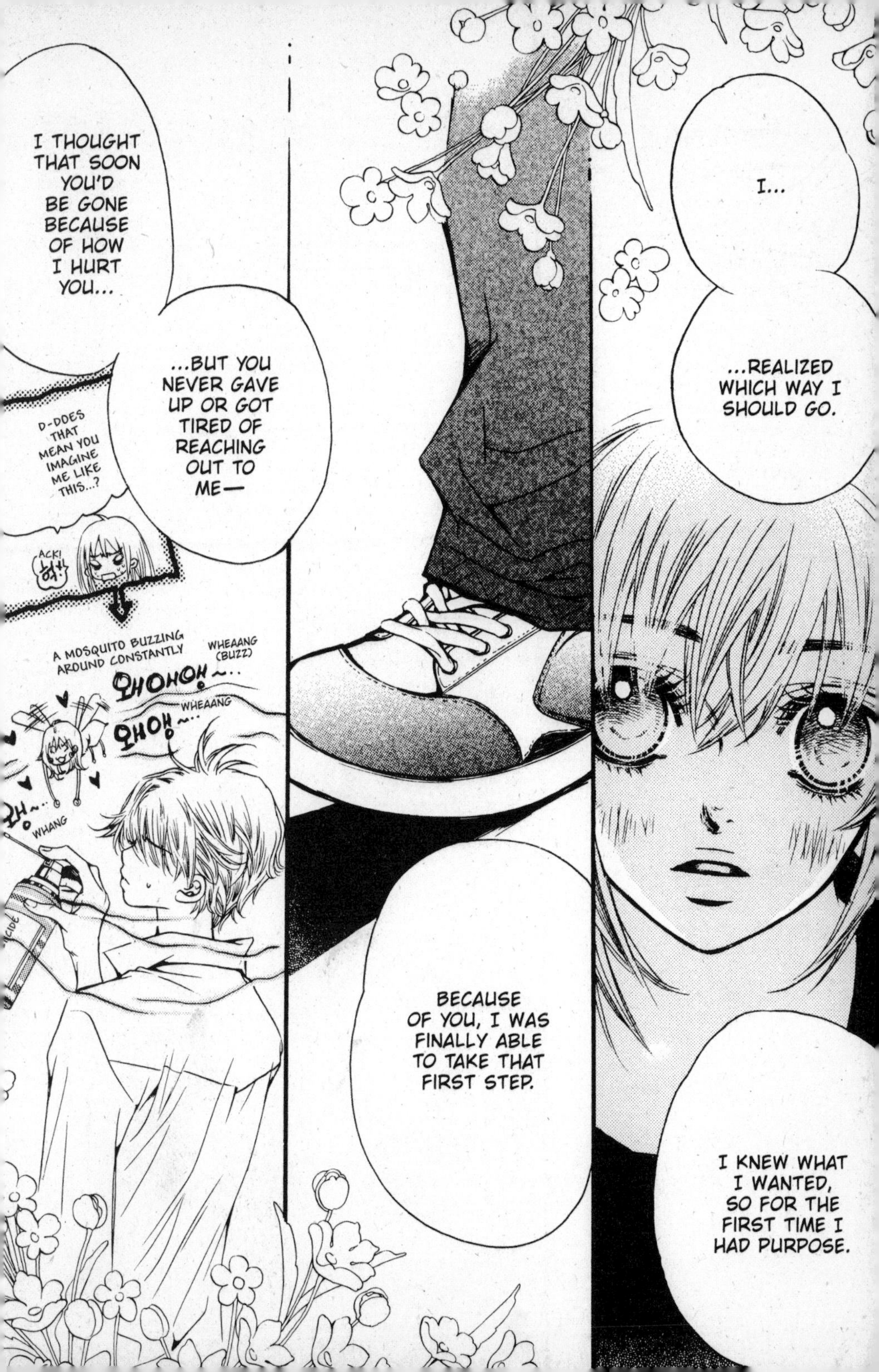
I THOUGHT THAT SOON YOU'D BE GONE BECAUSE OF HOW I HURT YOU...
...BUT YOU NEVER GAVE UP OR GOT TIRED OF REACHING OUT TO ME—
D-DOES THAT MEAN YOU IMAGINE ME LIKE THIS...?
ACK!
헉!
A MOSQUITO BUZZING AROUND CONSTANTLY
WHEAANG (BUZZ)
왜애애앵~...
WHEAANG
왜애앵~...
WHANG
BECAUSE OF YOU, I WAS FINALLY ABLE TO TAKE THAT FIRST STEP.
I...
...REALIZED WHICH WAY I SHOULD GO.
I KNEW WHAT I WANTED, SO FOR THE FIRST TIME I HAD PURPOSE.

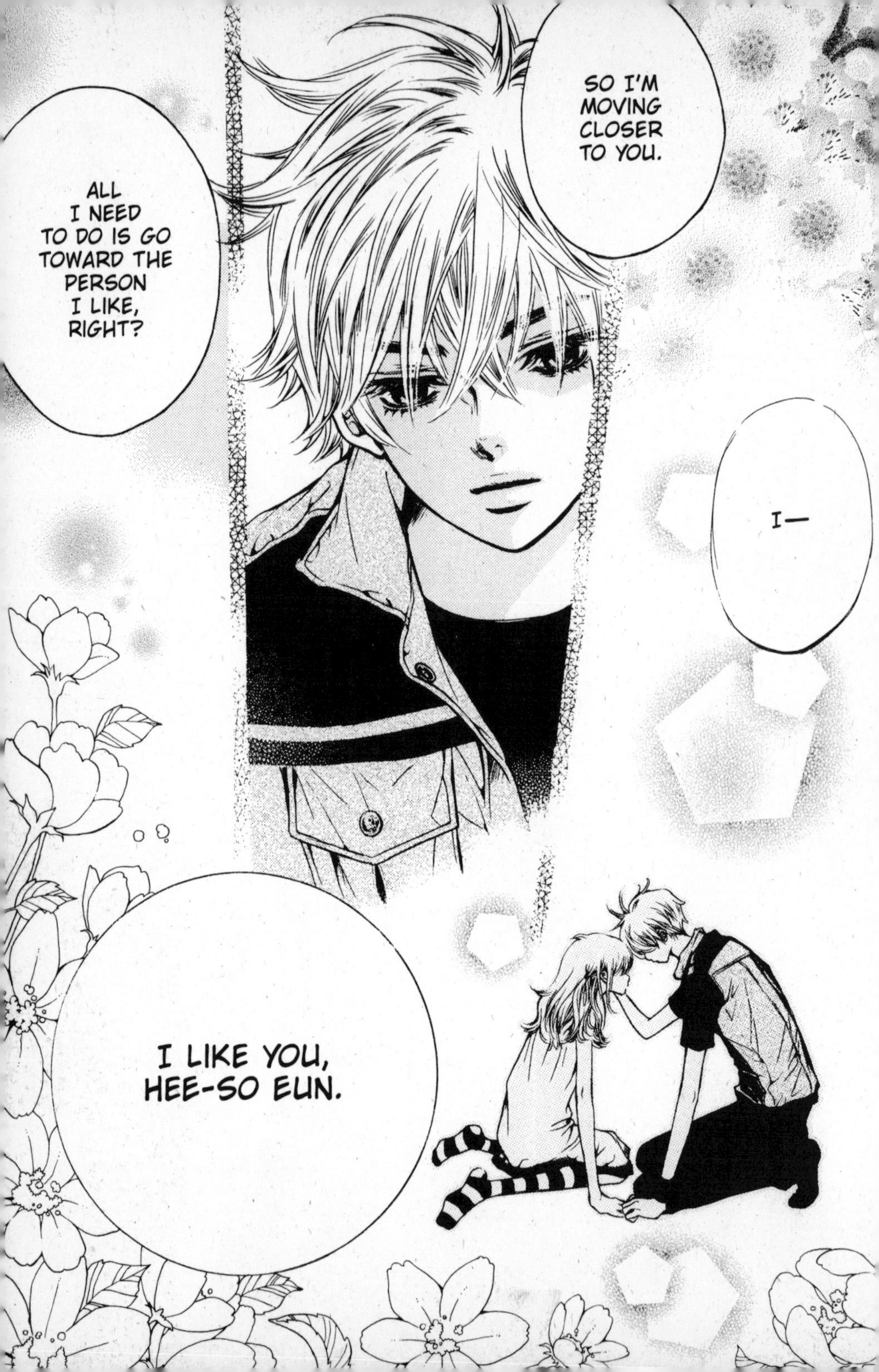
ALL I NEED TO DO IS GO TOWARD THE PERSON I LIKE, RIGHT?
SO I'M MOVING CLOSER TO YOU.
I—
I LIKE YOU, HEE-SO EUN.

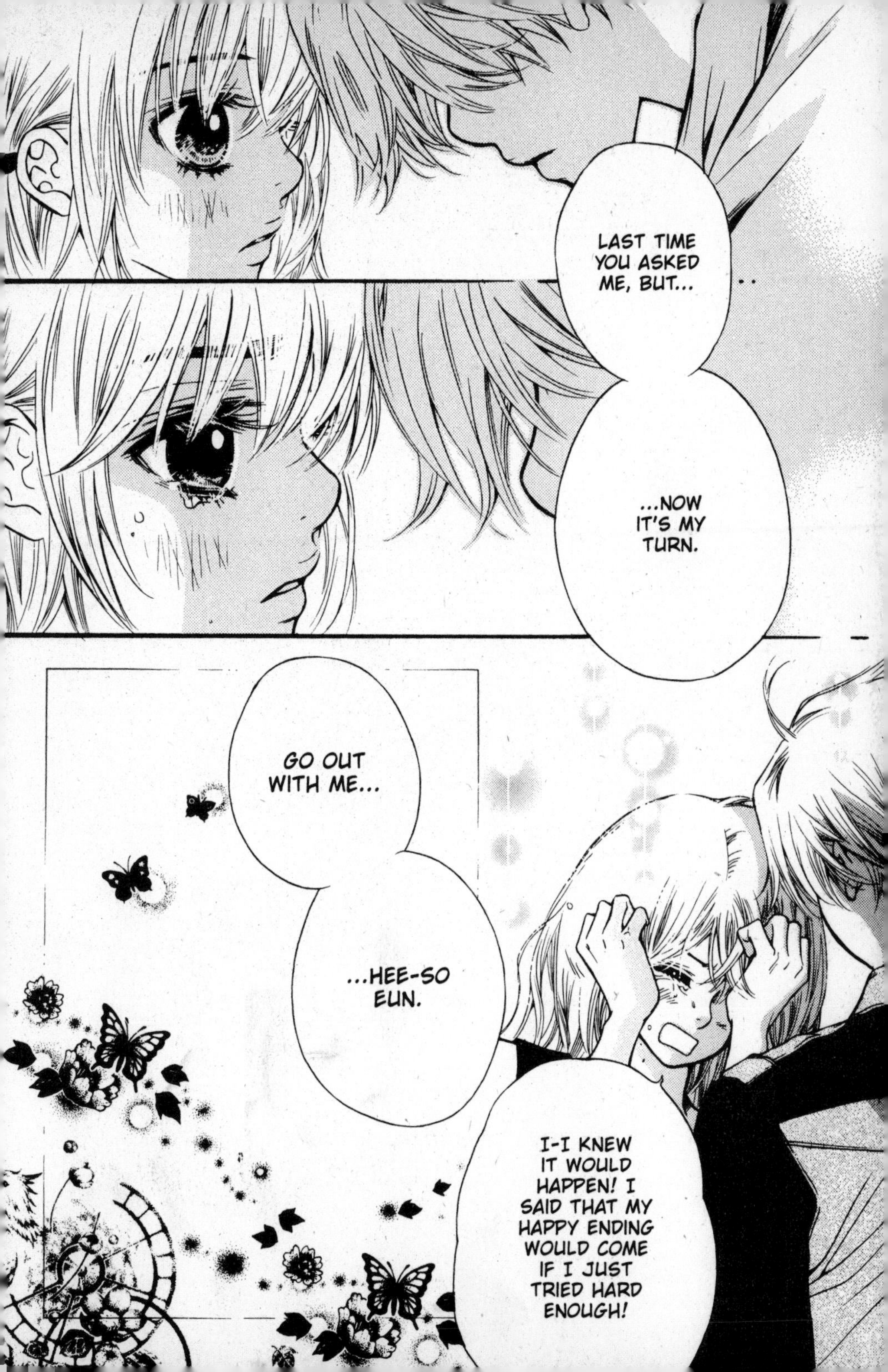
LAST TIME YOU ASKED ME, BUT...
...NOW IT'S MY TURN.
GO OUT WITH ME...
...HEE-SO EUN.
I-I KNEW IT WOULD HAPPEN! I SAID THAT MY HAPPY ENDING WOULD COME IF I JUST TRIED HARD ENOUGH!

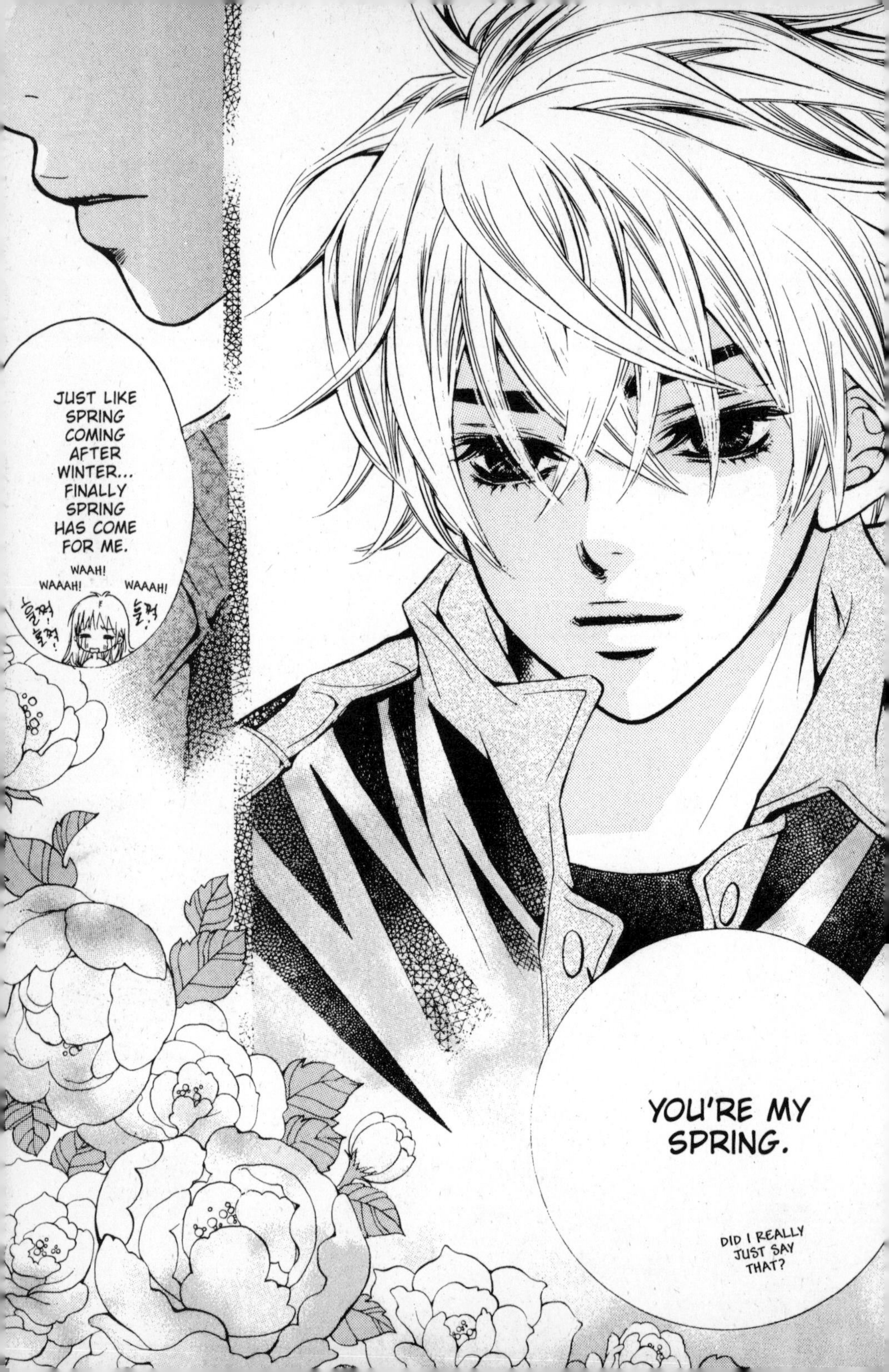
JUST LIKE SPRING COMING AFTER WINTER... FINALLY SPRING HAS COME FOR ME.
WAAAH!
WAAH!
WAAAH!
훌쩍! 훌쩍!
훌쩍!
YOU'RE MY SPRING.
DID I REALLY JUST SAY THAT?

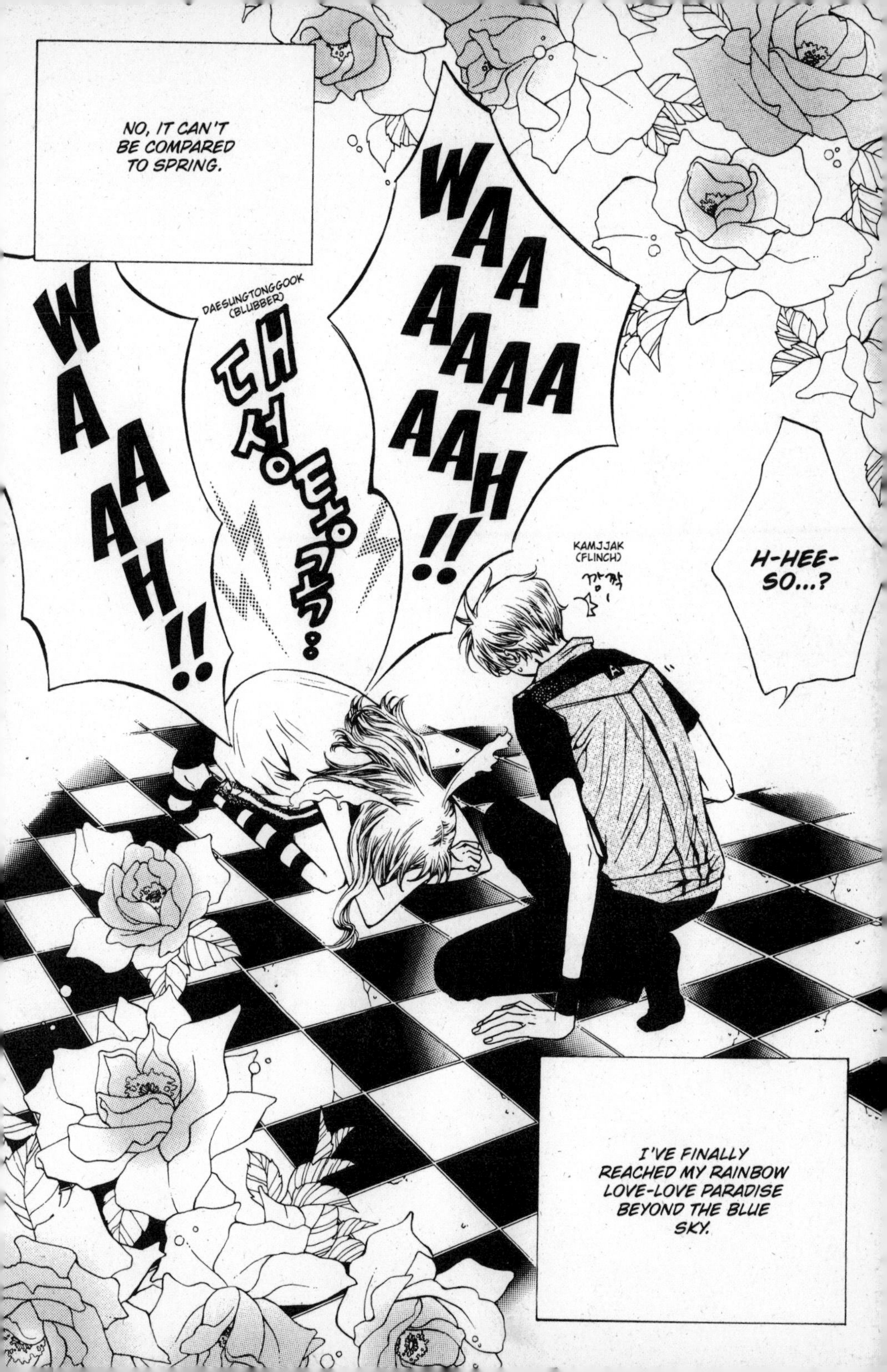

NO, IT CAN'T BE COMPARED TO SPRING.
WAAAH!!
DAESUNGTONGGOOK (BLUBBER)
대성통곡
WAAAAAAAAH!!
KAMJJAK (FLINCH)
깜짝
H-HEE-SO...?
I'VE FINALLY REACHED MY RAINBOW LOVE-LOVE PARADISE BEYOND THE BLUE SKY.

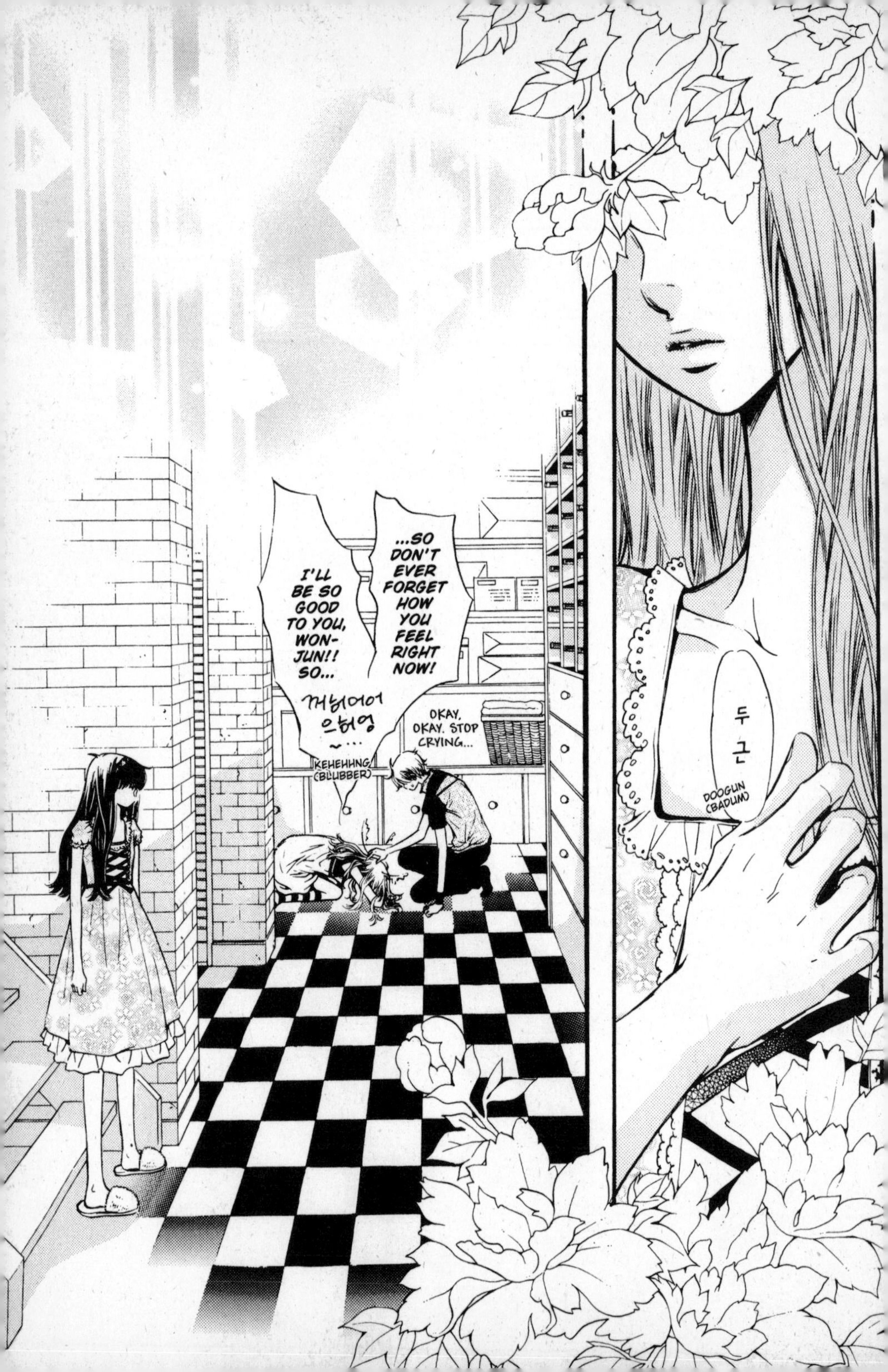

I'LL BE SO GOOD TO YOU, WON-JUN!! SO...
...SO DON'T EVER FORGET HOW YOU FEEL RIGHT NOW!
꺼버어어 으허엉 ~...
KEHEHHNG (BLUBBER)
OKAY, OKAY. STOP CRYING...
두근
DOOGUN (BADUM)

STEP 20. GOOD-BYE, TOE-TOE...

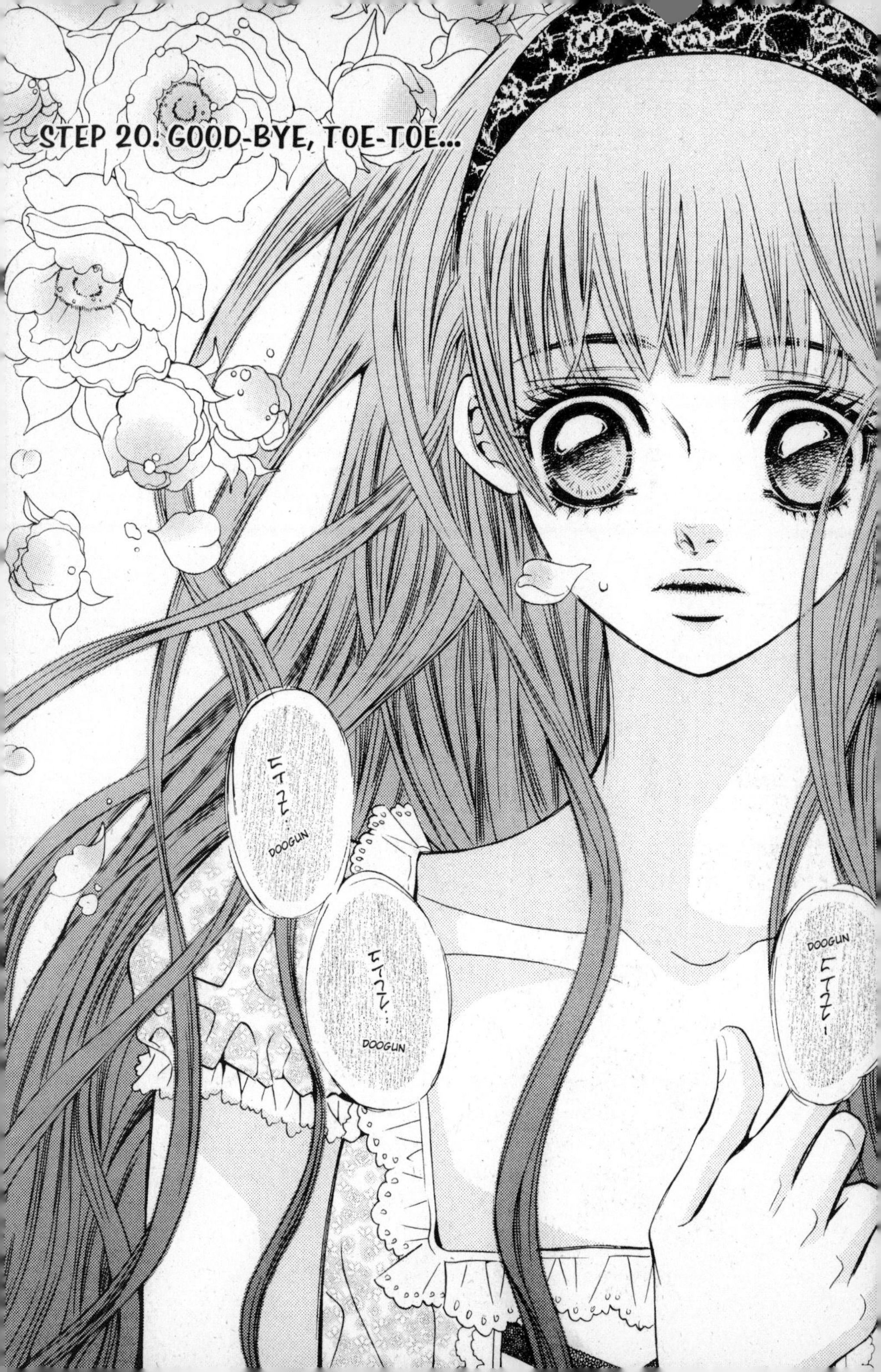
DOOGUN
DOOGUN
DOOGUN

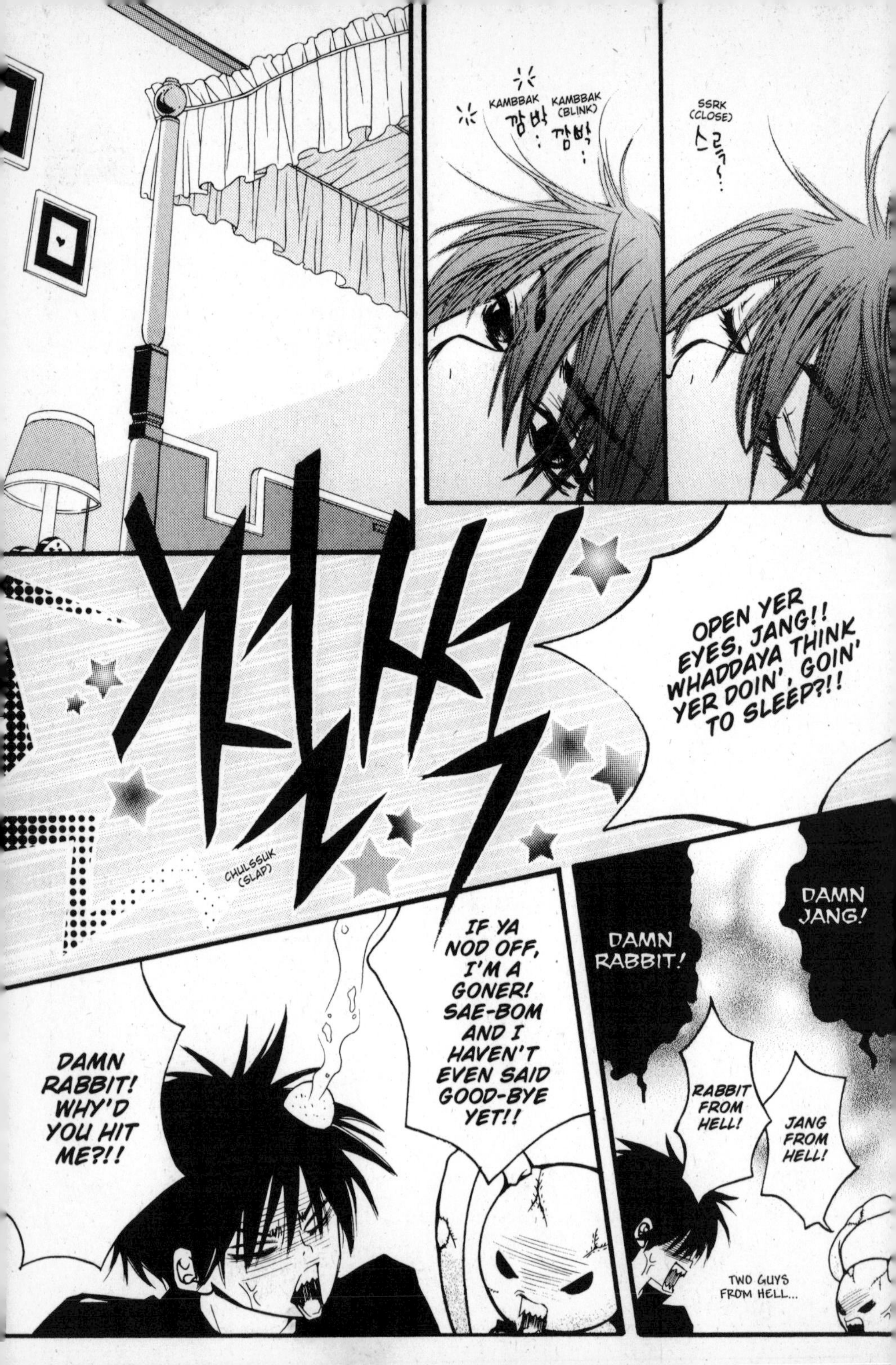
KAMBBAK
깜박
KAMBBAK (BLINK)
깜박
SSRK (CLOSE)
스르륵~...
CHULSSUK (SLAP)
OPEN YER EYES, JANG!! WHADDAYA THINK YER DOIN', GOIN' TO SLEEP?!!
DAMN RABBIT! WHY'D YOU HIT ME?!!
IF YA NOD OFF, I'M A GONER! SAE-BOM AND I HAVEN'T EVEN SAID GOOD-BYE YET!!
DAMN RABBIT!
DAMN JANG!
RABBIT FROM HELL!
JANG FROM HELL!
TWO GUYS FROM HELL...

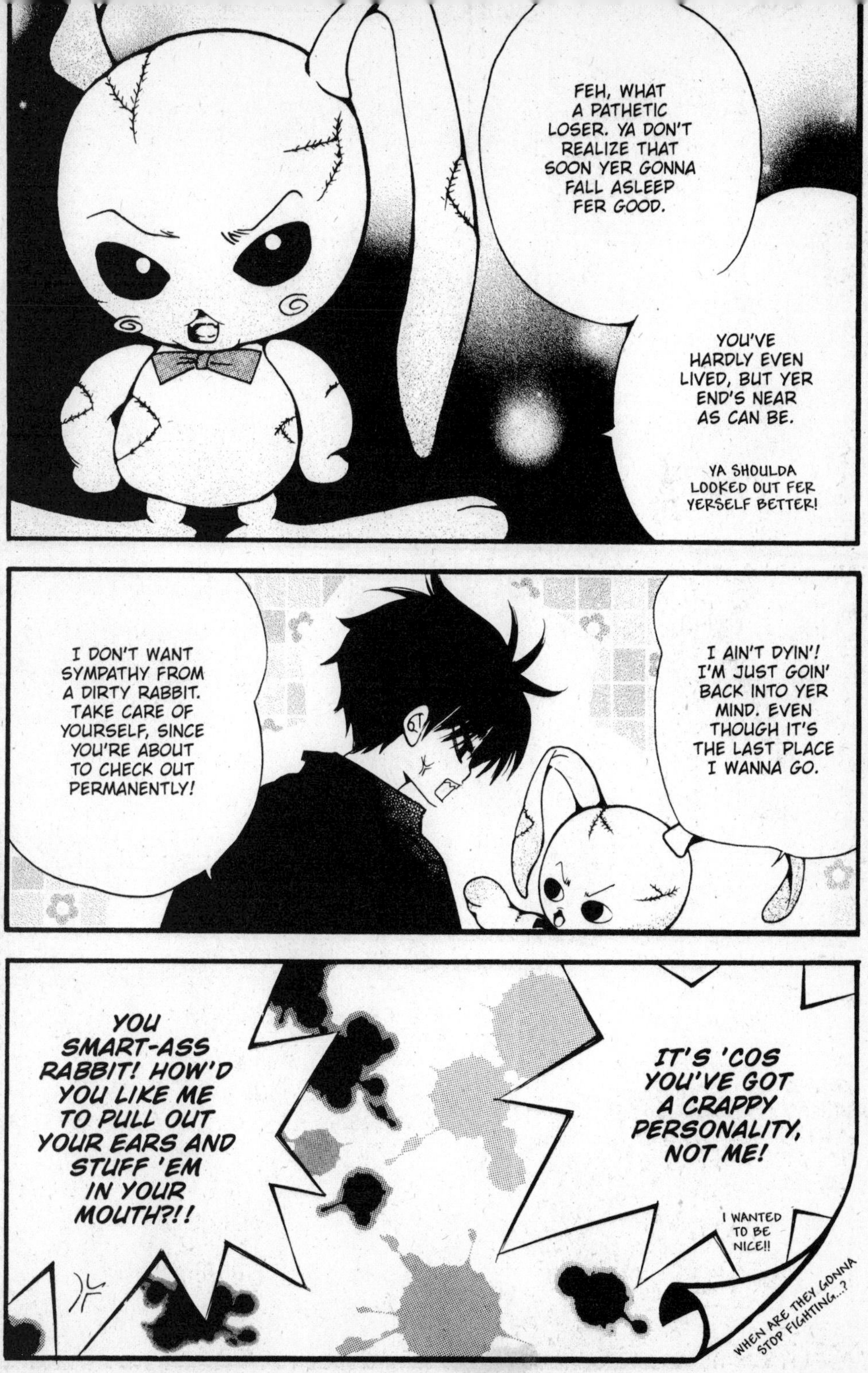
FEH, WHAT A PATHETIC LOSER. YA DON'T REALIZE THAT SOON YER GONNA FALL ASLEEP FER GOOD.
YOU'VE HARDLY EVEN LIVED, BUT YER END'S NEAR AS CAN BE.
YA SHOULDA LOOKED OUT FER YERSELF BETTER!
I DON'T WANT SYMPATHY FROM A DIRTY RABBIT. TAKE CARE OF YOURSELF, SINCE YOU'RE ABOUT TO CHECK OUT PERMANENTLY!
I AIN'T DYIN'! I'M JUST GOIN' BACK INTO YER MIND. EVEN THOUGH IT'S THE LAST PLACE I WANNA GO.
YOU SMART-ASS RABBIT! HOW'D YOU LIKE ME TO PULL OUT YOUR EARS AND STUFF 'EM IN YOUR MOUTH?!!
IT'S 'COS YOU'VE GOT A CRAPPY PERSONALITY, NOT ME!
I WANTED TO BE NICE!!
WHEN ARE THEY GONNA STOP FIGHTING...?

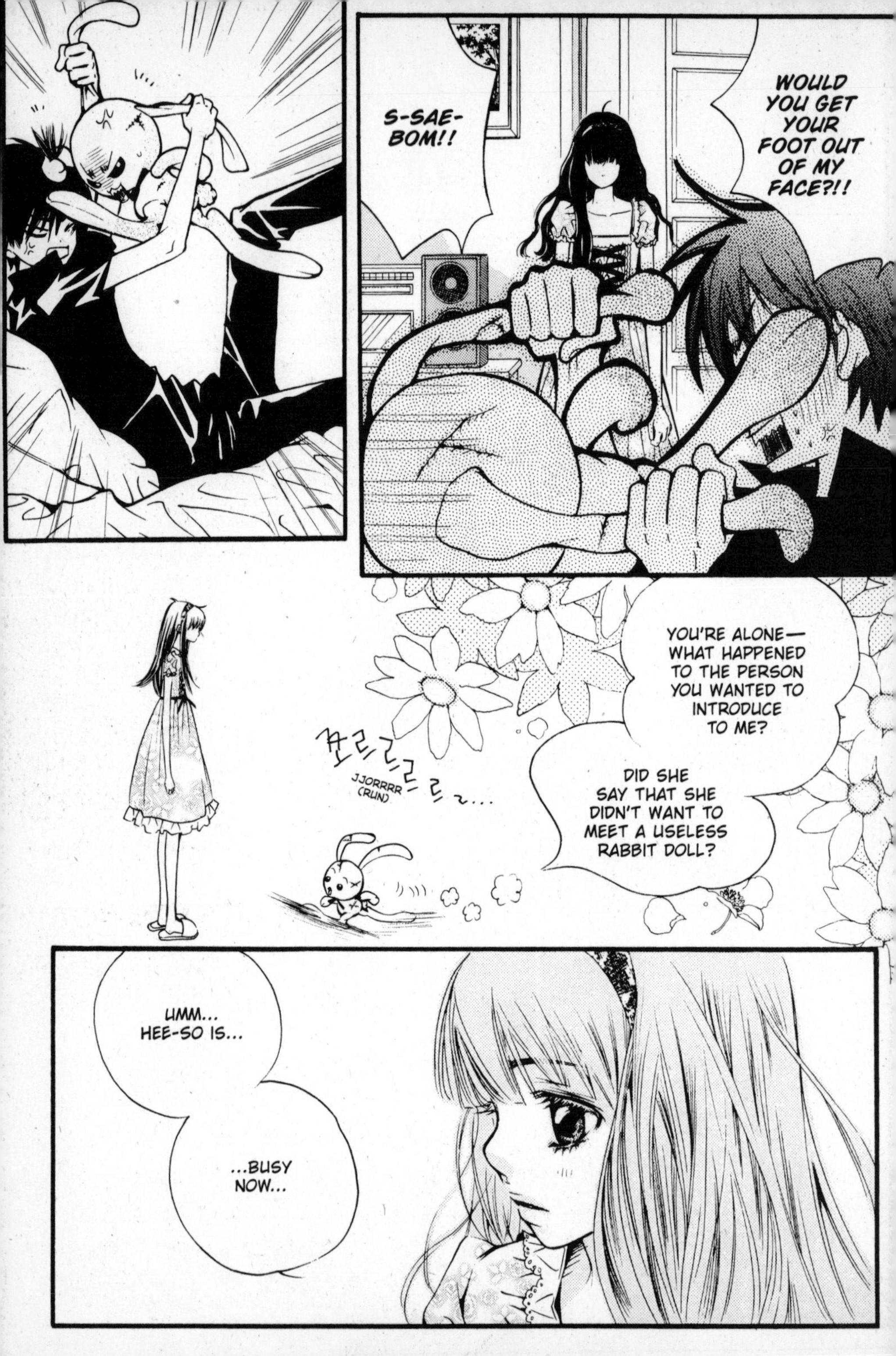
S-SAE-BOM!!
WOULD YOU GET YOUR FOOT OUT OF MY FACE?!!
JJORRRR (RUN)
YOU'RE ALONE—WHAT HAPPENED TO THE PERSON YOU WANTED TO INTRODUCE TO ME?
DID SHE SAY THAT SHE DIDN'T WANT TO MEET A USELESS RABBIT DOLL?
UMM... HEE-SO IS...
...BUSY NOW...

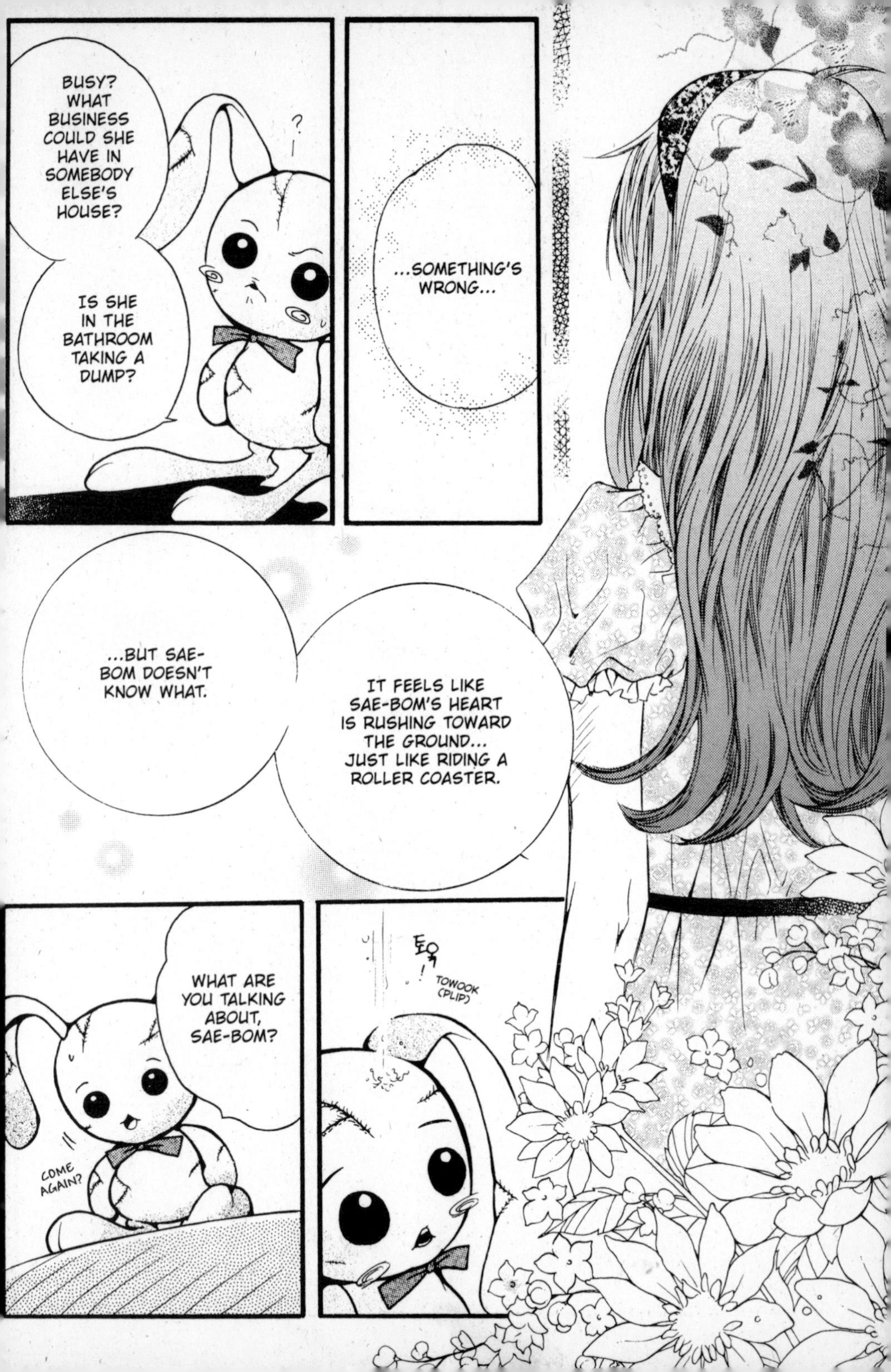
BUSY? WHAT BUSINESS COULD SHE HAVE IN SOMEBODY ELSE'S HOUSE?
IS SHE IN THE BATHROOM TAKING A DUMP?
?
...SOMETHING'S WRONG...
...BUT SAE-BOM DOESN'T KNOW WHAT.
IT FEELS LIKE SAE-BOM'S HEART IS RUSHING TOWARD THE GROUND... JUST LIKE RIDING A ROLLER COASTER.
WHAT ARE YOU TALKING ABOUT, SAE-BOM?
COME AGAIN?
TOWOOK (PLIP)

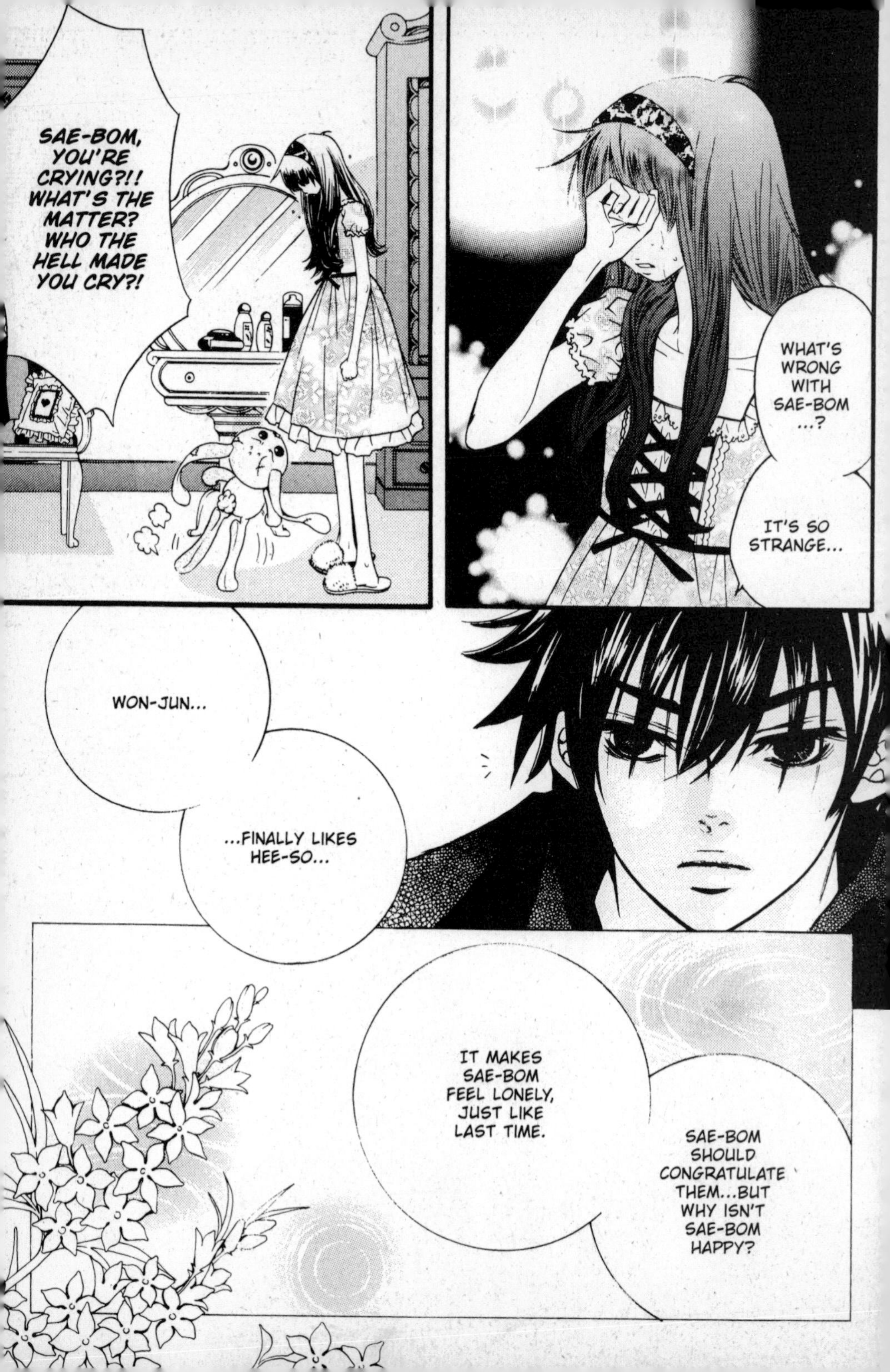
SAE-BOM, YOU'RE CRYING?!! WHAT'S THE MATTER? WHO THE HELL MADE YOU CRY?!
WHAT'S WRONG WITH SAE-BOM ...?
IT'S SO STRANGE...
WON-JUN...
...FINALLY LIKES HEE-SO...
IT MAKES SAE-BOM FEEL LONELY, JUST LIKE LAST TIME.
SAE-BOM SHOULD CONGRATULATE THEM...BUT WHY ISN'T SAE-BOM HAPPY?

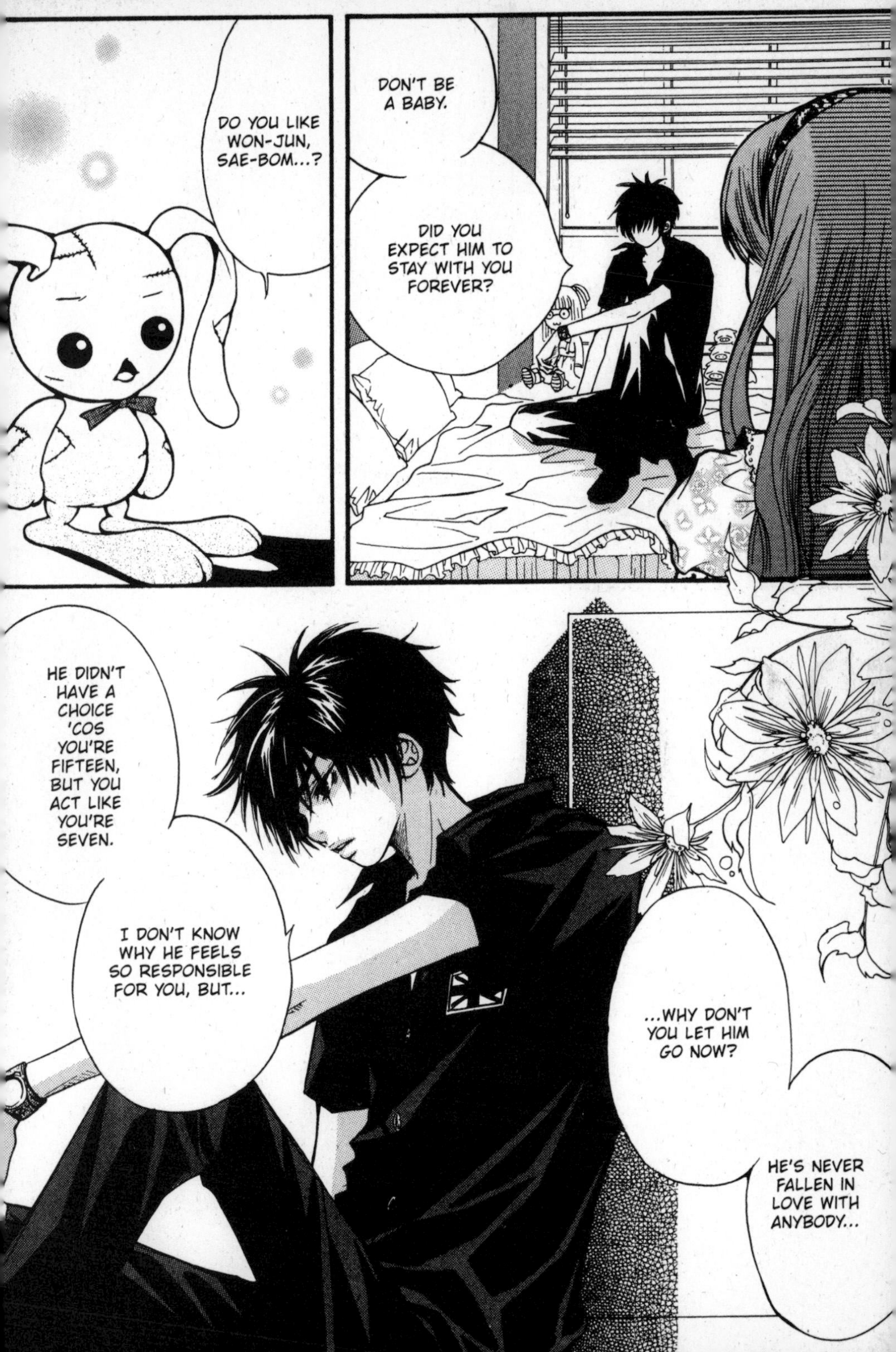
DO YOU LIKE WON-JUN, SAE-BOM...?
DON'T BE A BABY.
DID YOU EXPECT HIM TO STAY WITH YOU FOREVER?
HE DIDN'T HAVE A CHOICE 'COS YOU'RE FIFTEEN, BUT YOU ACT LIKE YOU'RE SEVEN.
I DON'T KNOW WHY HE FEELS SO RESPONSIBLE FOR YOU, BUT...
...WHY DON'T YOU LET HIM GO NOW?
HE'S NEVER FALLEN IN LOVE WITH ANYBODY...

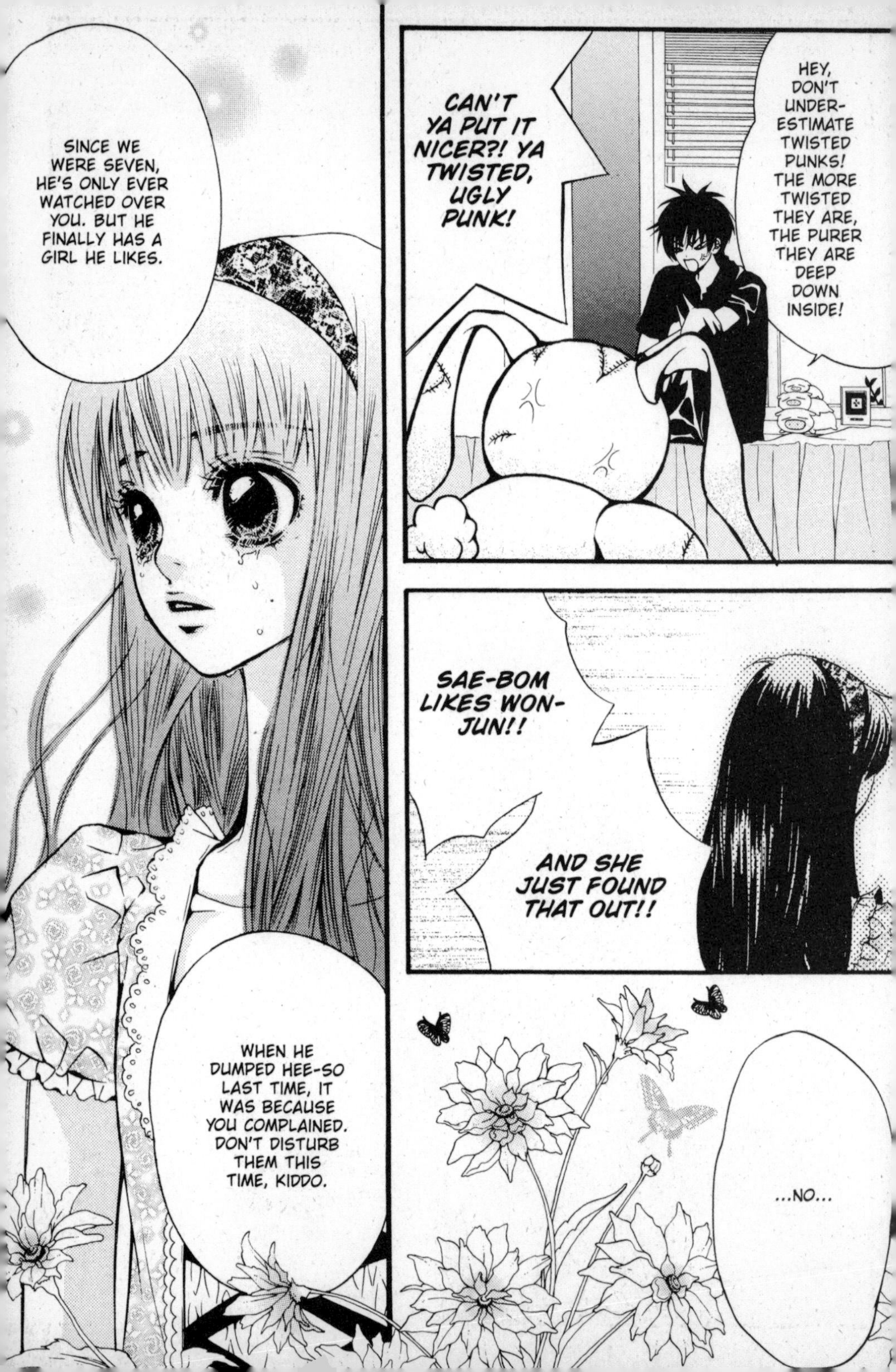
SINCE WE WERE SEVEN, HE'S ONLY EVER WATCHED OVER YOU. BUT HE FINALLY HAS A GIRL HE LIKES.
WHEN HE DUMPED HEE-SO LAST TIME, IT WAS BECAUSE YOU COMPLAINED. DON'T DISTURB THEM THIS TIME, KIDDO.
CAN'T YA PUT IT NICER?! YA TWISTED, UGLY PUNK!
HEY, DON'T UNDER-ESTIMATE TWISTED PUNKS! THE MORE TWISTED THEY ARE, THE PURER THEY ARE DEEP DOWN INSIDE!
SAE-BOM LIKES WON-JUN!!
AND SHE JUST FOUND THAT OUT!!
...NO...

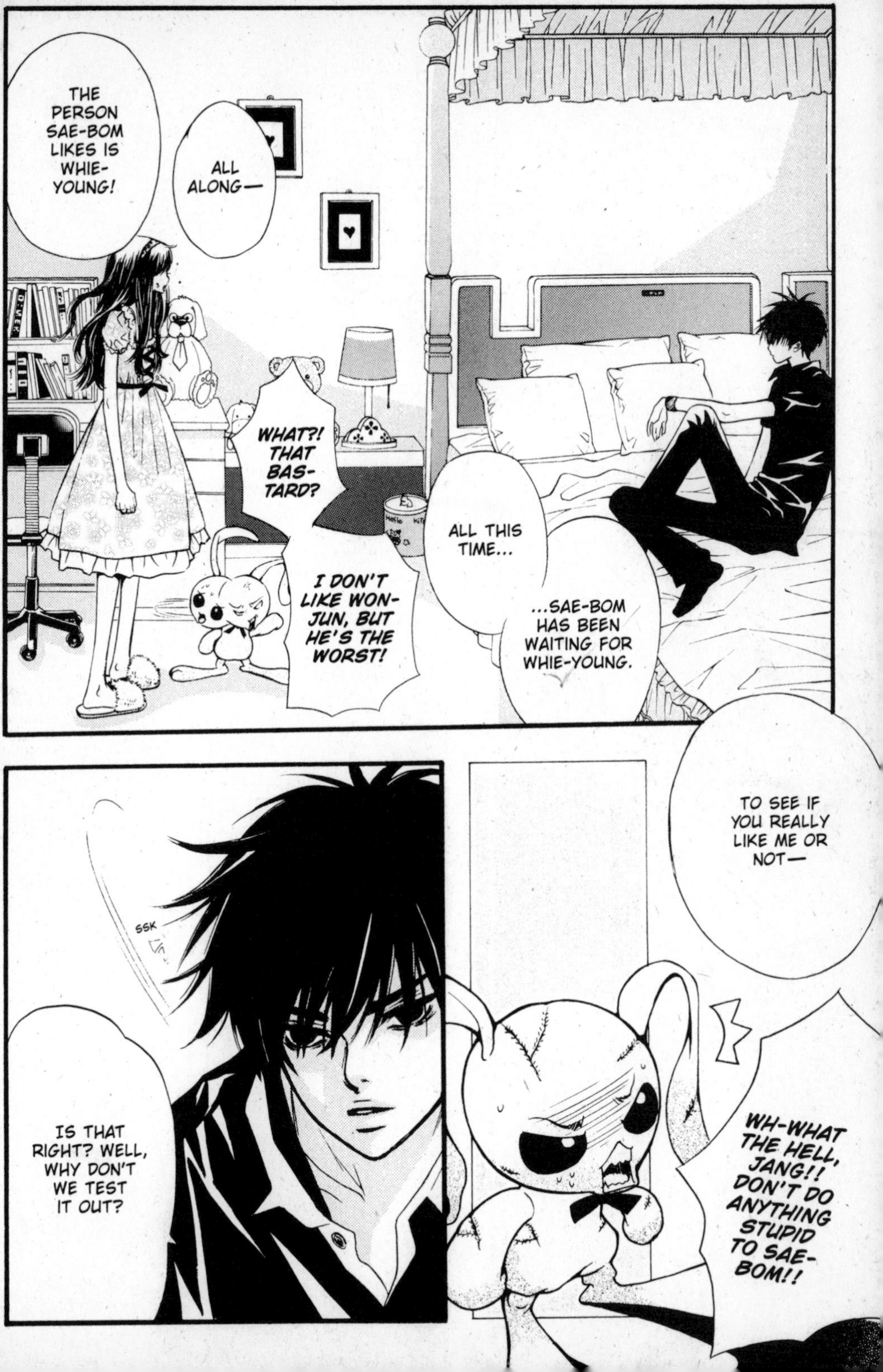

THE PERSON SAE-BOM LIKES IS WHIE-YOUNG!
ALL ALONG—
WHAT?! THAT BAS-TARD?
I DON'T LIKE WON-JUN, BUT HE'S THE WORST!
ALL THIS TIME...
...SAE-BOM HAS BEEN WAITING FOR WHIE-YOUNG.
SSK
IS THAT RIGHT? WELL, WHY DON'T WE TEST IT OUT?
TO SEE IF YOU REALLY LIKE ME OR NOT—
WH-WHAT THE HELL, JANG!! DON'T DO ANYTHING STUPID TO SAE-BOM!!

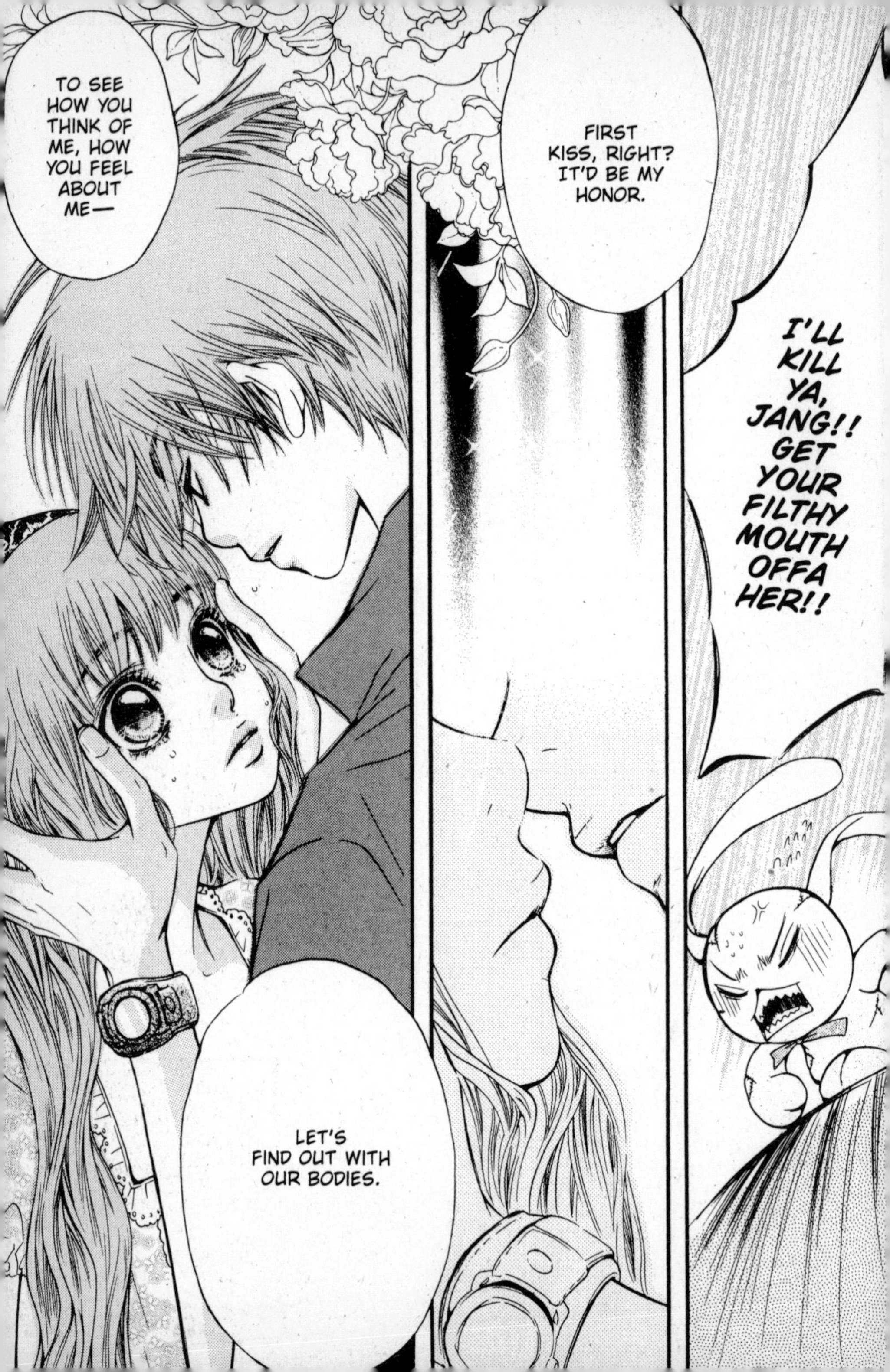
TO SEE HOW YOU THINK OF ME, HOW YOU FEEL ABOUT ME—
LET'S FIND OUT WITH OUR BODIES.
FIRST KISS, RIGHT? IT'D BE MY HONOR.
I'LL KILL YA, JANG!! GET YOUR FILTHY MOUTH OFFA HER!!

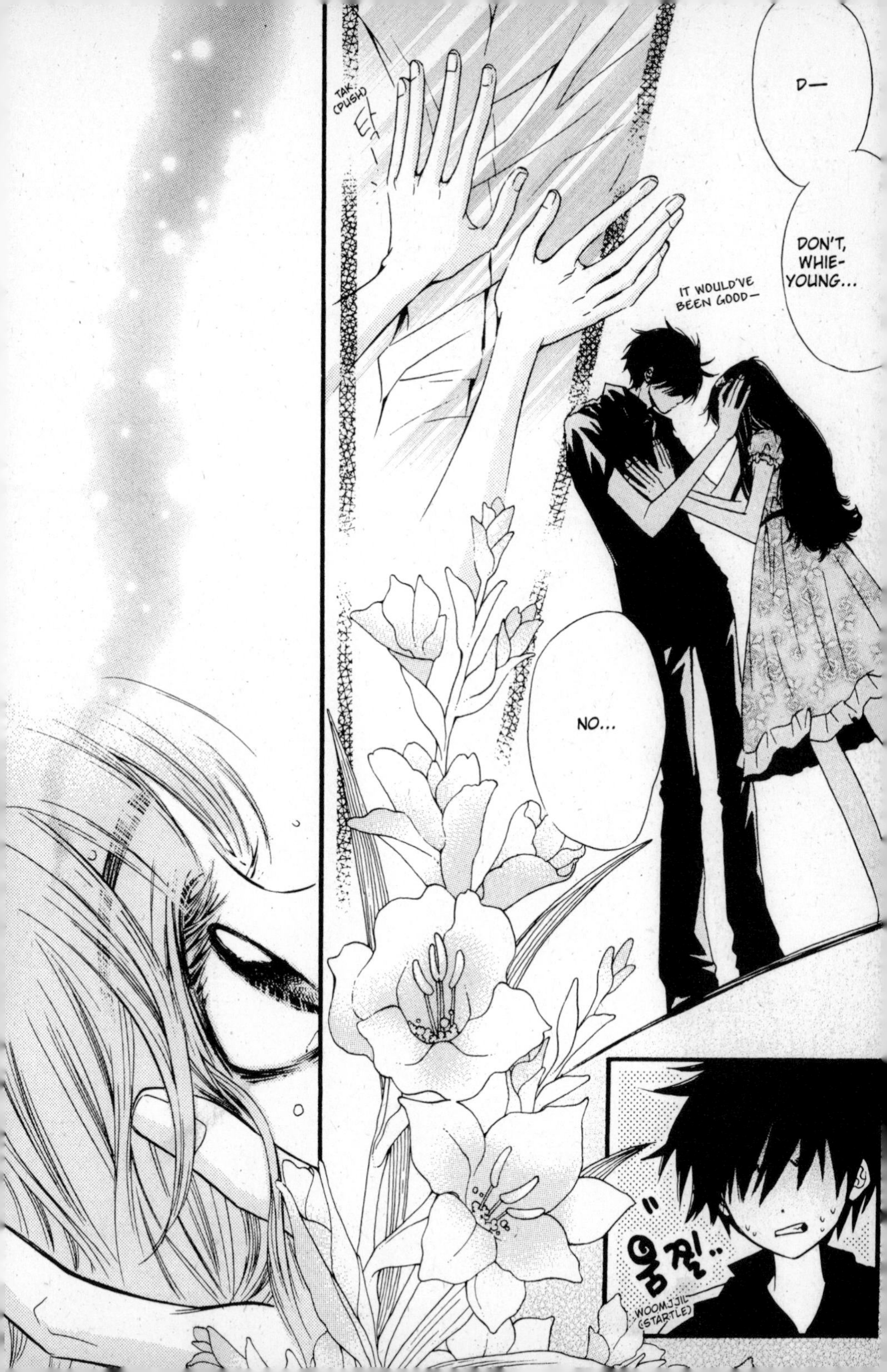

TAK (PUSH)
D—
DON'T, WHIE-YOUNG...
IT WOULD'VE BEEN GOOD—
NO...
움찔!..
WOOMJJIL (STARTLE)

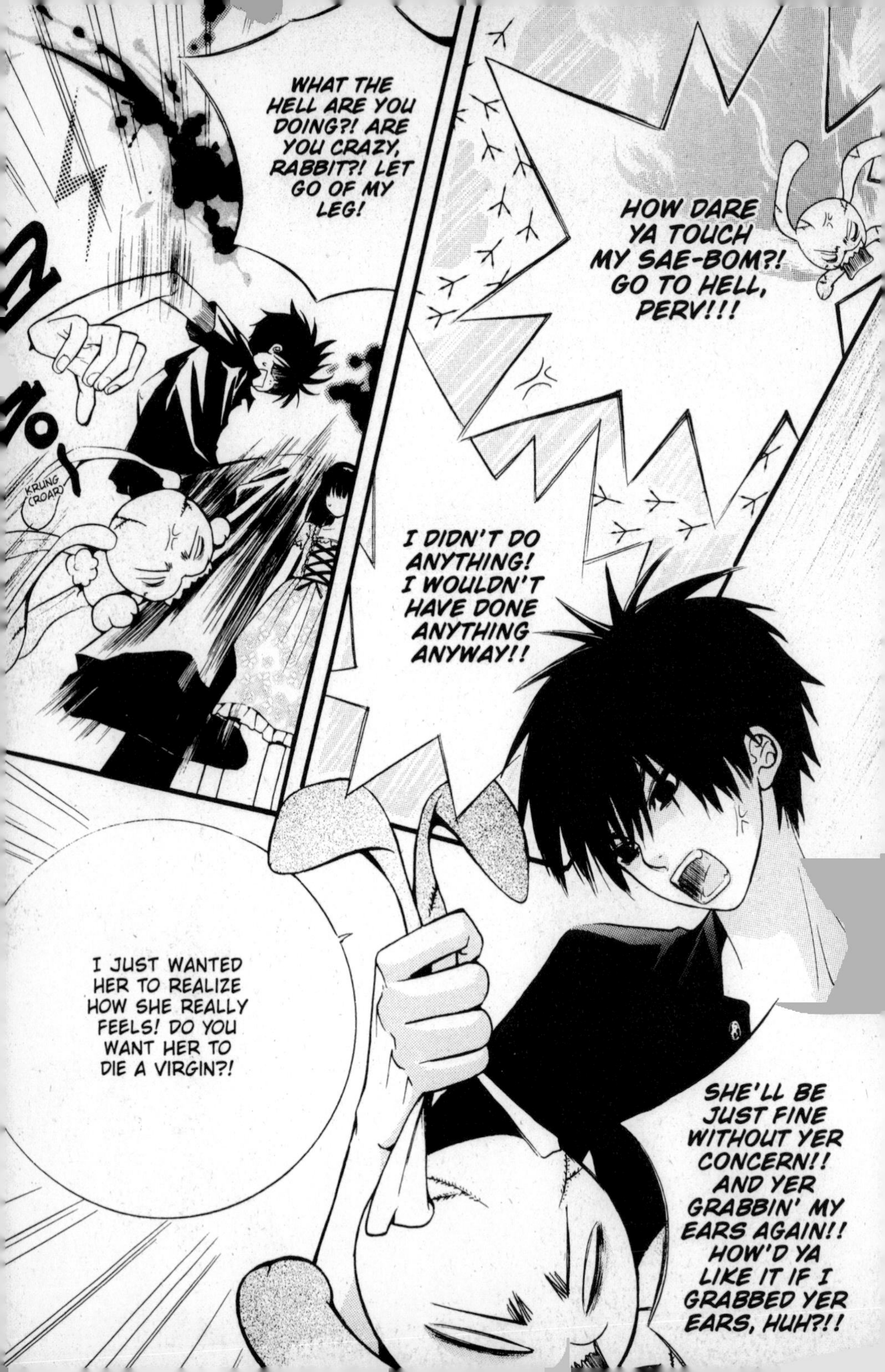
WHAT THE HELL ARE YOU DOING?! ARE YOU CRAZY, RABBIT?! LET GO OF MY LEG!
KRUNG (ROAR)
HOW DARE YA TOUCH MY SAE-BOM?! GO TO HELL, PERV!!!
I DIDN'T DO ANYTHING! I WOULDN'T HAVE DONE ANYTHING ANYWAY!!
I JUST WANTED HER TO REALIZE HOW SHE REALLY FEELS! DO YOU WANT HER TO DIE A VIRGIN?!
SHE'LL BE JUST FINE WITHOUT YER CONCERN!! AND YER GRABBIN' MY EARS AGAIN!! HOW'D YA LIKE IT IF I GRABBED YER EARS, HUH?!!

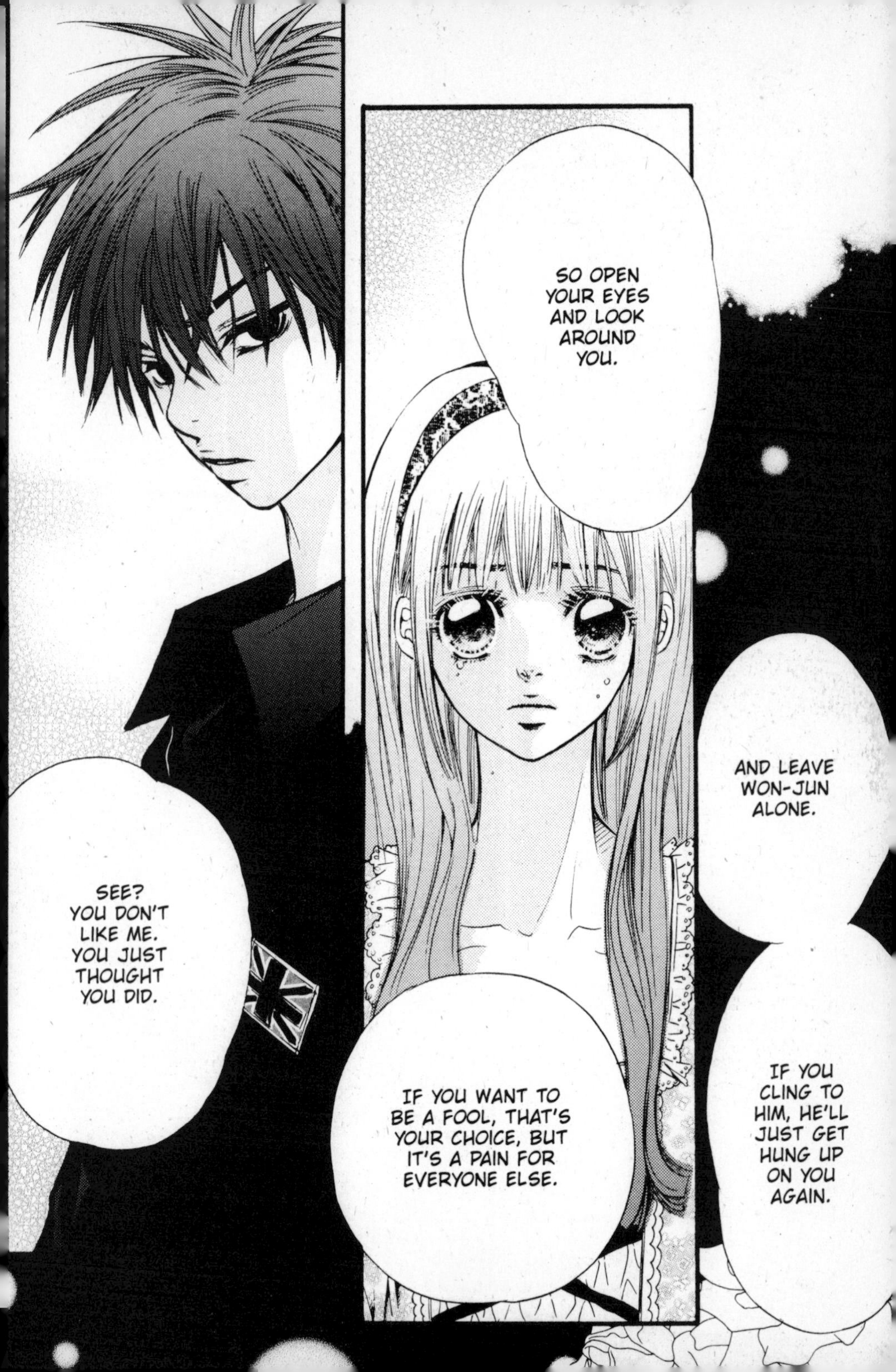
SEE? YOU DON'T LIKE ME. YOU JUST THOUGHT YOU DID.
SO OPEN YOUR EYES AND LOOK AROUND YOU.
IF YOU WANT TO BE A FOOL, THAT'S YOUR CHOICE, BUT IT'S A PAIN FOR EVERYONE ELSE.
AND LEAVE WON-JUN ALONE.
IF YOU CLING TO HIM, HE'LL JUST GET HUNG UP ON YOU AGAIN.

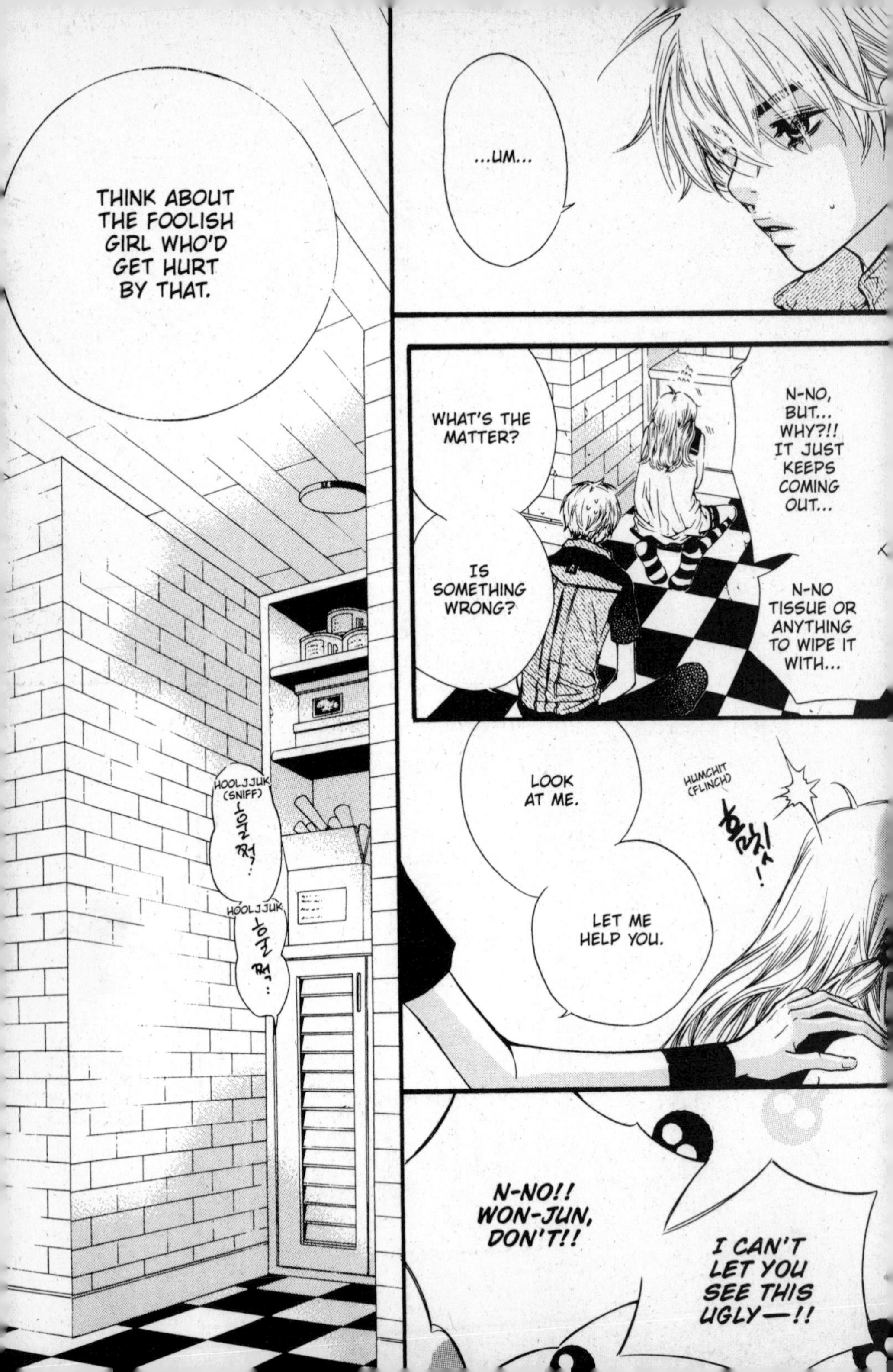
THINK ABOUT THE FOOLISH GIRL WHO'D GET HURT BY THAT.
HOOLJJUK (SNIFF)
훌쩍..
HOOLJJUK
훌쩍..
...UM...
WHAT'S THE MATTER?
IS SOMETHING WRONG?
N-NO, BUT... WHY?!! IT JUST KEEPS COMING OUT...
N-NO TISSUE OR ANYTHING TO WIPE IT WITH...
LOOK AT ME.
LET ME HELP YOU.
HUMCHIT (FLINCH)
흠칫!
N-NO!! WON-JUN, DON'T!!
I CAN'T LET YOU SEE THIS UGLY—!!

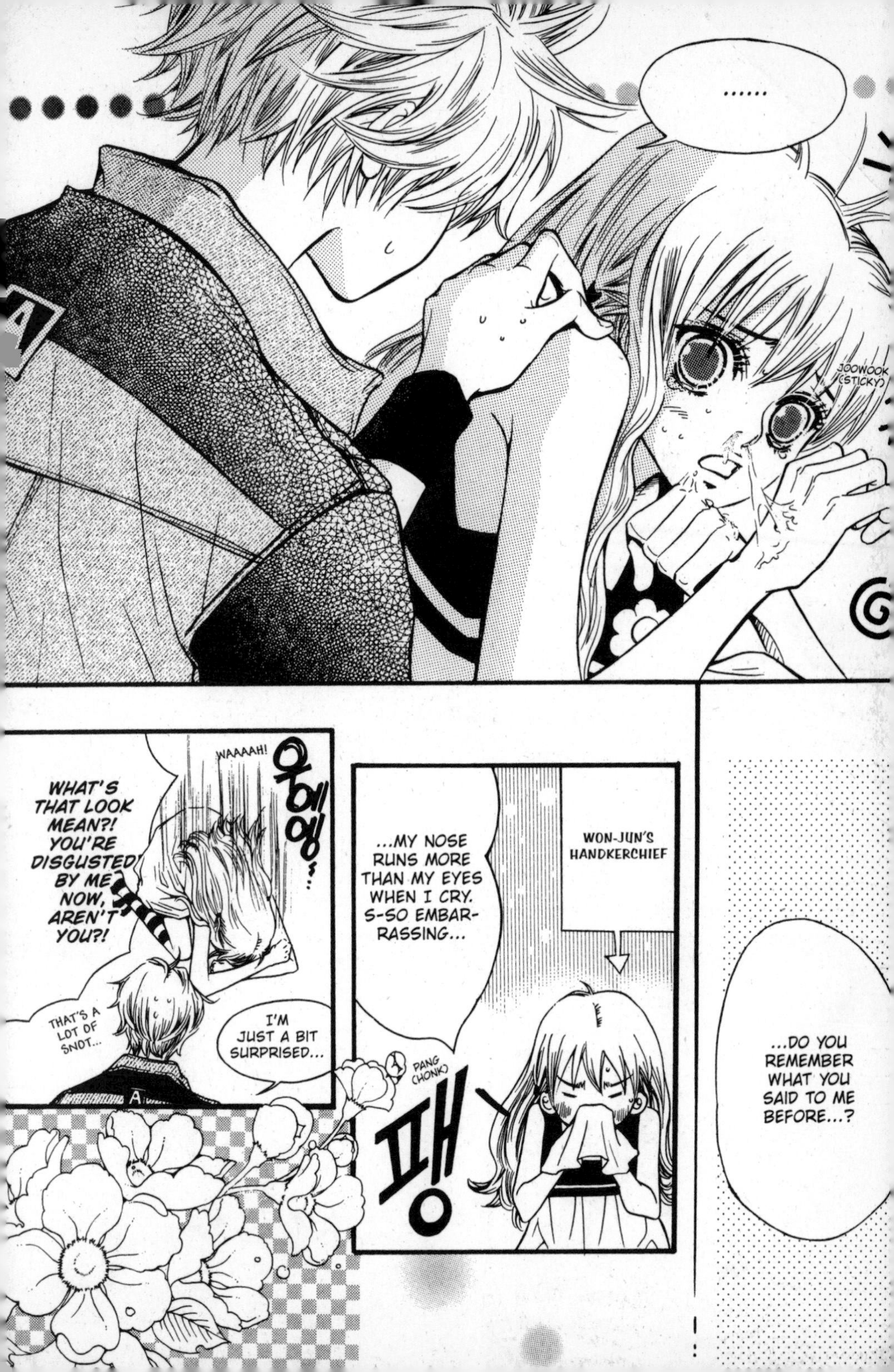
......
JOOWOOK (STICKY)
WAAAAH!
우에엥...
WHAT'S THAT LOOK MEAN?! YOU'RE DISGUSTED BY ME NOW, AREN'T YOU?!
THAT'S A LOT OF SNOT...
I'M JUST A BIT SURPRISED...
...MY NOSE RUNS MORE THAN MY EYES WHEN I CRY. S-SO EMBARRASSING...
WON-JUN'S HANDKERCHIEF
PANG (HONK)
팽!
...DO YOU REMEMBER WHAT YOU SAID TO ME BEFORE...?

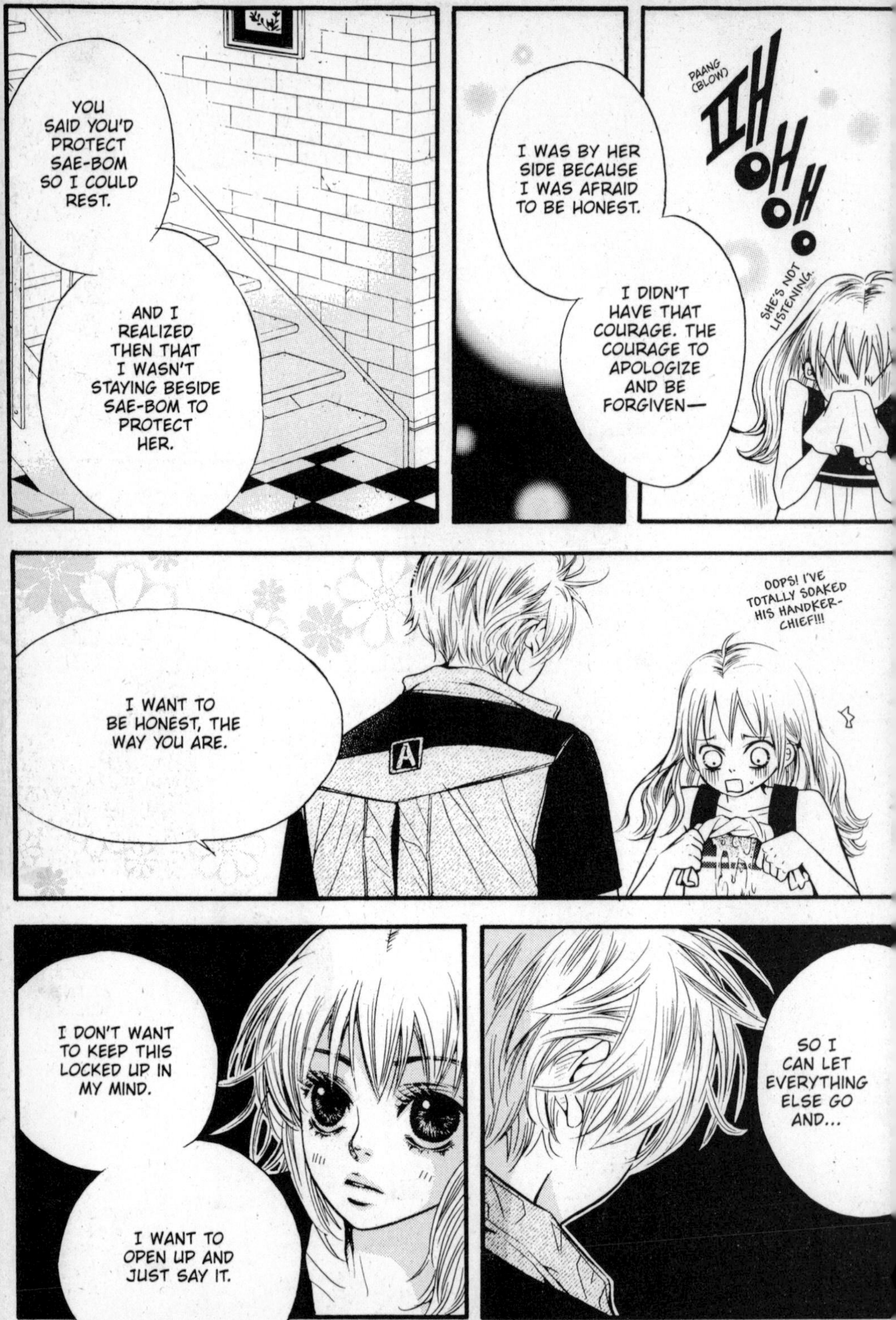
YOU SAID YOU'D PROTECT SAE-BOM SO I COULD REST.
AND I REALIZED THEN THAT I WASN'T STAYING BESIDE SAE-BOM TO PROTECT HER.
I WAS BY HER SIDE BECAUSE I WAS AFRAID TO BE HONEST.
I DIDN'T HAVE THAT COURAGE. THE COURAGE TO APOLOGIZE AND BE FORGIVEN—
PAANG (BLOW)
파앙!!
SHE'S NOT LISTENING.
I WANT TO BE HONEST, THE WAY YOU ARE.
OOPS! I'VE TOTALLY SOAKED HIS HANDKER-CHIEF!!!
I DON'T WANT TO KEEP THIS LOCKED UP IN MY MIND.
I WANT TO OPEN UP AND JUST SAY IT.
SO I CAN LET EVERYTHING ELSE GO AND...

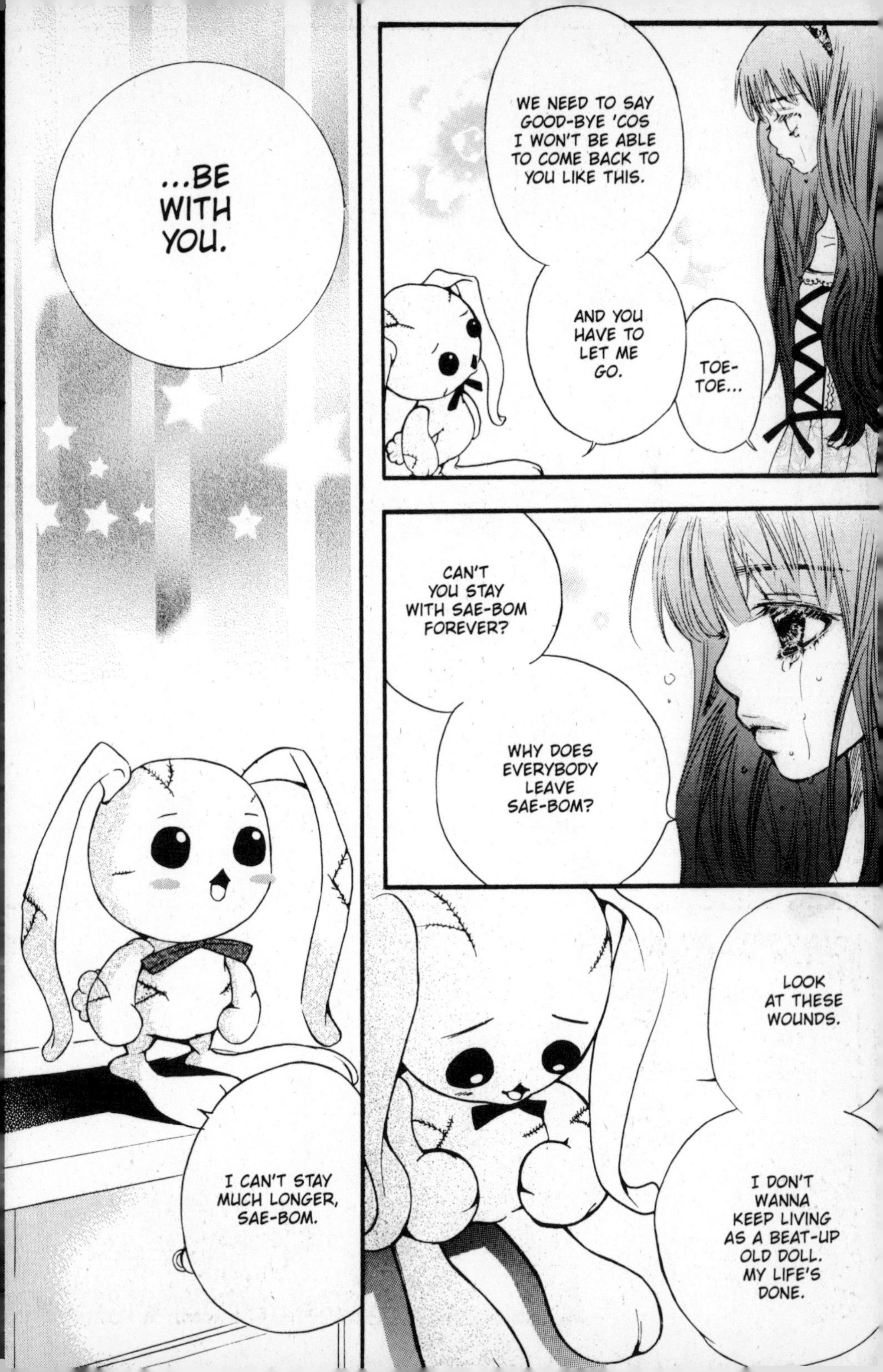
...BE WITH YOU.
I CAN'T STAY MUCH LONGER, SAE-BOM.
WE NEED TO SAY GOOD-BYE 'COS I WON'T BE ABLE TO COME BACK TO YOU LIKE THIS.
AND YOU HAVE TO LET ME GO.
TOE-TOE...
CAN'T YOU STAY WITH SAE-BOM FOREVER?
WHY DOES EVERYBODY LEAVE SAE-BOM?
LOOK AT THESE WOUNDS.
I DON'T WANNA KEEP LIVING AS A BEAT-UP OLD DOLL. MY LIFE'S DONE.

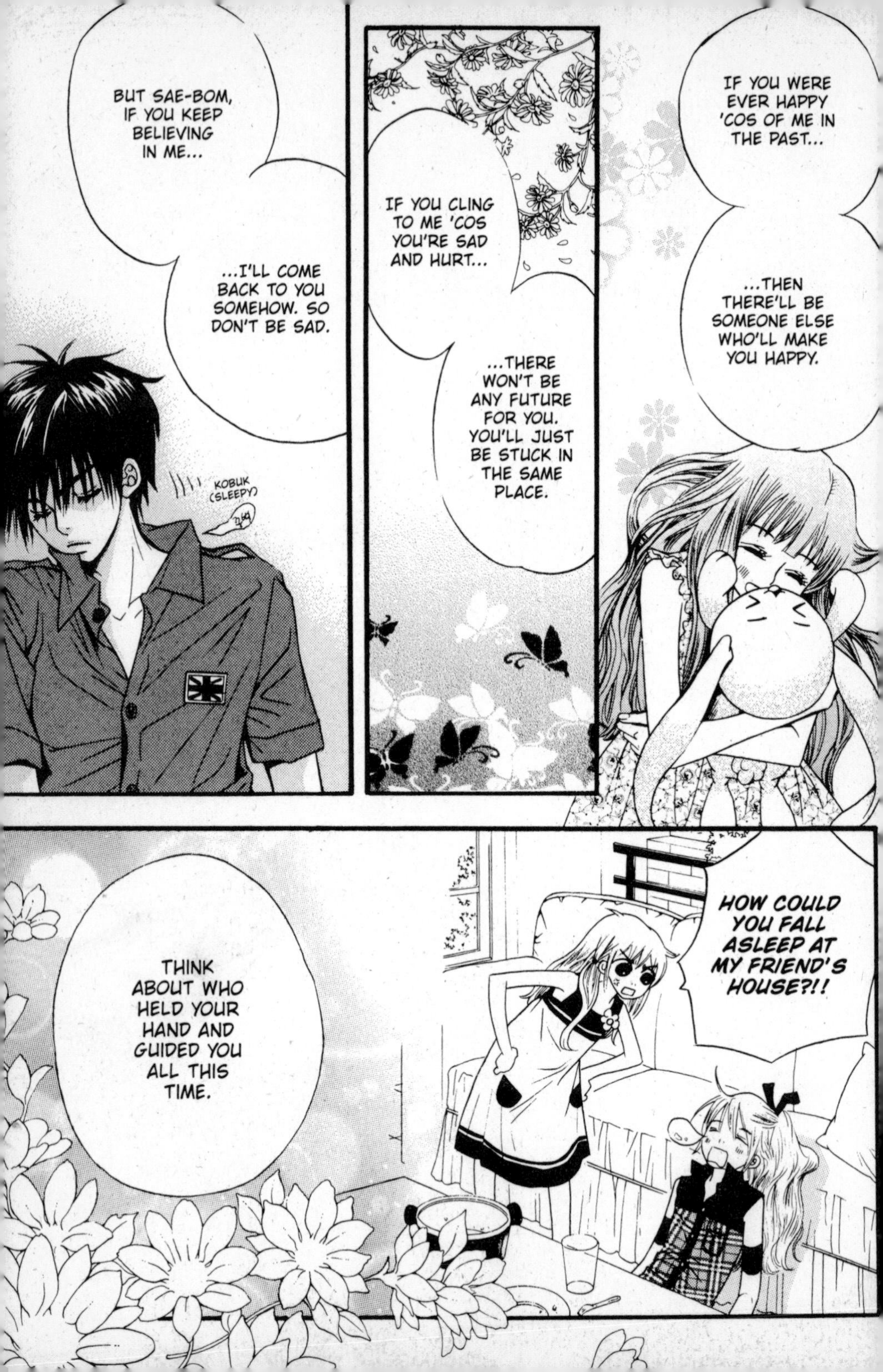
BUT SAE-BOM, IF YOU KEEP BELIEVING IN ME...
...I'LL COME BACK TO YOU SOMEHOW. SO DON'T BE SAD.
KOBUK (SLEEPY)
IF YOU CLING TO ME 'COS YOU'RE SAD AND HURT...
...THERE WON'T BE ANY FUTURE FOR YOU. YOU'LL JUST BE STUCK IN THE SAME PLACE.
IF YOU WERE EVER HAPPY 'COS OF ME IN THE PAST...
...THEN THERE'LL BE SOMEONE ELSE WHO'LL MAKE YOU HAPPY.
THINK ABOUT WHO HELD YOUR HAND AND GUIDED YOU ALL THIS TIME.
HOW COULD YOU FALL ASLEEP AT MY FRIEND'S HOUSE?!!

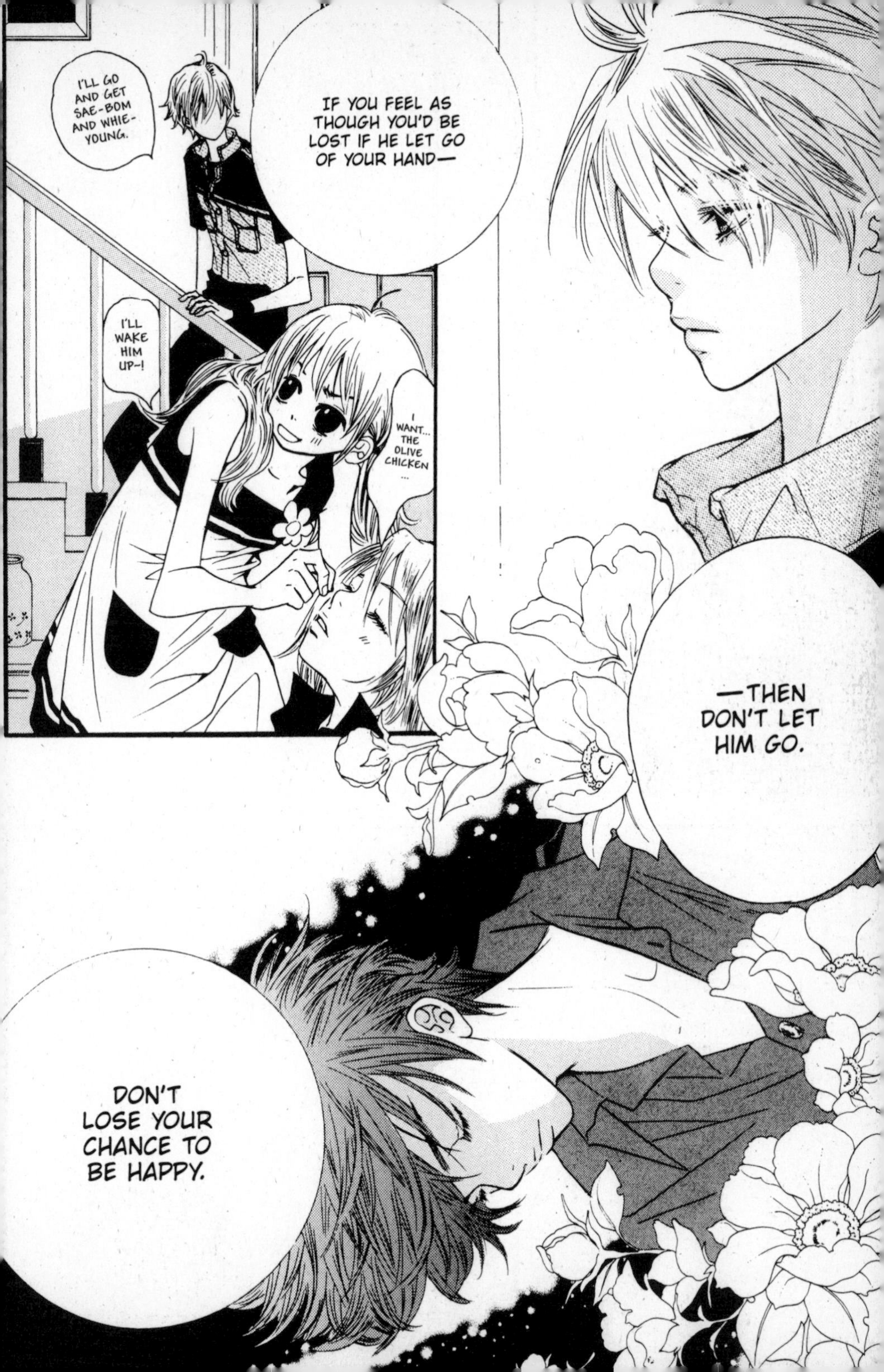
I'LL GO AND GET SAE-BOM AND WHIE-YOUNG.
I'LL WAKE HIM UP-!
I WANT... THE OLIVE CHICKEN ...
IF YOU FEEL AS THOUGH YOU'D BE LOST IF HE LET GO OF YOUR HAND—
—THEN DON'T LET HIM GO.
DON'T LOSE YOUR CHANCE TO BE HAPPY.

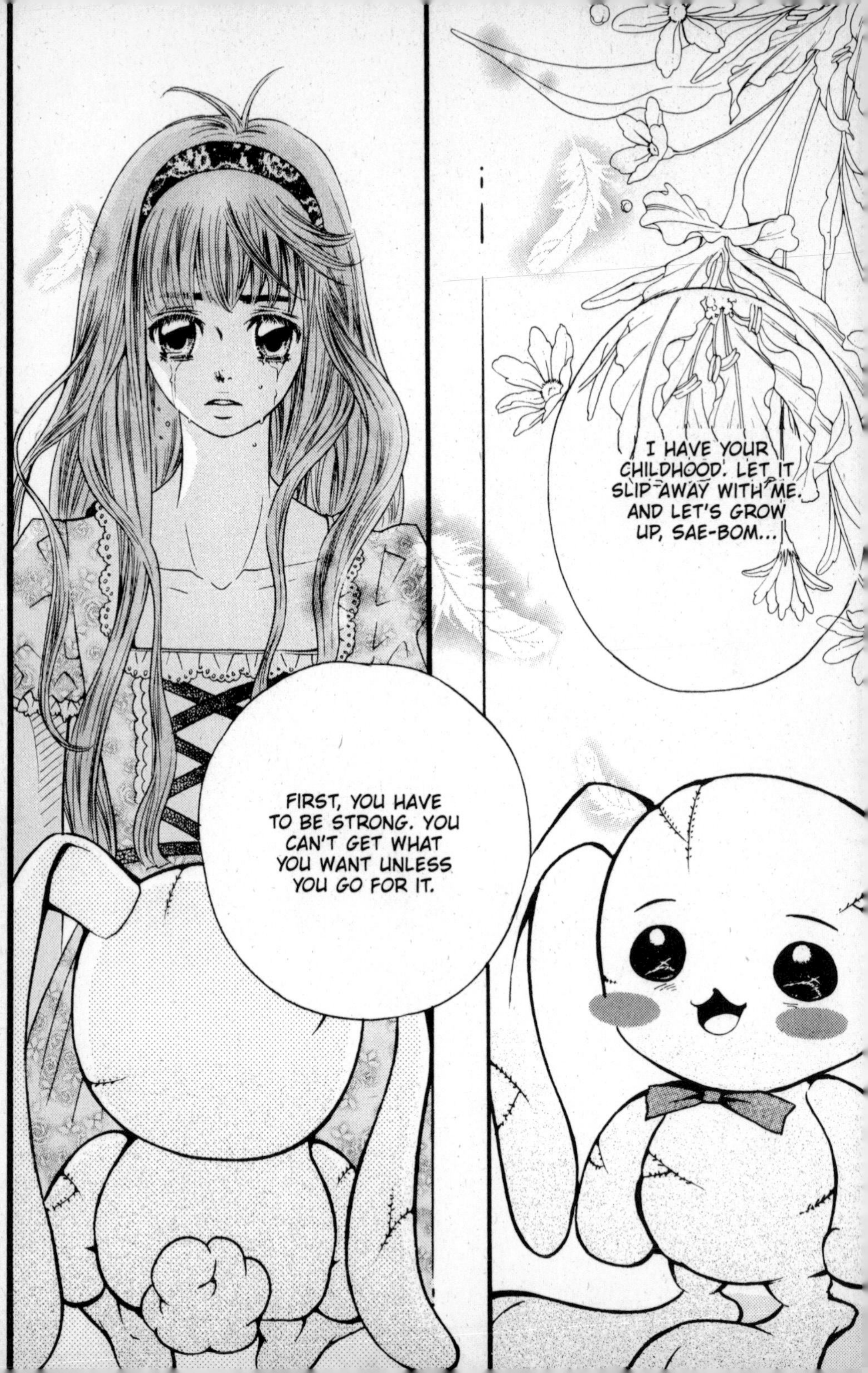
FIRST, YOU HAVE TO BE STRONG. YOU CAN'T GET WHAT YOU WANT UNLESS YOU GO FOR IT.
I HAVE YOUR CHILDHOOD. LET IT SLIP AWAY WITH ME. AND LET'S GROW UP, SAE-BOM...

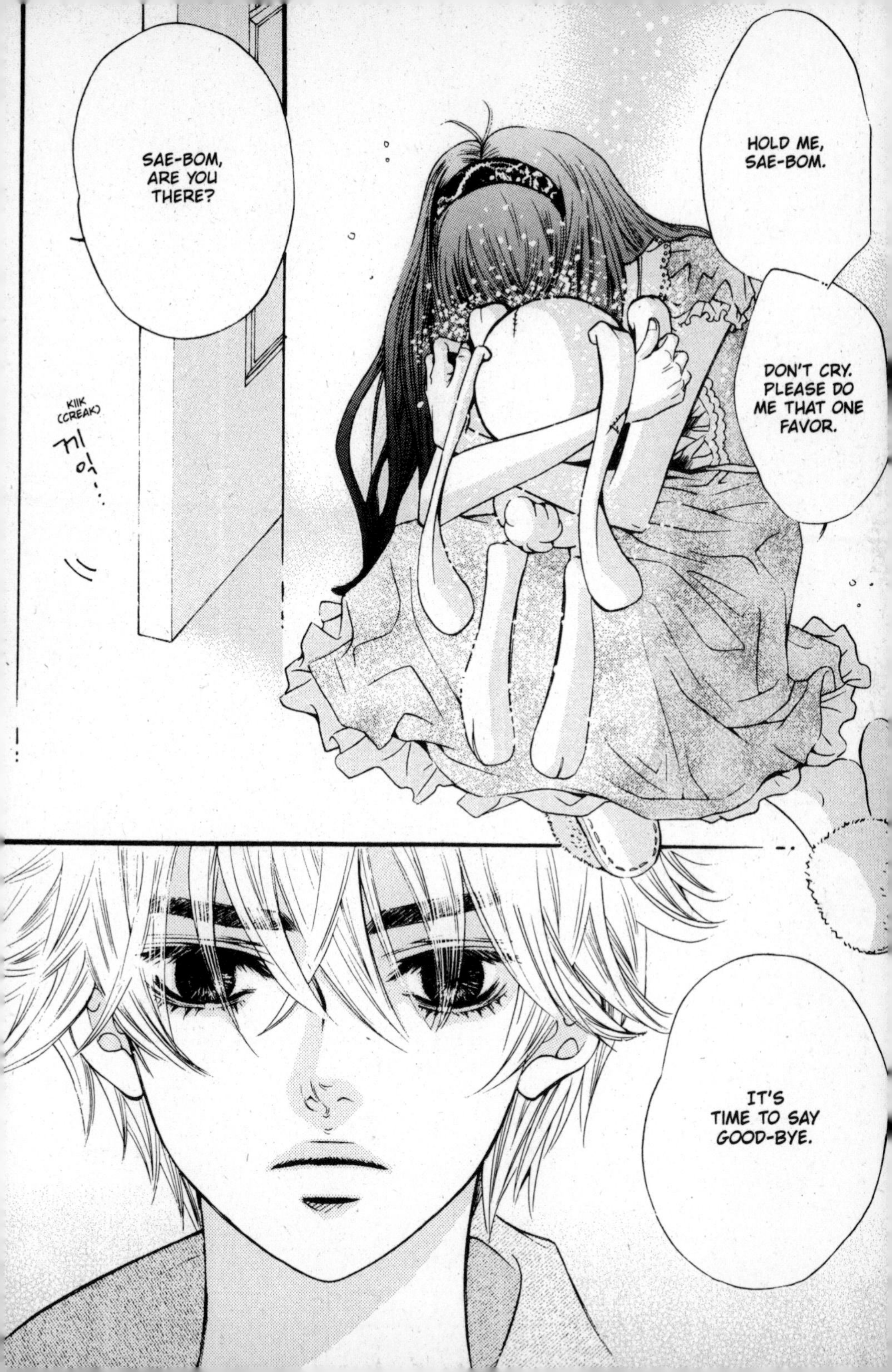
SAE-BOM, ARE YOU THERE?
KIIK (CREAK)
끼익...
HOLD ME, SAE-BOM.
DON'T CRY. PLEASE DO ME THAT ONE FAVOR.
IT'S TIME TO SAY GOOD-BYE.

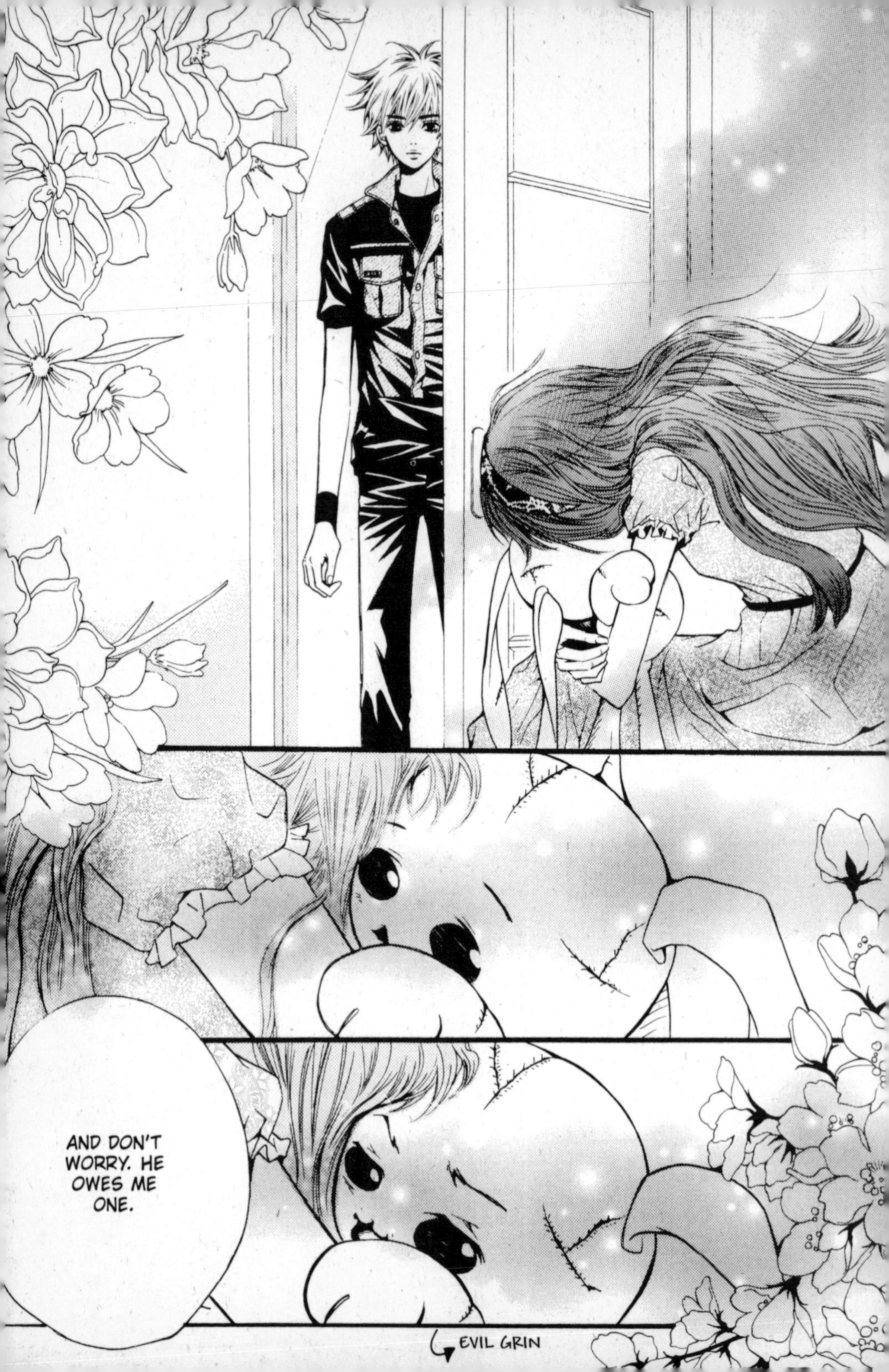
AND DON'T WORRY. HE OWES ME ONE.
EVIL GRIN

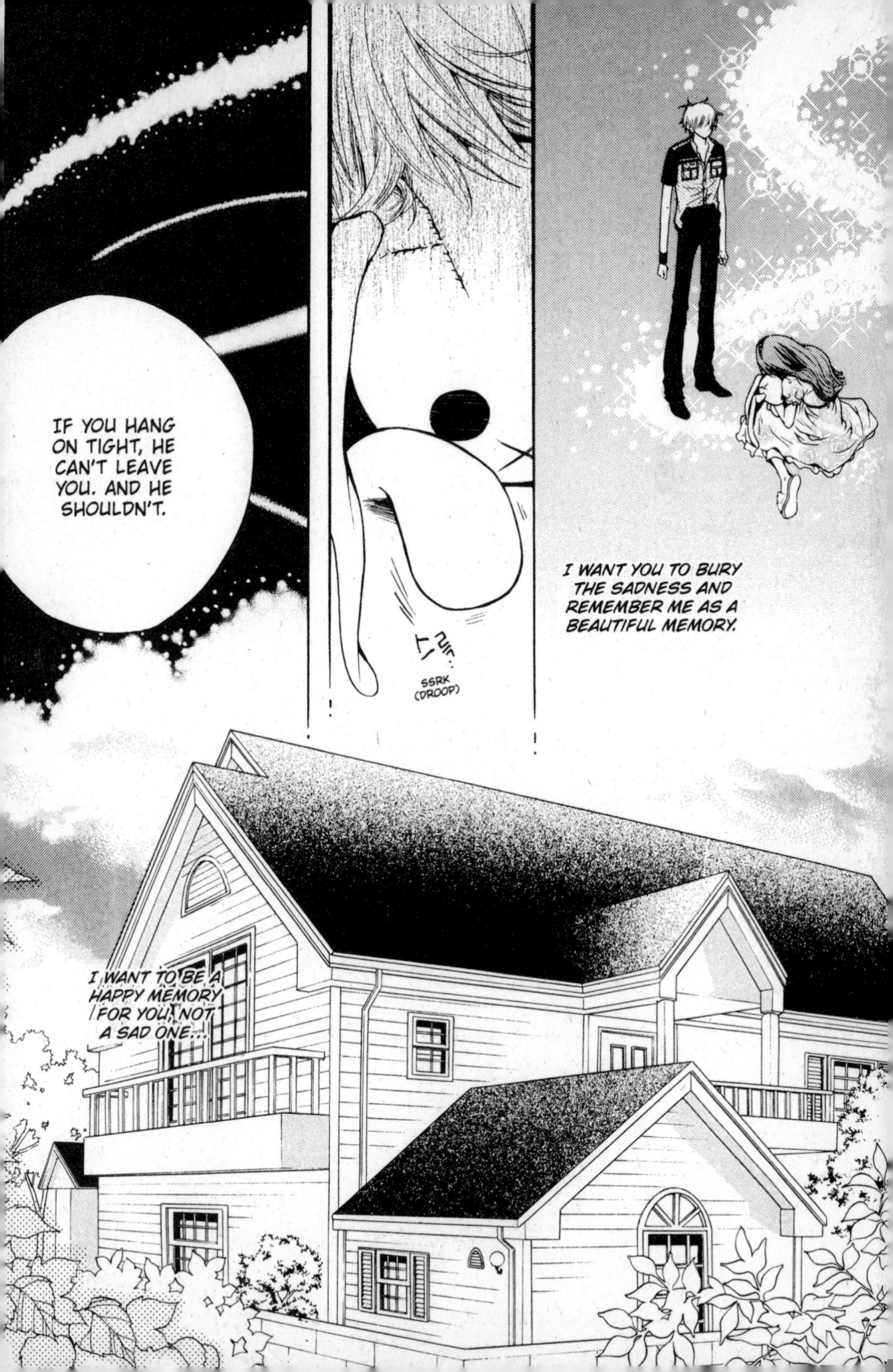
IF YOU HANG ON TIGHT, HE CAN'T LEAVE YOU. AND HE SHOULDN'T.
SSRK (DROOP)
I WANT YOU TO BURY THE SADNESS AND REMEMBER ME AS A BEAUTIFUL MEMORY.
I WANT TO BE A HAPPY MEMORY FOR YOU, NOT A SAD ONE...

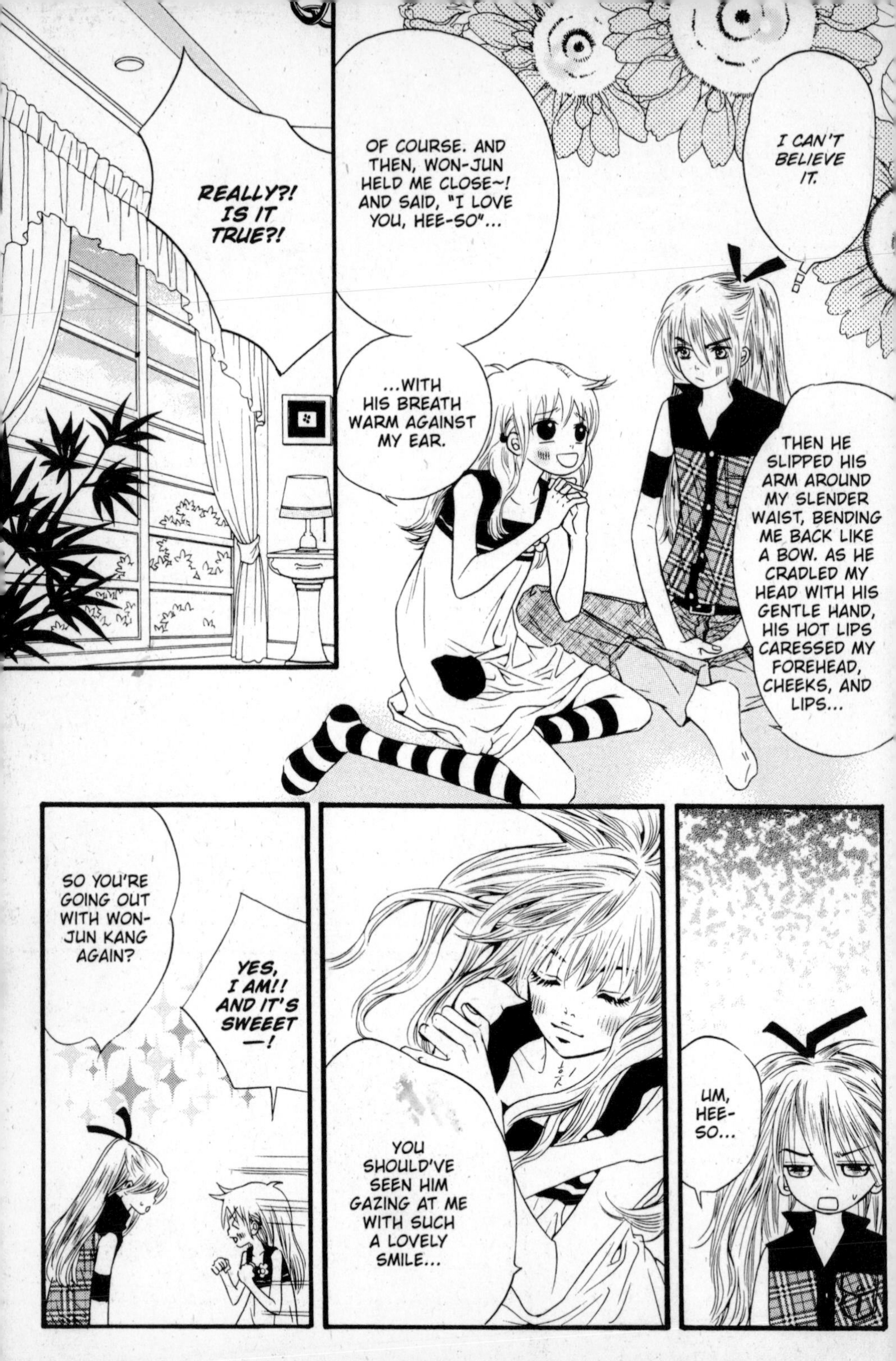
REALLY?! IS IT TRUE?!
OF COURSE. AND THEN, WON-JUN HELD ME CLOSE~! AND SAID, "I LOVE YOU, HEE-SO"...
I CAN'T BELIEVE IT.
...WITH HIS BREATH WARM AGAINST MY EAR.
THEN HE SLIPPED HIS ARM AROUND MY SLENDER WAIST, BENDING ME BACK LIKE A BOW. AS HE CRADLED MY HEAD WITH HIS GENTLE HAND, HIS HOT LIPS CARESSED MY FOREHEAD, CHEEKS, AND LIPS...
SO YOU'RE GOING OUT WITH WON-JUN KANG AGAIN?
YES, I AM!! AND IT'S SWEEET—!
YOU SHOULD'VE SEEN HIM GAZING AT ME WITH SUCH A LOVELY SMILE...
UM, HEE-SO...

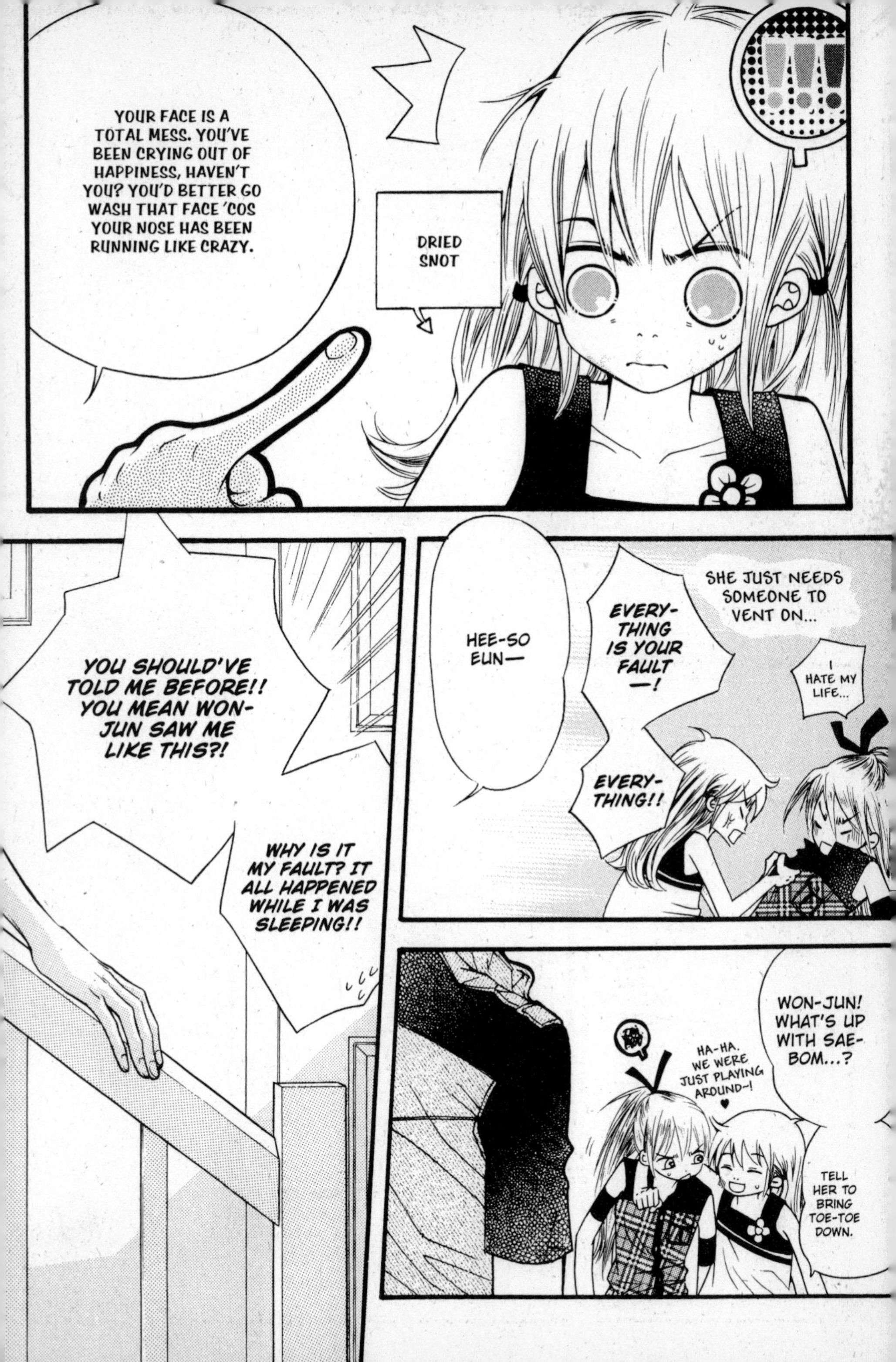
YOUR FACE IS A TOTAL MESS. YOU'VE BEEN CRYING OUT OF HAPPINESS, HAVEN'T YOU? YOU'D BETTER GO WASH THAT FACE 'COS YOUR NOSE HAS BEEN RUNNING LIKE CRAZY.
!!!
DRIED SNOT
YOU SHOULD'VE TOLD ME BEFORE!! YOU MEAN WON-JUN SAW ME LIKE THIS?!
WHY IS IT MY FAULT? IT ALL HAPPENED WHILE I WAS SLEEPING!!
HEE-SO EUN—
EVERY-THING IS YOUR FAULT —!
EVERY-THING!!
SHE JUST NEEDS SOMEONE TO VENT ON...
I HATE MY LIFE...
HA-HA. WE WERE JUST PLAYING AROUND~! ♥
WON-JUN! WHAT'S UP WITH SAE-BOM...?
TELL HER TO BRING TOE-TOE DOWN.

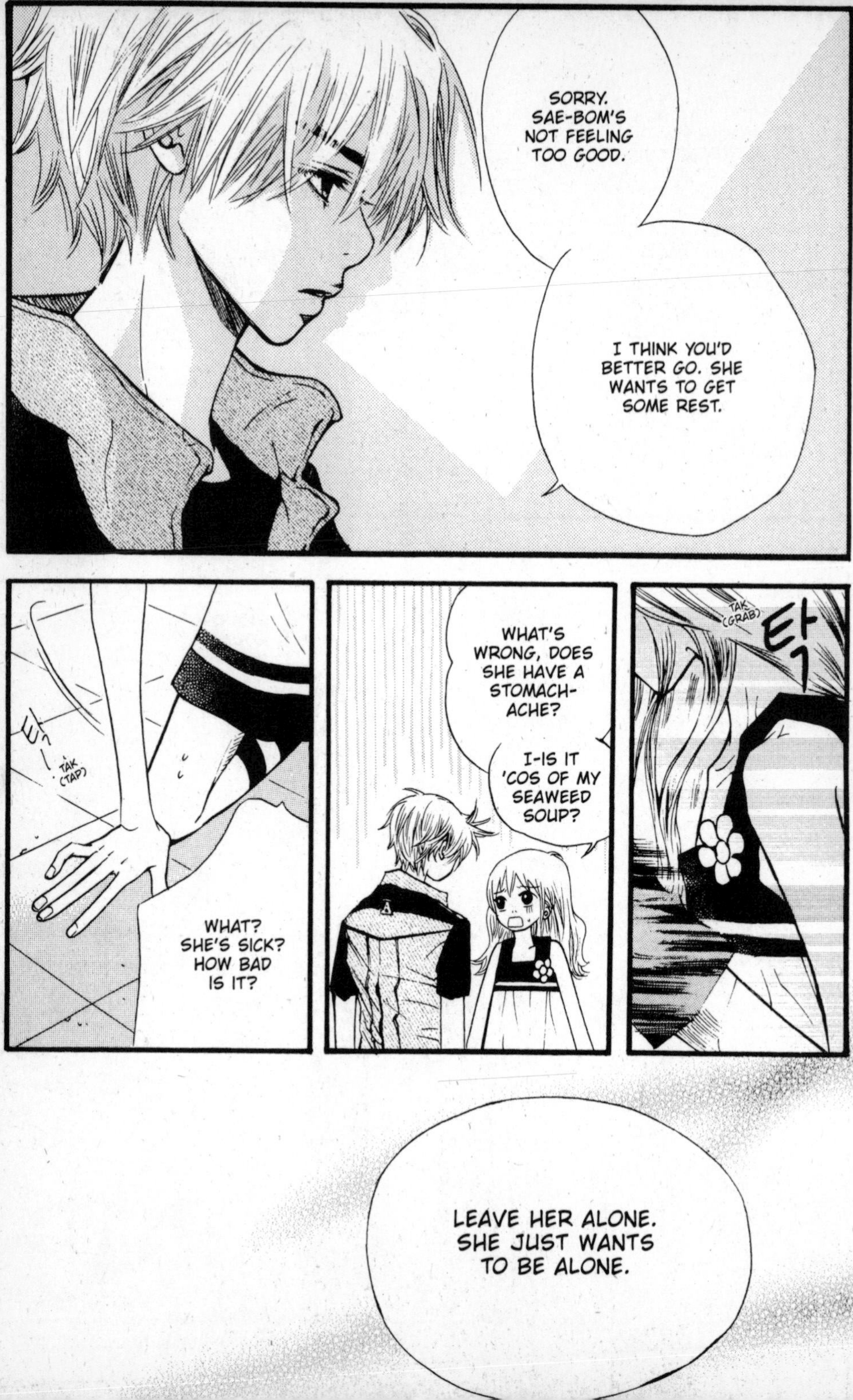
SORRY. SAE-BOM'S NOT FEELING TOO GOOD.
I THINK YOU'D BETTER GO. SHE WANTS TO GET SOME REST.
TAK (TAP)
WHAT? SHE'S SICK? HOW BAD IS IT?
WHAT'S WRONG, DOES SHE HAVE A STOMACH-ACHE?
I-IS IT 'COS OF MY SEAWEED SOUP?
TAK (GRAB)
LEAVE HER ALONE. SHE JUST WANTS TO BE ALONE.

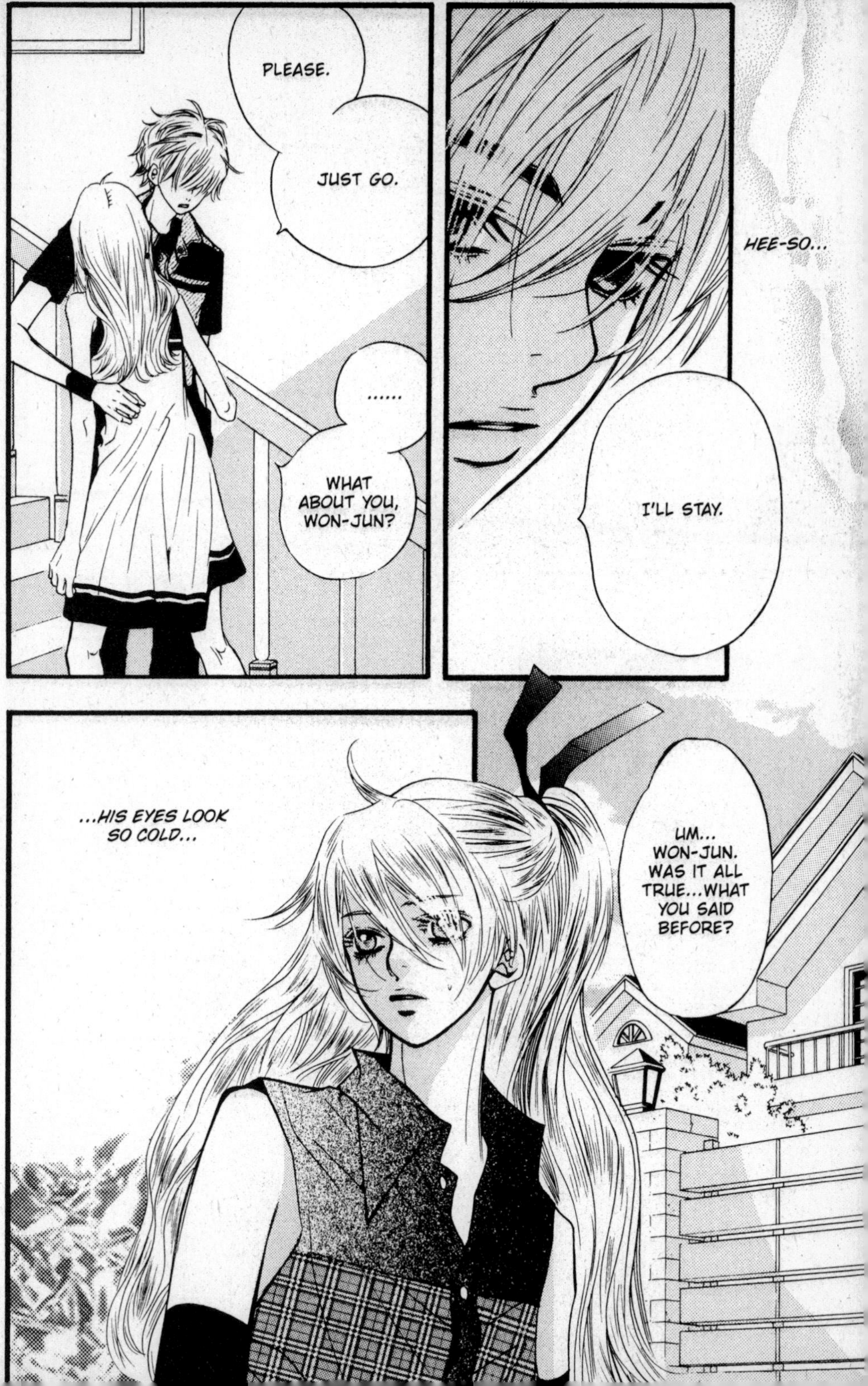

PLEASE.
JUST GO.
......
WHAT ABOUT YOU, WON-JUN?
HEE-SO...
I'LL STAY.
...HIS EYES LOOK SO COLD...
UM... WON-JUN. WAS IT ALL TRUE...WHAT YOU SAID BEFORE?

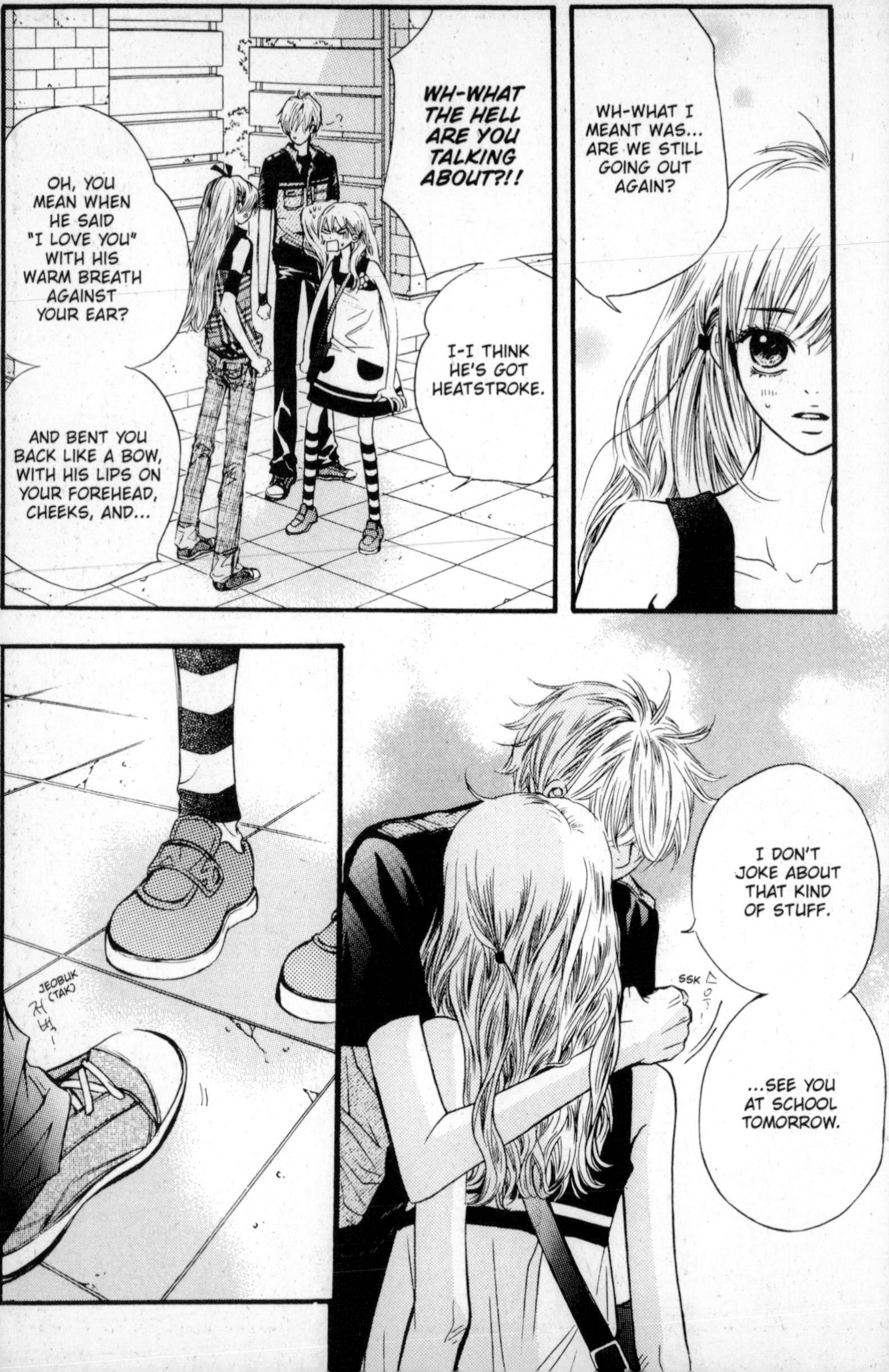
OH, YOU MEAN WHEN HE SAID "I LOVE YOU" WITH HIS WARM BREATH AGAINST YOUR EAR?
AND BENT YOU BACK LIKE A BOW, WITH HIS LIPS ON YOUR FOREHEAD, CHEEKS, AND...
WH-WHAT THE HELL ARE YOU TALKING ABOUT?!!
I-I THINK HE'S GOT HEATSTROKE.
WH-WHAT I MEANT WAS... ARE WE STILL GOING OUT AGAIN?
JEOBUK (TAK)
저벅
I DON'T JOKE ABOUT THAT KIND OF STUFF.
SSK
...SEE YOU AT SCHOOL TOMORROW.

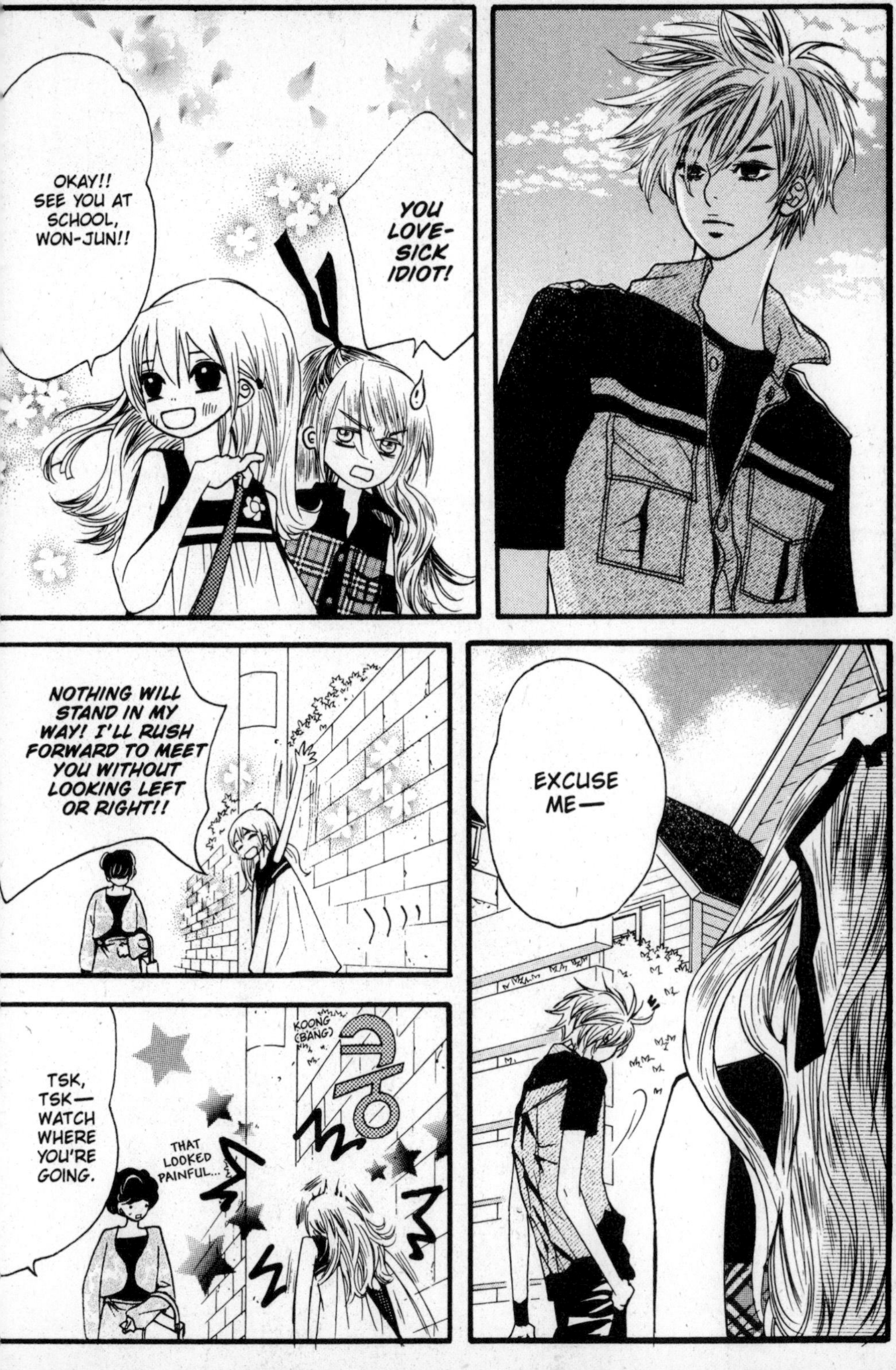
OKAY!! SEE YOU AT SCHOOL, WON-JUN!!
YOU LOVE-SICK IDIOT!
NOTHING WILL STAND IN MY WAY! I'LL RUSH FORWARD TO MEET YOU WITHOUT LOOKING LEFT OR RIGHT!!
TSK, TSK— WATCH WHERE YOU'RE GOING.
KOONG (BANG)
THAT LOOKED PAINFUL...
EXCUSE ME—

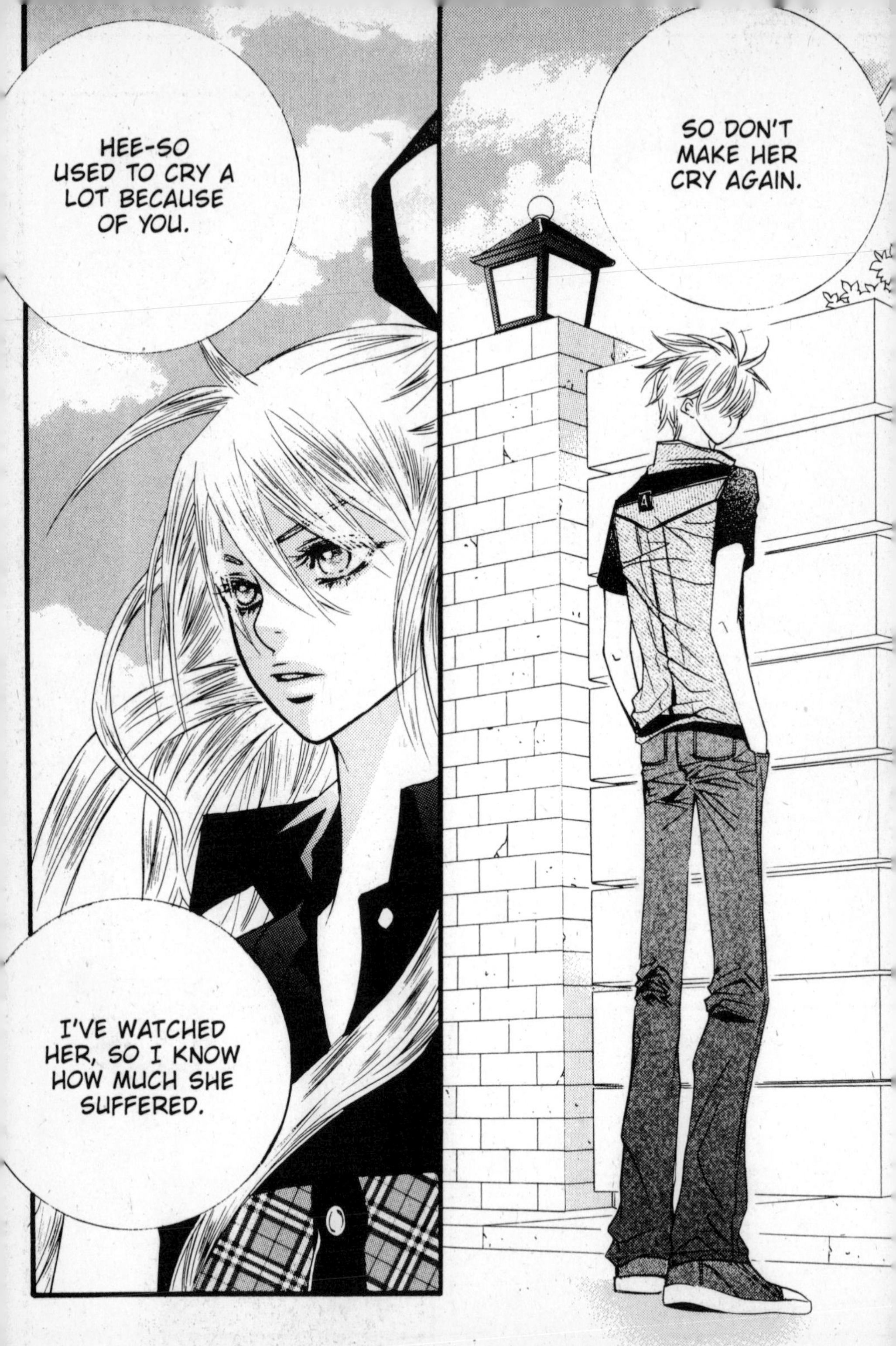
HEE-SO USED TO CRY A LOT BECAUSE OF YOU.
I'VE WATCHED HER, SO I KNOW HOW MUCH SHE SUFFERED.
SO DON'T MAKE HER CRY AGAIN.

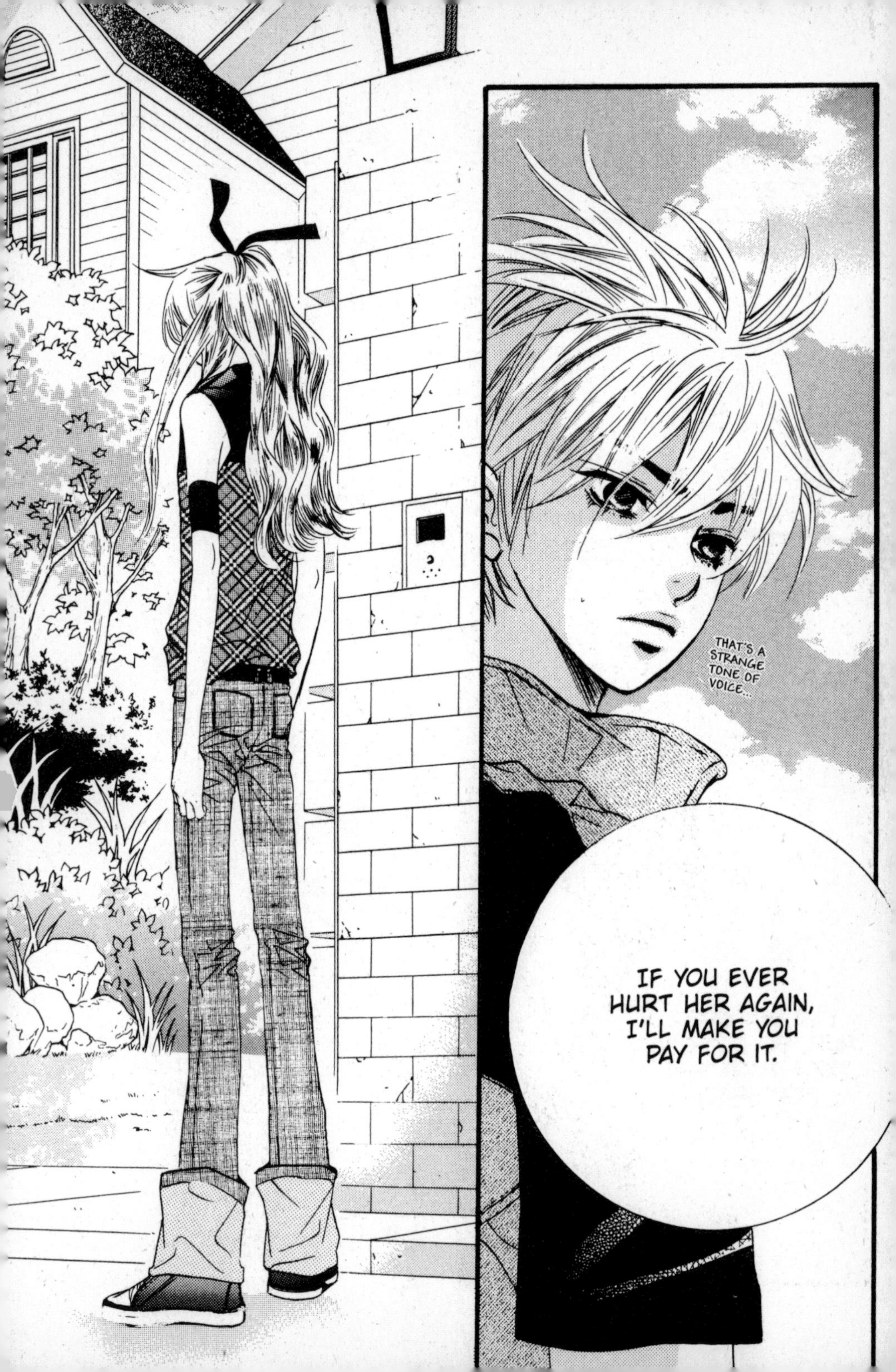
THAT'S A STRANGE TONE OF VOICE...
IF YOU EVER HURT HER AGAIN, I'LL MAKE YOU PAY FOR IT.

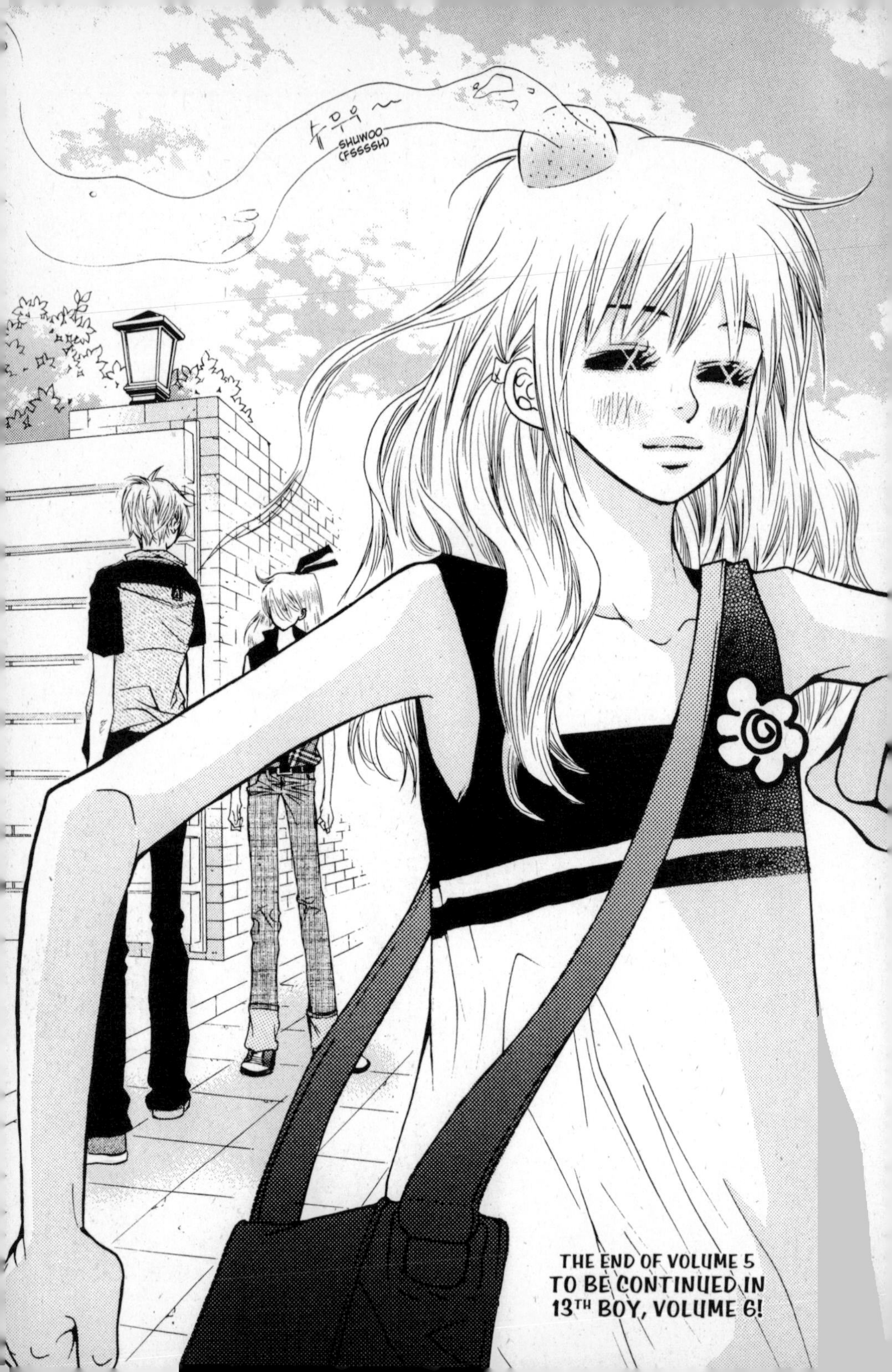
SHUWOO
(FSSSSH)
THE END OF VOLUME 5
TO BE CONTINUED IN
13TH BOY, VOLUME 6!

13th Boy

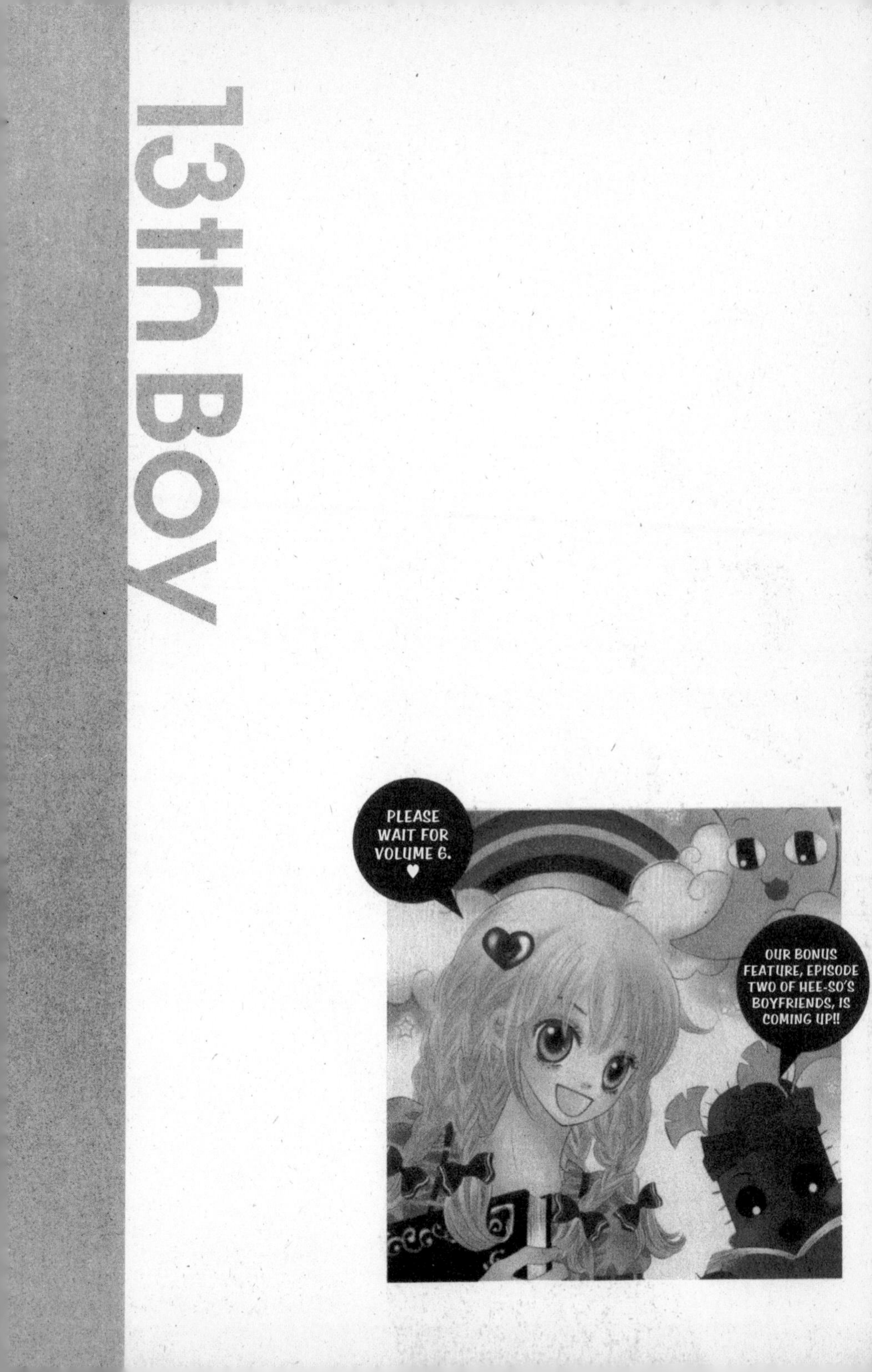
PLEASE WAIT FOR VOLUME 6. ♥
OUR BONUS FEATURE, EPISODE TWO OF HEE-SO'S BOYFRIENDS, IS COMING UP!!

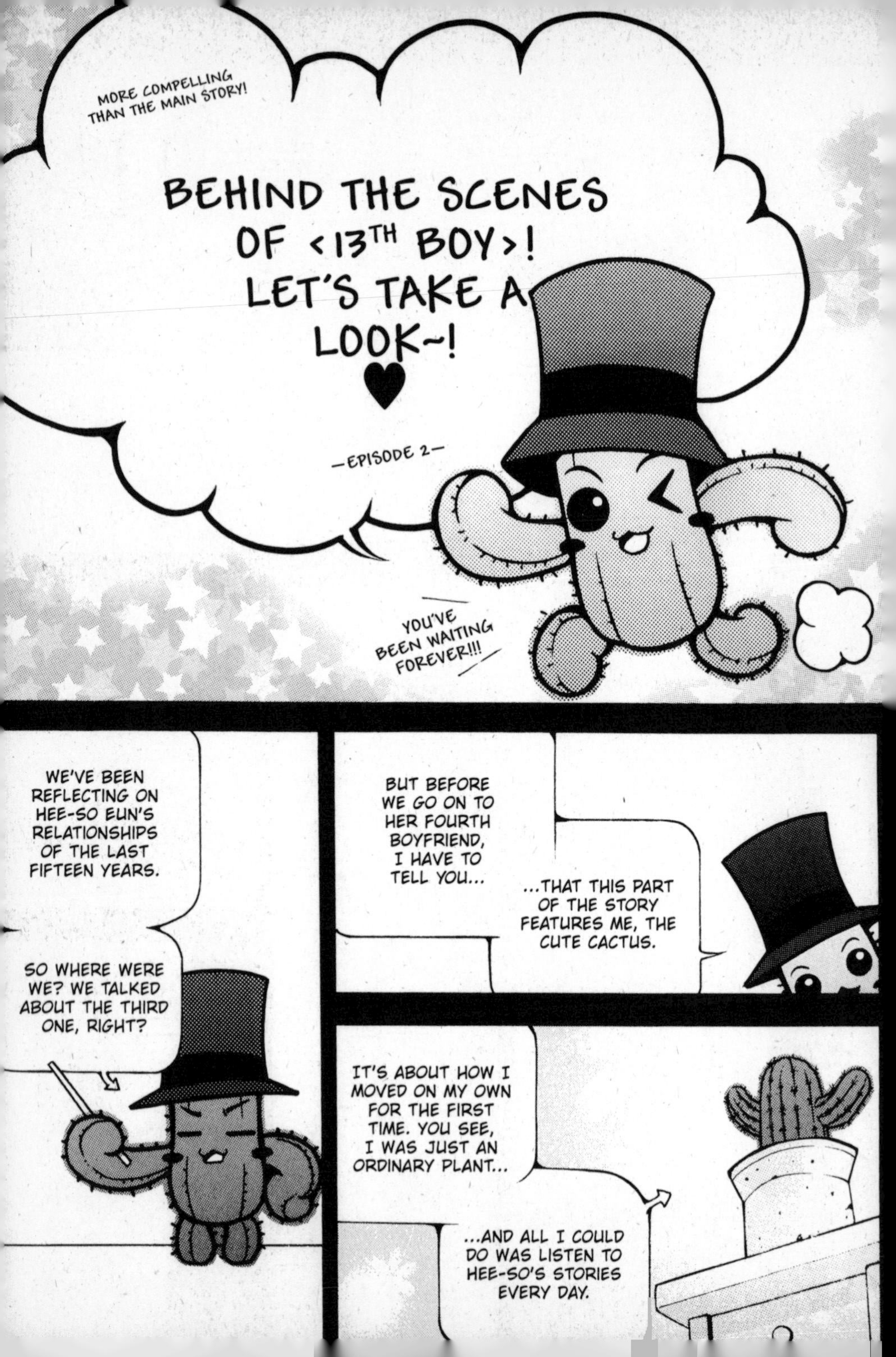
MORE COMPELLING THAN THE MAIN STORY!
BEHIND THE SCENES OF <13TH BOY>! LET'S TAKE A LOOK~! ♥
—EPISODE 2—
YOU'VE BEEN WAITING FOREVER!!!
WE'VE BEEN REFLECTING ON HEE-SO EUN'S RELATIONSHIPS OF THE LAST FIFTEEN YEARS.
SO WHERE WERE WE? WE TALKED ABOUT THE THIRD ONE, RIGHT?
BUT BEFORE WE GO ON TO HER FOURTH BOYFRIEND, I HAVE TO TELL YOU...
...THAT THIS PART OF THE STORY FEATURES ME, THE CUTE CACTUS.
IT'S ABOUT HOW I MOVED ON MY OWN FOR THE FIRST TIME. YOU SEE, I WAS JUST AN ORDINARY PLANT...
...AND ALL I COULD DO WAS LISTEN TO HEE-SO'S STORIES EVERY DAY.

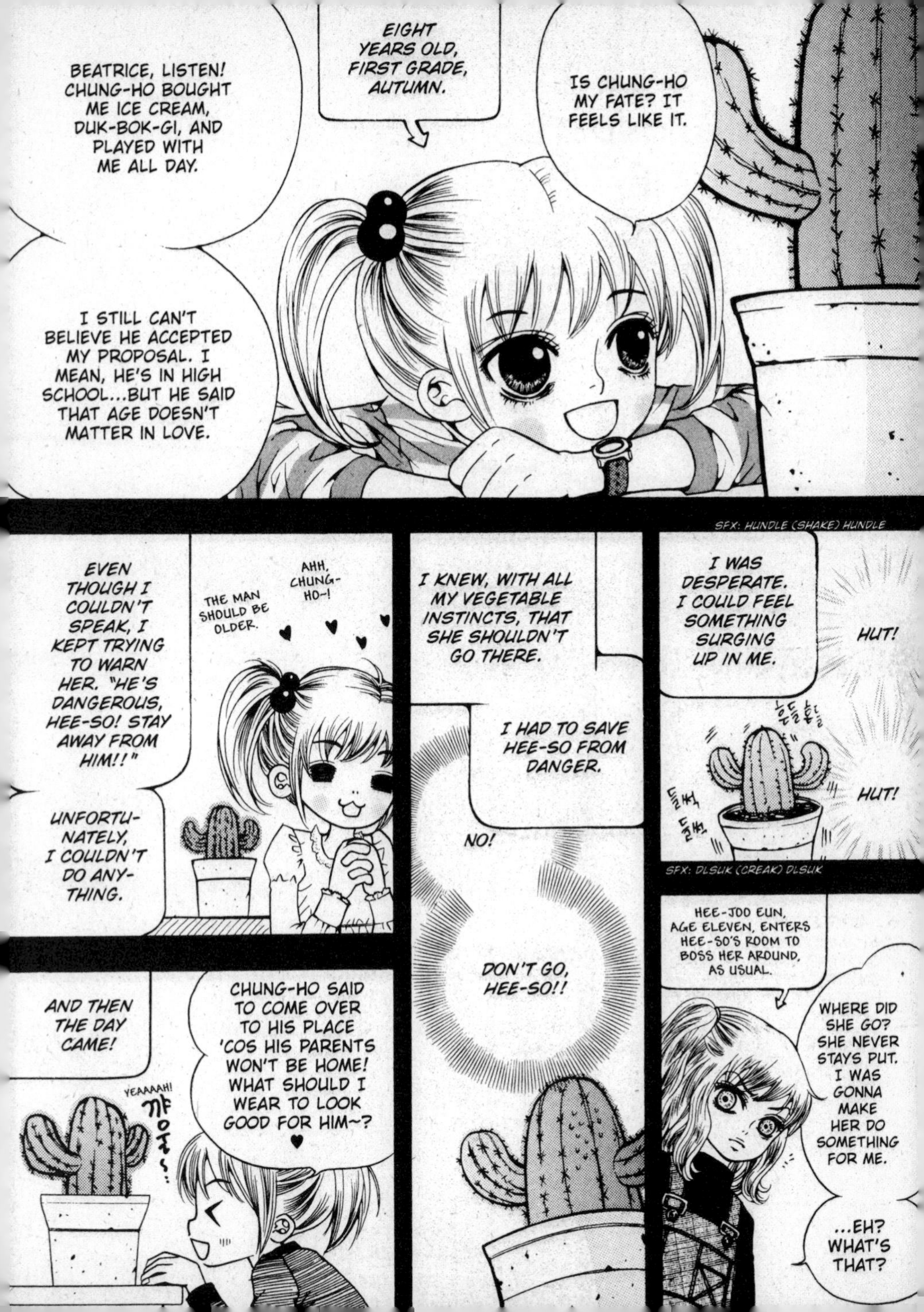

BEATRICE, LISTEN! CHUNG-HO BOUGHT ME ICE CREAM, DUK-BOK-GI, AND PLAYED WITH ME ALL DAY.
EIGHT YEARS OLD, FIRST GRADE, AUTUMN.
IS CHUNG-HO MY FATE? IT FEELS LIKE IT.
I STILL CAN'T BELIEVE HE ACCEPTED MY PROPOSAL. I MEAN, HE'S IN HIGH SCHOOL...BUT HE SAID THAT AGE DOESN'T MATTER IN LOVE.
SFX: HUNDLE (SHAKE) HUNDLE
EVEN THOUGH I COULDN'T SPEAK, I KEPT TRYING TO WARN HER. "HE'S DANGEROUS, HEE-SO! STAY AWAY FROM HIM!!"
THE MAN SHOULD BE OLDER.
AHH, CHUNG-HO~!
UNFORTU-NATELY, I COULDN'T DO ANY-THING.
AND THEN THE DAY CAME!
CHUNG-HO SAID TO COME OVER TO HIS PLACE 'COS HIS PARENTS WON'T BE HOME! WHAT SHOULD I WEAR TO LOOK GOOD FOR HIM~?
YEAAAAH!
I KNEW, WITH ALL MY VEGETABLE INSTINCTS, THAT SHE SHOULDN'T GO THERE.
I HAD TO SAVE HEE-SO FROM DANGER.
NO!
DON'T GO, HEE-SO!!
I WAS DESPERATE. I COULD FEEL SOMETHING SURGING UP IN ME.
HUT!
HUT!
SFX: DLSUK (CREAK) DLSUK
HEE-JOO EUN, AGE ELEVEN, ENTERS HEE-SO'S ROOM TO BOSS HER AROUND, AS USUAL.
WHERE DID SHE GO? SHE NEVER STAYS PUT. I WAS GONNA MAKE HER DO SOMETHING FOR ME.
...EH? WHAT'S THAT?

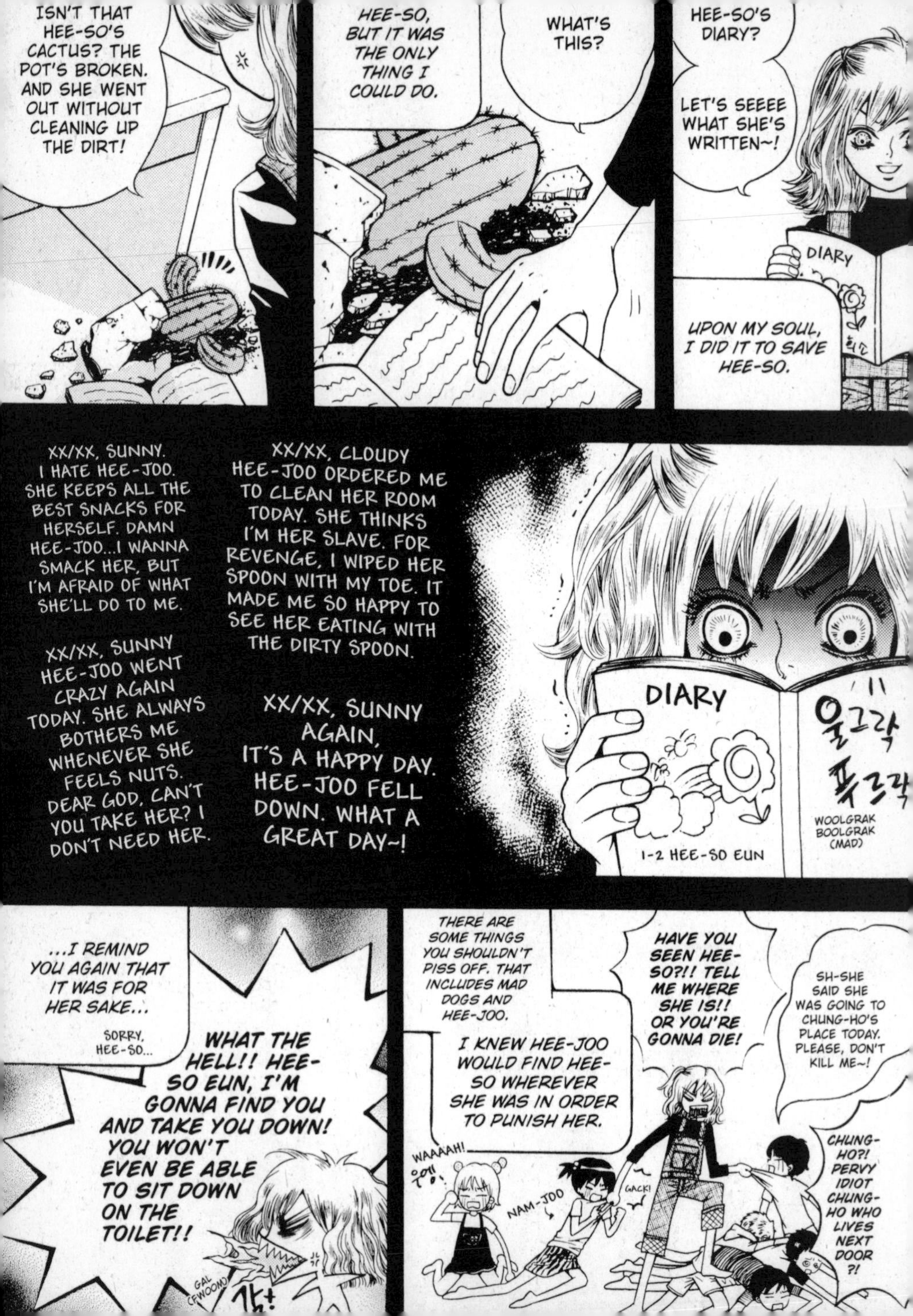
ISN'T THAT HEE-SO'S CACTUS? THE POT'S BROKEN. AND SHE WENT OUT WITHOUT CLEANING UP THE DIRT!
HEE-SO, BUT IT WAS THE ONLY THING I COULD DO.
WHAT'S THIS?
HEE-SO'S DIARY?
LET'S SEEEE WHAT SHE'S WRITTEN~!
DIARY
UPON MY SOUL, I DID IT TO SAVE HEE-SO.
XX/XX, SUNNY. I HATE HEE-JOO. SHE KEEPS ALL THE BEST SNACKS FOR HERSELF. DAMN HEE-JOO...I WANNA SMACK HER, BUT I'M AFRAID OF WHAT SHE'LL DO TO ME.
XX/XX, SUNNY HEE-JOO WENT CRAZY AGAIN TODAY. SHE ALWAYS BOTHERS ME WHENEVER SHE FEELS NUTS. DEAR GOD, CAN'T YOU TAKE HER? I DON'T NEED HER.
XX/XX, CLOUDY HEE-JOO ORDERED ME TO CLEAN HER ROOM TODAY. SHE THINKS I'M HER SLAVE. FOR REVENGE, I WIPED HER SPOON WITH MY TOE. IT MADE ME SO HAPPY TO SEE HER EATING WITH THE DIRTY SPOON.
XX/XX, SUNNY AGAIN, IT'S A HAPPY DAY. HEE-JOO FELL DOWN. WHAT A GREAT DAY~!
DIARY
1-2 HEE-SO EUN
울그락 푸르락
WOOLGRAK BOOLGRAK (MAD)
...I REMIND YOU AGAIN THAT IT WAS FOR HER SAKE...
SORRY, HEE-SO...
WHAT THE HELL!! HEE-SO EUN, I'M GONNA FIND YOU AND TAKE YOU DOWN! YOU WON'T EVEN BE ABLE TO SIT DOWN ON THE TOILET!!
GAL (FWOOM)
THERE ARE SOME THINGS YOU SHOULDN'T PISS OFF. THAT INCLUDES MAD DOGS AND HEE-JOO.
I KNEW HEE-JOO WOULD FIND HEE-SO WHEREVER SHE WAS IN ORDER TO PUNISH HER.
HAVE YOU SEEN HEE-SO?!! TELL ME WHERE SHE IS!! OR YOU'RE GONNA DIE!
SH-SHE SAID SHE WAS GOING TO CHUNG-HO'S PLACE TODAY. PLEASE, DON'T KILL ME~!
CHUNG-HO?! PERVY IDIOT CHUNG-HO WHO LIVES NEXT DOOR?!
WAAAAH!
NAM-JOO
GACK!

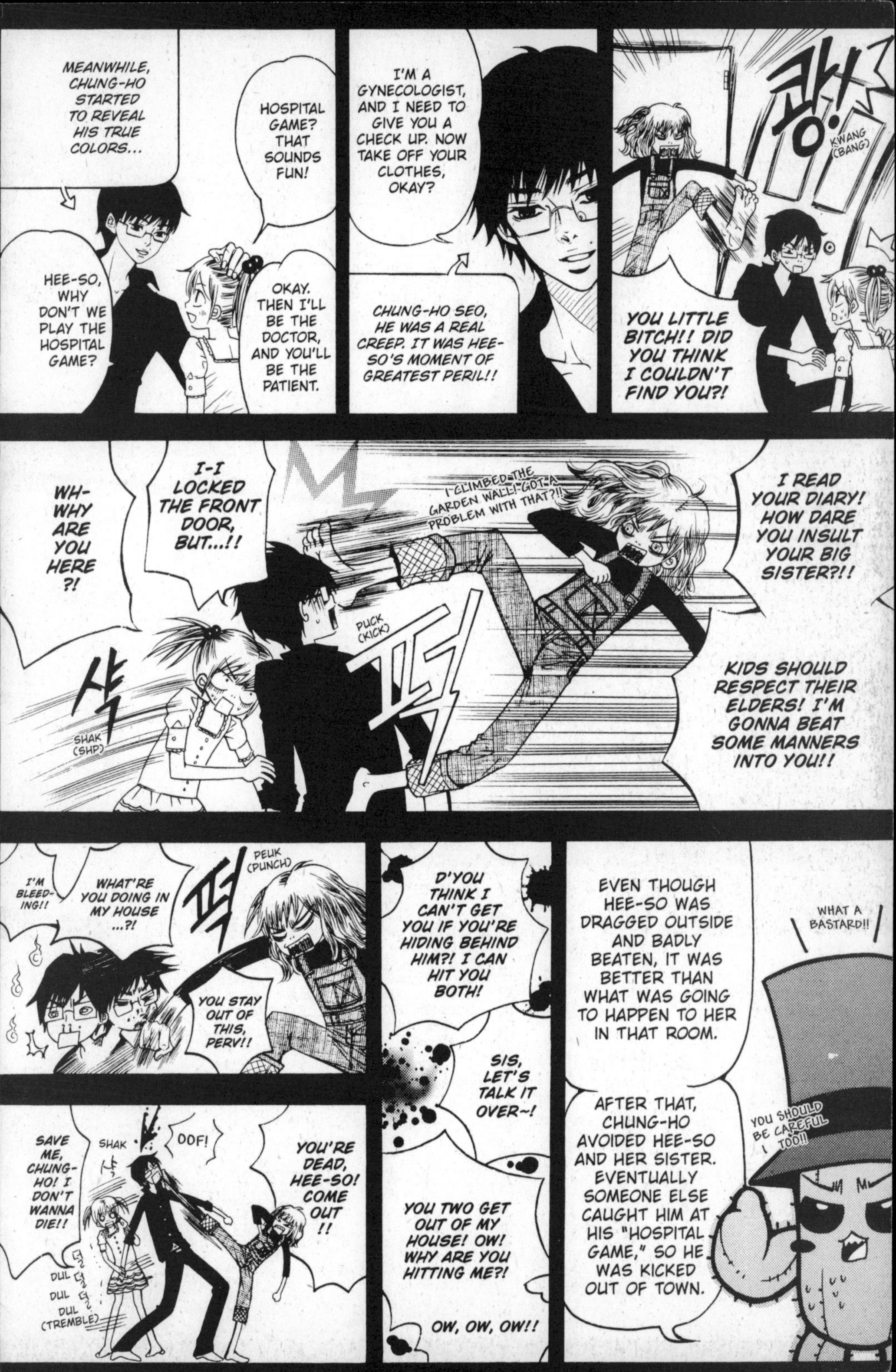

MEANWHILE, CHUNG-HO STARTED TO REVEAL HIS TRUE COLORS...
HOSPITAL GAME? THAT SOUNDS FUN!
HEE-SO, WHY DON'T WE PLAY THE HOSPITAL GAME?
OKAY. THEN I'LL BE THE DOCTOR, AND YOU'LL BE THE PATIENT.
I'M A GYNECOLOGIST, AND I NEED TO GIVE YOU A CHECK UP. NOW TAKE OFF YOUR CLOTHES, OKAY?
CHUNG-HO SEO, HE WAS A REAL CREEP. IT WAS HEE-SO'S MOMENT OF GREATEST PERIL!!
쾅!
KWANG (BANG)
YOU LITTLE BITCH!! DID YOU THINK I COULDN'T FIND YOU?!
WH-WHY ARE YOU HERE?!
I-I LOCKED THE FRONT DOOR, BUT...!!
I CLIMBED THE GARDEN WALL! GOT A PROBLEM WITH THAT?!!
I READ YOUR DIARY! HOW DARE YOU INSULT YOUR BIG SISTER?!!
PUCK (KICK)
퍽
샥
SHAK (SHP)
KIDS SHOULD RESPECT THEIR ELDERS! I'M GONNA BEAT SOME MANNERS INTO YOU!!
I'M BLEEDING!!
WHAT'RE YOU DOING IN MY HOUSE ...?!
PEUK (PUNCH)
퍽
YOU STAY OUT OF THIS, PERV!!
SAVE ME, CHUNG-HO! I DON'T WANNA DIE!!
SHAK
샥
OOF!
YOU'RE DEAD, HEE-SO! COME OUT !!
덜 덜 덜
DUL DUL DUL (TREMBLE)
D'YOU THINK I CAN'T GET YOU IF YOU'RE HIDING BEHIND HIM?! I CAN HIT YOU BOTH!
SIS, LET'S TALK IT OVER~!
YOU TWO GET OUT OF MY HOUSE! OW! WHY ARE YOU HITTING ME?!
OW, OW, OW!!
EVEN THOUGH HEE-SO WAS DRAGGED OUTSIDE AND BADLY BEATEN, IT WAS BETTER THAN WHAT WAS GOING TO HAPPEN TO HER IN THAT ROOM.
WHAT A BASTARD!!
AFTER THAT, CHUNG-HO AVOIDED HEE-SO AND HER SISTER. EVENTUALLY SOMEONE ELSE CAUGHT HIM AT HIS "HOSPITAL GAME," SO HE WAS KICKED OUT OF TOWN.
YOU SHOULD BE CAREFUL TOO!!

OH WOW...THE STORY OF HEE-SO'S FOURTH BOYFRIEND RAN LONGER THAN EXPECTED. ANYWAY, WHAT I WANT TO POINT OUT IS THAT THIS IS WHEN I FIRST STARTED TO HAVE FREE WILL.

MY SELF-AWARENESS AWAKENED, AND IT AFFECTED MY DEVELOPMENT.

HOOT (SNEER)

SO SHALL WE TALK ABOUT HER FIFTH BOYFRIEND, DAE-HEE BAEK? HE APPEARED ONCE IN VOLUME TWO.

UNLIKE OTHER BOYS HIS AGE, DAE-HEE WAS A VERY MELANCHOLY AND SOLITARY CHILD.

NO ONE WOULD EVER BELIEVE HE WAS A NINE-YEAR-OLD BOY. HE WAS SO SMART.

HEE-SO FELL IN LOVE WITH HIM FOR THAT, BUT SHE GOT TURNED OFF FOR THE SAME REASON.

SCHOPENHAUER SAID THAT IN SOLITUDE ONE FINDS THE TRUE SELF.

BUT CARL JUNG SAID THAT THE MOST FRIGHTENING THING WOULD BE TO ACCEPT MYSELF THE WAY I AM.

AS SARTRE MENTIONED, EXISTENCE PRECEDES ESSENCE. HEIDEGGER SAID THAT THE ESSENTIAL MOOD OF BEING HUMAN IS ANXIETY.

JUST LIKE NIETZSCHE INSISTED, GOD IS DEAD.

IN SHORT, HE WAS SMART, BUT IT MADE HER FEEL STUPID.

INTRO TO FREUD

......

WHAT THE...?

DAE-HEE BAEK'S SHORT LIFE ENDED AT THE AGE OF NINE DUE TO A CAR ACCIDENT.

IT TOOK A LONG TIME FOR HEE-SO TO GET OVER HER GRIEF.

AND THEN, IN THE SPRING OF HER TENTH YEAR, THERE WAS HER SIXTH LOVE. IT CAME TO HER LIKE A FLOWER-SCENTED BREEZE IN THE PERSON OF JI-HWAN SONG, A BOY WITH MODEL GOOD LOOKS WHO WAS JUST HER AGE.

BUT THERE WAS A TRAGEDY LOOMING IN THEIR RELATIONSHIP. HEE-SO EUN'S FORBIDDEN SIXTH LOVE...

...I'LL REVEAL IT IN VOLUME SIX! BE READY~! ♥

Bye Bye!

SO PLEASE BUY VOLUME SIX TOO~!

13th BOY Translation Notes

Page 12
Bananomilk.♥: A parody of a Korean banana milk brand.

Page 13
Dae-Gu subway fire: A serious incident that occurred in 2003 when a stopped train in the South Korean city of Dae-Gu was set on fire by an arsonist. The fire spread to another incoming train and resulted in numerous casualties and fatalities.

Page 119
***Saltoja*:** A play on words. In Korean, "murderer" is *salinja* (literally, something like "one who kills a person"), with the *in* meaning "person." But Toe-Toe switches out the "person" for "rabbit" (*to*).

Page 184
Duk-bok-gi: Spicy rice cake with vegetables.

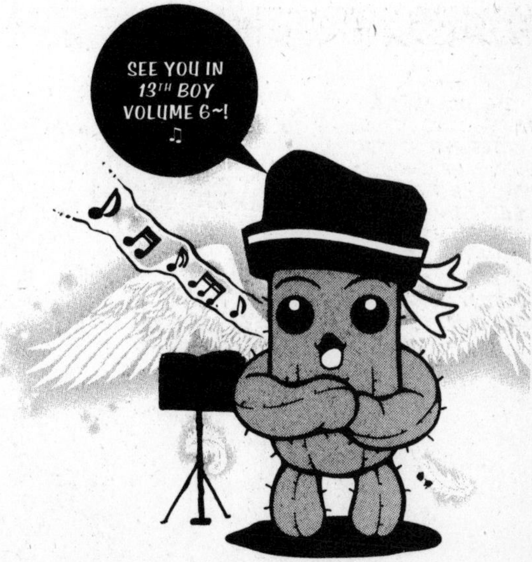
SEE YOU IN 13TH BOY VOLUME 6~! ♫

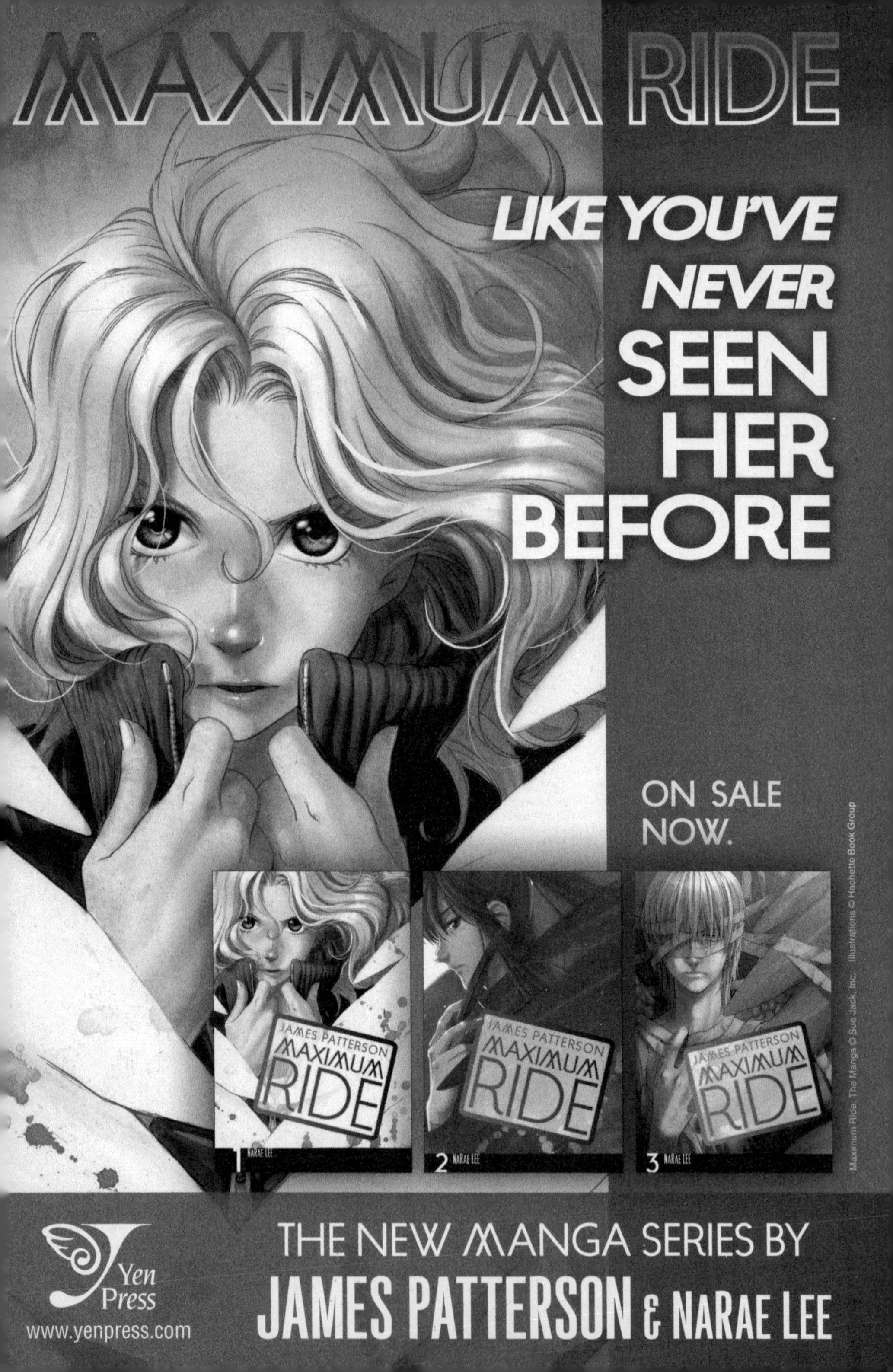
MAXIMUM RIDE
LIKE YOU'VE NEVER SEEN HER BEFORE
ON SALE NOW.
Maximum Ride: The Manga © Sue Jack, Inc. Illustrations © Hachette Book Group
JAMES PATTERSON MAXIMUM RIDE 1 NARAE LEE
JAMES PATTERSON MAXIMUM RIDE 2 NARAE LEE
JAMES PATTERSON MAXIMUM RIDE 3 NARAE LEE
THE NEW MANGA SERIES BY
JAMES PATTERSON & NARAE LEE
Yen Press
www.yenpress.com

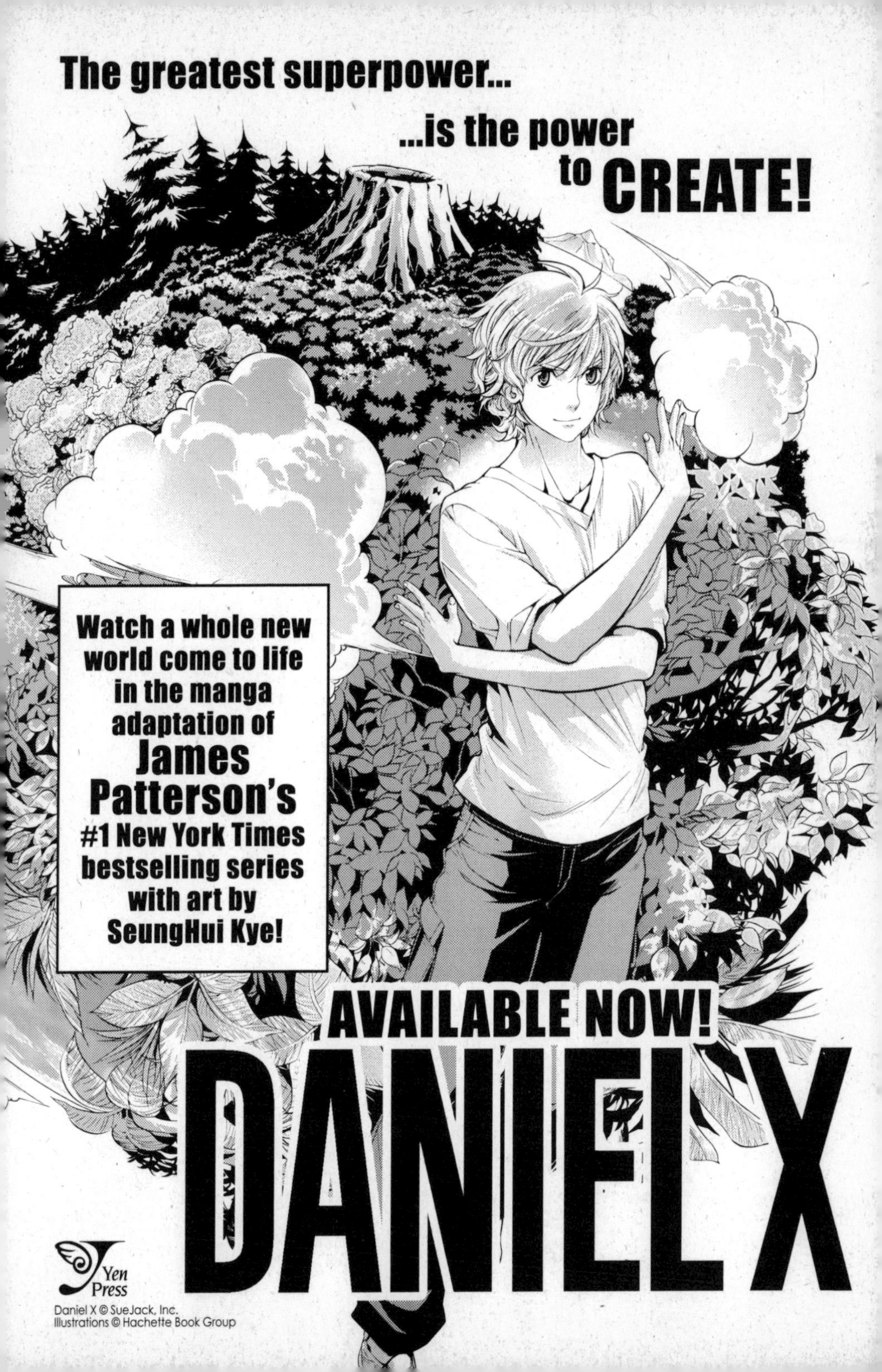
The greatest superpower...
...is the power to CREATE!
Watch a whole new world come to life in the manga adaptation of James Patterson's #1 New York Times bestselling series with art by SeungHui Kye!
AVAILABLE NOW!
DANIEL X
Yen Press
Daniel X © SueJack, Inc.
Illustrations © Hachette Book Group

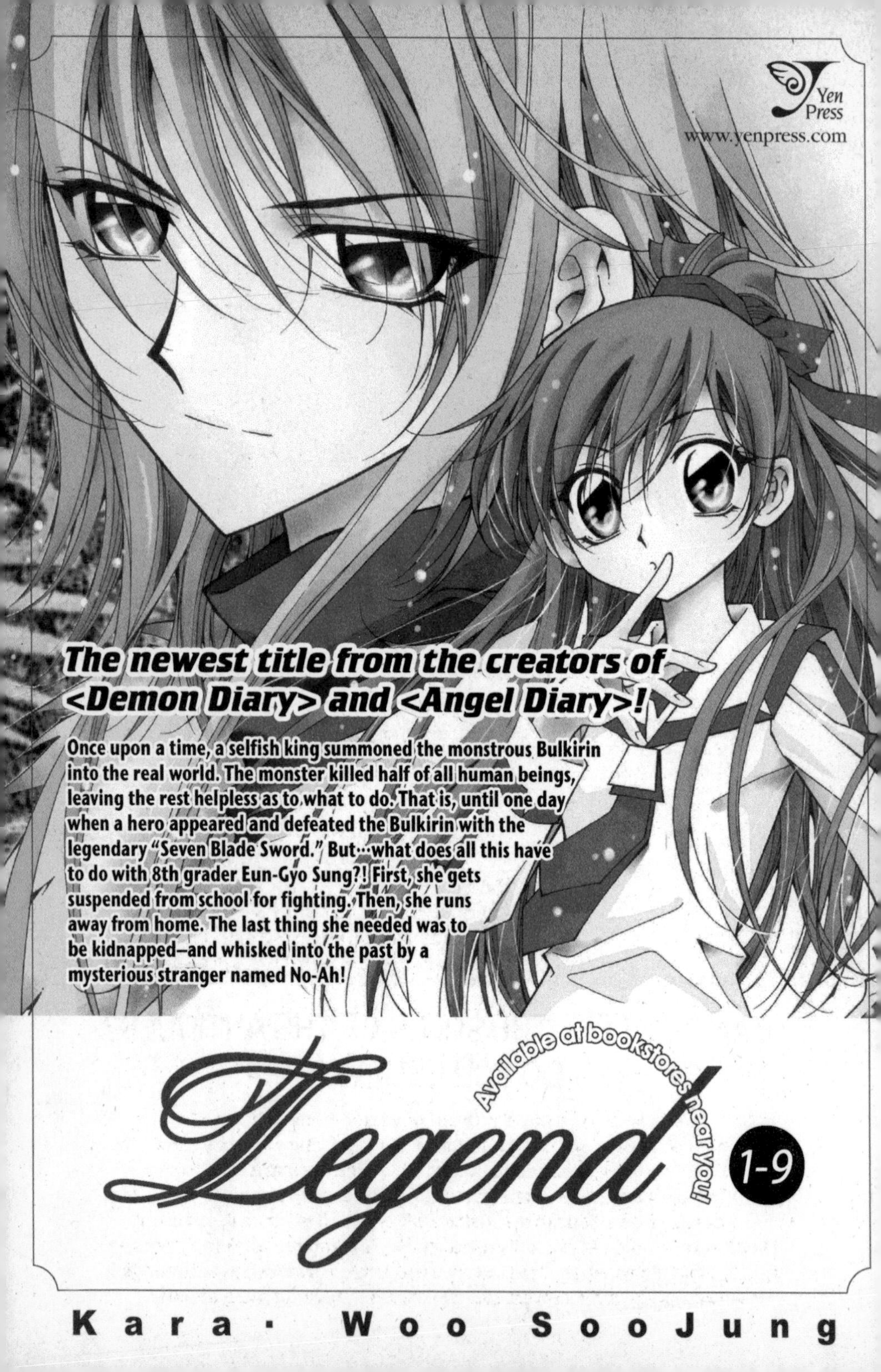
Yen Press
www.yenpress.com
The newest title from the creators of <Demon Diary> and <Angel Diary>!
Once upon a time, a selfish king summoned the monstrous Bulkirin into the real world. The monster killed half of all human beings, leaving the rest helpless as to what to do. That is, until one day when a hero appeared and defeated the Bulkirin with the legendary "Seven Blade Sword." But…what does all this have to do with 8th grader Eun-Gyo Sung?! First, she gets suspended from school for fighting. Then, she runs away from home. The last thing she needed was to be kidnapped–and whisked into the past by a mysterious stranger named No-Ah!
Legend
1-9
Available at bookstores near you!
Kara · Woo SooJung

The Antique Gift Shop 1~10

Lee Eun

Available at bookstores near you!

Yen Press
www.yenpress.com

CAN YOU FEEL THE SOULS OF THE ANTIQUES? DO YOU BELIEVE?

Did you know that an antique possesses a soul of its own?
The Antique Gift Shop specializes in such items that charm and captivate the buyers they are destined to belong to. Guided by a mysterious and charismatic shopkeeper, the enchanted relics lead their new owners on a journey into an alternate cosmic universe to their true destinies. Eerily bittersweet and dolefully melancholy, The Antique Gift Shop opens up a portal to a world where torn lovers unite, broken friendships are mended, and regrets are resolved. Can you feel the power of the antiques?

Yen Press
www.yenpress.com

THE MOST BEAUTIFUL FACE, THE PERFECT BODY,
AND A SINCERE PERSONALITY. . .THAT'S WHAT HYE-MIN HWANG HAS.
NATURALLY, SHE'S THE CENTER OF EVERYONE'S ATTENTION.
EVERY BOY IN SCHOOL LOVES HER, WHILE EVERY GIRL HATES HER OUT OF JEALOUSY.
EVERY SINGLE DAY, SHE HAS TO ENDURE TORTURES AND HARDSHIPS FROM THE GIRLS.

A PRETTY FACE COMES WITH A PRICE.

THERE IS NOTHING MORE SATISFYING THAN GETTING THEM BACK.
WELL, EXCEPT FOR ONE PROBLEM . . . HER SECRET CRUSH, JUNG-YUN.
BECAUSE OF HIM, SHE HAS TO HIDE HER CYNICAL AND DARK SIDE
AND DAILY PUT ON AN INNOCENT FACE. THEN ONE DAY, SHE FINDS OUT
THAT HE DISLIKES HER ANYWAY!! WHAT?! THAT'S IT! NO MORE NICE GIRL!
AND THE FIRST VICTIM OF HER RAGE IS A PLAYBOY SHE JUST MET, MA-HA.

vol.1~9

Cynical Orange

Yun JiUn

A totally new Arabian nights, where Scheherazade is a guy!

Everyone knows the story of Scheherazade and her wonderful tales from the Arabian Nights. For one thousand and one nights, the stories that she created entertained the mad Sultan and eventually saved her life. In this version, Scheherazade is a guy who disguises himself as a woman to save his sister from the mad Sultan. When he puts his life on the line, what kind of strange and unique stories will he tell? This new twist on one of the greatest classical tales might just keep you awake for another ONE THOUSAND AND ONE NIGHTS!

Yen Press
www.yenpress.com

Available at bookstores near you!

One thousand and one nights 1~11 final

Han SeungHee · Jeon JinSeok

Yen
Press
www.yenpress.com

Becoming the princess... Isn't that every girl's dream?!

Monarchy rule ended long ago in Korea, but there are still other countries with kings, queens, princes and princesses. What if Korea had continued monarchism? What if all the beautiful palaces, which are now only historical relics, were actually filled with people? What if the glamorous royal family still maintained the palace customs? Welcome to a world where Korea still has the royal family living in their everyday lives! Only for this one high school girl, Chae-Kyung, is this a tragedy, since she has to marry the prince — who apparently is a total bastard!

THE ROYAL PALACE
Goong

vol. 1~9

Park SoHee

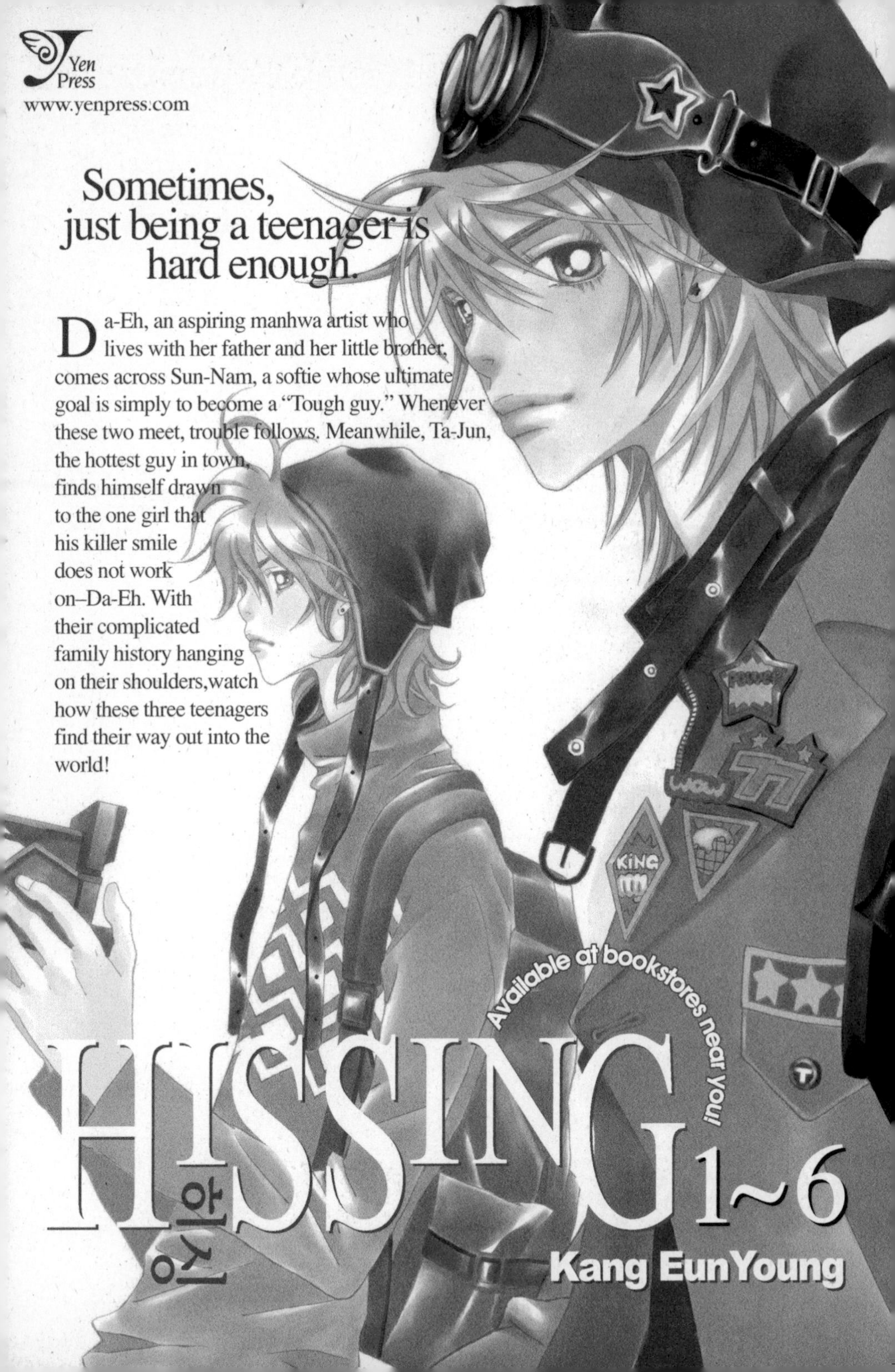
Yen Press
www.yenpress.com
Sometimes, just being a teenager is hard enough.
Da-Eh, an aspiring manhwa artist who lives with her father and her little brother, comes across Sun-Nam, a softie whose ultimate goal is simply to become a "Tough guy." Whenever these two meet, trouble follows. Meanwhile, Ta-Jun, the hottest guy in town, finds himself drawn to the one girl that his killer smile does not work on–Da-Eh. With their complicated family history hanging on their shoulders,watch how these three teenagers find their way out into the world!
Available at bookstores near you!
HISSING 1~6
하이싱
Kang EunYoung

Available at bookstores near you!

CHOCOLAT
1~7

Shin JiSang · Geo

Kum-ji was a little late getting under the spell of the chart-topping band, DDL. Unable to join the DDL fan club, she almost gives up on meeting her idols, until she develops a cunning plan–to become a member of a rival fan club for the brand-new boy band Yo-I. This way she can act as Yo-I's fan club member and also be near Yo-I,

How far would you go to meet your favorite boy band?

who always seem to be in the same shows as DDL. Perfect plan...except being a fanatic is a lot more complicated than she expects. Especially when you're actually a fan of someone else. This full-blown love comedy about a fan club will make you laugh, cry, and laugh some more.

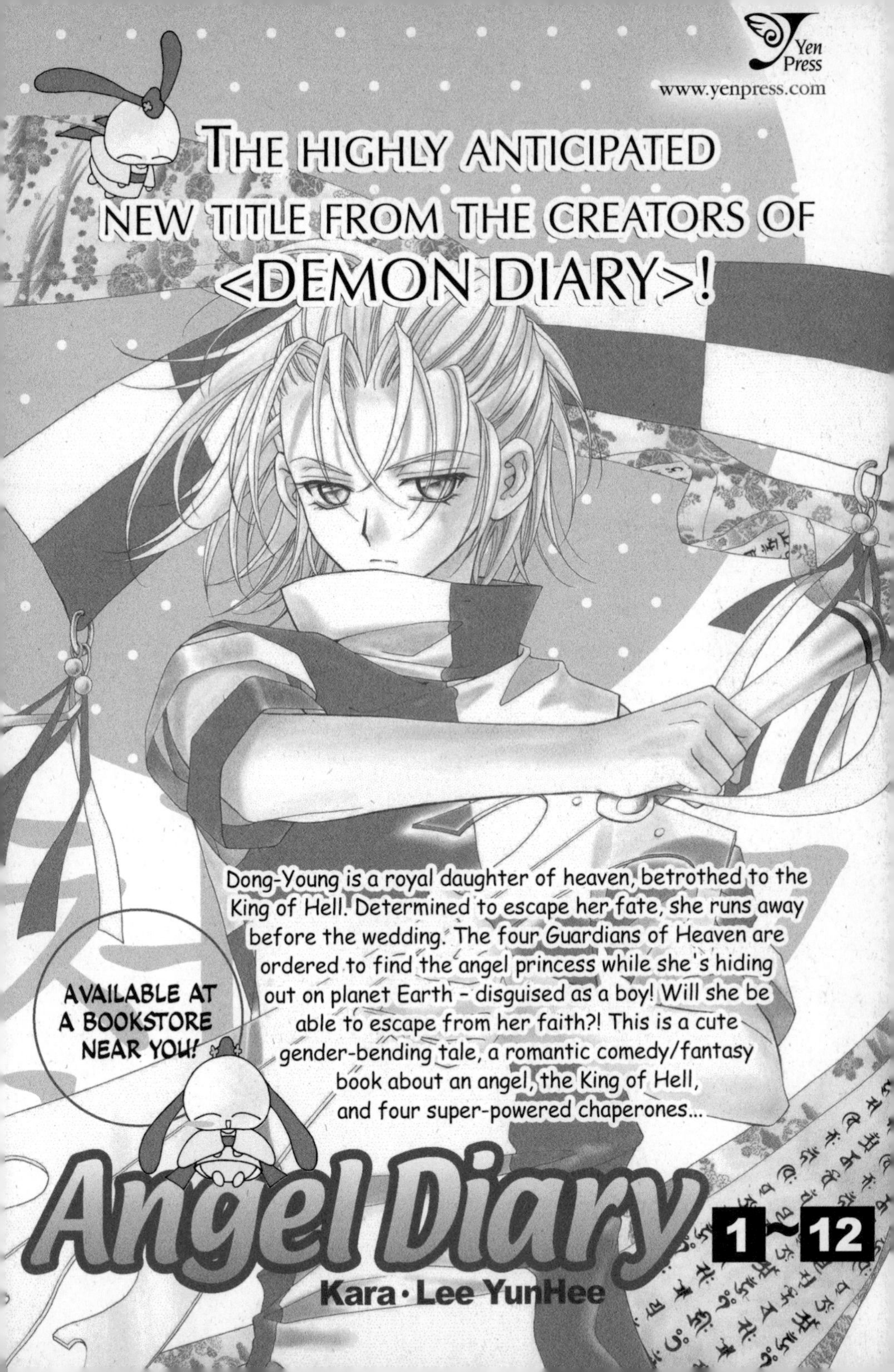
Yen Press
www.yenpress.com
THE HIGHLY ANTICIPATED
NEW TITLE FROM THE CREATORS OF
<DEMON DIARY>!
Dong-Young is a royal daughter of heaven, betrothed to the King of Hell. Determined to escape her fate, she runs away before the wedding. The four Guardians of Heaven are ordered to find the angel princess while she's hiding out on planet Earth – disguised as a boy! Will she be able to escape from her faith?! This is a cute gender-bending tale, a romantic comedy/fantasy book about an angel, the King of Hell, and four super-powered chaperones...
AVAILABLE AT A BOOKSTORE NEAR YOU!
Angel Diary
1~12
Kara · Lee YunHee

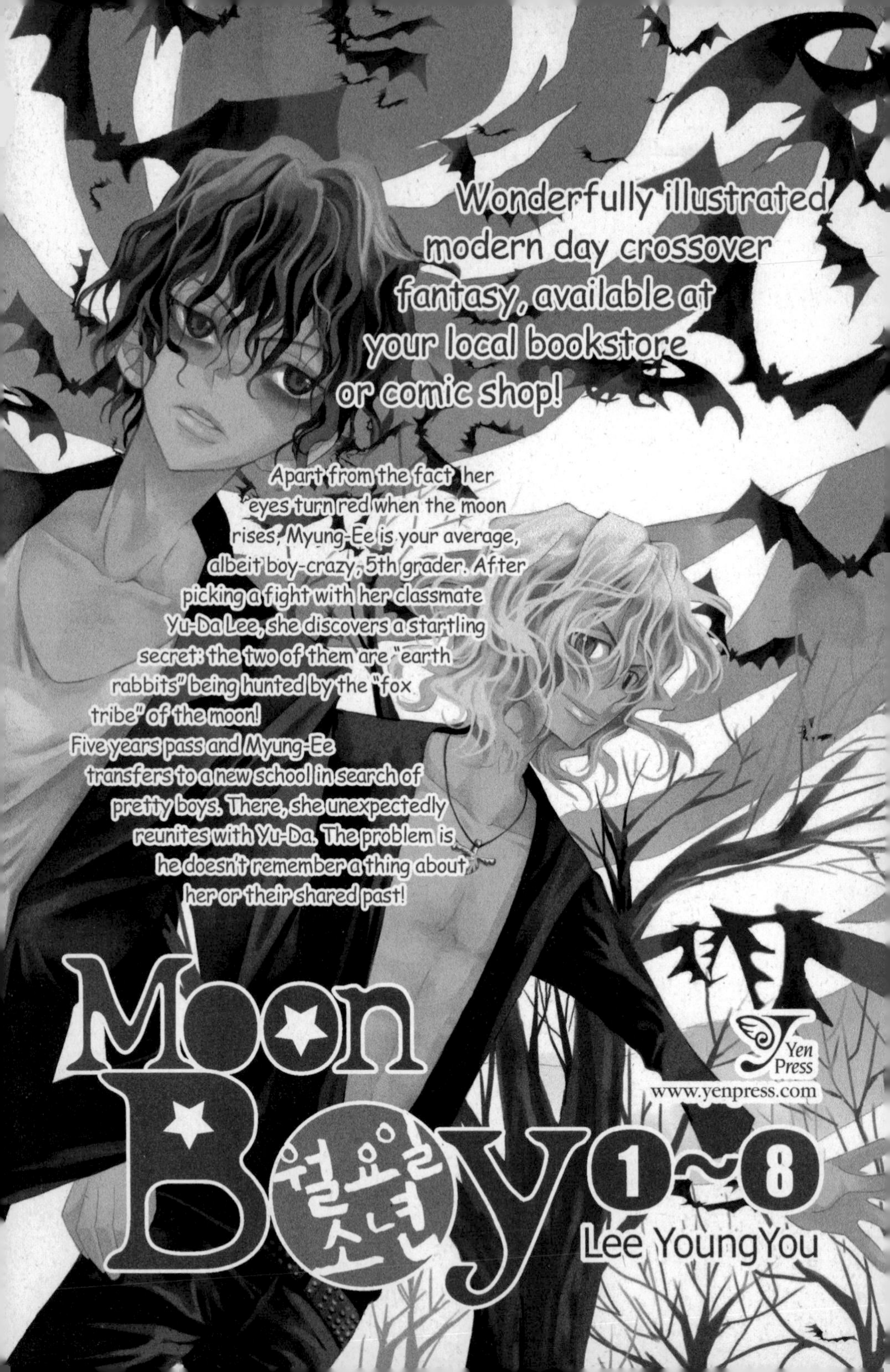
Wonderfully illustrated modern day crossover fantasy, available at your local bookstore or comic shop!
Apart from the fact her eyes turn red when the moon rises, Myung-Ee is your average, albeit boy-crazy, 5th grader. After picking a fight with her classmate Yu-Da Lee, she discovers a startling secret: the two of them are "earth rabbits" being hunted by the "fox tribe" of the moon!
Five years pass and Myung-Ee transfers to a new school in search of pretty boys. There, she unexpectedly reunites with Yu-Da. The problem is he doesn't remember a thing about her or their shared past!
Moon Boy 1~8
월요일 소년
Lee YoungYou
Yen Press
www.yenpress.com

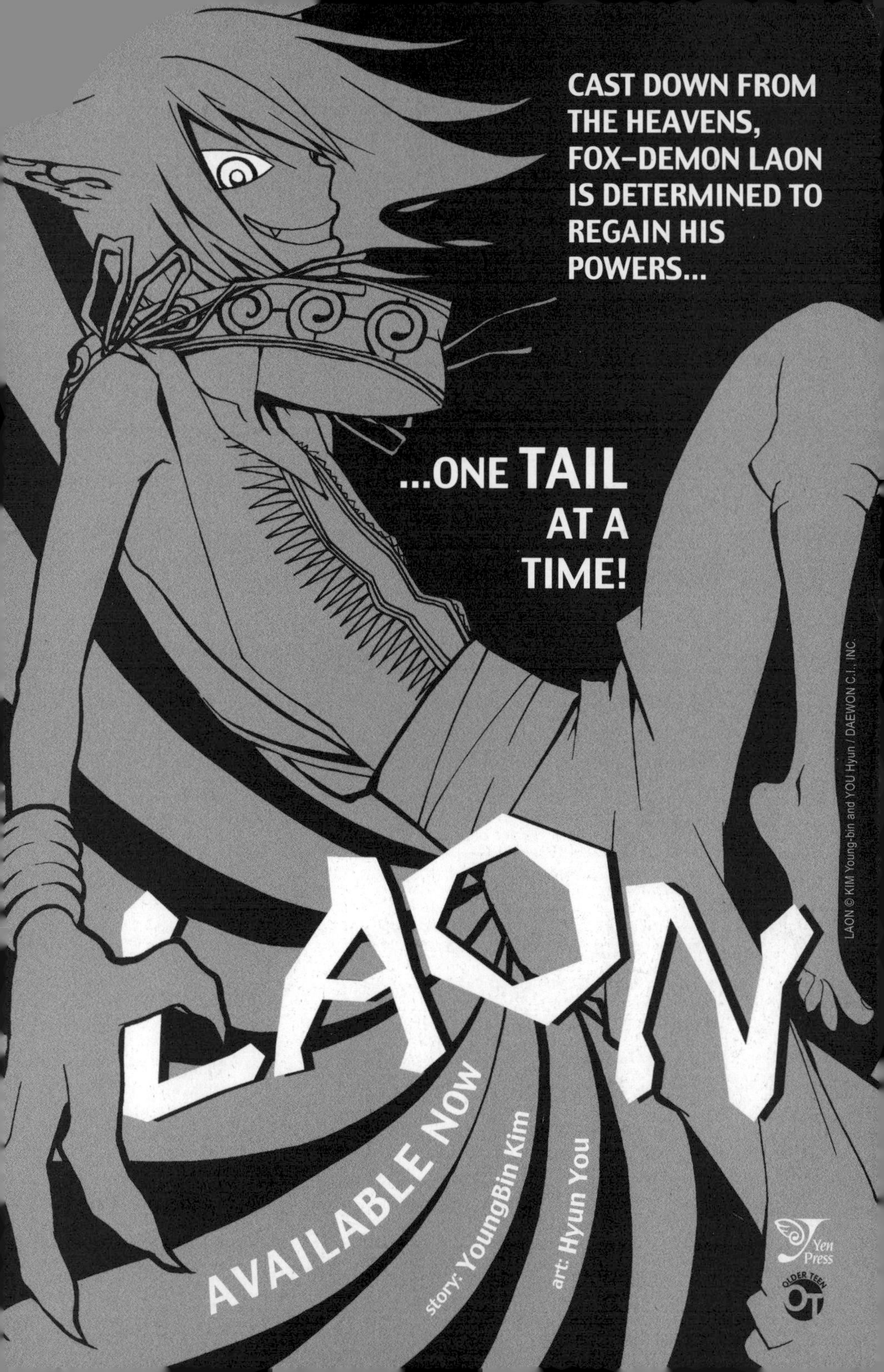
CAST DOWN FROM THE HEAVENS, FOX-DEMON LAON IS DETERMINED TO REGAIN HIS POWERS...
...ONE TAIL AT A TIME!
LAON
AVAILABLE NOW
story: YoungBin Kim
art: Hyun You
Yen Press
OLDER TEEN
OT
LAON © KIM Young-bin and YOU Hyun / DAEWON C.I., INC.

13th BOY ⑤

SANGEUN LEE

Translation: JiEun Park
English Adaptation: Natalie Baan

Lettering: Terri Delgado

13th Boy, Vol. 5 © 2006 SangEun Lee. All rights reserved. First published in Korea in 2006 by Haksan Publishing Co., Ltd. English translation rights in U.S.A., Canada, UK, and Republic of Ireland arranged with Haksan Publishing Co., Ltd.

English translation © 2010 Hachette Book Group, Inc.

Yen Press
Hachette Book Group
237 Park Avenue, New York, NY 10017

www.HachetteBookGroup.com
www.YenPress.com

Yen Press is an imprint of Hachette Book Group, Inc.
The Yen Press name and logo are trademarks of Hachette Book Group, Inc.

First Yen Press Edition: October 2010

ISBN: 978-0-7595-2998-4

10 9 8 7 6 5 4 3 2 1

BVG

Printed in the United States of America